F. L. Bauer J. B. Dennis G. Goos C. C. Gotlieb
R. M. Graham M. Griffiths H. J. Helms B. Morton
P. C. Poole D. Tsichritzis W. M. Waite

Software
Engineering

An Advanced Course

Edited by F. L. Bauer

Springer-Verlag
New York Heidelberg Berlin

Editor

Prof. Dr. F. L. Bauer
Mathematisches Institut
TU München
Arcisstraße 21
8000 München 2/BRD

Originally published in the series
Lecture Notes in Computer Science Vol. 30
Springer-Verlag Berlin Heidelberg New York
First Edition 1973
Reprint of the First Edition 1975

AMS Subject Classifications (1970): 68 A 05
CR Subject Classifications (1974): 4.

ISBN 0-387-08364-2 Springer-Verlag New York · Heidelberg · Berlin
ISBN 0-540-08364-2 Springer-Verlag Berlin · Heidelberg · New York

Printed in Germany
Printing and binding: Beltz Offsetdruck, Hemsbach/Bergstr.
2145/3140-54321

Contents

CHAPTER 2: <u>DESCRIPTIONAL TOOLS</u>

SOFTWARE ENGINEERING

An Advanced Course

by

J.B.Dennis	(Cambridge, Mass.)
G.Goos	(Karlsruhe)
C.C.Gotlieb	(Toronto)
R.M.Graham	(Berkeley, Cal.)
M.Griffiths	(Grenoble)
H.J.Helms	(Copenhagen)
B.Morton	(Reading, England)
P.C.Poole	(Abingdon, England)
D.Tsichritzis	(Toronto)
W.M.Waite	(Boulder, Colo.)

edited by   F.L.Bauer   (Munich)

The Advanced Course took place February 21 - March 3, 1972,
organized by the Mathematical Institute of the Technical
University of Munich and the Leibniz Computing Center of
the Bavarian Academy of Sciences,
in cooperation with the European Communities,
sponsored by the Ministry of Education and Science of the
Federal Republic of Germany.

PREFACE

It is not necessary to start with a definition of Software Engineering:
the present book, a consolidated effort of a group of experts, carefully prepared in a two-week seminar in Garmisch, Dec. 71/Jan. 72, and
presented at a EEC sponsored course in Febr.-March 72, illustrates the
use of the term.

In 1967 and 1968, the word 'Software Engineering' has been used in a
provocative way, in order to demonstrate that something was wrong in
the existing design, production and servicing of software. The situation has considerably changed since then; many people show concern
about the problems of software engineering and some of the manufacturers, to which the provocation was mainly addressed, claim that they
already obey the principles of software engineering, whatever this may
mean. Soon 'software engineering' will turn up in the advertisements.
But although the problems are indeed much better understood, the material is still not concentrated and systematized. The reports of the
NATO Science Committee sponsored conferences of Garmisch and Rome are
a useful collection of material, but not much more. In order to have
teaching material available, more has to be done. This book brings a
first step in this direction.

Our intention in the planning of this course was to cover as much as we
can at the moment of all the aspects of the theme, and to contribute
further to the systematization of the field. We do not actually debate
whether there is a need for software engineering. Instead, we think it
is essential to point out where the ideas of software engineering should
influence Computer Science and should penetrate in its curricula.
Thus we will try to find out as much as possible whether a topic of
software engineering is something you can mention as a kind of a theme
to your students in an academic environment.

In this respect, my major concern was that today one still finds it
extremely difficult, as many people told to me, to digest the material
at hand so that it could be used in a course. Therefore, we envisaged
publication of the lecture notes despite their somewhat tentative nature.

In selecting the participants we took some effort to assure that whatever they may learn here is spread out, in particular is propagated in the universities and the major manufacturers.

It is not quite accidental that efforts on 'Software Engineering' have been carried on to a large extent outside the United States. The poverty of the computer situation in Europe, at least on the continent, which is in sharp contrast to the affluent US computer community, leads to the demand for the most economical solution. But the roots of the software misery go deeper. It comes from the fact that people are forced to live with machines that they do not want. They have not constructed them, they simply receive them and have to make the best out of it. Sometimes, with the chance of buying a new machine, there is some hope that the situation will improve, but for simple market consideration, the manufacturer does everything he can do to make the customer stay with the product, and this usually ends all hopes for improvements. Thus, software engineering, for the time being, is partly a defense stratagem. But I hope that some day this situation will turn around, I hope one day software engineering considerations will dictate how machines are to be built and then to be used. Thus, what we have to work for is also preparing the ground for our future life. On the other hand, failure in mastering the software crisis may lead to strangulation of scientific users that depend on the computer today, in particular in 'Big Science', and may thus do harm also to science and economy in a rich nation.

In the preparation of the Advanced Course, I enjoyed the advice and help of colleagues and friends. I owe thanks to the co-director, Prof.L.Bolliet, and to the lecturers for their encouraging support. In particular, I am obliged to the German representative in the subgroup for education in informatics of group PREST of the EEC, Dr.R.Gnatz, for his help; in this connection the moral support from Mr.J.Desfosses (EEC) and the financial support from the Ministry of Education and Science of the Federal Republic of Germany should be gratefully acknowledged.The Conference Staff will forgive me for not mentioning all of them, my thanks to them go by the name of Mr.Hans Kuss of the Mathematics Institute of the Technical University Munich, who also was the responsible redactor of this publication.

Munich, June 1972   Friedrich L.Bauer

CHAPTER 1.A

WHAT THE SOFTWARE ENGINEER CAN DO FOR THE COMPUTER USER

Prof. Dr. K. W. Morton
Culham Laboratory, Abingdon, Berkshire
Great Britain

1. INTRODUCTION

There can be little doubt that there is at present an air of disillu-
sion in the computer community. Computers are not living up to their
potential and, in particular, the promises of the so-called third
generation systems have been largely unfulfilled. As a result users
have become more conservative and critical and are less ready to
invest in new equipment. The reason does not lie with the computer
hardware which continues to show a remarkable capacity to advance by
orders of magnitude. But how often do we find software becoming ten
times more reliable, ten times cheaper, ten times more efficient? It
is more likely that it is ten times more complex both to maintain and
to use and these more desirable qualities have been sacrificed as the
sophistication of concept has outstripped the capacity for practical
implementation. In short, software in general shows all the signs of
poor and inadequate engineering.

While computer science has flourished in the 1960's with the establishment of journals, degree courses in universities, etc., the software engineering aspects of the subject have struggled for support,
what techniques exist have been poorly disseminated and there is very
little software in the hands of users which has been built on the best
available engineering principles. In fact, many people are still
arguing about what is software engineering and how is it related to
computer science. As a mathematician, I am struck by the similarity of
both the controversy and the actual relationship with that existing
between mathematics in general and applied mathematics: in my view, it
is not the subject matter itself that forms the important distinction
but rather the use made of it and the attitude adopted toward it.
Computer science gave us Algol 60: it also gave us the prospect of
time sharing. But when we sit down at a console to write an Algol
program, it is software engineering which determines how easy it is to

achieve this end or, alternatively, the frustrations that we have to go through.

In his address to IFIP Congress 71, reproduced in this volume, Professor Bauer has given an excellent introduction to the subject and the more important references. In this lecture I want to draw attention to just three problems which are of particular concern to the computer user at the moment and where an increased application of software engineering principles could be of immense benefit to him. They are

(i)   program duplication - duplication in one's own programming because of ignorance of the work of others, differing languages, change of computing systems or partial change of requirements, and duplication of system software, which in the last analysis one has to pay for;
(ii)   the poor design and implementation of user images and their irrational variation from system to system;
(iii)   the management of large application program suites - getting them written, used and maintained.

2. PROGRAM DUPLICATION

The earliest response to this problem was the subroutine library. Every computer range, every programming language, every computer installation now has its subroutine library - but to a large extent they are all different. Some of the reasons for this higher level duplication are undoubtedly human but it is also astonishing how many technical barriers are placed in the way of users sharing subroutines more widely.

Routines implementing numerical algorithms are probably most widely distributed and most often form the basis of libraries. Indeed the last year or so has seen a great deal of progress in setting up machine and/or manufacturer independent libraries in this area. The appearance of the second volume of the Handbook of Automatic Computation [1] has been a great stimulus and the proceedings of the Mathematical Software Symposium [2] held at Purdue University in 1970 clearly show the increasing awareness of the benefits and problems of widely used mathematical software. In the United Kingdom, after several false starts stretching back over many years, a large number of numerical analysts and computing service people have now pooled their efforts

in the NAG library project [3] . I am doubtful whether this would have
materialised had it not been for the fact that the six universities
originally involved had orders for the same computers (ICL 1906As)
approved at about the same time. But now that it has started the project is being encouraged to cover IBM and CDC machines as well as
other ICL machines.

As one of the best available within current operating systems, the
NAG library is a good illustration of the practical limitations imposed by these systems. For example:

(a) The library covers the needs of both Fortran and Algol programmers
but to do so it has to contain duplicate routines - a waste of
both development effort and storage space as well as preventing
the exploitation of the most suitable language for each particular
algorithm. Many of the problems of mixed language programming,
especially between this pair of languages, have been overcome in
other operating systems and it is highly desirable that this interface should be properly defined and engineered once and for all.

(b) Routines in Fortran have to be in the ANSI dialect. This again
means that any extra features of the local Fortran dialect cannot
be exploited and a great deal of conversion work carried out. It
could well be possible that some of the techniques described in
this course could provide automatic dialect conversion tools to
avoid this limitation. Indeed it would seem that the proper engineering approach would be to insist that such conversion tools
should be an integral part of any proposed extension to a language.

(c) To increase portability, other limitations are placed on the subsets of the languages that may be used - for example, no I/O statements are allowed, nor are COMMON variables in Fortran. These are
important restrictions leading to poor programming practices and
result largely from imcompatibilities in run-time packages between
machines and languages. A properly engineered solution is to base
a library on a family of portable compilers with a shared run-time
package.

(d) Accuracy is generally given priority over efficiency: when such a
decision entails severe penalties several versions of a routine
are held. This requirement of "adaptability" is a common one and
forms a major target of software engineering techniques - the name
'generic components' has been given to program modules which can

be used to generate executable code meeting differing requirements.

In commercial data-processing, libraries of sub-routines are less
common though the disadvantages of duplication are no less great.
This is largely because the sort of restrictions described above
would be so severe in practice as to be unacceptable. The problems
they raise are more akin to those which appear in scientific programming when larger modules or whole programs from differing sources
are combined. These include
(a)   formats for input and output;
(b)   file access and storage mechanisms;
(c)   data security, private files and archiving;
(d)   data storage layout and variable dimensioning of arrays;
(e)   program segmentation and overlays;
(f)   overlapped execution of independent tasks (parallelism).

At this level the problems of sharing program modules become very
great and are hardly touched by the use of conventional programming
languages except between people using the same installation. The
choices entailed are highly machine dependent and this is reflected
in the differing implementations of the language facilities that are
needed. Nevertheless the difficulties met in practice are an order of
magnitude greater than those which are logically defensible. The
whole structure of high level programming involving compilers,
linkage editors, supervisor calls, etc. has evolved in a rather un-
disciplined way and simplifying advances like paging and the one-level
store have not won general acceptance.

These difficulties merge almost imperceptibly into those of non-
standard utility programs and expensive, difficult-to-use operating
systems. I look to the software engineers to so reorganise computer
systems and the way in which users construct large program suites
that it becomes
(a)   easier and more efficient to construct them;
(b)   possible to share program modules more widely and over more
       levels;
(c)   through application of these benefits to system software,
       cheaper and easier to use good system software.

3. USER IMAGES

In today's pattern of computer usage, the user image of a computer system is only to a quite small extent formed by the high level languages that it supports. The user has to carry in his head great masses of information about system facilities, job control and command languages, installation procedures and how the job queues are organised at different times of the day, right down to the key conventions of the various consoles made available to him. And hardly any of these are as logical or well designed as the common high level languages.

To learn all this for just one system might be acceptable, especially if, as for second generation machines, it happens gradually as the system evolves. But when one has to replace the hardware, and sometimes even when one does not, one usually has to face a complete change of system right down to the last detail. Moreover, whatever the degree of portability for program packages that one may reasonably hope for in the near future, many users are going to want to access several different systems because of the packages which they alone support. Thus there is a crying need for drastic simplification, rationalisation and stabilisation of these user images.

On the hardware side a strong pattern is now emerging which indicates the way in which computer networking may eventually be reached. The user image begins at his terminal. This may be a teletype, VDU or some more sophisticated online terminal: on the other hand, it may be a card-reader/line printer terminal connected to either a local or a remote batch stream. When there are several users on the same site, the logical next step is to combine these into a so-called intelligent terminal, consisting of a small computer controlling all user-orinted peripherals and handling all communications with any main frame computer which a user wishes to access. Thus there is a clear separation of function: the main frame computer provides the main processing and file storage capability which may be local or remote; the 'front-end' or terminal computer handles the users' peripherals.

It seems to me that the front-end should therefore become more and more responsible for providing the user image. This can then become stabilised against differences between main frame computers and adapted to the local needs of the user community. Building such front-end systems is very much a job for the software engineers: there are no new techniques really required and the all important requirements are for reliability, good design and stability. Several groups are already working on these problems and we have a small team so engaged at Culham Laboratory [4] .

Some of the tasks which it is envisaged may be handled by such a system include the following:

(a) User communication-controlling the consoles and other peripherals, determining which keys are used for which purpose and providing in-line text editing and format control of output; queuing requests and providing information about the state of accessible main-frame systems; checking user identity and access protocol; handling messages to and from other users; giving a first line information retrieval service.

(b) Main frame communication - controlling all information transfers; optimising use of communications lines; providing spooling facilities for I/O; providing for file transfers.

(c) Job control and console command language - providing a common core of language with translation to the main frame machine to be accessed; executing commands appropriate to itself (in many cases it will have its own filing system which will be accessed through the command language and which, by means of editors, syntax checkers etc., may be used for program preparation and job set-up); providing escape mechanisms into the JCL of particular main-frames when necessary; otherwise checking all input and providing prompts where appropriate.

(d) Scheduling - providing for local job queues and allocating priorities so that a maximum amount of local control is maintained; relaying as required up-to-date information to users on job status.

(e) Special device handling - this could range from handling fairly normal devices such as graph plotters and displays to acquiring data from special measuring devices.

(f) Utilities - providing many of the common utilities such as media conversion.

Front-end systems such as this will vary from the very simple to the very complex and there are many different ways in which the interface between the main-frame and front-end tasks will develop. The lead in these developments is unlikely to be taken by major manufacturers since it cuts across them and is very user-oriented. Thus we are likely to be faced by a very confused situation which is no improvement on the present unless this work is very firmly based on sound software engineering principles.

4. APPLICATION PROGRAM SUITES

Managing and planning the production and maintenance of large applications programs raises similar problems to those met in systems software. The use of software engineering techniques is just as relevant and indeed historically the early support for their development came from this direction.

Since most of the topics are dealt with at length in the main lectures, I will only highlight some of the most pertinent:

(a) Project management - training of staff in appropriate programming techniques; setting up standards; sub-dividing work into manageable parts; monitoring progress and quality.

(b) Product definition - specifying its function; defining user image; effects of host operating system.

(c) Documentation - selecting levels, methods and automatic aids; controlling quality; disseminating and updating.

(d) Design and implementation - this is a very large area but there is a particular problem with designing general purpose packages to operate in a multiprogramming environment where storage is at a premium - namely, how to combine generality and comprehensiveness with small size at run-time when applied to a simple particular case. This problem is of increasing importance and has design implications not only for the package but also for the operating system in which it runs.

(e) Problem-oriented languages - a recurrent theme of the course is the use of levels of language or hierarchies of abstract machines. to provide a structure within which a programming problem may be solved. Most application programs use only two levels, one at the Fortran or Cobol level and one at assembly code, although sometimes a less formal flow chart level can be recognised. Techniques now exist for readily creating levels which are matched to the problem at hand and which can be automatically translated from one level to the next lower one. In my own field, several groups are using very high level languages in which one merely specifies system of differential equations and the broad numerical methods to be used in their solution.

(f) Testing - generation of test data; use of test beds.

(g) Performance measurement - simulation; measurement tools; monitoring and optimisation.

(h) Maintenance and enhancement.

5. CONCLUSION

The help that the software engineer can provide the computer user falls into two parts: improvements to the computer systems that he has to use; and tools and techniques that he can make use of in his own work. In the former case greatest benefit will result if there is no sharp distinction drawn between software and hardware engineering.

6. REFERENCES

1   Wilkinson, J.H. & Reinsh, C. "Handbook for Automatic Computation, Vol. II Linear Algebra", Springer-Verlang, Berlin, 1971.

2   Rice, J. R. (Ed.), "Mathematical Software", Academic Press, New York, 1971.

3   Ford, B. "Developing a Numerical Algorithms Library", to appear in IMA Bulletin.

4   Poole, M.D., "Interim Report on A Stable User Image", Culham Laboratory Internal Report SEN 2/72.

THE DESIGN AND CONSTRUCTION OF SOFTWARE SYSTEMS

Jack B. Dennis [+]

Massachusetts Institute of Technology

Cambridge, Massachusetts, USA

1. INTRODUCTION

Software Engineering is the application of principles, skills and art to the design and construction of programs and systems of programs. It is often asserted that software engineering is largely art and based very little on sound principle. Yet trends are visible and new ideas are developing that promise to substantially increase the role of theory and principle in the design and construction of software systems. In this lecture, I wish to present a frame of reference for relating the material to be presented in this course. In addition, I shall try to assess the limitations of known principles for the practical needs of software engineering, and the prospects for broad future application of principle to the design and construction of software. This sketch will certainly be a very personal view of the field, for there is little published material that attempts to characterize software engineering.

The theme of this talk is that behind the absence of a satisfactory set of principles for the practice of software engineering lies the lack of adequate means for representing software and hardware system designs. Further development of the theoretical foundation for programming language semantics and system representation is required to overcome the limitations of contemporary software engineering.

[+]
The preparation of these notes was supported in part by the National Science Foundation under grant GJ-432 and in part by the Advanced Research Projects Agency, Department of Defense, under Office of Naval Research Contract Nonr-N00014-70-A-0362-0001.

2. TERMINOLOGY

In presenting a framework for discussing principles of software engineering we immediately encounter problems of terminology: What is
"software"? What do we mean by "computer system"?

2.1. COMPUTER SYSTEMS

We shall use the term *computer system* to mean a combination of hardware
and software components that provides a definite form of service to a
group of "users". A particular computer installation appears as many
different computer systems depending on the group of users considered.
For example, in a general purpose computer installation that offers
the ability to edit and interpret programs expressed in the language
Basic [1], we can identify at least three distinct computer systems
and corresponding user groups.

system	*user group*
1. the computer hardware	operating system implementers
2. hardware plus operating system	subsystem implementers
3. hardware, operating system and Basic language subsystem	users of Basic

Any computer system defines a language in terms of which all software
run on the computer system is expressed. I mean this in a very exact
sense: A computer system provides representations for certain data
types and information structures, and implements a set of primitive
operations on these data types and structures. Let us consider the
three cases mentioned above.

Suppose the computer system consists only of hardware (a processing
unit and main memory, say). Then the data types correspond to the in-
terpretations of memory words that are implicit in the built-in operations of the processor -- usually fixed and floating point representations for numerical quantities. In the absence of base registers
in the processor, the information structures of this computer system
are simply all possible contents of the main memory, selection of a
desired component of a structure being accomplished through indexing
or address computation. The effect of the interrupt feature of the computer must also be modelled in the language. The possibility of asyn-

chronous interrupts makes the language defined by a hardware computer
system nondeterministic; that is, there may be many successor states
possible for a given state of the system.

When the central hardware is augmented by peripheral devices and an
operating system, additional data types and classes of information
structures are represented, new primitive operations are defined, and
some features of the hardware are made inaccessible. One important
addition is the availability of files as a representation for information structures -- data and programs. Separate address spaces are
provided for each concurrent computation and a generalized means of
referencing data items and programs is implemented. The absolute addressing mechanism of the hardware is often not available to the user.
Similarly, the hardware facilities for process switching and interrupt
processing are replaced by software primitives for interprocess communication, which are implemented by the scheduling modules of the
operating system.

The operations and data structures of the language defined by hardware and operating system may be complex. For example, in this view,
the action of a program linking loader must be considered as a primitive operation that transforms one information structure (representing
a set of program modules generated by compilers) into a new information
structure (a set of procedures linked together and assigned to the
address space of a computation).

The inclusion of peripheral devices may alter the view the user has of
the language of the computer system. In the absence of peripherals, the
machine appears as a device into which one puts programs for execution.
The language of the computer system is then the set of programs that
can be represented in memory according to the computer system's instruction code. If users interact with a computer system from peripheral
terminals, the system behaves as a device having a set of internal
configurations and which responds to messages with answers depending
on its extant configuration. The language of the system now appears to
the user as a set of meaningful messages together with corresponding
state transitions and conditioned respondes.

Adding a software subsystem for the Basic programming language yields
a third computer system. The language defined by it is a model for the
commands and responses by which one interacts with the Basic subsystem

from a user's terminal. In this language, the primitive data types and operations are those of Basic. Users have access to the language of the operating system only through use of the subsystem.

2.2. SOFTWARE SYSTEMS

The environment for a program consists of the computer system on which the program runs, together with any hardware components, other than those of the computer system, required by the program. By the term *software system* we mean the software and hardware components that must be added to a specific computer system, called the *host system*, in order to realize some desired function.

We may illustrate in terms of the example cited above: For an operating system the host system may be the processing units and main memory hardware. The operating system is then a software system having many software modules and appropriate mass storage devices to hold files. This computer system may then serve as the host system for a software system that implements the language Basic. This software system consists of an editor, an interpreter, and a command processor. If the host system does not include a communications line controller, the implementer of Basic would find it necessary to add one to the host as part of the new computer system.

2.3. HIERARCHY

Hierarchical relationships occur in many forms in computer systems. Here, we will discuss just one form of hierarchy: the hierarchy of *linguistic levels* defined by successive layers of software. Each level of this hierarchy is a computer system characterized by the data types and primitive operations of its language. Each level is (or, is potentially) the host system for the definition of new linguistic levels through the addition of further software systems.

Hierarchy is a tool of software engineering which, if properly used, permits the components of several levels to be designed and developed separately. Of course, separate development of system levels is only possible if the languages corresponding to the boundaries between layers of software have been precisely specified and agreed to. For success, the implementers of a software system should not find it necessary to alter any component of the host system. Such need would expose incompleteness or inefficiency of the host language for the objectives of the software system. This principle is often violated in practice, for example, when an inner layer of an operating system is modified so an accounting procedure may be implemented within an outer software layer.

We distinguish three techniques used to define a new linguistic level by a software system: *extension, translation* and *interpretation*. Often combinations of the three techniques are used.

1. *Extension:* In defining a new linguistic level by procedural extension, the software system added to the host system is simply a collection of procedures that express the primitive operations of the new level in terms of the primitive operations of the host system. New data types or structure classes are implemented in this way and made available to users of the extended system in addition to the primitives and data types of the host system. In using extension the internal representations for procedures at both levels, host and new, are identical, syntactically and semantically.

2. *Translation:* Defining a new linguistic level by translation consists of writing a compiler to run on the host system that translates programs at the new linguistic level into programs in the language of the host system. The necessity of compilation as a step in running a program is characteristic of this technique. Representations of programs expressed in the language of the new level are not directly executed.

3. *Interpretation:* Defining a new linguistic level by interpretation consists of writing an interpreter for the language of the new level in terms of the data types and primitive operations of the host system. Programs at the new linguistic level are represented in directly executable form.

A software system may be designed so that all persons using the host system are required to do so at the linguistic level of the software system. An example is a computer run under a specific operating system which all users of the computer must use. Alternatively, several software systems may share the same host, as in the case that several programming language systems operate under the same executive control program.

Further, the definition of a new level may or may not deny the user access to part or all of the linguistic features of the host. The difference between use of extension and interpretation is that in extension the primitives of the host system remain available at the new level whereas this is usually not the case when interpretation is used.

It would seem that procedural extension ought not be considered as defining a new linguistic level unless the added procedures are grouped in a way that hierarchical relations are defined. Examples are the use of the technique for application packages and in the implementation of command languages of operating systems. In these cases, a collection of procedures defines the new linguistic level. Users of the new level are often prevented from using procedures outside the collection, and then the collection of provedures is essentially an interpreter for the new linguistic level.

Translation and interpretation are fundamentally different in the following respect: Two compilers for different source languages, if implemented for the same host system, produce compiled procedures in the language of the host. If standard procedure interfacing conventions of the host are honored by both compilers, then programs expressed in the two source languages may be operated together successfully. In contrast, interpretation is usually done because of a need to utilize a fundamentally different form of data organization from the host, or to obtain program monitoring and control features not possible at the host level. That is, the host level is *incomplete* for the objectives of the software system. If interpreters for two source languages are written in the language of the host, then communication between procedures expressed in the two languages will be difficult if not impossible, unless carefully coordinated planning is done by the implementers. Each interpreter will likely use entirely different representations for equivalent data types, hence each call on a procedure expressed in the other language would have to cause switching of interpreters and translation of all data to be communicated.

2.4. *SYSTEM AND APPLICATION SOFTWARE*

Traditionally "system program" r efers to the layers of software that "belong" to a computer installation and are available to all clients of the installation; "application software" refers to the software brought to an installation by a client for performing his desired computation. This distinction between system and application software has lost meaning with the evolution of more sophisticated uses of computer systems. For example, one client of an installation may implement a new programming language and make it available to other clients of the installation. Or an installation may be devoted entirely to a particular application as in the case of real-time systems such as reservation and inventory systems.

Nevertheless, by using the concepts and terminology discussed above, we may list certain distinguishing characteristics that will serve to crudely classify software as *system software* or *application software* for the purposes of subsequent discussion.

system software: A collection of system programs usually forms a hierarchy of software systems having these properties:

1. The collection of programs are implemented under one authority.

2. The hierarchy of software systems defines a single linguistic level which applies to all users of the collection of programs.

3. Inner linguistic levels of the hierarchy are hidden from the user.

4. The outer linguistic level of the hierarchy is "complete" for the goals of the implementing authority.

5. The primary means of defining new linguistic levels is partial interpretation.

application software: An application program or software system usually has these properties:

1. The programs are expressed in terms of a "complete" linguistic level

2. The programs define a new linguistic level by extension, translation interpretation, or by some combination of these techniques.

3. The linguistic level defined by the program or software system is inadequate for defining further linguistic levels.

4. A variety of such programs or software systems are available to clients of an installation, and are often implemented under different authorities.

3. DESCRIPTION OF SOFTWARE SYSTEMS

The design and construction of a software system is, fundamentally, the creation of a complete and precise description of the system. The description of a software system is a collection of descriptions of its software and hardware components.

The complete and precise description of a software component is in reality a program expressed in a well-defined programming language. If this language is the language of the host system, or the translation of the program to the linguistic level defined by the host is strictly a clerical operation, then preparing the program completes the process of constructing the system component. Otherwise implementation of the component is incomplete until a correct representation of the component is prepared at the linguistic level of the host system.

In the case of a hardware component, a description is adequate only if it permits the designer of the software system to determine exactly the relevant behavior of the component for all situations that may occur during operation of the software system. Statements of interfacing conventions are insufficient, for these do not describe the function performed by the hardware component. Usually, an adequate description must take the form of a model of the internal operation of the component.

Besides descriptions of its hardware and software components, two further descriptions are required: A description of the host system, and a description of the linguistic level the software system is intended to realize. The semantics of the linguistic level of the host system must be known before the components of outer software layers can have exact representations. Of course, the objectives of the system must be known before final designs of all of its components can be specified.

4. FUNCTION, CORRECTNESS, PERFORMANCE AND RELIABILITY

The designer of a software system wishes to achieve certain goals. The goals are expressed in terms of four kinds of properties desired of the completed software system: function, correctness, performance, and reliability. Let us consider the state-of-the-art in each of these four aspects of software systems and the directions in which further development of principle is needed.

4.1. FUNCTION

The function of a software system is the correspondence desired of output with input. Input is all information absorbed by the software system from outside the host system; output is all information delivered outside the host system. Information held by a software system between interactions with the outside is covered by this view, since such information either is the result of processing information received as input, or should be considered part of the software system, its effect then being incorporated in the mapping of inputs to outputs.

In the case of application software, the function of a software system depends on what one takes as the host system. For example, the data base for an application may be internal if the host system provides a data management facility, or it may be external if the data base is on a set of tapes not part of the host system.

In the case of system programs, the function of a collection of system programs is to implement a specified linguistic level. A linguistic level is adequately defined only by a model of a class of system states, and a state-transition function which, together, give the equivalent of a formal interpreter for the level.

There is a rapidly growing body of formal knowledge applicable to many aspects of the representation of programs and systems. Some of this material is listed below:

1. Semantic models for programming languages.
    the lambda calculus [2]
    the contour model [3, 4]
    Vienna definition method [5, 6]
    program schemas [7, 8]

2. Concepts relating to interacting concurrent activities
    Petri nets [9]
    processes, semaphores, determinacy [10]
    modularity [11]

3. Fundamentals of classes of algorithms
    numerical methods
    symbolic algorithms (e.g. sorting, theorem proving)

parsing methods

Although the theoretical foundation for programs and systems is fast developing, there is a yet no generally accepted representation scheme that has a precisely known semantics and is sufficiently general to meet the descriptive needs of software system designers. Areas in which the theoretical development has not yet provided an accepted synthesis of concepts are:

1. Representation of concurrent activities and their interaction.

2. The sharing of procedures and data among computations.

3. Representation of data structures which change in content and extent during computation.

4. The notions of ownership, protection, and monitoring.

The consequence of this state of affairs is that designers of computer systems adopt different sets of primitive data types and operations as the basis for the design of the inner layers of hardware and software. Then, in realizing a standardized linguistic level such as a *FORTRAN* programming system the system designer employs these primitives to implement the standardized aspects of the language. Nevertheless, the **implementer** is usually forced to implement extensions of the language so application programmers may make use of unstandardized linguistic features of the host. Since the primitives in terms of which these extensions are defined are different for different computer systems, the extensions are unlikely to be compatible, and portability of the application software is lost.

This discussion underscores the need for better understanding of the semantic issues listed above.

Suppose a computer system is developed as a hierarchy of several linguistic levels. Then the data types and primitive operations used at each linguistic level are restricted to those implemented at deeper levels. Often a single language (a *system programming language)* is advocated for representing software components at all levels within the system. In this case, either the language can include only the linguistic features implemented at the innermost level (the hardware), or restrictions must be placed on use of linguistic features depending on the level for which software is being written. Certain essential hard-

ware features such as interrupt mechanisms, processor faults, and protection features are not usually incorporated as linguistic features
of the system programming language, and recourse must be made to machine
language procedures. In this way, the system programming language is
extended to encompass the primitives required to implement its higher
level features, and linguistic features of the computer system that
are not directly encompassed by the system programming language.

Thus a system programming language provides primarily a syntactic structure permitting easy use of linguistic features common to all linguistic
levels at which it is used. The degree to which a system programming
language aids in simplifying the design and programming of system software depends critically on the generality of the set of linguistic
features common to all software levels.

4.2. CORRECTNESS

Correctness of a software system means correctness of its description
with respect to the objective of the software system as specified by
the semantic description of the linguistic level it defines. Regardless
of the approach adopted to favor correctness of a software system, it
is always the responsibility of the designer of the system or system
component to convince himself of the correctness of *some* description
of the system or component. One would like this description to be as
simple as possible, for example, a simple relation of output to input.

Two approaches to the correctness of systems have been suggested:

1. Structured programming [12]: The use of a programming style that
    makes the correctness of a program self-evident to the author.

Greater use of structured programming is limited by the need for linguis
tic features not found in established programming languages. Use of
structured programming may be encouraged by use of languages that dis-
allow troublesome linguistic features such as *goto* statements and side
effects.

2. Proof of correctness [13]: To prove correctness of a software system
    or component, one establishes by logical deduction that some descrip
    tion of the system or component asserted to be correct by the desig-

ner is equivalent to the description of the system or component
expressed at the host level.

In the case that the host level description is the result of automatically
translating the designer's description, proving the correctness of the
translator suffices. In other cases mechanically generated proofs or
man-machine proof generating systems are required for this approach to
be effective, and the semantics of the host language must be correctly
axiomatized for the proof generator. This approach is beginning to be
used experimentally. Although it is questionable whether establishing
correctness by proof will become a practical technique, the research is
yielding useful knowledge for improving the design of programs and
languages.

4.3. PERFORMANCE

Performance of a software system is the effectiveness with which resources
of the host system are utilized toward meeting the objective of the software system.

The demands on a contemporary software system usually cannot be modelled
exactly, and statistical characterizations must be employed. The theoretical foundation for performance studies is Markov processes and
queuing models, for these models of stochastic service systems are amenable to analysis. In software systems where the demands can be reasonably
well determined by observation, for example, in real-time transaction
systems, statistical analysis has provided valuable predictions of performance to system designers.

On the other hand, performance analysis has so far failed to provide
adequate methods for predicting the performance of software systems
where the applications to be implemented at the new linguistic level
are unknown. This state of affairs is due to two difficulties, both
stemming from the lack of generally accepted representation schemes
for software. One difficulty is the absence of a satisfactory model
of resource usage for application programs represented at the new linguistic level. For each design of a software system, a new model of
program behavior has to be formulated and validated before it can be
used to extrapolate performance data. These models have not been useful for predicting performance of a tentative system design. The other

difficulty is that the software system itself is not represented in a generally accepted notation, and no standard techniques of performance analysis are available for direct application to the descriptions of software systems.

The main point of these remarks is that our ability to analyze and predict performance of software systems is limited by the inadequacies of available description schemes rather than by the inadequacy of statistical methods. After all, approximate answers to performance questions are often satisfactory, but there is no such thing as a satisfactory approximate description of function.

4.4. *RELIABILITY*

Reliability is the ability of a software system to perform its function correctly in spite of failures of computer system components. By *failure* of a component we mean a temporary or permanent change in its characteristics that alters its function. Software does not fail. What is often referred to as "software failure" is a matter of correctness.

Nevertheless, one must recognize the high likelihood of incorrect software being present in a complex software system. The design of a system as a set of minimally interacting modules using principles of structured programming can limit effects of software bugs to the modules and data structures that depend on correctness of the module in error. The possibility of realizing practical systems constructed according to this principle depends on new fundamental knowledge of structured programming and modular systems.

If a software system has no hardware components, then component failures can only occur within the hardware components of the host computer system. In the ideal host system, failures of its hardware would not be observable at the linguistic level defined. Some current work [14] on fault-tolerant and self testing and repair computer architecture is directed toward realizing this ideal, but is still far from solving the problem in the context of general purpose computer systems. Most reported work on reliability is concerned with the detection of failures and does not attempt to cope with the loss of information that inevitably accompanies hardware failure. We need concepts of computer organization that will permit the construction of computer systems in which single internal failures do not produce observable effects.

Since the ideal host system is not now available, some hardware failures will affect operation of software systems implemented at the linguistic level of the host. Then a description of the host system is not complete without a specification of the possible modes of failure, and the resulting effects observed at the host linguistic level. A software system to be implemented on such a host is not completely described unless the action to be taken for each failure mode of the host is specified.

At present we must be satisfied with software systems even if they occasionally fail with irrecoverable loss of information. For it is not known how to construct an infallible software system using a fallible computer system as host. Although there are systems (such as the American Airlines Sabre system and the Bell System's Electronic Switching System No. 1 ESS) that come close to providing complete protection against all single failures, the techniques used do not generalize easily to computer systems intended for general application.

5. SOFTWARE PROJECTS

Large projects for the design and construction of software systems are notorious for their delays in meeting specified objectives. A large project is one in which two or more levels of management are required, and hence the key personnel of the project are not in continous communication with one another. In a large project it is necessary to divide the work to be done into units for assignment to project teams. Any unit of work which in itself amounts to a large project must be further subdivided.

The best division of work into units is the division that minimizes the interaction between units. Two kinds of structure may be used as a basis for the subdivision of work: hierarchy and modularity.

Suppose a project team is assigned the construction of some module of a software system. The team's task is completely defined by a precise specification of:

1. The function of the module.

2.   The linguistic level of the host system.
3.   The performance required of the module.
4.   The performance capability of the host.

In practice this information is at best only partially known by a project team at the time it is expected to begin work. It is often still
incomplete   at the time the team is expected to have a usable version
of the module ready for integration with other system components.

Clearly, the most crucial information required by a project team is a
precise definition of the linguistic level of the host system: for it
is impossible for the team to produce a correct description of any part
of the module unless the semantics of the host system are known.

Iteration of design is frequently found to be necessary in large software projects. Iteration occurs when it is found that decisions already
made prevent realization of overall system objectives. The most serious
design iteration is where more than one linguistic level is affected,
as the description of all modules in outer software layers may be in-
validated by a change to a host system. The need for iteration arises
in several ways: Sometimes it is discovered that certain linguistic
features needed to implement a software system are impossible to realize
in terms of the primitive constructs of the host level. Then the semantic
of the host level must be revised to meet the need. In other cases, it
is found that the performance objectives of a software system cannot be
achieved without altering the specification of host level function.

These observations bring out the importance of having a precise specification of the host system before beginning construction of components
of a software system. For each additional layer included in a software
system, either the project must be extended to allow time for the precise
formulation of the new linguistic level, or work on several levels must
overlap, raising the risk that design iteration will be required. The
need to implement several linguistic levels within one project would be
circumvented if a host computer system were available that realized a
complete and satisfactory linguistic level for the objectives of the project.

These arguments reinforce the need for better understanding of fundamental linguistic constructs for building software systems and the
development of corresponding principles of computer system architecture.

When this understanding has been gained, perhaps there will no longer
be any need for large software projects.

6. *ACKNOWLEDGEMENT*

The author wishes to express his thanks to Professor Jerome Saltzer,
whose incisive comments on an early draft have been valuable in the
preparation of these notes.

7. *REFERENCES*

1. J. G. Kemeny and T.E. Kurtz, *BASIC Programming*. John Wiley and Sons,
   Inc., New York 1967.

2. P. J. Landin, A correspondence between *ALGOL 60* and Church's lambda-
   notation, Part I: *Comm. of the ACM, Vol. 8, No. 2* (February 1965),
   pp 89 - 101.
   Part II: *Comm. of the ACM, Vol. 8, No. 3* (March 1965), pp 158 - 169

3. J. B. Johnston, The contour model of block structured processes.
   *Proceedings of a Symposium on Data Structures in Programming
   Languages, SIGPLAN Notices, Vol. 6, No. 2* (February 1971), pp 55 -
   82.

4. D. M. Berry, Block structure: retention or deletion?
   Proceedings of the 3rd Annual ACM Symposium on Theory of Computing,
   May 1971, pp 86 - 100.

5. P. Lucas and K. Walk, On the formal description of PL/I. *Annual
   Review in Automatic Programming, Vol. 6, Part 3,* Pergamon Press,
   1969.

6. P. Lucas, P. Lauer, and H. Stigleitner, *Method and Notation for
   the Formal Definition of Programming Languages*. Technical Report
   TR 25.087, IBM Laboratory Vienna, June 1968.

7. M. S. Paterson, Decision problems in computational models. *Proceedings of an ACM Conference on Proving Assertions About Programs,
   SIGPLAN Notices, Vol. 7, No. 1* (January 1972), pp 74 - 82.

8. A. P. Ershov, Survey paper on program schemata, presented at the
    IFIP Congress, Ljubljana, 1971.

9. A. Holt, F. Commoner, S. Even, and A. Pnueli, Marked directed
    graphs. *J. of Computer and System Sciences, Vol. 5, No.* (1971),
    pp 511 - 523.

10. E. W. Dijkstra, Co-operating sequential processes. *Programming
    Languages*, F. Genuys, Ed., Academic Press, New York 1968. (First
    published as Report EWD 123, Department of Mathematics, Technolo-
    gical University, Eindhoven, The Netherlands, 1965.)

11. S. S. Patil, Closure Properties of interconnections of determinate
    systems. *Record of the Project MAC Conference on Concurrent
    System and Parallel Computation*, ACM, New York 1970, pp 107 - 116

12. E. W. Dijkstra, A constructive approach to the problem of program
    correctness. *BIT* (Nordisk Tidskrift for Informations-behandling),
    Vol. 8, No. 3 (1968), pp 174 - 186.

13. Z. Manna and R. J. Waldinger, Toward automatic program synthesis.
    Comm. of the ACM, Vol. 14, No. 3 (March 1971), pp 151 - 165.

14. A. Avizienis, G. C. Gilley, F. P. Mathur, D. A. Rennels, J.A.Rohr,
    and D. K. Rubin, The STAR (Self-Testing and Repairing) computer:
    an investigation of the theory and practice of fault-tolerant
    computer design. *IEEE Trans. on Computers, Vol. C-20, No. 11*
    (November 1971), pp 1312 - 1321.

HIERARCHIES

Gerhard Goos, Karlsruhe
University of Karlsruhe, Germany

0.   INTRODUCTION

Large software systems are usually subdivided into many components;
every component solves a subproblem into which the original problem can
be split. The decomposition influences not only the properties of the
final system; the implementation effort itself is influenced in several respects.

There are very few ideas only about the methodological question how the
decomposition can be achieved best. The most elaborated one is the
well-known engineering principle of building complex components from
simpler ones, establishing a hierarchical order of components. This
lecture is concerned with the application of this principle of software
construction and programming languages.

1.   HIERARCHICAL ORDERING AS A DESIGN STRATEGY

The design of a software system starts from a description of the problem to be solved and the available host system (in the sense of [1]).
The problem may be formally represented by an abstract machine which
from the input-data, a *program* for this machine, produces some out-
put-data solving a particular case of the problem.

The gap between the host system and the problem is now bridged in two
steps :

First a set of program components (procedures, coroutines, asynchro-
neous processes) is defined by specifying their interfaces to the outside. Every component either solves a part of the original problem,
i.e. it implements some functions of the abstract machine, or it implements some functions needed in defining other components. Via their
interfaces the components communicate with each other by various interconnections : procedure calls, use of common data, exchange-jumps (in
case of coroutines), synchronization primitives. We call this first
step the gross design of the system.

As a second step the internal behaviour of each component is defined. Since we know the interfaces of the component to the outside the component can be separately considered and the same principles can be applied to the design of the component as to the system as a whole.

The ideas may be illustrated by considering the construction of a file-system of an operating system. The file-system may be subdivided into four components :

- the basic I/O routines for the disc
- the storage allocation on disc
- the handling of directories, protection-mechanisms
  etc. for the files
- the implementation of access functions to files,
  and directories based on the I/O routines mentioned before.

The result of the gross design can be represented as a network of components (fig. 1.). Every arrow represents an asymmetric communication line between components, e.g. a possible procedure call. Symmetric communication lines, e.g., use of common data, is represented by two arrows. The network is a directed graph of arbitrary complexity. This complexity may cause trouble concerning the following objektives of software-design :

- The design should allow at every stage to convince
  oneself of the correctness of the designed program as
  far as it is already known. One should not use design
  techniques which increase the probability that one must
  go back revising large parts of earlier design decisions because of errors found to late. In practice
  such techniques very often imply that errors are never
  corrected.

- Programs are very often modified either during design,
  production or later to meet modified requirements or
  different resources. Therefore the original design
  should produce a program structure in which the
  components are as independent from each other as possible. At least an overview on all consequences of
  changing a particular design decision must be possible.

31

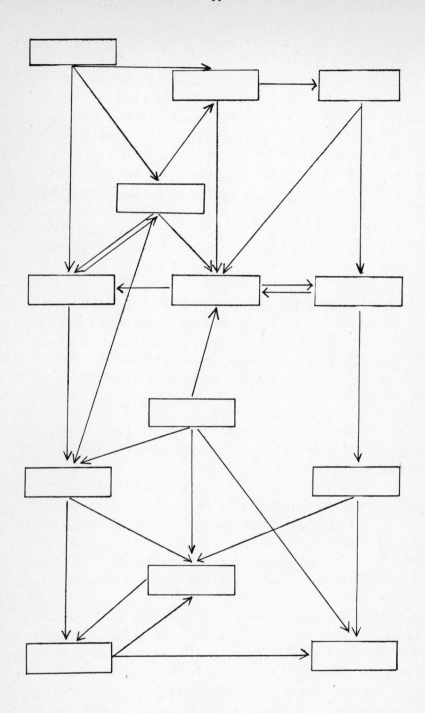

Fig. 1   Network of Program Components

- Design, production and maintenance of software must be
  manageable tasks. This also requires that the interde-
  pendence of components is kept to a minimum. At the
  same time the dependencies must be clearly presented
  not only in detail but also in principle. Otherwise
  one cannot split the problem into subtasks to be solved
  by a larger group of people since these people will always have trouble in communicating with each other :
  Either they have to spend too much time in getting the
  necessary informations about the environment in which
  their work is to be used. Or they do not get the information at all since they do not know which information
  they need and where it can be found.

These objectives are hardly met when - as in figure 1 - the network
shows interdependencies, e.g. cycles, between the program parts which
cause difficulties in overviewing all the implications of design decisions and modifications. Obviously such difficulties will also make it
impossible to overview the grounds on which further desisions have to
be based.

Hence the objective is to reduce the interrelations between program
parts. Since cycles cannot be excluded completely - every set of cooperation processes in the sense of Dijkstra [2] constitutes such a cycle - all what we can do is to minimize the number of program parts belonging to a cycle. We arrive at a partially ordered set of program
layers (fig. 2.) each of which is either a single program component
or a cycle of program components. Very often the set of layers forms
a tree (fig. 3.) or a linearly ordered set (fig. 4.). The term layer
was originally introduced for the latter case only by Dijkstra [3].

The principle of structuring a system into a partially ordered set of
layers is called *hierarchical ordering*. Hierarchical ordering is a
successful technique because it allows to build systems from more elementary program components - layers - in a clearly conceived way. We
get maximum insight in the completeness and correctness of the gross
design. At the same time, we are forced to set up a clear scheme for
interfacing the different layers. Hierarchical ordering splits the system into components in such a way that we can hope everybody will get
a clear picture of what the interface to other components is and how a
component contributes to the tasks of the system as a whole.

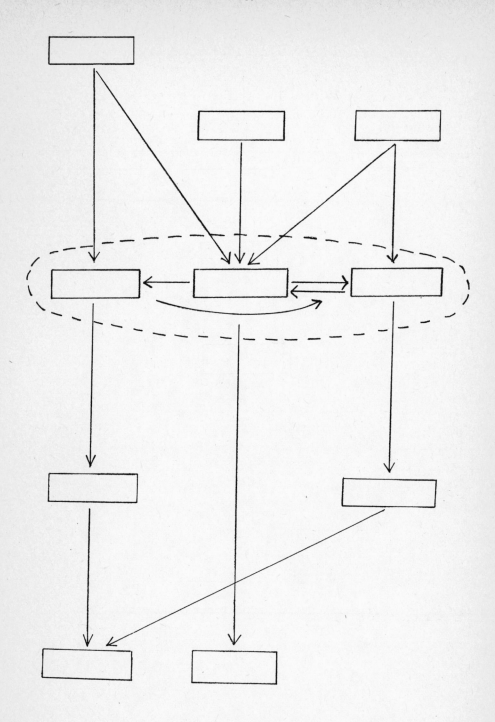

Fig. 2   Partially ordered Set of Layers

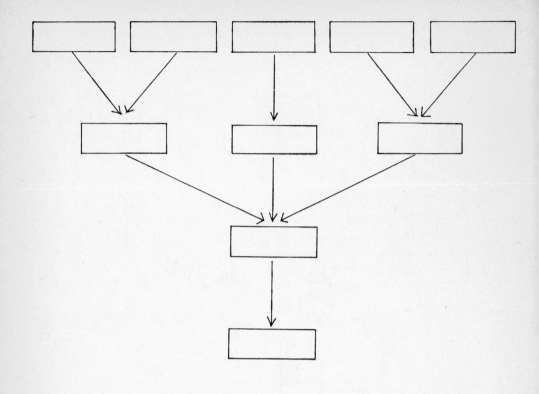

Fig. 3   Tree-like structured Program

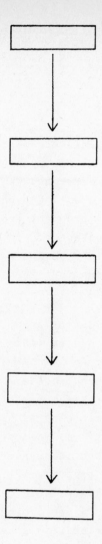

Fig. 4   Linearly ordered set of Layers

Hierarchical ordering is achieved by a systematic way of thinking about how the objectives of the system can be met. This is our next subject.

1.1. *LEVELS OF ABSTRACTION*

Let us assume we have to solve some numerical problem P_0 on some computer. Usually we shall solve P_0 by a program written in some high-level language, e.g. *ALGOL*. Provided we know the mathematical algorithms for solving our problem well enough this program is straightforward and causes no particular problems from the programmers point of view. This, however, is a consequence of the fact that it is relatively well-known which programming tools are required for numerical applications and that *ALGOL* allows for expressing algorithms fairly easily by these tools.

In fact, we have not yet solved our problem by programming it in *ALGOL*. In addition we must supply an implementation of *ALGOL* on our computer. Hence our solution up to now was only a reduction of the original problem P_0 to another problem P_1, the implementation of (a compiler and) a run-time system for *ALGOL*. On smaller machines this run-time system may be implemented directly, incorporating routines for storage-allocation, storage-access - e.g. addressing of multi-dimensional arrays -, I/O and standard functions. In a multi-programming environment we run many programs written in different high-level languages simultaneously. Thus we have to implement many run-time systems. Each of these reduces a problem of type P_1 to the problem P_2 of implementing a resource allocation scheme which distributes the resources available on the computer to the different *users*, represented by a run-time system and a program running on it. P_2 is solved by the operating system.

This example shows the following significant properties :

- The original problem P_0 is solved not by one program but by a number of program layers : *ALGOL* program, run-time system, operating system.
- Each of these layers solves a problem P_i by means of a certain set of programming tools. The implementation of these tools constitutes problem P_{i+1}.

- The tools for the final problem are the properties of the hardware.

- Except that every layer implements the tools for the foregoing one, the layers are completely independent. At least conceptually, when writing the *ALGOL* program we are not concerned with the details of how the elementary constructs of *ALGOL* are implemented. Conversely, when writing the operating system or the run-time system we are not concerned with the properties of *ALGOL* programs for which we supply the tools. (Exceptions from this rule of independence may arise from efficiency considerations.)

To be more general, the method which we have applied to this example may be expressed as follows :

To solve a problem we choose an appropriate abstract machine, e.g. the *ALGOL* machine in the example above, on which the problem is implemented. The machine is appropriate if it implements the basic notions by which we have expressed the algorithm for the problem. Of course, these notions must contribute to reducing the original problem to the capabilities of the host system. Repetitive application of this principle yields a sequence of abstract machines the last of which is identical to the given host system.

By every abstract machine of this sequence we abstract from some details of the previous one and of the original problem. It constitutes a *level of abstraction* on the way from the original problem to the host system. Conversely : Every abstract machine abstracts from some properties of the host system using it for implementing some new tools which are better suited for the intended application. So it constitutes a *level of abstraction* on the way from the host system to the original problem.

In introducing the term *level of abstraction*, E. W. Dijkstra used the bottom-up approach and stated the following properties of the abstract machines (which are now numbered $A_0, A_1, \ldots, A_n$, starting from the host system) :

- The resources and the functions provided by A_i form the the complete basis on which to build A_{i+1}. There is

no way to use properties of A_{i-1} in building A_{i+1}.
Hence, every A_i is a complete interface-description
in the hierarchy.

- Resources of A_{i-1} used in defining new resources of
  A_i can no longer be present in A_i.

- The correctness of the solution of the final problem
  can be asserted by stepwise proving the correctness of
  the implementation of each abstract machine A_{i+1} on A_i.

The last assertion is obvious. The second rule is trivial but it is
mentioned here because it is often overlooked and violated in practice.
Modularity is achieved by the first property. However, there may be properties of A_i identical to some properties of A_{i-1}. But in using
these for constructing A_{i+1} we have to consider them as properties of
A_i and we have to forget about whether a property is newly constructed
in the layer yielding A_i or merely preserved from the previous level.

The bottom-up approach also shows the way in which we achieve tree-like
hierarchical structures : Based on an abstract machine A_i many different machines A_{i+1} may be implemented sharing the resources provided
by A_i. Top-down design shows one path in the tree only because it assumes that there is only one problem to be solved.

1.2.   *THE ORDER OF DESIGN DECISIONS*

The last remark shows that top-down design is not always appropriate.
In fact, if the problem to be solved can be split into various sub-pro-
blems which have to be solved simultaneously, we shall get layers implementing sharing of resources and the possibly necessary synchronization between different program components. These layers cannot be designed working downwards from a subproblem creating a sequence of abstractions. In this case bottom-up is more appropriate.

Obviously this consideration is concerned with the order in time in
which design decisions are taken. The conceptual ordering is a consequence of the ordering in time.

In general working through the levels only once is insufficient. Instead we must iterate one or more times revising earlier decisions until we get the system balanced. Although such iterations show that these earlier decisions were based on wrong assumptions we must often start from unproven assumptions if we want to start at all. This raises the question how to get a stable and correct gross design as fast as possible.

Top-down design without iteration is useful for that purpose if the problems discussed in the beginning of the paragraph are not involved and if moreover the following conditions are met :

- The problem is described in a fairly constructive manner
- it must be known in advance, e.g., by experience that from the given description of the problem a solution can be derived, efficiently implementable by available resources.

Conversely, for using bottom-up design the host system must be precisely known and experience must allow to derive the next levels such that we really approach the problem to be solved. In either case we must assure for each layer that we have not forgotten any major feature needed in the abstract machines below and above respectively.

The first of the conditons mentioned above is satisfied by most problems stated by a set of formal conditions to be satisfied by the solution. It is never fulfilled when the validity of the solution depends not only on correctness and efficiency but also on such terms as convenience to the user, range of applicability etc. as in the case of operating systems. Analogously bottom-up design should not be applied if the underlying hardware configurations may vary in a wide range or if the resulting software has to be portable.

Whether the second condition is satisfied or not depends mostly on the people involved. One must be able to make a useful choice amongst different alternatives for solving partial problems knowing in advance that the decision never has to be revised. Of course, one must use iteration when one starts by investigating whether the problem description is suitable for implementaion. E.g., since language definitions usually do not allow for straightforward solutions, compilers are designed with iteration.

To avoid iterations efficiency problems must be considered carefully.
It must be noted that every abstract machine A_i is slower than all
the underlying machines. The execution of some *machine-instructions*
for that machine involves the call of some procedures of the layer below. So the latter works using a smaller *grain of time*. Unfortunately this remark may apply to operations occuring very frequently which
perhaps could be implemented much more efficiently by circumventing the
hierarchical order. Careful analysis should exhibit such critical
operations in advance so that they can be placed in a layer as low as
possible in order to speed them up.

To summarize, design without iteration looks like throwing a ball into
a hole. Whether we succeed depends on the size of the hole and of the
ball as well as on our knowledge about the position of the hole and
our experience in throwing.

In general we cannot hope to succeed by top-down or bottom-up design
only. There are too many problem areas which cannot be related together correctly in the first attempt. Another reason might be that the
implications of introducing certain algorithms or data structures cannot be overviewed immediately. Apparently whether or not such arguments apply to a particular design depends on the previous experience
of the designers.

In such cases we can start using any design strategy mentioned above.
But after we have gone through once we have to go back revising earlier
decisions or - in the worst case - starting over again from the beginning. Revisions are based on the insights we have got in designing
other parts of the system or in developing details of the proposed
gross design.

If there are subproblems whose solution seems to influence strongly the
design of other parts of the system, we can also start the design somewhere in the middle of the system instead of proceeding top-down or
bottom-up. Operating systems are often designed in this way starting
from decisions on memory allocation. Also simulation experiments may
be a good starting point. Those problems are further discussed by S.
Gill [4], Zurcher and Randell [5] and Randell [6].

As Dijkstra [3] points out, it is useful that the final design is
thought to be achieved in the bottom-up manner regardless how it really
was achieved : At least during testing it is much better to consider

the layers in sequence starting from the bottom than to provide a test environment for each layer. - In practice, such artificial environments are only useful if the interfaces are very simple.

2. *HIERARCHICAL ORDERING AND LANGUAGES*

Each level of abstraction in a hierarchically ordered system introduces a new programming language. The skeleton of this language is given by the catalogue of admissible operations on that level. Other concepts - data types, resources etc. - are introduced as the attributes of parameters of these operations. The set of operations may be viewed as the set of instructions of a computer and it is this view which leads to the term *abstract machine*. Of course, to be a convenient basis for programming the language should have some *flesh* around this skeleton.

Considering levels of abstractions as programming languages introduces a set of criteria, e.g. programming convenience, portability, adaptability, range of applicability and implementability. These criteria are particularly important in the development of application software. Our subject is not to apply them to a particular level of abstraction but to relate them to the hierarchy of levels.

2.1.   *ABSTRACT MACHINES AND THE PRODUCTION PROCESS*

Hierarchical ordering was introduced as a means for structuring the design and thus the final product. However, it influences the production and maintenance phase also. Therefore we must observe some additional rules in designing the different abstract machines.

The first rule is very simple : system programmers are also programmers. Therefore convenient test facilities, appropriate means of storage administration, procedures converting between different data types etc. should belong to the lowest possible level, not only to the user oriented topmost level.

Secondly the production of *portable* software requires that there is an intermediate level which easily can be implemented on all available computers. This level is not necessarily the lowest one. E.g., to im-

plement a string manipulation system the lowest level should provide
for the basic string operations on a word-oriented computer. If these
facilities are already provided by a certain hardware then we can transfer the system to this computer implementing the second level as the
lowest one. Apparently, all layers below that level which is thought
to be the common base for all computers must implement machine dependent features only.

Thirdly adaptability to new applications can be best achieved if there
is an intermediate level yielding those and only those functions substantial to the system. Thus *adapting* means changing some algorithms
on top of this level only.

From rule 2 and 3 it follows that we have two levels so that all layers between these levels can be engineered to maximum efficiency without hampering portability or adaptability of the system.

The fourth rule says that all algorithms should be made available as
generally as possible. Counterexamples are found very often in operating system design. E. g. there exist very often procedures for text
editing accesssible by the command language interpreter but not by normal user programs. Thus, for implementing more powerful text editors
we have to implement the functions already present again.

The last rule is concerned with the control of efficiency. It is commonly observed that designers do not make the correct estimates about
the *critical paths* for efficiency in time or space. Hence it is required that the actual implementation of the basic operations of any
abstract machine contains means to record the frequency and the required amount of space and time for executing these operations. Otherwise
we will never know the critical path through the system concerning efficiency.

2.2.   *HIERARCHIES OF LANGUAGES*

As Dennis [1] points out the programming language corresponding to
an abstract machine A_{i+1} may be obtained by three different techniques from the language corresponding to A_i : Procedural extension,
translation and interpretation.

The primary concern of a new language in the hierarchy is the introduc-

tion of the new operations, data types and data structures corresponding to the new abstract machine. In addition, at least by using translation or interpretation one can protect against misuse of tools no
longer available on level A_{i+1}.

On the other hand, there is no reason why languages corresponding to
two different levels should have a different control structure. E.g.
it is not useful to have a hierarchy of languages with loops, case-
expressions, procedures etc. available on each level but expressed differently. In fact, by using procedural extension the control statements of the base language are automatically taken over from one level
to the next one. But also in case of a hierarchy based on two different languages, e.g. a system programming language and a high-level
language, an unified approach is preferable.

A good example for such an unified set of languages is provided by Burroughs [7, 8]. *ESPOL*, the language used in writing operating systems,
and Burroughs *Extended ALGOL* are both extensions of *ALGOL 60*. *ESPOL*
allows for some machine-oriented operations and data types not provided
by *Extended ALGOL*. The latter allows for file-handling implemented
by the operating system and thus this is not available in *ESPOL*. Both
languages define the operations *disable* and *enable interrupts*. In
ESPOL these operations denote the corresponding machine instructions;
in *Extended ALGOL* the operations denote system calls which protect
the current sequential process from being logically interrupted or allow for such interrupts.

Intentionally, *ESPOL* and *Extended ALGOL* are called a *set* of languages, not a hierarchy of languages. Each of these languages only defines a basis from which a hierarchy of languages may be developped by
procedural extensions. E.g., after we have added the usual procedures
for matrix-calculations *ALGOL* corresponds to another abstract machine
than before. Thus, statements as 'program *A* is written in assembly language' or 'program *B* is written in *ALGOL*' give a very
rough idea only of the level of abstraction used as the basis of program *A* or *B*.

By specifying a certain language out of a hierarchy of languages the
technique for implementing this language is not always implied. This
fact may be illustrated by the hierarchy of macro-languages used by
Waite and Poole [9]. The set of primitive instructions of one of these macro languages may be implemented by writing a procedure for each

instruction. But in-line coding by macro-substitution, a particular
case of compiling , is also possible. On a suitable computer some instructions may even directly correspond to machine instructions while
other instructions must be implemented by one of the other techniques.

3. *PROTECTION BY HIERARCHICAL ORDERING*

So far we have dealt with hierarchical ordering as an engineering aid
in design and production of software. The main assumption was that operations and data structures present on a level A_{i-1} but not on level
A_i cannot be used by programs running on A_i. However, this rule introduces hierarchical ordering as a tool in testing and debugging also :
To protect against misuse of operations and data we have to place these
operations and data in a different level.

There are three ways to apply this principle :

The most efficient way is separate compilation of different layers.
There is no price to be paid at run-time and it is guaranteed that different modules communicate only via clearly defined communication lines
specified by entry and external declarations. However, the protection
can be circumvented if the language allows for explicit address calculations or if the implementation does not check against indices exceeding the bounds. Moreover virtually no programming language allows for
read-only access to data in certain parts of a program while writing
is permitted elsewhere.

The second means is protection supported by hardware. By using different addressing schemes we can protect lower layers against any misuse
of data and operations provided by higher layers. Usually it is also
possible to exclude higher layers from writing certain data which nevertheless can be read. This well-known method has two disadvantages :
We can distinguish very few levels only because the hierarchy of addressing schemes is very limited. Moreover, we often waste memory space
because the protection mechanism does not apply to logical records
(one table or procedure) but to rather large physical records.

By some additional software the number of levels which can be distinguished by hardware-protection mechanisms can be increased. Suppose we
have two processes P, Q running in slave mode and the corresponding

address spaces are hardware-protected against each other. Usually this
means that P and Q are running on the same abstract machine. However, we can construct a control procedure running in master mode which
sends certain system-calls coming from Q back to P. In this way P
may become a layer below Q which is protected against Q and still
programs running in master mode are protected against P.

All these protection mechanisms protect lower layers against disallowed
access from higher layers. There is no method generally available to
protect in the converse direction. Neither does there exist any hardware-protection against wrong programs running in absolute addressing
mode nor does any method help against misuse of addresses which were
passed to a procedure as actual parameter. Those mistakes can be detected only by careful debugging of the interfaces between the layers.

4.   R E F E R E N C E S

1   Dennis, J.B. *The Design and Construction of Software*. These
     Lecture Notes.

2   Dijkstra, E.W. *Cooperating Sequential Processes*. In : F. Genuys
     (ed.), Programming Languages. London-New York : Academic Press,
     1968.

3   Dijkstra, E.W. *The Structure of the 'T.H.E.' Multiprogramming
     System*. Comm. ACM 11 (1968), 341-346.

4   Gill, S. *Thoughts on the Sequence of Writing Software*. In :
     P. Naur and B. Randell (ed.), Report on a Conference on Software
     Engineering. Brussels : NATO Science Committee, 1969.

5   Zurcher, F.W. and Randell, B. *Iterative Multilevel Modelling,
     A Methodology for Computer System Design*. In : Proceedings IFIP
     Congress 1969. Groningen : North-Holland Publ. Comp. 1969.

6   Randell, B. *Towards a Methodology of Computing System Design*.
     In : P. Naur and B. Randell (ed.). Report on a Conference on
     Software Engineering. Brussels : NATO Science Committee, 1969.

7   Burroughs *B6700 ESPOL Language,* Information Manual. Detroit :
     Burroughs Comp. # 5000094, 1970.

8   Burroughs *B6700 Extended ALGOL Language,* Information Manual,
     Detroit : Burroughs Comp. # 5000128, 1971.

9   Waite, W.M., Poole P. *Portability and Adaptability*. These Lec-
     ture Notes.

CHAPTER 2.B.

L A N G U A G E   C H A R A C T E R I S T I C S
PROGRAMMING LANGUAGES AS A TOOL IN WRITING SYSTEM SOFTWARE

Gerhard Goos

University of Karlsruhe, Germany

0. INTRODUCTION

There are various aspects in judging the quality of a programming language. From the engineering point of view we are interested how programming languages influence the process of program creation and the
properties of the final program. Theoretically a program written in
assembly language can have all desired properties except portability. In
practice this is not true because the use of assembly language influences the programmer and his thinking habits. The same remark applies
to every other programming language.

This lecture investigates the relationship between language properties
and properties of programs written in the language in order to get some
idea which characteristics a good programming language should have. This
is most important in practice for the design of system programming languages replacing the use of assembly language. We therefore concentrate
our discussion on system software and not on application software. After
discussing which program properties can be influenced we study various
language constructs taken from languages like FORTRAN, ALGOL 60 [1] ,
SIMULA 67 [2], ALGOL 68 [3], PL 360 [4], ESPOL [5], BLISS [6], PS 440 [7]
and PASCAL [8]. Our general approach is to use a high-level language
for writing system software. Our starting point is ALGOL 68.

1. THE INFLUENCE OF LANGUAGE PROPERTIES ON SOFTWARE CREATION

There is a well-known relationship between a natural language and the
thinking habits of people using the language. The language mirrors the
habits of those creating it, conversely people are forced to think and
to express themselves in the language. If they find this difficult they
must develop it further inventing new notions and idioms or they must
use another language.

The same applies to programming languages. Additionally they reflect the structure of present-day computers and what computers are thought to be good for. Therefore a programming language influences its user at least with respect to the following:

- The conceptual understanding how a problem can be solved by computer

- The range of problems which can be attacked by programming

- The set of basic notions available for programming

- The style of programming (clarity, robustness, readability etc.)

- The meaning of "portability"

- The meaning of "efficiency"

It is the purpose of this paragraph to make these points more concrete.

1.1. *LANGUAGE CONSTRUCTS AS MODELS FOR PROGRAM BEHAVIOR*

Except for storage limitations every Turing-machine can be represented by a program written in assembly language. The question arises why in this context we automatically speak about Turing-machines and why not about theoretically equivalent formulations, e.g. recursive functions or Markov-algorithms.

The answer is: It is very easy to formulate a Turing-machine in assembly language. To implement recursion or the pattern matching facilities required by Markov-algorithms is much more complicated. If we had used SNOBOL 4 instead, we probably had thought about Markov-algorithms; the use of LISP had implied the use of -definable functions.

Nobody will implement top-down syntax analysis when forced to use FORTRAN because recursive procedures are not allowed in this language. Somebody using ALGOL 68 might come to the conclusion that it is useful to solve a problem P by constructing two algorithms to be executed in paralel. Probably he will not have this idea if his implementation of ALGOL 68 does not allow for parallel processing. On the other hand, using SIMULA 67, the problem will be solved using coroutines because these, but no parallel processes, are available in this language.

Without mentioning details these examples show that programming languag influence our choice of the theoretical model by which we want to solve a problem.

Analogous remarks can be made on data structures. Apparently the widespread use of FORTRAN and ALGOL 60 in the Sixties has severely hampered
the development of string manipulation and nonnumerical applications.
The use of languages like EULER [9] will imply linear lists as models
for structuring data. Tree-like structures are presented when using
languages as SIMULA 67, ALGOL 68 or PASCAL.

These considerations show that the choice of a certain programming language very much influences the design of the algorithms and data structures solving a given problem. Thus the programming language does not
only determine *how* to express programs; it also determines the scheme
choosen for the problem solution. Of course, the latter statement is true
only if the language was known and used in the design stage already.

1.2. *INFLUENCE ON PROGRAMMING STYLE AND PROGRAM DOCUMENTATION*

Programs can be tricky or straightforward. They can be subdivided into
modules or they can be unstructured. They can look like an ad-hoc collection of statements or they can show a systematic treatment of the
subject.

For a very long time tricky programming - the art of programming - was
thought to be more efficient and therefore more economic. However, the
financial calculation behind such reasoning is doubtful. Firstly the
expenses for design and construction are considered negligible compared
to the costs of actual program execution. Secondly maintenance and
portability are usually neglected completely. Thirdly in most cases there
is no evidence that tricky programming really leads to programs more
efficient in time and space than others.

Analogous remarks apply to the two other alternatives. Of course, at
least today it is very difficult to define the meaning of "tricky" or
"structured programming" precisely and we shall not attempt to do that.
For example, it depends on the circumstances whether the use of Jensen's-
device in ALGOL 60 is considered as tricky programming or not.

The properties of the programming language in use play an important rôle
in guiding programmers to express themselves in a well-organized fashion.
A few examples are as follows:

Most programming languages do not allow to attach an identifier and a
data type to a subfield of· a computer word.(An exception is PASCAL [8],
but this can be found from the implementation only, not from the definition). Instead,packing and unpacking of data must be described by
shifts etc. Therefore there are no mnemnonic names for packed data.
When reading a program operating on such data the identification of the
data must be decoded from the operations accessing the data. Moreover
the programmer usually considers any subfield of a word as a collection
of bits. He does never state explicitly whether these bits are a set
of Boolean variables, an unsigned integer, a signed integer, etc. All
these informations and in case of integers the admissible range of value
must be derived implicitly from the program text instead of being mentioned explicitly. Thus automatically the programs are badly readable.
Moreover, also in designing such programs the programmer is misguided
since he is not asked to define his data structures clearly. Lastly it
is an open question why the programmer should be concerned on coding
the access to subfields of words explicitly. This clerical task should
be done by a compiler with a much smaller number of mistakes.

The existence of a while-construction
          while condition do statement
or some generalization of it guides the programmer to say clearly where
loops do occur in his program. Otherwise he must describe the construction by a conditional jump and the information "loop" must be recon-
structed by the reader. This is an easy job if the statement to be repeated is short. To see that a "long-distance jump" constitutes a loop
might be very difficult.

Another example of language characteristics influencing programming
style is the use or misuse of global variables. Labelled COMMON was
introduced in FORTRAN to suggest a subdivision of all global data of a
program such that for every subprogram it is clearly defined which glob-
als may be accessed or not. In ALGOL 60 and its successors we do not fin
such a construct. In using these languages we therefore find many examples of uncontrolled and unpermitted use of global variables (see section 2.2 for an attempt to remove this problem).

Our claim behind these examples is that good programming style means
to express oneself straightforward and without deviating too much from
the original description of the algorithm (loops should be expressed as
loops etc.). This leads to logical clarity and correctness. Speeding
up programs is not the first but the second step in programming. There
is no need to make an incorrect program more efficient.

Logical clarity can be measured in terms of readability: it should be easy to reconstruct the conceptual algorithm from the written program. In that way good programming style also means to get the maximum contribution to the program documentation from the program text itself.

Besides this there is also an explicit relation between language characterstics and documentation already demonstrated in the first example of this paragraph. Program documentation does not only mean to formulate readable statements in the program and to add a sufficient number of comments. It mostly requires also some coherent description of the algorithms and data structures supplied independently of the program. To get the maximum benefits of this additional information the description must be clearly related to the different parts of the program. To this purpose the data and program parts should be named consistently throughout the program and the documentation. This requires at least that it is possible to have identifiers for all data including parts of a word.

1.3. MACHINE INDEPENDENCE AND PORTABILITY

Machine independence refers to those properties of a program making it independent of the details of the computer structure such as the word length, addressing scheme, number and kind of registers etc. Portability requires in addition that the program is independent from special properties of the operating system, or, more generally, it requires that an appropriate environment for the program can be provided on most current computers.

Both properties can be approximately achieved by using a high-level programming language. Programs written in such languages are machine dependent only with respect to the accuracy of real arithmetic, range of arithmetic values and the character-set. The machine dependency concerning character sets can be removed by using only a set consisting of the capital letters, the digits and a small number of other characters which are widely available (together ca. 48 characters). Programs written in high-level languages are portable if the use of I/O is restricted to the use of sequential files (input-file, printer-file, scratch-file). There do not yet exist widely implemented standards for more sophisticated access-methods on files.

Considering system programming languages there are a number of unsolved problems concerning portability. Poole and Waite [10] have developped abstract machines to be programmed in an assembly-like manner which have proven being successful languages for portable software. However, the basic operations of these abstract machines are specially adapted to the problem at hand. Using a language which is structured similarly to a high-level language such as PL360, PS440, PASCAL or BCPL [11] causes some problems concerning machine independence. There must by a way of packing and accessing data within a computer word. The descriptio of packing should be independent of the word length. Additionally in-dexing is done in steps of different size on different computers. (Step-size for integers is 1 on the UNIVAC 1108, CDC 6400, 2 on the TR4, TR440, 4 on the IBM System 360). Using a unique scheme for indexing arrays implies therefore multiplication by different powers of 2 on different computers, a serious inefficiency.

The best we can achieve today to solve these problems is splitting the programs into a data description and an algorithmic section. The algo-rithmic section should be machine independent as far as possible. The data description might need some modifications for adapting it to other computers. The splitting is a logical one. It is not required that the data description and the algorithmic section are physically split. De-clarations belonging to the data description can be inserted anywhere in the algorithmic section. However, future applications involving data interchange in computer networks might require complete physical and logical splitting of the data description and the algorithmic section the former being supplied together with the data.

1.4. PORTABILITY VERSUS EFFICIENCY

It is often claimed that portable software automatically means inef-ficient software. Whether this is true or not largely depends on the language used. Inefficiency may arise from

- storage allocation and data packing schemes not suited to the proble
- data packing schemes not suited to give fast access on the computer
  at hand
- too complicated interfaces to the environment (e.g. the operating
  system
- inefficient code generated for very heavily used loops.

The first two problems can be removed by using methods as presented in PASCAL. The third problem is a problem of the future. It requires fur-

ther standardization of the interface. Today we must try to avoid it
by using very simple interfaces only. If this seems to be impossible
we must apply hierarchical ordering constructing the required sophisticated tools based on more simple ones. The final program consists of
two layers: The top layer solves the programming problem on the basis
of an appropriate system interface. The lower layer implements this
interface assuming the existence of a simpler interface. E.g., if
index-sequential access to files is required the lower layer may provide for this access-method assuming that direct access is available.
Hence, the program can run on every host system providing for direct
access to files. Of course, on a system which itself supplies index-
sequential access we may remove or simplify the lower layer using the
more elaborate system interface.

The fourth problem requires additional language properties. There is
no reason why portable software should not be fine tuned to a computer
after being adapted. First we write the program in a standard version
which perhaps is inefficient in inner loops. On any given computer the
statements known to be critical for the performance of the program are rewritten in a more efficient form. To this purpose we need the possibility to insert machine-code not only by calling a closed subroutine but
by in-line coding, a facility for which our language should provide.
The call of closed code-procedures is not sufficient because very often
the subroutine-jump and the parameter-transmission is too slow.

Providing the insertion of machine-code also solves another problem encountered at least in writing operating systems in a useful language.
It is impossible to supply a language-construct for every special instruction used for starting I/O, interrupt-handling, moving the CPU
around the processes in the system, etc. These tasks and the instructions used are not only machine dependent, but also critical in time.
Experience shows that inserting these instructions directly into the
program leads to less than 5 % of the system being expressed in a machine
dependent manner.

1.5. LIMITATIONS OF PROGRAMMING LANGUAGES

From the preceding paragraphs there evolved a set of criteria which
language properties are useful or requested for writing good system
programs. Of course, these criteria are partly contradictory. It depends on the problem at hand in which order the criteria get priority.

At least the last paragraph showed that there are a number of problems
which should not be considered as being tasks to be solved by supplying
appropriate language constructs. Moreover, it must be stressed that no
language does force programmers to write "good" programs. Good design
and proper engineering can be influenced by a programming language but
it cannot be enforced. Lastly it should be noted that every language contains a certain freedom for misusing it. Therefore programming discipline is an absolute necessity.

2. REQUIREMENTS FOR STRUCTURED PROGRAMMING AND PROGRAM MODULARITY

We discuss   some means for better structuring programs whether they
are present in existing programming languages or not. The significant
rôle played by procedures and their proper use is assumed to be known
and is not discussed.

2.1. MODULARITY

Modularity denotes the ability to combine arbitrary program modules into larger modules without knowledge of the construction of the modules.
With respect to programming languages we are concerned with the following questions:

- Which syntactic units are suited to represent program modules
- How to express the interfaces used in combining modules
- Technical aspects of the process of combination.

A module must be described independently from other modules. Therefore
all syntactic units are appropriate which can be compiled independently.
Usually this means procedures or parts of the data description (BLOCK
DATA in Fortran). Simula 67 supplies some additional facilities. Class
definitions

    class A(B,C); integer B,C; begin <Declarations, and/or statements,> end
                                          Decl.A   Stat.A

serve to define procedures leaving their local address space as a record after they have been executed. Classes can be compiled separately.
Moreover they can be used as prefixes of other classes or normal blocks:

```
  class D; begin  <Decl.D> ;  <Stat.D1> ;  inner; <Stat.D2>end
D class E; begin  <Decl.E> ;  <Stat.E>  end
```

means:

```
  class E; begin<Decl.D> ;  <Decl.E>;<Stat.D1>;<Stat.E>;<Stat.D2>end
```

A slight generalization of this scheme would allow to compile any number of ALGOL-blocks separately and to build programs as follows:

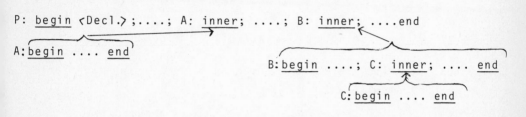

Any of these lines could be compiled separately. So the general rule is
that every parenthesized set of declarations and statements should be
separately compileable whether it is a procedure or not. Additionally
every definition of a data structure can be compiled separately provided it is allocated in store separately from the push-down.

The main difficulty in separate compilation is correct interfacing of
different modules. There are no problems if the interface consists only
of the calling sequence of a procedure including parameter transmission
and of supplying a result on return. Also statically allocated global
data are simple to handle. In case of other global parameters, e.g.,
variables on some block level $\neq$ 0 or Boolean variables located somewhere
in the middle of a computer word, the compiler either must be supplied
with an algorithm for accessing these parameters or it can generate macro-
calls only which must be replaced by the correct access sequence at
binding time. The first method requires that all modules supplying global parameters are translated in advance. The second method is more general, however, it may hamper code optimization severely.

Of course, in case of separate compilation of blocks for later insertion
somewhere in other blocks the block level of that block is part of the
necessary interface. Lastly the discussion shows that the simple notions
of external data and entry points as used by most assembly languages are
not sufficient.

The way we choose to supply information about global parameters determines the sequence of steps required in compiling and binding the modules together. Assume that in the example above modules A and B use glob-

al parameters from P and C uses parameters from B. If we want to have the access algorithms for these parameters known at compile-time we get the sequence:

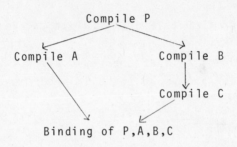

If the access algorithms are represented by macros during compilation the order is not significant:

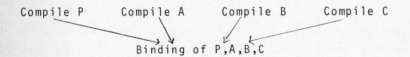

If. however, the binding should occur as an appendix to the compilation of the outermost block we get the sequence

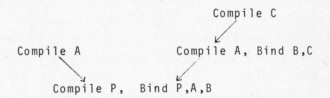

2.2. *HIERARCHIES, NESTING AND SCOPE RULES*

The last example shows that hierarchical ordering can be achieved by means of nested blocks:

$$
\begin{array}{ll}
\text{P} & \text{is the base layer} \\
\text{A, B} & \text{is the second layer} \\
\text{C} & \text{is the top layer}
\end{array}
$$

Of course, nesting of blocks may also serve purely syntactic purposes as in the ALGOL 60 - construction.

```
begin  integer n;
       read (n);
       begin array a [1:n];
```

Or it might be used to minimizing storage requirements by deleting arrays
as soon as possible from the push-down. Therefore it is useful to mark
such blocks serving as new layers:

<u>level</u> A <u>begin</u> ......<u>end</u>

"<u>level</u> A" defines A to be a label. The availability of such a construction reminds the programmer that he should think on structuring his program hierarchically.

Hierarchical ordering by nesting blocks is a well-known principle. It
seems that the success of nesting as a programming principle mostly
rests upon hierarchical ordering. The principle is taught to beginners
by such rough advices as: "Distribute your algorithms to procedures declared in the outer blocks; then write a main program as the innermost
block consisting mainly of procedure calls". This advice tells to define
a set of new basic operations (procedures) such that the problem can be
solved easily on the next level using these operations. Hierarchical
ordering is also present in describing standard declarations and library
functions as being declared in an outer block enclosing the given program.

Hierarchical ordering requires that no layer uses local data of another
layer. In a nested block structure this rule is guaranteed in one way
only: No outer block can access data declared in inner blocks. Conversely: global parameters are open for any kind of misuse. To enforce good
programming practice it is necessary to define means by which data can
be protected against unpermitted access from the next layer. This is
necessary for all data serving as global parameters to a set of procedures on one same level. No member of the ALGOL-family provides a means
for doing that.

A solution would be to restrict the scope of identifiers such that inner
blocks can be taken out from the scope arbitrarily. The following example is self-explanatory:

```
                                           Scope of x:

      begin  except   A   real x;          ⎤
                       ⋮
             level A begin                 ⎦

                       end ;
                       ⋮
      end                                  ⎤
                                           ⎦
```

2.3. CONCURRENT PROCESSES

ALGOL 68 allows for formulating collateral execution of expressions $E_1....E_n$ by writing

$$(E_1, E_2, ..., E_n)$$

It is requested that no expression E_i changes the value of any variable accessed by any other expression. Collateral expressions are useful in the future for 3 reasons:

- The programmer can describe independent sequential processes as being independent. Thus he achieves a better insight into his algorithms.
- Computers having more than one arithmetic unit can compute the results of these expressions in parallel.
- Compilers can optimize the resulting code by searching for common subexpressions not only of one but of many expressions.

The last two objectives can be achieved also by constructing more sophisticated compilers. But why should we do that when the other way contributes to clarity of programming?

Collateral expressions can be also executed one after another. Parallel or quasi-parallel (time-shared) execution is needed only if the different processes contain critical sections in which they access and change common data. In these cases synchronization is required by means of P- and V-operations (Dijkstra [12]) or by operations built on these basic operations (event-operations, message systems). To allow for these operations the compiler must be told in advance that some expressions are executed in parallel and that sequential execution is not appropriate. The compiler must generate code to allocate a new stack for every such process. ALGOL 68 indicates parallel execution by

$$\underline{par} \; (E_1, E_2, ..., E_n)$$

based upon Dijkstra's notion

$$\underline{parbegin} \; E_1, E_2, ..., E_n \; \underline{parend}$$

These constructs assume that the number of processes running in parallel is known in advance and that they all start at the same time. This very systematic assumption is nevertheless somewhat artificial when considering operating systems: User jobs are started whenever they arrive and the number of parallel jobs is limited only by the length of some system tables and by storage requirements.

BLISS, acting on a more elementary level, provides for a special statement creating a process:

> <u>create</u> P (AP1, ..., APn) <u>at</u> ⟨reference expression⟩ <u>length</u>
> ⟨integral expression⟩ <u>then</u> ⟨statement⟩

P is the pure procedure to be executed as a separate process. A stack
is allocated starting at the address given by the reference expression
and having the prescribed length. The last statement is executed after
the process has finished. It frees the stack and indicates the successor-
statement.

This construction is not only useful for starting an independent process.
Coroutines can be handled in the same way.

3. DATA STRUCTURES IN SYSTEM PROGRAMMING

The term "data structure" refers to an object which can be manipulated
by a program. Data structures are built recursively from more elementary
ones. The most elementary data structures are simple values which loose
their meaning if subdivided further. They are classified by the monadic
and dyadic operations applicable to them. Each class of values is of a
certain "data-type", i.e. integer, real, long integer, long real, Boolean,
character, reference or address etc.

More complex data structures can be described theoretically as follows
(Lucas and Walk [13]): Given the set of simple values EO (elementary
objects) and a set of elementary selectors S we build the set of all
objects O as follows:

> (1) $EO \subseteq O$
> (2) If $x_1, \ldots, x_n \in O$ and $s_1, \ldots, s_n \in S, s_i \neq s_j$ for $i \neq j$ then
> $x = (\langle s_1 : x_1 \rangle, \ldots, \langle s_n : x_n \rangle) \in O$

$\langle s_i : x_i \rangle$ is called a component of x consisting of an object x_i and its
selector or name s_i. By definition

> $s_i(x) := \langle s_i : x_i \rangle$

A special case is given when using integers as selectors:

$$(\langle 1:x_1 \rangle, \ldots, \langle n:x_n \rangle)$$

or

$$\langle x_1, \ldots, x_n \rangle$$

denotes the array of objects $x_1, \ldots, x_n$.

Obviously all such objects can be described as rooted trees. The branches are labelled by selectors. Subtrees describe components of the object. The final nodes of the tree are labelled by elementary objects:

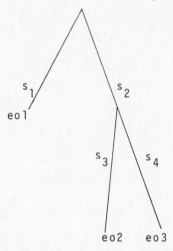

$$(\langle s_1:eo1 \rangle, \ \langle s_2:(\langle s_3:eo2 \rangle, \ \langle s_4:eo3 \rangle) \rangle)$$

It turns out that these objects are general enough to describe most data structures occurring in practice if one adds one additional rule:

- It is allowed to insert one same subtree at different nodes in a tree.

To apply this theoretical construction we must investigate how a selection s(x) can be implemented. There are four ways:

- x is an array and all selectors are integers. Thus selection is mapped on indexing.

- x is a structured value (record). Selection is represented as a prefix or postfix operation: s of x or x.s in the program. Internally selection is mapped on indexing.

- Every node of the tree is represented by a record. References are used as components of the record. They represent selectors by pointing to another record.

- Selection is represented by user-defined operations.

Nothing general can be said on the last case. The first alternative is well-known. The remaining two are discussed in 3.2.

3.1.   SIMPLE VALUES

In system programming the only simple values are the bits 0 and L. Since this is no   useful unit for most applications it is necessary to define some larger unit as the basic one. Two different directions can be followed:

The *operation-oriented* approach mentioned before classifies objects according to the admissible operations regardless of the number of bits used to represent the object. Besides the data types mentioned before it is useful to have some means of defining new types describing a finite, ordered set of values:

   (Sunday, Monday, Tuesday, Wednesday, Thursday, Friday, Saturday)
or

   (0..9)   (the numbers 0,1,2,...,9)

The basic assumption of the operation-oriented approach is that the binary coding of values bears no relation to and has no influence on the algorithm handling them. This assumption is true conceptually and it *must* be true in practice if the algorithm should be portable. From the engineering point of view there are, however, severe disadvantages of the operation-oriented approach:

- Storage cells can contain values of arbitrary type. Our approach does prohibit the use of this freedom. Hence we may waste space by using two cells instead of one although the contents of the cells may be significant at different times only.

- There is a practical need for having variables whose content is of different type at different times. Inspection of the union-mode in ALGOL 68 and analogous constructions in other languages show that it is impossible to implement these constructs by one storage cell only.

- It is difficult to construct sophisticated storage allocation schemes. For that purpose we must be able to access storage as a linear array and to use the information found. At least it must be moved around. However, our approach does not allow to access the interior of records by explicit indexing. The mapping of selectors onto indices is left to the compiler.

ESPOL, PASCAL and all high-level languages use the operation-oriented
approach. (ESPOL allows for using words as basic units too).

The other languages quoted in the beginning are *word-oriented*: They
use the computer word (4 bytes on a byte-oriented machine) as the basic
unit. Thus we get the same properties as within assembly languages including all the freedom. The disadvantages of this approach are:

- Software is not portable when the word size decreases significantly
  because most programmers try to fill the words with data to the
  utmost.

- There are no good testing and debugging facilities since the system
  cannot interpret the data types. Thus we have to live with octal
  and hexadecimal memory-dumps.

- There is no automatic control of correct use of references in dynamic storage allocation systems. Thus it is very easy to make such
  well-known mistakes as accessing data having died or accessing data
  which have been moved in the meantime.

- Programmers think in terms of words and groups of bits. They are
  never enforced to describe precisely the information represented by
  these bits. Hence the method is useful for "good" and disciplined
  programmers only.

3.2. RECORDS

Records are classified according to their length (word-oriented) or
according to the types and names of their components. The mapping of
selectors onto indices can be done in both cases by the compiler. In
the word-oriented case the user can control it or he may define it
explicitly as in PS440:

> The declaration
>
> > full select s = $[2]$
>
> allows for
>
> > s of x
>
> yielding
>
> > x $[2]$.

In both cases it must be possible to pack more than one component into
one word in order not to vaste space. When using operation-defined types

finite types like (0...9) are useful for the compiler to determine the
number of bits necessary for the component. The engineering problem
presented by packing is the minimization of space and of access-time
by one same construction:

Packing can be controlled by the compiler, i.e., the compiler can re-
arrange the order of the components for better use of space or for using
optimized instruction sequences in accessing the components. Or it can
be controlled by the user, i.e., the order of components and the subdivision of words always remains as described in the program. Although
the latter method is machine-dependent it is recommended here. It has
the advantage of being able to describe hardware- or system-dependent
records within the frame of the language. E.g., the subdivision of
instructions into operation-code, address-fields etc. or the building
of parameter-records for a SVC-instruction does not cause problems. When
adapting the program to another computer system the record-declaration
must be rewritten, but the algorithms remain unchanged as far as data
access is concerned.

Records containing references as components can be used to represent
trees. If the tree is simplified to a linear chain we get a "list". In
the usual list-processing languages the list-cells (the records) contain
two additional components:

| Value tag |
| reference field |
| value field |

The value tag specifies the type of the present content of the value
field. The value field can contain values of different types, especially
references to other lists are allowed. Thus the pair (value tag, value
field) is a union-variable in the sense of ALGOL 68.

It is interesting to compare the internal treatment of the reference
field and the value field: The compiler as well as the run-time-organi-
zation know that the reference field contains a reference. Therefore
the user must not handle the reference field explicitly. The system-
routines and the generated code are optimized. However, the occurrence
of a reference in the value field is mostly handled as an exception and
is never dealt with in an optimal fashion.

The latter remark applies generally to all user-defined record-components of type reference. Thus representing a tree of records within a list-processing system yields better efficiency in time than the use of a record oriented system. For efficiency in space the converse is true.

3.3.   STORAGE-ALLOCATION FOR RECORDS

ALGOL 68 provides *one* heap for storing all records generated dynamically (records in the stack cause no problems). This implies the existence of a sophisticated garbage-collector handling records of different size. There must exist templates at run-time for every record and for all objects in the stack indicating which storage cells contain valid references to a record of a certain type. Moreover, it is possible to reference components of a record directly. Such references must be represented such that it is possible to find the beginning of the record.

All these problems should be avoided in system programming. The last one because references to components do add nothing to the expressive power of the language. Instead, procedures such as

> proc store = (ref record x, fieldtype w):s of x:=w;
> proc load = (ref record x) fieldtype : s of x ;

should be used where record is some record-mode containing a component of fieldtype selected by the selector s.

The former problems concerning garbage-collection are mostly induced by using one heap only. In most system-programs, e.g. compilers, the set of records can be logically subdivided into classes such that all records of a class show a common behavior concerning storage allocation: From a symbol table entries are never removed; tables containing information about declarations may behave similar to a stack; other classes contain records of the list-cell type; thus garbage-collection can be replaced by a more efficient free-list-administration.

If we assign to each such class a separate storage zone we can use for every class a storage administration scheme making use of the particular properties of the records of the class. The different routines for storage administration can be supplied from a library; the requested routines are specified by the declaration of the storage zone. Every declaration of a record-mode specifies in which zone records of this mode are allocated.

The ideas explained here can be found in PASCAL. But N.Wirth went only
half the way: All records of a class must have the same mode and the
free list administration must be organized by the user himself. Moreover the length of the zones is fixed at compile-time. There is no
means for expanding one zone by shortening others as used in many
system programs.

A more general method can be developed by combining hierarchical ordering and ideas from SIMULA 67 and ESPOL: SIMULA 67 demonstrates how
records can be enhanced by additional components by prefixing the declaration of the record-mode by another one. The queue-declarations of
Burroughs' ESPOL contain algorithms used to allocate space for new
records in the queue, to remove records, to insert records at appropriate places of the queue etc. Hierarchical ordering suggests that
storage-administration should be done one level below that level where
the storage is used; information local to the storage-administration
should be protected against misuse from the higher level.

We therefore propose the following:

- Every zone is declared to be an array.

- The zone-declaration contains algorithms for storage allocation etc.,
  including a garbage-collector if necessary. The array-structure of the
  zone is accessible within these algorithms only.

- The zone-declaration may specify a record-mode which is used as a prefix to all records allocated in the zone. The prefix specifies those
  components of the record containing information for the storage administration. By declaring it through
      struct prefix = (except user level bool marking bit,...)
  the components of the prefix are inaccessible from the higher levels.

- The higher level prefixes every record-generator by the appropriate
  zone-identifier. This automatically supplies the additional components
  of the record-mode mentioned in the zone-declaration. Storage allocation is done by calling implicitly the allocation-algorithm of the
  zone-declaration.

- Other algorithms of the zone-declaration can be called by explicit
  calls, e.g. REMOVE (reference to record, zone identifier).

This proposal is not yet implemented. Therefore no comment can be made
how to extend the scheme such that it allows zones of varying length.

4. SYSTEM-DEPENDENT LANGUAGE FEATURES AND PORTABILITY

Compilers are machine dependent at least in their code generating section. They depend on the operating system with respect to the file-handling facilities. This dependency compilers have in common with most utility routines (cf. 1.4 for proposals how to weaken this dependency). Operating systems of today are machine dependent on purpose: Interrupt handling is based solely on hardware properties, storage allocation depends on the addressing scheme (linear, paged, segmented using base registers, etc.). The performance of many parts of the system depends on careful analysis of the speed ratios between different components of the computer system.

In all programs performance might be increased by recoding small parts of the program directly in machine code. There are two methods in use for doing that:

- If the compiler of the system programming language in use translates into assembly language we can use assembly language strings as parts of the program. These strings are transmitted without any change to the assembler positioned correctly in the assembly program generated by the compiler. PS440 uses this method.
- Machine instructions can be introduced written as procedure calls anywhere in the program. This method requires that it is possible to access registers explicitly in the language. It is used in PL 360 and partly in ESPOL.

Other methods can be derived from these two by macro substitution.

The first method has the advantage that the programmer can get explicit control on static storage allocation by writing appropriate pseudo-instructions to the assembler. This feature is needed in writing the nucleus of an operating system. There we have to store certain data, jumps and other instructions into hardware-defined storage cells. In case of the second method we have to supply an additional feature for achieving the same: It must be possible to specify the address of certain objects and labels explicitly in the declaration or label definition.

Both methods allow for statically allocated objects only to be parameters of the machine-instructions. This appears to be a very undesired restriction.

Machine instructions and hardware-registers are word-oriented. To introduce them into a language using operation-oriented data types involves
some inconsistency. In particular it is possible to by-pass all consistency checks and protection mechanisms of the compiler. Since the programmer assumes that these checks and protection mechanisms work correctly it is difficult for him to detect when they fail.

Using machine code is necessary not only for increasing performance. It
is needed in any case where the expressive power of the language does
not suffice for dealing with hardware problems. On the other hand many
machine dependent data structures and algorithms can be expressed by
machine independent language constructs. E.g., the code generation of
a compiler may be formulated without referring to machine dependent
constructs.

Thus portability of a program requires not only that the program is
written in a language sufficiently machine independent. It depends on
the content of the program and the way it uses the language whether it
is portable or not.

5. SOME OPEN PROBLEMS

The most serious problem of today's system programming languages is the
non-existence of a basic model for file-handling and I/O. All models
either are developed with a certain operating system in mind and are
difficult to adapt to other operating systems. Or they are to simple
allowing for sequential files only while random-devices are modelled
by unstructured linear address spaces. Basically this problem is a
problem of standardizing the interfaces of operating systems.

Most system programming languages allow for stacks. All other data are
allocated statically. On the one hand this is done on purpose: the
programmer should control the use of memory as far as possible. On the
other hand the programmer is served better when he gets standardized
tools for handling complex data structures instead of being forced to
write such tools himself. The AED Free Storage Package (Ross [14]) is
a good example how the situation can be changed.

To use operation-defined data types requires more efficient solutions
to the problem of union-modes than are available today. In the same
context the implementation of indexing is not yet solved satisfactorily.
Most schemes imply much more shifts or multiplications by powers of

two than any assembler programmer would ever write.

Concerning the overall situation of system programming languages I feel
that we are still in the beginning of knowing what is needed. Most languages are critized either for being too high-level or for being too machine-oriented. But we learn only very slowly where good compromises
between these two extremes must be looked for. It seems to be very
difficult to distinguish between language constructs systems programmers
really need and those which they believe they need because they have
used them for a long time.

6. REFERENCES

1. Naur, P. (ed): Revised report on the Algorithmic Language ALGOL 60. Num.Mathematik 4 (1963), 420-453.

2. Dahl, O.-J., Myhrhaug, B., Nygaard, K.: SIMULA 67, Common Base Language, revised edition. Oslo: Norwegian Computing Center, 1970.

3. v.Wijngaarden, A.: Report on the Algorithmic Language ALGOL 68. Num. Mathematik 14 (1969), 79-218.

4. Wirth, N.: Pl 360, A Programming Language for the 360 Computer. J.ACM 15 (1968).

5. Burroughs B 6700 ESPOL Language, Information Manual. Detroit: Burroughs Comp. 5000094, 1970.

6. Wulf, W.A. et al.:BLISS Reference Manual. Computer Science Department Report, Carnegie-Mellon Univ. Pittsburgh (Penn.), 1969.

7. Goos, G., Lagally, K., Sapper, G.:PS440 - Eine niedere Programmiersprache -, Rechenzentrum der Technischen Hochschule München, Bericht 7002. München 1970.

8. Wirth, N.: The Programming Language PASCAL. Acta Informatica 1 (1971), 35-63.

9. Wirth, N. and Weber, H.:EULER:A Generalization of ALGOL, and its Formal Definition: Part II. Comm. ACM 9 (1966), 89-99.

10. Waite, W.M., Poole, P.: Portability and Adaptability. These Lecture Notes.

11. Richards, M.: BCPL Reference Manual. Technical Memorandum 69/1, University of Cambridge, Computing Laboratory, 1969.

12. Dijkstra, E.W.: Cooperating sequential processes. In:F.Genuys (ed.) Programming Languages. London - New York: Academic Press, 1968.

13. Lucas, P., Walk, K.: On the formal description of PL/I. in: Annual Reviews in Automatic Programming, vol.6, Pergamon Press, 1970.

14. Ross, D.T.: The AED Free Storage Package. Comm.ACM 10 (1967), 481-491.

CHAPTER 2.C.

L O W   L E V E L   L A N G U A G E S
S U M M A R Y   O F   A   D I S C U S S I O N   S E S S I O N

edited by M. Griffiths
University of Grenoble, France

1. INTRODUCTION

This chapter is a summary of a discussion on low-level languages, during which prepared contributions were presented by BAUER, GOOS,
GRIFFITHS and RAIN, together with pertinent comments from GOBIN,
GOTLIEB, NIEVERGELT, SONNENBERG, WAITE and WEGNER. The text will not
differentiate the contributions of the different speakers.

Over the last five years we have experienced a proliferation of new
languages, loosely called 'low-level languages'. The first, well-known
example was PL 360 [1], which was rapidly followed by many others. The
number of these languages would seem to indicate that programmers felt,
and continue to feel, a need for tools which were not normally available.
It is our aim to try and analyse this need, to discover whether it is
real or psychological and to draw the relevant conclusions concerning
the desirable features of such a language.

Questions which occur, and which are nearly all still under discussion,
include those of generality, machine-independence, degree of efficiency,
programming style and education.

2. JUSTIFICATION

The immediate replies to the question 'why create a new low-level language?' are usually either to avoid using assembler or machine code,
or because the available languages were inefficient and did not allow
complete control of the computer. It is this second answer which merits
some thought, since it implies a criticism of existing languages. Would
it not therefore be sufficient to improve current, general-purpose languages, in including a selected number of supplementary features, and

in improving the efficiency of certain parts of the implementation? In long term, the answer to this question rests under discussion, but on a short term basis, the consensus of opinion seems to be that we do not yet know how to allow the necessary feature in a satisfactory manner within the framework of existing languages and compilers.

A fundamental question seems to be concerned with storage allocation. Users of low-level languages are usually producing software, and are capable of programming their own storage allocation. Since their methods are adapted to the particular task in hand, they are more efficient, and often clearer, than a general method. Not only does it seem difficult to allow sufficient control over storage allocation in a language which, for the general user, does this automatically, but even were the language designed satisfactorily, the user would need to know too much about the compiler to exploit it successfully.

Another important justification is more difficult to define, but can be described roughly as programming style. Implementers often wish to think in terms of machines, and less in terms of algorithms then other users. Whether they can write their program or not in a general-purpose language is less important than the clear exposition of their thought patterns. This sensation is not difficult to pin down, but is also an unproved assertion. It has been said that the implementer would do better to rethink in terms of a higher level.

3. FEATURES

The contents of low-level languages have varied from minimal additions to the assembler which are considered as a departure point to full-blown languages with a complete range of data and control structures. Examples of these extremes are [2] and [3]. The differences depend, of course, on the use to which the language is to be put, either as the lowest readable level in the language hierarchy, or as the highest level which still knows about the computer.

Some measure of agreement exists as to the minimum control structure necessary in such a language - loops, conditions, procedures, and so on, all implemented in the most efficient manner. For example loops tend to be of the form *while ... do* or to have constant and once-evaluated step functions. On the other hand, different points of view are presented concerning block structure, parameter passing, and even recursion,

although few people defend the elimination of this last possibility.
As far as data structure is concerned, the subject is very open, since
suggestions vary from a language without declarations and hence without any given data structures, to complex systems allowing various
types with checking and sometimes conversion, indexing, structures and
pointer manipulation.

A further point of discussion lies in the links between the language
defined and the machine or assembly language. Most, if not all, of the
languages proposed allow the use of machine language in one form or
another. The interface requires thought, especially in addressing mechanisms.

In view of the wide differences which exist between different projects,
we may perhaps try to distinguish two groups. The first of these would
contain the very simple, special-purpose efforts, which are less languages than different styles of programming. This is not a criticism
of such work, which has considerably helped the formulation of certain
products. If we eliminate this first group, the languages which remain
are not, in fact, low-level, and many of their designers prefer the
term 'machine-oriented'. It seems important to point out that machine-
oriented languages can be high-level, and that low-level languages can
be problem oriented. Languages such as those described in [3] and [4]
are sophisticated programming tools which allow tight control of the
computer.

4.   MACHINE DEPENDENCE

One problem which arises when we consider machine-oriented languages
is whether these languages must be fully machine dependent. It would
seem regrettable that we design a new language for each computer, but
on the other hand, in order to have complete control, the language must
know about the particular machine. In this context there are two different aims to consider. The first is to make algorithms readable, understandable by programmers working in other systems, and the second
is to make programs portable. Neither aim can be achieved all the time
in a machine-oriented language, which implies that programmers must
consider more carefully the structure of their programs.

Opinions differ concerning the proportion of the language definition
which takes account of the particular computer, but agreement is reached

on the fact that, even if the language is heavily machine dependent, particular programs should not be so. The major part of any program is machine independent, and it is up to the programmer to isolate those parts which are not. These machine dependent sections require particularly careful documentation.

5. EFFICIENCY

We consider three types of efficiency, those of programmer effort, machine time, and memory space. The machine oriented language is often a means to obtain all three kinds of efficiency. Memory space is kept at a minimum by the use of assembler programs, and it has been said that this also minimises run-time. Recent work would suggest that this is not necessarily true, for example in MULTICS, written in PL/1, the important gains in run-time efficiency have come from global optimisation and not from recoding on a local basis (see Graham[5]).In any case, programmer efficiency using an assembler is unacceptable.The machine-oriented language should encourage programmer efficiency in the same way as any high-level language, produce compact code as in assembler, and allows both local and global optimisation at run-time. In general the best of both worlds. The fact that this best of both worlds is not necessarily utopic may well have an impact on general-purpose programming languages.

6. STYLE AND EDUCATION

Language designers have at last become conscious of the fact that their design influences the programming style of their users. The result has been an effort to enforce a more elegant programming style, together with a lot of discussion concerning, for example, *goto* statements. Machine oriented language designers often have a point of view which is more flexible, by trying to design a language which allows the user to find (or usually to continue to use) his own style. This decision, which is in any case a good thing, comes from the fact that system programmers are often irreductible as far as changes in their methods are concerned, and they have usually much more experience than the average programmer.

We are aware of the fact that good programming style is created by education, and merely encouraged by good tools. Since the machine-oriented language may well be used in the education of young system programmers it is of vital importance that these languages should allow clear, elegant and clean programming. Flexibility in the design should help, at least for the present time, since we are not yet able to define completely these features which lead to 'good' programming.

7. CONCLUSION

In general, the speakers assume that the arrival of machine-oriented, sometimes called low-level, languages respond to a need in software engineering. Thought and effort need to be put into their design and implementation, and we should consider the interface between these languages and the more classical general-purpose languages. Many points which have already received attention over the last fifteen years are being reconsidered in this new context. This effort is not wasted, but should not ignore what already exists.

8. ACKNOWLEDGEMENTS

We thank all the speakers at the session concerned, and hope that they will not consider that their thoughts have been misrepresented. The ideas in the paper are a concensus of opinion, and it should not therefore be supposed that any particular speaker agrees with all of the contents.

9. REFERENCES

[1]   N.WIRTH
      A Programming Language for the 360 Computer
      J A C M, Jan. 1968

[2]   M.GRIFFITHS, M.PELTIER
      A Macro-Generable Language for the 360 Computer
      Computer Bulletin, Nov. 1969

[3]   M.RAIN
      MARY
      SINTEF, Technical University of Norway, 1972

[4]   G.GOOS, K.LAGALLY, G.SAPPER
      PS 440, Eine niedere Programmiersprache
      Technische Universität, München 1970

[5]   R.GRAHAM
      Notes from this school

CHAPTER 2. D.

RELATIONSHIP BETWEEN DEFINITION

AND IMPLEMENTATION

OF A LANGUAGE

M. Griffiths
University of Grenoble
France

1. INTRODUCTION

The non-specialist sometimes accuses both computer scientists
and software engineers of spending all their time on discussions about
languages, to the detriment of all the 'real' problems. Whilst this
accusation is not without foundation, it must be clearly understood that
language is central to the whole problem of software engineering. If we
cannot supply powerful, well-defined, understandable languages with
corresponding, economic implementations on existing computing equipment,
then the programmer can hardly be expected to express himself in a way
which will permit us to use the term which is the theme of this school.

In these lectures we will discuss the impact of language
definition on the programs written in the language and on the methods
used to execute these programs in the computer. Defining a language is
a two-fold process : the future user must be allowed ways of saying
what he will wish to say, which means that the language content must be
suitable, and the way in which this content is expressed is also important, although this importance may be greater for the implementer than
for the user. The ultimate aim of compiler writers is to find a way of
automatically converting a language definition into an implementation.
We are of course a long way from this ultimate aim, but this should not
stop us from trying to define languages in a way that is reasonably
close to the way in which they are implemented.

1.1 - REQUIREMENTS OF DIFFERENT PEOPLE -

Three main groups of people are possible readers of a language
definition, the users, implementors, and theoreticiens. Each of these
groups has its own particular requirements, and these requirements can
be seen to contain certain incompatibilities. In particular, it seems

that no existing language definition can be used satisfactorily by all three sections of the community.

The user of a programming language requires a document which will answer the question : 'How do I obtain such an effect?'. His aim is to create programs, and he is not interested by the programs he will not write. No user exploits all the features of a language, and few are capable of so doing. Their approach is thus synthetic and limited, which means that user requirements are met by a description, with examples, which may well be restricted in order to encourage programming clarity. A standard example of this type of restriction is that of side-effects. Consider the ALGOL 60 program :

```
begin integer procedure a;
      begin b:=b+2;
            a:=sqrt(b)

      end;
      integer x, b;
      b:=8;
      x:=a+b


      end
```

Obviously, since a changes the value of b, the result of the assignment

$$x := a+b$$

depends on the order of evaluation of the operands of an expression. This order is in fact defined in ALGOL 60, but the users' manual may well say : 'do not use expressions in which one operand changes the value of another'. The manual may even suggest that procedures should only change the values of their parameters, but this is a more doubtful axiom under certain conditions. We may consider that keeping the user in ignorance of certain parts of the language is a bad thing, but it is certain that language designers would do well to consider to what degree it is possible to encourage, or even force, users to write clear programs. Modern languages, like ALGOL 68, have made some considerable improvements in this field. In the example program, ALGOL68 does not define the order of evaluation of operands, and indeed says it is arbitrary. One property of a language definition is thus to be such as to encourage clear, clean programming. This can almost be rephrased to say that programs written by a user who exploits all the details of a language should be as easy to understand as those written in a subset.

For the implementer of a language the definition is not just
a guide, but a bible. He requires a complete list of every type of phrase
which can be written, together with a precise and complete definition of
their effects. This analytic point of view is in opposition to the user's
synthetic one, and the implementer does not worry whether it is reasonable or not to write certain programs, but simply to apply the law. As
in real life, the law may often be an ass, but this is not an excuse to
change it unilaterally. One of the measures of the degree to which the
definition is unreasonable can be found in the amount of time the implementer spends in working on details which are exploited by few programmers who should not use such knowledge anyway   Side effects due to
procedure calls were the first example ot this phenomenon, which we may
term the phenomenon of 'over-definition'. A corollary of this is that
the implementor should not inform his users in what order he does evaluate expressions in ALGOL68, ever though this order may well be fixed
in a particular compiler.

To say that an implementor requires a complete, precise
definition is of course not sufficient. He is extremely interested in
the form of the definition, and in particular in the degree to which
it is possible to transform the definition into an implementation.
Descriptions of existing languages are not usually in a form which
facilitates this transformation, and it is our view that the language
definition should be in terms which are much closer to those of the
implementor then is presently the case. For example, some of the more
modern languages are defined in terms of an abstract or hypothetical
machine which acts like an interpreter. The idea is basically a good
one, since it is to be hoped that the algorithms written for the
abstract machine will correspond closely to the algorithms written
for a real machine in the translating process. However two factors
make this more difficult then is desirable. The first of these is the
fact that the abstract machine usually corresponds to a full interpreter, whereas the translation process more usually used is in two
distinct parts. The implementor has therefore the problem of separating
the interpreter for the abstract machine between the operations which
will be performed at compile time and those which are left to the execution. In the next chapter we will introduce the terms 'static semantics' and 'dynamic semantics' and attempt to indicate how a definition
should be given in terms of these two concepts. The second difficulty
comes from the level at which the abstract machine is defined. In as
much as we discuss high-level, general-purpose languages, the abstract
machine is not usually defined in such a way as to be implemented directly on any existing computer, which means that its use is strictly

conceptual. In making this criticism, we must of course remain aware
of the opposite trap, which consists in defining a language in terms
so close to those of a particular computer that the definition is not
applicable to other circumstances.

For the theoretician, a language description must be a
complete, formal, mathematically consistent set of statements which
conform to the usual mathematical principles of a minimal number of
axioms to which everything is formally related. In principle his
point of view is nearer to that of the implementor then is the user's,
since both are analytic. However, the method used to define axioms
will often seem more closely related to the theory of automata then
to the way in which computers really work. Their aims are to prove
that algorithms can be expressed in the language, or are correct, or
to discover the more efficient algorithm in theoretical terms.

The remarks in this section were mostly concerned with
the definition of high-level, general-purpose languages. The
conclusionwe would draw applies also to other types of language, and
is that the basic definition of a language should be in implementor's
terms, that a user discription should be drawn from it, as also may
be deduced a satisfactory model. We will suggest in a later section
that the definition should also be accompanied by a form of implementation which has been mapped onto a real machine. When all these
forms of language definition and description become one document
the problem will have been solved ; until then we need a constant
search for points of reasonable balance.

1.2. DESIGN OF LANGUAGE FOR GOOD PROGRAMMING

We may approach this topic by criticising the contents of
current languages, and trying to find remedies. The main problems are
concerned with a lack of obviousness, and the phenomena of over-ordering
and over-definition, which lead to problems of dependence of different
elements of a program. The example of side-effects seen above is a
typical one and we should consider it very carefully.

Side effects can be created by procedure calls, use of
parameters (in particular of parameters by name) and with loops of
various sorts. All three are in fact different forms of procedure.
Collateral evaluation is one of the ways of eliminating side effects,
since if the user does not know what the order of evaluation is, then
he cannot rely on it. In statement like

$$x := a + b$$

the evaluation of a and b in either order normally gives the same result, as is also true in

<pre>   a := 1,   b := 2.</pre>

Whichever assignment is obeyed first in irrelevant. However, what should happen if a and b are not mutually independent ? ALGOL68 says that the result is arbitrary, but we are tempted to go further and forebid mutual dependence in collaterals. Unfortunately this could lead to criticism from users, who may find it normal to write

<pre>   a := random,   b := random</pre>

since whichever is done first leaves them indifferent. Similar problems arise in input/output statements, but we feel that the price paid would be worth-while.

A second aid towards a solution is to eliminate the problem at its source. In the case of loops, to forbid interference with control variable, step size and limit, and in the case of name parameters, their simple elimination, leaving parameters of type procedure, or by reference. These measures are already taken in modern languages. For procedures, we may suggest

- no goto to an external label
- no assignment to external variables.

The first suggestion requires no comment, being the centre of considerable discussion already, but the second has some disadvantages. If it is decided not to apply the strict rule, it would be possible at least to insist on a declaration listing non-locals which change values. This list could perhaps be given by the compiler. Not only would this lead to clearer programs, but the resulting information is typical of that required in documentation. Aid to documentation by the compiler is a subject which could give rise to further study.

Further design points which should help the programmer are concerned with over-ordering, for example in loops. To set a vector to zero in ALGOL 60, we write :

<pre>   for i := 1 step 1 until n do   a[i] := 0</pre>

It is clearer, and less error-susceptible, to write 'for all the elements of a do', or as in ALGOL68 :

<pre>   for i := lub a to up b a do   a[i] := 0</pre>

Where <u>lwb</u> and <u>upb</u> are the lower and upper bounds of their operands. This is an example of 'defensive programming', which is programming against errors.

1.3. DESIGN FOR TESTING

The concept of defensive programming was seen above as a counter-measure to over-ordering. The user had to say too much. It has a further application in testing, where the user knows more about the program than does the compiler. The programmer should be able to write what he knows. As a typical example, he should indicate ranges of values at certain points, in particular after input statements, or at procedure entry for parameters. He may wish to write :

read (x) ; <u>note</u> x > 0 ; ...

or   <u>real</u> <u>procedure</u> sin (x) ; <u>value</u> <u>integer</u> x ;

<u>note</u> -1<x<1 ; ...

The <u>note</u> statement should not have any side effects. This rejoins some of the automatic proof mechanisms for programs. The tests implied by the <u>note</u> statement may be performed only in debug mode, but this depends on the implementation.

During the discussion concerning side-effects we stated a preference for languages which did not define them. An associated question for the implementor is to know what he should do if a user writes expressions in which the operands are not independent. By following the rules this will produce some arbitrary result, but it would be a kind action to indicate to the user that his program may well be badly written . However, the process of discovering mutual dependence is a long one, since it consists of building large matrices to which transitive closures must be applied. Thus the warning would probably only be printed in the debugging compiler.

Further examples of the price of finding all nonsensical statements in a program can be found in the testing that array indices are between their declared bounds. This can slow the execution of certain programs by a factor. In the same way, in a language manipulating lists, testing the type of an atom can be very expensive. In ALGOL68, such an atom would be a union of a number of modes, and its use would be via a 'conforms to and becomes' symbol. For example :

```
mode atom = union (int,char) ;
atom a; int i; char p;
a := 1;
i ::= a
```

The use of this construction implies that the compiler will
not trust the user to know that a particular atom is an integer, but
will produce code which tests for this at runtime, whether the compiler
is in debug mode or not. Whether we can pay this price for security or
not is still a matter for discussion.

A further example which was shown up by ALGOL68 is that
of testing the scopes of references. Should pointers be allowed to
point at values which have a shorter lifetime than the lifetime of
the pointer ? The ALGOL68 answer is no, but we could conceive of a
language which allowed this, going wrong only when necessary, or
printing a warning. Howewer, these alternative solutions de not
appear to be very satisfactory.

2. LANGUAGE DEFINITION

In this section we consider the technical problem of
defining a language, that is to say the form of the document which
is the bible for the language concerned. We will look at this problem
from the point of view of the implementor, with the theory that he is
the person most affected by the strict definition. The requirements
of the other two classes of readers will be considered separately.

For the purposes of definition it seems convenient to
consider not only a separation between syntax and semantics. Static
semantics is that part of the semantics which does not depend upon
the execution of a program, like the relationship between the use of
an identifier and its declaration. Dynamic semantics considers the
actual manipulations of objects and of values which takes place during
the execution of a program. In a classical implementation, the compiler will normally perform that which is defined as static semantics,
and will produce machine code which will in its turn obey the rules
defined by the dynamic semantics.

2.1. SYNTAX

If a language description is to based on a syntax, and we

84

will not in this section discuss any languages which are not, then the
form of the grammar is important to the implementor. Since he wishes to
make an anlyser out of this grammar he requires it to conform to certain
criteria, some of which depend on the method of analysis to be used.
Since the criteria differ for different methods, it is reasonable to
suppose that the definition will make a decision concerning the method
of analysis. Since efficiency is to be hoped for the method chosen will
be one which can only treat a subset of the context-free languages, for
example simple precedence [4] or left-factored (otherwise known as
LL(1)) [5]. The choice of one of these methods implies the more important
property of being non-ambiguous, since if the grammar is analysable by
means of one of these restricted methods, standard tools can be applied
to prove the conformity of the grammar. These tools will also ensure
the absence of parasites, non-producing symbols and undefined symbols.
Not using tools will often mean that there will be errors in the grammar.

This attitude may lead to critism on several grounds. First
of all one can suggest that it is a way of stifling progress, and this
would have been true ten to fifteen years ago. At that time no techniques were available, and so we could not insist on using them. At
present, it is merely good engineering practice to make products using
proven techniques, leaving research workers in computer science departments to prove new ones. We do not consider a new language to have
reached its final form until its definition and implementation have been
proved in the laboratory, since weak points in the definition will always
need to be changed as a result of implementation. Until this stage is
reached, user programmers should not have access to new languages. The
feedback is best obtained by carrying out implementation and design at
the same time ; even if the implementation is sketchy, this idea is
extremely important.

Grammars should also be shortened, if not minimised. For
example it is unreasonable to read :

<Boolean assignment> ::= <Boolean variable> :=

<Boolean expression>

<Arithmetic assignment> ::= <Arithmetic variable> :=
<Arithmetic expression>

Not only are these rules ambiguous, since

a := b

is not known syntactically to be boolean or arithmetic, but also they
confuse concepts which are syntactic with the semantic notion of type.
The difference between boolean and arithmetic objects is static semantics, and putting this in the syntax helps nobody.

2.2. STATIC SEMANTICS

Static semantics is that part of the definition which can
normally be treated at compile-time, that is to say the static relationships between elements of the program. These concern mostly the
association of uses of identifiers with their declarations and the
corresponding type information, that is to say with the classical
problems of static scope.

The relationships will be expressed in terms of the syntax
tree produced automatically by the analyser. In some cases the tree will
be transformed to a form which is more convenient, and then information
will be attached to individual nodes of the tree. This information will
serve later for the expression of the dynamic semantics. We will use
the term 'property' of a node for the information which is attached to
it. These concepts will be seen in the example in section 2.4.

2.3. DYNAMIC SEMANTICS

The dynamic semantics describe an interpreter of the program
which operates on the revised form of the syntactic tree which results
from the static semantics. They correspond to the execution of the
program, and are thus concerned with the data structures which correspond
to each declaration, accessing functions, the control structure of the
program, and other functions of that sort. Like the static semantics,
the dynamic semantics will be illustrated by the example in the next
section.

2.4. EXAMPLE TAKEN FROM ALGOL60

The following example is included with the aim of clarifying
the brief escriptions of the different concepts given above. It is simply
illustrative and is both incomplete and untested by implementation.
Further work would therefore be necessary before it could become useful
in the practical sense.

2.4.1. Syntax

The syntax which follows is of ALGOL60 without own, string or numerical labels. The method used is a simplification of the scheme used in [6]. The brackets { and } indicate that their contents may or may not be present, an asterisk indicates repetition and (and) group their contents. The symbol → stands for the Backus-Naur [7] symbol ::= and the vertical bar has the same sense as in the Backus-Naur form. Rule numbering is for later reference. The rules are LL(1), except in a limited number of cases where their transformation would make comprehension less easy. An LL(1) equivalent of these rules is given later. The axiom of the grammar is 'Block'.

1. Block   → begin (D ;)* S { ; S }* end

2. D   → Declarer (Idlist | Arrayd | Procd) |
          Arrayd | Procd |
          Switch Id := Desex { , Desex }*

3. Arrayd   → array Bounds { , Bounds }*

4. Procd   → procedure Id Formals S

5. Idlist   → Id { , Id }*

6. Declarer → real | integer | boolean

7. Bounds   → Idlist [Ex : Ex { , Ex : Ex}*]

8. Desex   → Id {[Ex] } |
          if Ex then (Id { [Ex] } |
          (Desex)) else Desex

9. Formals   → ; | (Idlist) ; Specs

10. Specs   → { value Idlist ; } (Specifier Idlist;)*

11. Specifier→ Declarer{procedure | array} | procedure |
          array | label | switch

12. S   → NLUS | NLCS | Id : S

13. NLCS   → if Ex then {Id:}* NLUS {else S} |
          for Var := Forlist do S

14. NLUS   → begin S {;S}* end | Block | goto Desex |
          (Var :=)* Ex | Id {(Exlist)} |

15. Exlist   Ex { , Ex }*

16. Var   → Id {[Exlist]}

17. Forlist → Forel {, Forel}*

18. Forel   → Ex {while Ex | step Ex until Ex}

19. Ex   → Ex1 {⊃ Ex1 }

20. Ex1   → Ex2 {≡ Ex2 }

21. Ex2   → Ex3 {or Ex3 }*

22. Ex3   → Ex4 {and Ex4 }*

23. Ex4   → {not}* Ex5 {Relop Ex5 }

24. Relop   → > | ≥ | < | ≤ | = | ≠

25. Ex5   → Ex6 {(+ | -) Ex7 }*

26. Ex6   → {+ | -} Ex7

27. Ex7   → Ex8 {(* | / | ÷) Ex8 }*

28. Ex8   → Prim {↑Prim}*

29. Prim   → Simplex|if Ex then Simplex else Simplex

30. Simplex → (Ex) | true | false | Intno | Realno |
               Id {[Exlist] | (Exlist)}

The lexical analyser is assumed to eliminate comments and layout characters, and to furnish underlined words, identifiers, numerical constants and symbols. The grammar could still be shortened, but this would be of strictly limited interest.

The above grammar would be accepted by the LL(1) analyser-producing program made by Bordier [8] based on Foster's SID program [9] if rules 12 to 14 were rewritten as follows :

12. S   → Id {:S | S1} | S2 | if Ex then S3 {else S} |
           for Forlist do S

13. S1   → {[Exlist]} := {Var :=}* Ex | (Exlist)

14. S2   → begin {D;}* S {;S}* end | goto Desex

31. S3   → S2 | Id {:S3 | S1}

This version is LL(1) if the lexical analyser distinguishes : from :=. The semantics will use the numbers of the rules of the original grammar, since the transformations applied can be shown to be correct. Thus we have a clear, unambiguous, compact grammar which conforms to the criteria developed above.

The syntax tree which is produced by the analyser of the
above grammar has the obvious form for the constructions without asterisks. In the case of repetitions, these are done at the same level in
the tree ; for example the tree for a block has the form :

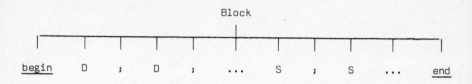

2.4.2.   Static semantics

Three essential actions are accomplished by this part of the
definition :

- Declarative information is accumulated in declaration tables,
  which are the properties of nodes which are 'scope' nodes (in
  ALGOL60 blocks and procedure declarations).

- Uses of identifiers are identified with their relevant declarations

- Some trivial transformations of the tree make it more suitable for
  the dynamic semantics.

These three actions are accomplished by means of functions
which are brought into play at the different nodes of the syntax tree,
in connection with the relevant syntax rules.

1) - A Block node has two properties. It is a scope mode, and it
possesses a declaration table. The entries in the declaration table are
provided by the D and S nodes in the expansion of Block. Each entry corresponds to an identifier (Id). No identifier may correspond to two
entries in the declaration table.

2) - The term 'nearest declaration table to a node N' is defined to
mean the declaration table attached to the first scope node encountered
in ascending the tree from node N. Each expansion of D puts one or more
entries in its nearest declaration table. The contents of this entry are
different for the different expansions :

- Declarer Idlist creates one entry for each Id of the Idlist, the
  contents of the entry specifying a type which is the expansion of
  Declarer given by rule 6.

- Declarer Arrayd creates the entries given by the property of the
  mode Arrayd, to which are attached the type X <u>array</u> where X is
  the expansion of Declarer by rule 6.

- Declarer Procd creates the entry given by the property of the
  node Procd, to which is attached the type X <u>proc</u> where X is
  the expansion of Declarer by rule 6.

- Arrayd has the same effect as Declarer Arrayd has when Declarer
  expands to <u>real</u>.

- Procd creates the entry given by the property of its node together
  with the type <u>proc</u>.

- <u>Switch</u> ... creates an entry of type <u>switch</u> which correponds to
  the identifier.

3) - The property of Arrayd is the union of the properties of the
Bounds.

4) - The property of Procd passed to the D immediately above it is
the identifier Id. In addition Procd is a scope node and has a declaration
table. The entries in this declaration are, firstly those provided by
Formals, followed by those provided by S.

5) - The property of Idlist is the list of its identifiers. No identifier may occur twice in Idlist.

7) - The property of Bounds is the list of identifiers from Idlist.
No identifier used in any of the expressions (Ex) must correspond to
an entry in the nearest declaration table.

8) - The identifier (if it occurs) of the first or of the second
alternative is identified. The process of identification proceeds as
follows. The nearest declaration table is consulted. If the identifier
corresponds to an entry in that declaration table, the identifier indicates that entry in that table, otherwise the nearest declaration
table of the scope node is taken and the process repeated. If the identifier canot be identified its use is illegal.
The type of the entry indicated by the identifier must be <u>switch</u> if the
identifier is followed by [Ex], otherwise it must be label. The Ex of
[Ex] must be of type <u>integer</u>, or of type <u>real</u>, in which case it receives

the property 'convert to <u>integer</u>'. The Ex after <u>if</u> must be of type
<u>boolean</u>.

9) - Formals provides entries in the nearest declaration table for
each of the identifiers in (Idlist). The contents of these entries are
provided by Specs.

10) - Each identifier in the Idlist following <u>value</u> must occur in one
of the Idlists following specifier. The type <u>value</u> is added to the type
of the corresponding entry in the declaration table. The identifiers in
the Idlist following specifier must correspond one to one with the identifiers in the Idlist of Formals. The type given by the specifier is
inserted in the corresponding entry in the declaration table.

11) - The type given by specifier is its expansion, with Declarer
being replaced by its expansion from rule 6, together with the type
<u>parameter</u>.

12) - The identifier creates an entry in the nearest declaration table
with type <u>label</u>.

13) - The Ex after <u>if</u> must be of type <u>boolean</u>. The Id creates an entry
in the nearest declaration table with type <u>label</u>.

14) - In the expansion Id {(Exlist)} the following rules must be observed. The Id is identified and must indicate an entry of type <u>procedure</u>.
The Procd which created this entry is compared with the expansion under
consideration as follows. If the Exlist of the expansion is absent, then
the Formals of the Procd must have been accepted by the first expansion
of rule 9. Otherwise the second expansion of rule 9 must have been applied.
The number of Ex in the Exlist must be equal to the number of elements in
the Idlist of the second expansion of rule 9. In addition, comparing the
elements of the Exlist with the elements of the Idlist in left-to-right
order, the type of each Ex must be the same as the type indicated by the
identification of its corresponding Id without the words <u>parameter</u> or
<u>value</u>.
In the expansion (Var :=)^{x} Ex the type of each Var must be the same. The
type of Ex is made compatible with this type. The phrase 'expression E
made compatible with type T' has the following meaning : If E has type T,
no action is taken. If the type of E is different from T and one of the

types is _boolean_ then the program is incorrect, otherwise E takes the property 'convert to T'.

16) The Id is identified. If the Exlist is present, the type indica-ted by Id must include _array_ and the number of elements of Exlist must be equal to half the number of Ex in the Bounds which created the cor-responding entry in the declaration table. Each Ex in the Exlist is made compatible with the type _integer_. The type of Var is that one of _integer_, _real_ or _boolean_ to be found in the type indicated by Id.

18) - The Ex after _while_ must be of type _boolean_. The first Ex is made compatible with the type of Var of rule 13 which preceeds the Forlist which expands to this Forel. If _step_ is present, the type of this Var must not be _boolean_, and the Ex after _step_, together with the Ex after _until_ are made compatible with this type.

19) - If ⊃ is present, Ex takes the type _boolean_, and the two Ex 1 must be of type _boolean_, otherwise Ex takes the type of the Ex 1.

20) - As 19 with ≡, Ex 1 and Ex 2 substituted for ⊃ , Ex and Ex 1 respectively.

21) - If _or_ is present, Ex 2 takes the type _boolean_ and all the Ex 3 must be of type _boolean_, otherwise Ex 2 takes the type of Ex 3.

22) - As 21 with _and_, Ex 3 and Ex 4 substituted for _or_, Ex 2 and Ex 3 respectively.

23) - If _not_ is present, Ex 4 takes the type _boolean_ and the Ex 5 must be of type _boolean_. If Relop is present, Ex 4 takes the type _boolean_ and the two examples of Ex 5 must not have type _boolean_. If neither _not_ nor Relop is present, Ex 4 takes the type of Ex 5.

25) - If + or - is present, no example of Ex 6 may be of type _boolean_ and if all the Ex 6 are of type _integer_ Ex 5 takes the type _integer_, otherwise Ex 5 takes the type _real_. If + and - are absent Ex 5 takes the type of the Ex 6.

26) - If + - ✕ / ÷ are all absent, Ex 6 takes the type of Ex 7. If any of them are present, no Ex 7 may be of type _boolean_. If any Ex 7 which

neither preceeds nor immediately follows ÷ is <u>real</u> the
Ex 6 takes the type <u>real</u>, otherwise the type <u>integer</u>.

27) - If ↑ is present the Ex 7 takes the type <u>real</u>, otherwise Ex 7 takes
the type of Prim.

28) - For the first alternative, Prim takes the type of Simplex. In
the second alternative, the expression after <u>if</u> must be <u>boolean</u>. If
either Simplex is of type <u>boolean</u> then both must be and Prim takes the
type <u>boolean</u>, otherwise if both are <u>integer</u> the Prim takes the type
<u>integer</u>, otherwise Prim takes the type <u>real</u>.

29) - Simplex takes the type of its applied alternative as follows :

  - The type of (Ex) is the type of the Ex

  - The types of <u>true</u> and <u>false</u> are <u>boolean</u>

  - Intno is <u>integer</u> and Realno is <u>real</u>

  - The Id is identified and the Prim is that one of <u>integer</u>, <u>real</u>
    or <u>boolean</u> which is indicated. If [ ] are present the relevant
    parts of rule 16 are applied. If ( ) are present the relevant
    parts of rule 14 are applied.

2.4.3 - Dynamic semantics -

The dynamic semantics have knowledge of the stack in which
all information is stored. They are again given in terms of syntax rule
numbers. The result of a program is the result of evaluating its syntax
tree.

1) - The evaluation of a block is preceeded by the stacking of

  - An indication of the position in the stack of the preceeding block
    or Procd on the stack.

  - Data space corresponding to each entry in its declaration table
    which is of type <u>real</u>, <u>integer</u> or <u>boolean</u>.

  - Data space corresponding to each entry in its declaration table
    whose type contains the word <u>array</u>. The definition of this part
    of the language will not be given here.

The evaluation of a block is the successive evaluation of each constituent S until either the <u>end</u> is reached or a <u>goto</u> statement terminates
the block (see rules 8 and 14). The termination of a block removes from
the stack those objects which were put on to it at the start of the
block.

2) - The evaluation of <u>switch</u> ... is the evaluation of the n.th Desex,
where n is the index passed by the object which provoked the evaluation
of the <u>switch</u>.

4) - The evaluation of a Procd is preceeded by the stacking of the
following :

- An indication of the position in the stack of the preceeding
  Block or Procd on the stack. This will be refered to as the
  'dynamic scope pointer'.

- An indication of the position in the stack of the block in the
  declaration table of which occurs the identifier of the Procd.
  If this block occurs more than once in the stack, the most recent
  occurrence is indicated.
  This will be referred to as the 'static scope pointer'.

- For each member of the Idlist (if it exists) of Formals whose
  corresponding type in the declaration table is <u>real</u> <u>value</u> parameter,
  integer value parameter or <u>boolean</u> <u>value</u> parameter, a data-space
  for a <u>real</u>, <u>integer</u> or <u>boolean</u> object, respectively. This data-
  space is filled with the value provided by the evaluation of the
  object which provoked the evaluation of Procd.

The evaluation of Procd is the evaluation of the S. The termination of the
evaluation of Procd requires the removal from the stack of the objects
which were stacked at the beginning of its evaluation.

8) - If the form of Desex was Id, the Id is found (see below). Those
Blocks and Procd which have been stacked more recently than the one is
which the Id was found are terminated. The evaluation proceeds with the
statement following the ocurrence of the Id which provoked the entry in
the declaration table.

If the form of Desex was Id [Ex], the Expression is evaluated,
the Id is found and the more recent Blocks and Procds terminated. The
value of the expression is passed as index to the <u>switch</u> corresponding
to the entry corresponding to Id in the declaration table. This <u>switch</u>

is evaluated.

If the form of the Desex was _if_ ..., the Ex after _if_ is evaluated. If its value is _true_ then the part between _then_ and _else_ is evaluated as a Desex, otherwise the Desex after _else_ is evaluated.

12) - The evaluation of S is the evaluation of the relevant alternative.

13) - If the form of the NLCS is _if_..., the value of the Ex is evaluated. If this value is _true_ then the NLUS is evaluated, otherwise the S (if it exists).

The evaluation of _for_ ... is not given.

14) - The evaluation of the different alternatives is as follows :

- _begin_ ..., each S is evaluated in turn.

- The Block is evaluated

- the Desex is evaluated

- the Variables are found, the expression is evaluated, and the value is put into the data-space corresponding to each Variable.

- the Id is found. If the Exlist exists, each Ex of the Exlist which corresponds to an entry is the declaration table of the found Id which is of a type which contains _value_ is evaluated. The values are passed to the Procd corresponding to the found Id, which is evaluated.

16) - Array references are not described. Finding Var is equivalent to finding the Id.

19 - 28) - The evaluation of the different levels of expression will not be given.

29) - The evaluation of simplex is the evaluation of the corresponding alternative, as follows :

- the Ex is evaluated

- the constants have their obvious value

- the Id is found, and the value is the contents of its corresponding data-space

- See the last alternative of rule 14. The value is the value of the Procd.

Many details have been omitted in this exposition of the dynamic semantics, for example _for_ statements, array references and the value of functions. The aim of the example is to give ideas, and not a complete definition of ALGOL60. The most important part of the dynamic semantics is the concept of 'finding' an identifier, which will be defined as follows :

It is a property of the node of each identifier to indicate the block or procedure in whose declaration table the identifier occurs. Finding an identifier means therefore finding the data space in the stack corresponding to the entry in the declaration table. This data space is in the space taken in the stack at entry to the block or procedure. Consider the most recent block or procedure. If it is not the required block then consider the block or procedure indicated by this block or by the static pointer of the procedure and repeat the process,otherwise the data space is found.

2.4.4   Comments on the example

The example given above could not serve as a definition of ALGOL60, since it is incomplete and untested. The aim of this course is not, howewer, to redefine ALGOL60, but to try to indicate the way in which we might define a language to be implementable. Thus we will continue to develope the example by making it resemble more and more the program (compiler) which is its equivalent.

In order to produce a compiler from the definition, it will be necessary to rewrite it in more machine-like terms, or at least in more symbolic terms. The next step is therefore to find a definition/implementation language which allows us to express the information we considered necessary in the definition. This language should be able to be implemented on different machines. It should be noted that this way of working is not a return to UNCOL [10] or to any system, in which the 'universal' intermediate language is defined, since the definition language is particular to the high level language which is being defined. We also suggest that the implementation of the definition language be left open, since it is probable that the implementor will rewrite in any case.

3. FROM DEFINITION TO IMPLEMENTATION

Since our ideal of an automatic transformation of a definition into an implementation is not yet feasible, the programmer must perform this transformation by hand. His method of working is to separate the subject matter into a number of logical steps, firstly in deciding what can be done at compile time and what must wait until run-time, and then in dividing the compiler into a number of passes. This division depende on the order of arrival of information in the source text. Problems which arise can be trivial but may often not be so. They are often due to using an object which is declared 'lower down the page'. This occurs with identifiers in many languages, and is the principal logical reason for multi-pass compilers.

The division of work between different phases of the compiler is not helped by the type of language definition given above (apart from the separation of static and dynamic semantics, which splits compile time from run time). Thus we suggest that even the 'implementer-oriented' definition given in the preceeding chapter is not good enough, and the language should comport an "implementers' guide", which is essentially the design of an ideal compiler. This compiler could be specified, at least to some extent, by the use of syntax directed semantic routines, which are called semantic functions in what follows. We should consider carefully the language in which these semantic functions might be written.

3.1, SEMANTIC FUNCTIONS

Established compiler-compiler methods allow the insertion in the grammar of function calls to obey hand-written semantic procedures during the analysis process. The classic example, taken from [9] is the following evaluation of an integer :

Grammar : Integer ::=Digit f1 x

x   ::=Digit f2 x | ∅

Functions f1 : value ← digit

f2 : value ← value :: 10 + digit

Similar calls are allowed in bottom-up methods at each reduction. All the rules of static semantics can be written in terms of these functions, with the addition of the set of procedures or macros

which are frequently used. The difficult, and extremely important decision
is the choice of the language in which these functions will be written.

Before discussing possible ways in which this decision might be taken,
we look at a typical part of the static semantics in order to get some
idea of the facilities that the language might contain. We consider the
insertion of the declaration of a list of <u>real</u> variables in the declaration table.

The grammar rules concerned with this part of the example
are :

```
2. D        → Declarer Idlist | ...

5. Idlist   → Id {, Id}*

6. Declarer → real ...
```

Functions are inserted as follows :

```
2.D         → Declarer Idlist f1 | ...
5. Idlist   → Id f2 {, Id f3}*
6. Declarer → real f4 ...

    f1 : while listofids ≠ null do
         begin add (dectable (localblockno), (lastdeclarer,
               head (listofids))) ;
               listofids ← tail (listofids)

         end
    f2 : listofids ← null ;
         add (listofids, idnumber)
    f3 : add (listofids, idnumber)
    f4 : lastdeclarer ← 'real'
```

Within these functions, 'add' adds the second of its parameters to the
list which is the first parameter. 'Head' and 'tail' have their usual
list-like sense. The functions are meant to be understood, rather than
compiled.

The example shows that the implementation language for the
static semantics must contain a certain number of facilities which
are sometimes described as sophisticated, for example a minimum of list-
processing and the treatment of aggregates of various sorts. Individual
functions are likely to be short pieces of program, and hence the control structure of the language need not be complicated, but the data-
structures are very language-dependent (their implementation will also

be very machine-dependent).

3.2.   IMPLEMENTATION LANGUAGES

We have suggested above that the syntantic definition of a
language should have a particular analysis method in mind. In the same
way it would seem reasonable that the definition of the semantics of
the language be in terms of a particular implementation language. This
has the double advantage of forcing the language designer to consider
the implementer's terms, at the same time as approaching our aim of
automatic transformation of definition into implementation. This means
that consideration of specialised languages for the production of
software is an important topic [22].In addition this once again limits
the implementer, who either obeys the rules, or takes on his own head
any changes he may wish to make. This encouragement towards a certain
logical standardisation will also help in portability, adaptability and
maintenance, since different groups working in the same area should be
able to apply each others' results.

3.3.   EXECUTION MODEL

The Static semantics can be defined as they are programmed,
since they represent essentially that part of the language which is
treated at compile time. The dynamic semantics, in a normal compiler,
are obeyed at execution of the programme. They are thus expressed in
terms of an interpreter which works on a double data structure, the
first part of which is the representation of the program, the second
being the data. This representation of the dynamic semantics can be
expressed in natural language (as in ALGOL 68 [12] or in some algorithmic or mathematical one (an effort is made with PL/1 [13]). These
two examples will be examined in a later section. An essentiel rule
defining the execution model by a formal interpreter, or by a natural
language description of an interpreter, is that given a choice between
two ways of describing some phenomenon, it should be automatic to
choose the algorithm which most resembles what is likely to be implemented. This rule has not always been followed in definitions, since,
for example, the 'copy rule' is never implemented in pratice.

A slightly different idea is to give not an interpreter
for the dynamic semantics, but equivalences of each concept in some

lower form of language. This is the basis of the extensible language philosophy, and the language is simply defined as a level in a language hierarchy. These concepts will also be examined in a future section. They are not yet well-enough established to come under the heading of software engineering. One obvious way for defining equivalences is to use some macro system, with as many layers as desired.

The difference between these two methods is not as great as it would appear from their external form, the interpreter defining essentially equivalences in a hierarchy which is strictly limited. However, much more static semantics are necessary in the definition which uses the interpreter, since in the case of a language defined by extension from a lower-level language, static semantics need only be defined at the lower level. In pratice it should be noted that there may well be static semantics at each level. As an example of this, we may define a simple loop by its equivalence in terms of a test and goto, as follows :

while Expression do statement

is equivalent to

ℓ : if Expression then begin statement ;

goto ℓ end

The static semantics requiring the expression after while to be boolean are covered by those requiring an expression after if to be boolean. This would seen to be an advantage for the mechanism of extension, since the definition would seem to be more compact, but it is not yet clear how to implement this compact version with as much efficiency as the classical one.

A small point of terminology to conclude this section : a language which is defined by extension is not necessary itself an extensible language, this term being reserved for languages which contain within them definition mechanisms which allow them to be extended.

3.4 - FINAL COMMENTS ON IMPLEMENTATION

In this section we have not described particular implementation methods, but have tried to see what influence the definition of the language may have on its implementation. It is clear that the influence is considerable, since it is easier, safer and more efficient to implement a language by directly following its definition. It is this idea which prompts us to suggest that the definition of a language should foresee its implementation, and that the implementation should be strongly directed from the very start. There is here a parallel with the architecture of computer hardware, which is likely improve conceptually each time the hardware engineer works closely enough to the software engineer and hence considers the use to which the machine may be put. The use to which a language definition is put is in the first instance the implementation.

We consider, therefore, that a language definition should be in terms of an idealised implementation, or at least be accompanied by an "implementers' guide", which may be at two different levels. A language issued for general use should not be given to implementers as a challenge : "here it is, now it is your turn", since the two processes are mutually dependent and the feedback loop between them is of considerable importance.

4. A LOOK AT SOME DEFINITIONS

In this section we will look at some existing language definitions from the point of view which has been developed above. Since the definitions which we consider were not necessarily written for the same reasons as those we have exposed, criticisms of particular points in the definitions should not be taken as criticisms of the project concerned in the context in which the project was carried out.

4.1. ALGOL68

ALGOL68 is defined [12] in terms of the famous two-level grammar, together with a stylised English text describing the interpretation of a program on a hypothetical computer. It is not the intention of this course to present in detail this much-discussed document, but the concept of double grammar is important. For simplicity, we show an example from ALGOL60.

The double grammar can express compatibility of type, for example in the ALGOL60 assignment
Assignment : TYPE variable, assignment symbol, TYPE expression.
The two occurrences of TYPE must, in a given expansion of 'assignment', give rise to the same expansion in the rule

TYPE : Arithmetic type ; booleantype .

(Note that the colon corresponds in some sense to the **::=** of Backus
normal form, that the semi-colon separates alternatives and the com-
ma is the concatenation operator).

This example does not seem very powerful, but it becomes
so as soon as we allow recursion. In the ALGOL68 grammar, each object
carries its type along with it. The grammar recognises different
identifiers from the rule

TAG : LETTER ; TAG LETTER ; TAG DIGIT.

Thus, in a rule which contains two occurrences of TAG,

A: ... TAG ... TAG ...

The two occurrences refer to the same identifier. The type of an
object includes, amongst other information, the number of dimensions
in an array, and the number and description of parameters of a
procedure. The dimensionality of an array is found in :

ROWSETY:ROWS ; EMPTY.
ROWS : row of ; ROWS row of.

Parameter descriptions are found in the rules :

PROCEDURE : procedure PARAMETY MOID.
PARAMETY : with PARAMETERS ; EMPTY.
PARAMETERS : PARAMETER ; PARAMETERS and PARAMETER.
PARAMETER : MODE parameter.

Type conversion is also handled by this mechanism.

Much of the information which is included in static
semantics can therefore be handled directly by the syntax, and this
is an extremely powerful definitional feature. The power of this
definition method remains, however, a source of frustration for the
implementor, who is unable to profit from it for two reasons. The
first of these is that no satisfactory analyser has yet been built
for two-level grammars in general, which means that the grammar cannot be used directly. The second reason stems from the fact that the
most important immediate adavantage of the method is the automatic
treatment of types and type conversion. For this treatment to be
operative, the uses of the identifiers of a program must have been
associated with their relevant declarations in order to discover

their type. This in its turn implies a certain level of syntactic
analysis, since the association process depends on the program
structure. Thus the syntax must be applied in at least two independent
phases (there are also further reasons why this in necessary).

Computer science has not yet provided solutions to these
problems, which may reside, if solutions there are, in a transformation of the two-level grammar into another form. Efforts towards
this goal have been published, for example in [14]. In this sense
ALGOL68 represents an open challenge and does not correspond to our
aims of easy implementability. In practice it has proved to be the
language for which the delay between definition and implementation
has been the longest up till now. In defence of ALGOL68 it must be
said that its aims were not ours.

For the dynamic semantics, and for that part of the
static semantics not included in the grammar, ALGOL68 uses an
interpreter written in English together with a limited number of
extensions. The advantages and disadvantages of these techniques
have already been discussed. The extensions are not defined in a way
as to be implemented as such, which limits their use to the definition.

In conclusion, ALGOL68, while being an impressive and
important contribution to computer science, is   yet of limited
application in software engineering, since the techniques used are
more experimental than is desirable for a production engineer. The
immediate advantages in software engineering come from some of the
nicer touches in the language contents, for example the concept of
collateralism. A more complete evaluation of ALGOL68 is to be found
in [23].

4.2. VIENNA DEFINITIONS

The definition method developed at Vienna is used for the
formal definition of PL/1 [13] and other languages such as ALGOL60.
A formal definition is composed of a concrete syntax, an abstract
syntax is written in the form we have already seen [6], and concerns
the physical representation of phrases of the language.

The abstract syntax allows an abstract representation of the program based on predicates, with formal rules concerning relationships between different elements. The function 'translate' translates the abstract representation into an abstract program. The translator contains rules which perform the tests included above in static semantics, checking in particular for double declarations, and forming the declaration tables. As an example, taken from [15], consider the rule forebidding multiple declarations :

$$\text{trans - decllist (p)} =$$

$$\neg \; (\exists i,j) \; (i \neq j \; \& \; S_2 o S_i op(t) = S_2 o S_j op(t) \neq \Omega) \rightarrow$$

$$\mu o \; (\{<id : \text{trans-decl} \; (S_1 op) > \; |$$

$$id = S_2 o S_i op(t) \neq \Omega\})$$

$$T \rightarrow error$$

The first line of the definition says that there do not exist two entries (i and j) in the declaration table for which the identifiers (discovered by selectors) are equal and non-vide.
The second line defines the action to be taken when this condition is confirmed, that is to say the translation of the declaration list. If the condition is not confirmed, the error function is entered.

The translation of a concrete program, which is defined by concrete syntax, is an abstract program, defined by the abstract syntax. The highest level rules of the PL/1 abstract syntax have the following form :

$$\text{is-program} = (\{<id:is-body>||is-id \; (id)\})$$

$$\text{is-body} \quad = (is-block \; ;< s-param-list:is-id-list>)$$

$$\text{is-block} \quad = (<s-decl-part:is-decl-part>,$$

$$< s-st-list:is-st-list>)$$

$$\text{is-decl-part} = (\{<id:is-decl>||is-id(id)\}).$$

is-program defines the form of an object which is a program. The right-hand side of the equation says that a program is a set of objects which are bodies (is-body) selected by identifiers.

Each identifier is of type is-id (|| can be read as 'where'). An abstract program is thus a tree of the form

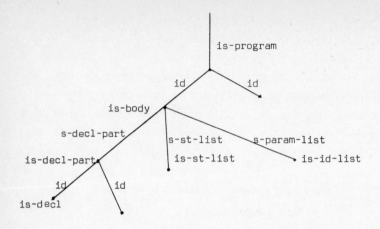

The interpreter is a formal set of transitions which are applied to give successive states of an abstract machine. A brief example, again taken from [15], is the evaluation of an expression :

$$
\begin{aligned}
&\underline{\text{int-expr}}(e) = \\
&\quad \text{is-bin}(e) \rightarrow \underline{\text{int-bin-op}}\ (\text{s-op}(e),a,b)\ ; \\
&\qquad\qquad\qquad a : \underline{\text{int-expr}}\ (\text{s-rd1}(e)), \\
&\qquad\qquad\qquad b : \underline{\text{int-expr}}\ (\text{s-rd2}(e)) \\
&\quad \text{is-unary}(e) \rightarrow \underline{\text{int-un-op}}\ (\text{s-op}(e),a)\ ; \\
&\qquad\qquad\qquad a : \underline{\text{int-expr}}\ (\text{s-rd}(e)) \\
&\quad \text{is-var}(e)\quad \rightarrow \text{PASS} : \text{content}\ (e,\xi) \\
&\quad \text{is-const}(e) \rightarrow \text{PASS} : \text{value}(e)
\end{aligned}
$$

This evaluation of an integer expression reads : 'if e is a binary expression than the evaluation is the evaluation of the binary operator applied to a and b, where a and b are the two operands, otherwise, if e is a unary expression ..., etc.

This formal definition corresponds closely to the scheme of definition/implementation which is desirable in practice. The interpreter knows about stacks and data-structures (although in a representation which may seen strange to an implementer), and contains all the necessary information for implementation. To our knowledge, no implementation based on the definition has been carried out, neither is one likely. Whether implementation is feasible remains doubtful. It is this project which shows up most clearly the gap between our formal knowledge and possibilities given by computer science research, and our possibilities of applying reasonable and clear techniques in software engineering practice.

4.3. EXTENSIBLE LANGUAGES

One approach to the problem of closing the gap between the formal definition, unusable (or unused) by the implementor, and the practical definition, which is very unsatisfying from the point of view of mathematical precision, may well turn out to be that of extensible languages. An extensible language consists of a rela- tively simple, but self-contained, base language, which itself contains extension mechanisms which allow the definition of new statement or data types. It is difficult to quote particular pieces of research without creating lists of projects, but two succes- sive international symposia give some idea for those particularly interested [16], [17]. The example uses the notation of [18].

Consider the loop already used as an example. We may write its syntax as :

<u>macro</u> $Statement_0$ → <u>while</u> Ex_1 <u>do</u> $Statement_1$

<u>where</u> type (Ex_1) = boolean

<u>means</u> $\ell 1$: <u>if</u> Ex_1 <u>then</u> <u>begin</u> $Statement_1$; <u>goto</u> $\ell 1$ <u>end</u>

This mechanism of syntactic macros allows conditions to be put on the parameters of the macro (<u>where</u> clause) and gives its expansion (<u>means</u> ....). Thus, given a base language, the new macros are automatically processed and the new compiler is produced auto- matically.

This line of research, which follows compiler-compiler and macro systems, can be considered promising, but the results are not yet sufficiently efficient to be considered as standard engine- enring practice. We may consider the <u>macro,</u> <u>where</u> and <u>means</u> parts of a definition to correspond respectively to the syntax, static seman- tics and dynamic semantics of the extended language. The base language must be defined by some other means, probably traditional.

5. CONCLUSION

We have tried to look at the impact of language definition on software engineering from three points of view. Firstly in considering the user, we see that certain aspects of a language may encourage the programmer to write better programs. Secondly we consider the needs of an implementor, who we consider should be more directly guided, and thirdly some attempts at formal definition.

One conclusion which may be drawn from this overview is that there is an unexplored gap between the work of formal language definition and compiler implementation which is extremely unsatisfactory. We hope and suggest that computer science research should work towards bridging this gap. If the miracle happens, then the implementor will have less work to do, since the definition will imply the implementation method. In the last resort, implementors become redundant, since the transformation from definition to implementation becomes automatic.

In the last section, a particular line of research which leads towards this goal was indicated. It must not be thought that no other research projects are of any interest. Indeed, one of the more recent tendencies has been away from the classical languages which we have considered, and towards new structures in different ways, for example APL [19] or ABSYS [20] and ABSET [21]. Our crystal ball is not tuned to foreseeing the language scene in 1985, nor is this part of software engineering.

One may also consider what is the domain of application of these reflections concerning languages and compilers. In our view they are not restricted only to general-purpose programming languages. It seems obvious that it is almost more important to apply sound techniques in the definition of special-purpose languages, since the limited application of these normally means that less effort is available for later clarification.

In addition to their application to other language situations, these techniques have much in common with any program, since it is always necessary to carry through the cycle of definition/implementation. Of course a program to be compiled represents for the moment the most complicated data structure usually treated by a computer (with the probable exception of natural language) and much more

effort is put into this data definition. It is possible to find a
parallel between syntax, static semantics and dynamic semantics on
the one hand, and data structure, defensive testing of the data and
the manipulations to be performed on the other.

In our efforts to eliminate the implementor, the definition and implementation of a language tend towards different forms
of the same object. This object becomes less and less understandable
to the user, who needs different documents to serve as description.
We do not at the moment see any way of making the definition serve
satisfactorily as this description.

It is perhaps to be regretted that this course presents
more problems than solutions. However, we must be aware of the
distance which separates our present techniques from those future ones
which will, optimistically, be mathematically provable, efficient,
and usable by programmers with little formal training outside their
own fields of application.

6. ACKNOWLEDGEMENTS

The author wishes to thank MM. BOUSSARD, JORRAND and
LOUIS for their helpful remarks during discussions.

7. REFERENCES

[1] - N. WIRTH
A Programming Language for the 360 Computers
JACM, Jan.1968.

[2] - G. GOOS, K. LAGALLY, G. SAPPER
PS440, Eine niedere Programmiersprache
Technischen Universität, Munich 1970

[3] - N. WIRTH
The Programming Language PASCAL
Acta Informatica I, 1971
and The Design of a PASCAL Compiler
Software Practice and Experience 1, 4, 1971

[4] - R.W. FLOYD
Syntactic Analysis and Operator Precedence
JACM, July 1963

[5] - D.E. KNUTH
Top -Down Syntax Analysis
Proceedings of a Summer School, Copenhagen, 1967

[6] - K. ALBER, P. ÓLIVA, G. URSCHLER
Concrete Syntax of PL/1
IBM Vienna Laboratory, TR 25.084, 1968

[7] - J.W. BACKUS et al.
Report on the Algorithmic Language ALGOL60
CACM Dec. 1960

[8] - J. BORDIER
Méthodes pour la mise au point de grammaires LL(1)
Thèse de Troisième Cycle, Grenoble, 1971

[9] - J.M. FOSTER
       A Syntax Improving Device
       Computer Journal, May 1968

[10] - T.B. STEEL
       UNCOL : The Myth and the Fact
       Ann. Rev. in Aut. Prog., 2, 1961

[11] - P.C. POOLE, W.M. WAITE, This school

[12] - A. Van WIJNGAARDEN et al.
       Report on the Alogorithmic Language ALGOL68
       Mathematisch Centrum, Amsterdam, MR101, Oct. 1969

[13] - P. LUCAS, K. WALK
       On the Formal Definition of PL/1
       Ann. Rev. of Aut. Prog. 6, Pergamon Press, 1971

[14] - C.H.A. KOSTER
       Affix Grammars
       in. J.E.L. Peck (Editor), ALGOL68 Implementation, 1971

[15] - P. LUCAS, P.LAUER, H.STIGLEITNER
       Method and Notation for the Formal Definition of
       Programming Languages
       IBM Laboratory Vienna, TR 25.087, 1968

[16] - Proceedings of the Extensible Languages Symposium
       SIGPLAN Notices, Aug. 1969

[17] - Proceedings of an Extensible Languages Symposium
       SIGPLAN Notices, Dec. 1971

[18] - S. SCHUMANN
       Specification des Langages de Programmation et de leurs
       Traducteurs au moyen de Macros Syntaxiques
       Proc. AFCET, 1970

[19] - K.E. IVERSON
       A Programming Language
       Wiley, New York, 1962

110

[20] - J.M. FOSTER, E.W. ELCOCK
       ABSYS1 : An Incremental Compiler for Assertions
       Machine Intelligence 4, Edinburgh University Press, 1969

[21] - E.W. ELCOCK, J.M. FOSTER, P.M.D. GRAY, J.M. Mc GREGOR,
       A.M. MURRAY
       ABSET, a Programming Language Based on Sets
       Machine Intelligence 6, Edinburgh University Press, 1971.

[22] - M. GRIFFITHS
       Low-Level Languages.
       Notes from this school.

[23] - J.C. BOUSSARD, J.J. DUBY (editors)
       Rapport d'évaluation ALGOL68
       RIRO, Feb. 1971

CHAPTER 2.E.

CONCURRENCY IN SOFTWARE SYSTEMS +)

Jack B. Dennis
Massachusetts Institute of Technology
Cambridge, Massachusetts, USA

1. INTRODUCTION

A large program such as an operating system, a compiler, or a real-
time control program is a precise representation of a system composed of
many interacting parts or modules. Due to the size of these programs,
it is essential that the parts be represented in such a way that the
descriptions of the parts are independent of the pattern in which they
are interconnected to form the whole system, and so the behavior of each
part is unambiguous and correctly understood regardless of the situation
in which it is used. For this to be possible, all interactions between
system parts must be through explicit points of communication established
by the designer of each part.

If two parts of a system are independently designed, then the timing
of events within one part can only be constrained with respect to events
in the other part as a result of interaction between the two parts. So
long as no interaction takes place, events in two parts of a system may
proceed concurrently and with no definite time relationship among
them. Imposing a time relation on independent actions of separate
parts of a system is a common source of overspecification. The
result is a system that is more difficult to comprehend, troublesome to
alter, and incorporates unnecessary delays that may reduce performance.
This reasoning shows that the notions of concurrency and asynchronous
operation are fundamental aspects of software systems.

In this lecture we consider a model for systems viewed as collections of concurrently operating subsystems that interact with one

+) The preparation of these notes was supported in part
by the National Science Foundation under grant GJ-432
and in part by the Advanced Research Projects Agency,
Department of Defense, under Office of Naval Research
Contract Nonr-N00014-70-A-0362-0001.

another through specific disciplines of communication. In many cases,
we desire that such a system have a behavior that is reproducible in
separate runs when presented with the same input data. This property
of systems is known as determinacy. We shall present and illustrate an
important result that if interactions between subsystems obey certain
natural conditions, then determinacy of the subsystems guarantees
determinacy of the whole system. We conclude by illustrating the application of this result to systems of concurrent processes that interact by means of semaphores using the primitives P and V of Dijkstra.

2. PETRI NETS

　　During the discussion we will illustrate concepts by reference
to particular examples of systems. Since we have found it convenient to use the formalism of Petri nets to represent these examples
of systems, we begin with a brief introduction to the notation and
semantics of Petri nets.

　　A Petri net [1, 2, 3] is a directed graph with two types of nodes
called places and transitions. Each arc must go from a place to a transition or from a transition to a place. In drawing a Petri net, places
are represented by circles and transitions by bars as in the example
shown in Figure 1. Places from which arcs are incident on a transition

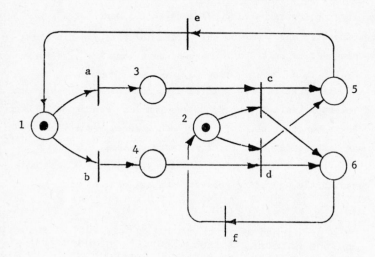

Figure 1. A Petri net.

are called <u>input places</u> of the transition, and places on which arcs
from a transition terminate are called its <u>output places</u>. Each place
may hold zero, one, or more <u>markers</u> or <u>tokens</u>. An arrangement of markers
in a net is called a <u>marking</u> of the net. A Petri net may assume any
series of markings consistent with the following <u>simulation rule</u>:

1. For a Petri net and a marking, each transition which has at
    least one token in each of its input places is <u>enabled</u>.
2. Any enabled transition may be chosen to <u>fire</u>.
3. Firing a transition consists of removing one token from each
    of its input places and adding one token to each of its output
    places.

Figure 2 shows a sequence of markings for a Petri net resulting from
the firing of transitions in the sequence a,c,e,f. Note that this firing
sequence returns the net to its original marking.

A marking of a Petri net is said to be <u>safe</u> if no simulation of the
net, starting from the given marking, yields a marking in which some
place holds more than one token. In a net having a safe marking no
transition is ever enabled when tokens are present in any of its output
places. A marking of a Petri net is <u>live</u> if, for any marking reachable
from the given marking, there is a firing sequence that will enable any
transition of the net. Liveness of a marked Petri net requires that no
part of the net ever reach a condition from which further activity of the
part is impossible. The Petri net in Figs. 1 and 2 is both live and
safe for all of the markings shown.

If simulation of a Petri net reaches a marking for which two transitions are enabled that share an input place, the two transitions are
said to be in <u>conflict</u> over the token in the shared place. In Fig. 2a
transitions a and b are in conflict at place 1. In this case, the conflict is resolved by making an arbitrary decision as to which transition
is to receive the token in place 1, hence this sort of conflict is
called a <u>free choice</u>.

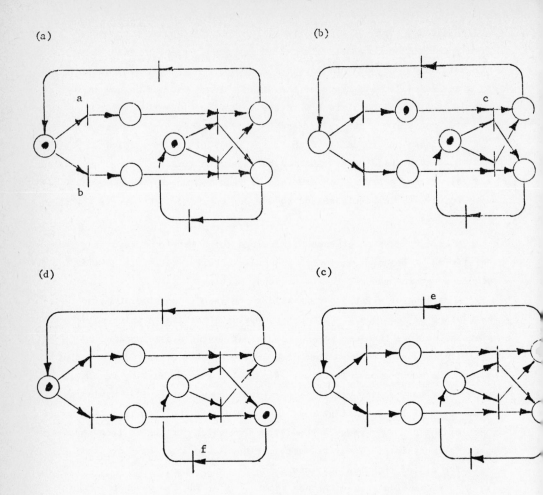

Figure 2. Simulation of a Petri net.

3. SYSTEMS

In Figure 3 we show a <u>system</u> S with m <u>inlets</u> and n <u>outlets</u>. The inlets are points at which the system receives signals from other systems or from the environment E in which the systems operate. The outlets

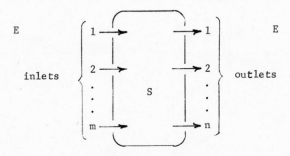

Figure 3. A system.

are points at which the system emits signals for reception by other systems or the environment. An alphabet of possible signals is associated with each inlet or outlet of the system.

Suppose system S begins operation from some internal configuration C_0 and makes transitions to successive configurations $C_1, C_2, \ldots, C_k, \ldots$. In some transitions symbols are absorbed at certain inlets; in other transitions symbols are delivered at outlets. Suppose the system has reached configuration C_i. During the activity from C_0 to C_i some definite sequence of signals was abosrbed by S at each inlet, and some definite sequence of signals was delivered at each outlet, as shown in Figure 4. The array of input sequences U is called an <u>input</u> of the system; the array of output sequences V is a corresponding <u>output</u> of the system.

In this way, the behavior of a system is given by a binary relation R_S containing each pair (U, V) such that S has some finite activity, starting from configuration C_0, during which it absorbs the input array U and emits the output array V.

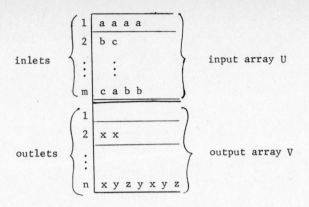

inlets   input array U

outlets   output array V

Figure 4

The domain of R_S consists of all inputs that can be absorbed by S
during some activity starting from C_0. The domain does not include
all possible arrays of finite sequences because S may cease absorbing
signals at some inlets either temporarily or permanently. The range of
the relation R_S contains each output S could emit for some input.

Let us consider some simple examples of systems to become familiar
with the kinds of behavior that may occur. The system of Figure 5,
shown in its initial configuration, transmits the pair of signals x,y for

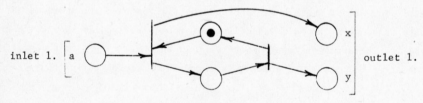

inlet 1.   outlet 1.

Figure 5.

each signal received at its inlet. Corresponding to the input

> 1. ⬚a a⬚

the output may be any one of the three possibilities:

> 1. ⬚x y⬚ ,   1. ⬚x y x⬚   or   1. ⬚x y x y⬚

In this case, a bounded input can yield only bounded outputs. Figure 6 shows a system that can have unbounded outputs for certain bounded inputs.

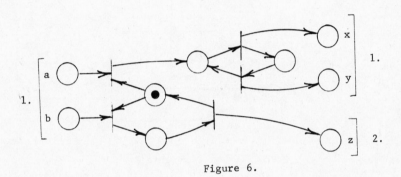

Figure 6.

For the input

> 1. ⬚b a⬚

the output may be any member of the infinite set of arrays

> 1. ⬚⬚
> 2. ⬚z⬚   1. ⬚x⬚
>   2. ⬚z⬚   1. ⬚x y⬚
>   2. ⬚z⬚   1. ⬚x y x⬚
>   2. ⬚z⬚   . . .

The example in Figure 7 shows how the order in which input signals are absorbed at different inlets may vary for different runs of a system

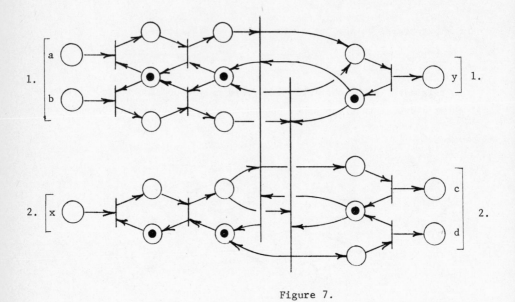

Figure 7.

without affecting the sequences that are emitted at each outlet. Two
input-output pairs are shown below:

<table>
<tr><td>1.</td><td>a b a</td><td></td><td>1.</td><td>b</td><td></td></tr>
<tr><td>2.</td><td>x</td><td></td><td>2.</td><td>x x x</td><td></td></tr>
<tr><td>1.</td><td></td><td></td><td>1.</td><td>y</td><td></td></tr>
<tr><td>2.</td><td>c</td><td></td><td>2.</td><td></td><td></td></tr>
</table>

4. DETERMINACY

Next we introduce the <u>ultimate output</u> Y of a system S for some
<u>presented input</u> X. We imagine that the symbol sequences of the array
X are made available for absorption at the inlets of S. Some of these
sequences may be infinite. Then an associated ultimate output of S
is an output array Y emitted by advancing the activity of S as far as
possible without absorbing input symbols beyond those in X. (In this
activity, it may be that S does not absorb all of X.) To state this
precisely, let us say that two sequences (possibly infinite)

$$x_1, \; x_2, \; \ldots, \; x_k, \; \ldots$$

$$y_1, \; y_2, \; \ldots, \; y_k, \; \ldots$$

are <u>similar</u> if $x_i = y_i$ for each index such that both x_i and y_i exist.
Two arrays are <u>similar</u> if corresponding rows are similar. Then Y is
an ultimate output of S for X if and only if

$$\left.\begin{array}{l} (U, \; V) \in R_S \\[4pt] U \text{ a prefix of } X \\[4pt] V \text{ similar to } Y \end{array}\right\} \text{ implies V is a prefix of Y}$$

Some examples of ultimate outputs for the systems shown in Figures 5,
6 and 7 are given below:

figure	presented input X	ultimate output Y
5	1. $\boxed{\text{a a}}$	1. $\boxed{\text{x y x y}}$
6	1. $\boxed{\text{b}}$	1. $\boxed{}$ 2. $\boxed{\text{z}}$
6	1. $\boxed{\text{b a}}$	1. $\boxed{\text{x y x y x y} \ldots\ldots}$ 2. $\boxed{\text{z}}$
7	1. $\boxed{\text{a b}}$ 2. $\boxed{\text{x}}$	1. $\boxed{\text{y}}$ 2. $\boxed{\text{c}}$

In these systems, there is a unique ultimate output for each presented input. We
call any system having this property a <u>determinate</u> <u>system</u>. Some examples
of systems that are not determinate are shown in Figures 8, 9, and 10.

1. $\begin{bmatrix} a \end{bmatrix}$ 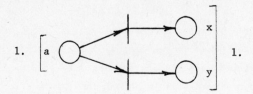 1.

Figure 8

1. $\begin{bmatrix} a \end{bmatrix}$ 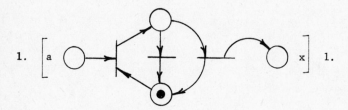 1.

Figure 9

1. $\begin{bmatrix} a \end{bmatrix}$ 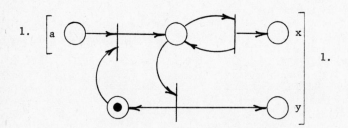 1.

Figure 10

figure	presented input	ultimate outputs	
8	1. $\boxed{a}$	1. $\boxed{x}$	1. $\boxed{y}$
9	1. $\boxed{a}$	1. $\vert$	1. $\boxed{x}$
10	1. $\boxed{a}$	1. $\boxed{x\ x\ y}$	1. $\boxed{x\ x\ x\ x}$ ... .

5. INTERCONNECTED SYSTEMS

In the examples of systems used above, arrival of a signal at an inlet occurs when a marker is put in one of the places of the inlet. We assume that no further input signals arrive until the system absorbs the signal by removing the marker from the place. An output signal is emitted when the system puts a marker in one of the places of an outlet. We assume the marker is immediately removed by the environment in which the system operates.

Suppose a finite collection of systems $\{S_i\}$ are assembled to form a larger system S by specifying associations of certain outlets and inlets, as illustrated by Figure 11. We may define the input-output relation R_S

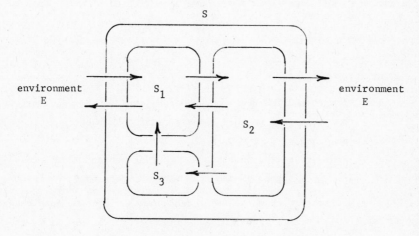

Figure 11

for the composite system by employing the following convention regarding the inputs and outputs of the constituent systems:

Suppose operation of S has reached a point where S has absorbed input U and emitted output V, and each subsystem S_i has absorbed input U_i and emitted output V_i. Then, if outlet p of S_i is associated with inlet q of S_j, the qth row of U_j must be a prefix of the pth row of V_i.

If the pth inlet of S_i is specified to be qth inlet of S, then row q of X and row p of X_i must be identical. If the pth outlet of S_i is specified to be the qth outlet of X, then row p of Y_i and row q of Y must be identical.

Using these conventions for defining the behavior of assembled systems, Patil [4] has established this important result:

Theorem   A system S formed by the assembly of systems $\{S_i\}$ is determinate if each system S_i is determinate. That is, the class of determinate systems is closed under the operation of assembly.

If, in an assembly of systems, outlet p of S_i is associated with inlet q of S_j, then more signals may have been emitted by outlet p than have been absorbed by inlet q. Thus, to apply the above result, we must connect outlet p to inlet q in such a way that signals emitted by p are fed to q in exactly the same order, and no signals are lost. Two ways of accomplishing this are:

1. Insert an FIFO queue of unbounded capacity between outlet p and inlet q to hold signals emitted by p but not yet absorbed by q.

2. Prevent S_i from emitting a signal at outlet p until the previous signal emitted has been absorbed by S_j at inlet q.

Suppose outlets are connected to inlets by means of unbounded queues. Then an event that emits a signal at an outlet enters the signal in the associated queue; an event that absorbs a signal at an inlet removes a signal from the queue, and can only occur if the queue is not empty. Under this communication discipline, the Theorem shows that interconnections of determinate systems are necessarily determinate.

To prevent a system from emitting signals before a previous signal has been absorbed, it is sufficient that an assembly of systems satisfy the following condition:

<u>α-condition</u>: For each association of an outlet p of some S_i with an
inlet q of some S_j, the assembly S must contain a path from
inlet q to outlet p by way of systems in $\{S_i\}$ and the environment of S such that each signal emitted at outlet p requires
the prior absorption of a signal at inlet q.

Figure 12 is an example of an assembly of systems that satisfies the
α-condition. If it can be verified that an assembly S of systems satisfies the α-condition, then the Theorem guarantees that S is determinate.

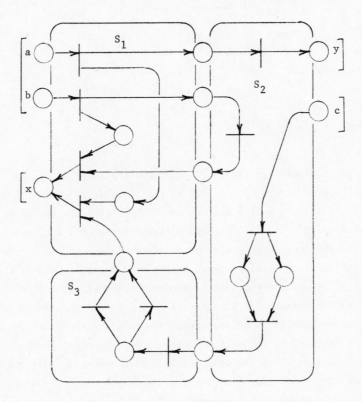

Figure 12

There is an important scheme for interconnecting systems that guarantees that the α-condition hold for the resulting system. The only
kind of connection permitted between systems is a <u>link</u> that connects an
<u>output</u> <u>port</u> of one system to an <u>input</u> <u>port</u> of another as shown in Fig-
ure 13. Each port consists of an inlet and an outlet. Systems are re-

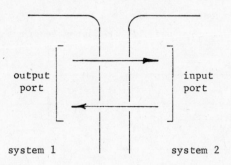

output   input
port   port

system 1   system 2

Figure 13

quired to obey the discipline of emitting a signal at the outlet of a
port only after receiving a signal at the associated inlet. In the
initial configuration of a system, each output port is considered to have
just received a (null) signal, and is prepared to emit a signal at the
outlet of the port. Each input port is prepared to absorb a signal at the
inlet, and will not emit a signal at the outlet until a signal arrives at
the inlet. We call systems that communicate according to this discipline
<u>β-systems</u>. Since any β-system satisfies the α-condition automatically,
and any interconnection of β-systems is also a β-system, the Theorem shows
that the class of determinate β-systems is closed under interconnection.

From Figure 14 we see that, since a FIFO queue is a determinate
β-system, it is also true that determinate β-systems interconnected by
queues yield determinate β-systems.

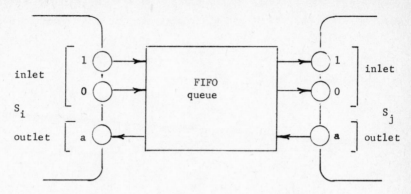

Figure 14

6. INTERPROCESS COMMUNICATION

A sequential process may be represented by a Petri net. An example is shown in Figure 15. Since there is one site of control, only one marker is ever present in the Petri net. Such Petri nets are called <u>state</u> <u>machines</u>. The location of the marker corresponds to the notion of "program counter" in a conventional computer.

(a) block diagram   (b) Petri net

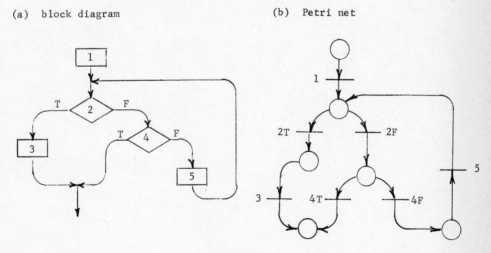

Figure 15

The synchronizing primitives of Dijkstra [5], as used to control
the interaction of pairs of processes, may be represented as in Figure 16.
The number of markers in place s represents the value of the semaphore.

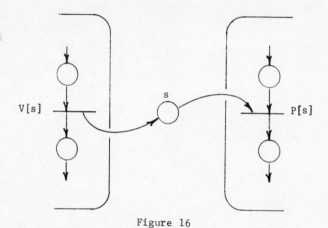

Figure 16

Suppose n sequential processes interact only in the two ways defined in Figure 17. Our development shows that such a system of processes is determinate.

(a) FIFO queue   (b) β-link

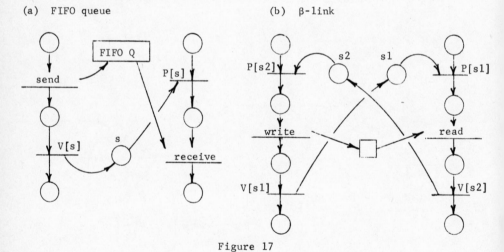

Figure 17

7. REFERENCES

1. C. A. Petri, Communication With Automata. Supplement 1 to Technical Report RADC-TR-65-377, Vol. 1, Griffiss Air Force Base, New York 1966. [Originally published in German: Kommunikation mit Automaten, University of Bonn, 1962.]

2. A. W. Holt and F. Commoner, Events and conditions. Record of the Project MAC Conference on Concurrent Systems and Parallel Computation, ACM, New York 1970, pp 3-52.

3. A. W. Holt, F. Commoner, S. Even, and A. Pnueli, Marked directed graphs. J. of Computer and System Sciences, Vol. 5 (1971), pp 511-523.

4. S. S. Patil, Closure properties of interconnections of determinate systems. Record of the Project MAC Conference on Concurrent Systems and Parallel Computation, ACM, New York 1970, pp 107-116.

5. E. W. Dijkstra, Co-operating sequential processes. Programming Languages, F. Genuys, Ed., Academic Press, New York 1968. [First published as Report EWD 123, Department of Mathematics, Technological University, Eindhoven, The Netherlands, 1965.]

CHAPTER 3.A.

M O D U L A R I T Y [+]

Jack B. Dennis
Project MAC, Massachusetts Institute of Technology
Cambridge, Massachusetts, USA

1. INTRODUCTORY CONCEPTS

The word "modular" means "constructed with standardized units or dimensions for flexibility and variety in use." Applied to software engineer
ing, modularity refers to the building of software systems by putting
together parts called *program modules.*

The dictionary meaning applies very well in, for example, the construction materials trade: In the United States floor tile comes in nine-
inch squares (the modules) which may be conveniently adjoined to fill
up any shape of floor area with just a bit of trimming at the boundary.
A great variety of patterns may be produced by using modules of differing color and texture.

In modular software, clearly the "standardized units or dimensions"
should be standards such that software modules meeting the standards
may be conveniently fitted together (without "trimming") to realize
large software systems. The reference to "variety of use" should mean
that the range of module types available should be sufficient for the
construction of a usefully large class of programs.

In July 1968 a two-day symposium was held in Boston on the subject of
Modular Programming [1]. The preprints of papers for this meeting
probably form the only collection of material representing a significant range of viewpoints on the nature and purpose of modular programming. In this collection of papers various concepts of program
modularity are described ranging from vaguely defined principles to

[+]The preparation of these notes was supported in part by the National
Science Foundation under grant GJ-432 and in part by the Advanced
Research Projects Agency, Department of Defense, under Office of
Naval Research Contract Nonr-N00014-70-A-0362-0001.

definitive formal concepts. Yet there is an important objective common
to all. It stems from recognition of the high cost of producing correctly functioning software systems; it is to realize the benefits promised by the saying: "*divide et impera*".

To many people in software practice, modular programming means the division of the whole of a program into parts so "the interactions between parts are minimized" or so "the parts have functional independence." Frequently, the assumption is made that in modular programming
the program and its parts are designed at the same time and under the
same authority. There is little appreciation that the objective of
simplifying program construction by dividing the task into parts has
definite implications regarding the structure of programs and the characteristics of computer systems.

Nevertheless, several thoughtful and precise notions were also expressed at the symposium. The designers of the Integrated Civil Engineering
System (ICES) [2] emphasized the importance of being able to use together independently written program modules. Boebert [3] also recognized that the success of modular programming depends on characteristics of the linguistic level at which the modules are expressed. He
points out that modularity should be regarded as a property of a computer system or linguistic level rather than a property possessed or
not possessed by some program. E. W. Dijkstra's concern [4] with principles of "structured programming" is closely related.

Our goal in these lectures is to develop further understanding of these
notions of modular programming, and to derive their implications for
the design of programming languages and computer systems.

1.1. DEFINITION OF MODULARITY

We take the following statements to be the objectives of modular programming:

1. One must be able to convince himself of the correctness of a program module, independently of the context of its use in building larger
units of software.

2. One must be able to conveniently put together program modules written under different authorities without knowledge of their inner workings.

These statements embody the concept of "context-independence" discussed by Boebert [3], and the concept of non-interference stated by Dijkstra [4].

We consider *modularity* to be a property of computer systems:

A computer system has modularity if the linguistic level defined by the computer system meets these conditions: Associated with the linguistic level is a class of objects that are the units of program representation. These objects are *program modules*. The linguistic level must provide a means of combining program modules into larger program modules without requiring changes to any of the component modules. Further, the meaning of a program module must be independent of the context in which it is used.

In previous publications [5,6] I have applied the term "programming generality" to computer systems that have this property of modularity.

Two relatively precise concepts regarding the form of a program module occur in the literature on modular programming. On one hand, a module is viewed as a procedure: At any point during the progress of a computation, one module (procedure) may initiate an activation of another procedure by specifying a set of input data. The new procedure activation is carried on, possibly making use of additional procedures, until it terminates, leaving a set of output data for use by the procedure from which it was activated. In this concept, a modular program is a collection of non-interferring procedures. Characteristic of programs constructed as combinations of procedures is the flow of control in a pattern described by a tree. The notion of procedure is a central feature of most modern programming languages, *ALGOL 60* being the classical model [7,8] . But, as we shall see, the procedure in its usual form does not meet our requirements for modular programming.

On the other hand, a module may be conceived as an entity that is joined to other modules by communication links. Each module receives data over its input links, transforms it in some way, and sends it on to other modules over its output links. In this picutre, each module is continously active, processing data so long as inputs are available. Concurrency of operation is an inherent part of this notion of modularity. The links connecting one module to another are thought of as channels through which data flow. First in-first out queues may be introduced in the links as a means of improving the efficienca of an implementation without altering the semantics of a modular program.

This form of modular programming is advocated [3,9] for data processing
applications where the links are implemented as "buffer files." The concept is closely related to Conway's coroutines [10] and Dijkstra's co-
operating sequential processes [11]. The only programming languages
having features suitable for this form of modular programming are certain simulation languages, in particular Simula 67 [12].

In these lectures, we study the limitations on modular programming
found in the linguistic levels defined by certain computer systems. We
consider the well-known programming languages, *FORTRAN* and *ALGOL 60*,
to understand the issue of clashes of identifiers. Wen then consider
the problems of handling dynamic data structures in modular programs
and the problems of combining program modules expressed in different
representations. Multics [13] is studied as a system in which sharing of
procedures and data is possible with considerable generality. Finally,
we consider the definition of a hypothetical linguistic level within
which a very general form of modular programming is possible.

1.2.   *MODULARITY IN FORTRAN*

Let us start by considering the forms of modular programming possible
at the linguistic level defined by the ANSI *FORTRAN* language standard.
We will not consider here the features of *FORTRAN* for input, output
and transfer of data between storage levels, and we assume that subprograms in other languages are not permitted.

A *FORTRAN program* consists of a sequence of statements that make up a
main program and a collection of separate sets of statements that represent *function subprograms* and *subroutine subprograms*. Since there is
no provision in the *FORTRAN* standard for combining separately written
FORTRAN programs, a complete *FORTRAN* program consisting of main program
and subprograms cannot serve as a program module at the linguistic level defined by the standard.

The obvious choice as a unit for modular programming is the *FORTRAN*
subprogram. We encounter one difficulty immediately: The only method
of combining several subprograms is to collect them together with a
main program, yielding an executable *FORTRAN* program. Alas, this is not
a program module, and therefore cannot be further combined with other
units to form larger modules.

Thus *FORTRAN* fails by not permitting hierarchical structure in a modular program. Nevertheless, let us disregard this defect and look for other problems. It will be useful to have in mind a picture of the computation states occurring during execution of a *FORTRAN* program. The structure of a state is shown in Fig. 1 as an *object* of the variety used by the IBM Vienna Group in their work on formal definition of programming languages. This object represents an execution state, and therefore the operation of putting several modules together to form a program has been performed. The 'text'-component of the state is an object having as its components the compiled form of each source language subprogram, including one subprogram identified as 'main', and the remaining subprograms identified by names chosen by their programmers. The 'private'-component of the state has, as its leaf nodes, data entities and other values that are accessed only during execution of the corresponding subprogram text (except, of course, when these values are passed as arguments to other subprograms). These values are values of *FORTRAN* variables and arrays not mentioned in COMMON statements of the source language subprogram, and additional variables generated by the compiler.

The 'common'-component of the state contains several vectors of data items that are accessed during execution of statements in several subprograms. The computation state of a *FORTRAN* program has a fixed structure during execution of the program, only values at the leaf nodes are changed (two exceptions: adjustable arrays and extension of COMMON).

Limitations on the generality of modular programming in a linguistic level arise from points of interaction between program modules. For *FORTRAN* subprograms these points of interaction are: calling a function or subroutine; the naming of subprograms; and the use and naming of COMMON.

If two authors have chosen the same name for their independently written subprograms, a clash of names occurs when these subprograms are used together. Similarly, two authors may choose to use blank COMMON for different pruposes, or may use the same names for labelled COMMON storage. These are violations of our definition of modularity since alteration of the representation of a module may be required before it can be correctly combined with other modules.

These names clashes may be removed by changing the names of subprograms and choosing new labels for COMMON storage areas. Matters would be more difficult if a program module were to consist of several subprograms, possibly independently written, working together. The problems intro-

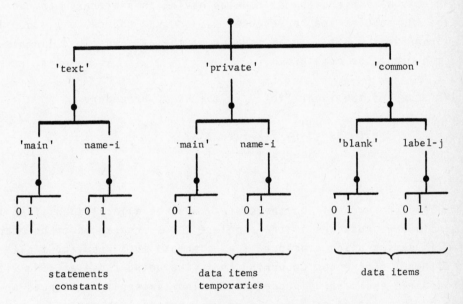

Figure 1. State of a Fortran program.

duced by attempting to remove clashes through substitution are discussed below.

1.3 MODULARITY IN ALGOL 60

In *ALGOL 60* the procedure is clearly the candidate for consideration as the form for program modules. Since procedures may be combined without modification to form larger procedures, a modular program in *ALGOL 60* may be a hierarchy of modules having an arbitrary depth of nesting. The modules are represented as *ALGOL 60* source text. Compiled *ALGOL* programs are not program modules of the *ALGOL*-defined linguistic level and cannot be combined.

The instances of the identifier y in the *ALGOL* procedure

$$\textit{real procedure } f(x); \textit{ real } x;$$
$$\textit{begin } f := x + y;$$
$$y := y + 1; \textit{ end}$$

are nonlocal references and therefore y must be a local identifier in some enclosing procedure if the complete *ALGOL* program is to be meaningful. A person using procedure f as a module must know about all such external references occurring in f (including those arising within procedures enclosed by procedure f) since external references are a form of interaction of a procedure with external objects. One may wish to use two *ALGOL* procedures, f and g, in the construction of a modular program where each procedure makes use of the identifier y to reference some external object. If both procedures are placed in the program as declarations within the same enclosing procedure, there is a clash of names. Thus the use of nonlocal references in an *ALGOL 60* program module is a violation of our concept of modularity.

Several means are available to remove or avoid clashes of names between procedures in *ALGOL 60* programs:

1. Substitute an alternate identifier for each appearance of y as an external reference in one of the procedures. For reasons to be discussed shortly, the use of substitution has significant disadvantages.

2. Enclose one of the procedures within an "interface procedure" that

renames the external object by assignment:

```
real procedure f1(x)  real x;
      begin real y;
      real procedure f(x); real x;
          begin f := x + y;
                  y := y + 1; end
      y := y1;
      f1 := f(x)
      y1 := y
      end
```

This would be awkward to do for arrays, and impossible in *ALGOL 60* if the external object is a procedure. Moreover the choice of identifier y1 depends on the text of the procedure that encloses f1.

3. Enclose one of the procedures in a procedure declaration in which y is a local identifier and formal parameter:

```
real procedure f1(x, y); real y
      begin
      real procedure f(x); real x;
          begin f := x + y;
                  y := y + 1; end
      f1 := f(x)
      end
```

This has the effect of substitution for y, but takes effect at procedure entry.

4. Organize the modular program that uses procedure f and g so that the scopes of y do not overlap, by placing the declarations of f and g within distinct procedures or blocks of the program.

The need for any of these schemes would be avoided if y were included as one of the formal parameters of procedures f and g.

The mechanism of non-local reference in *ALGOL 60* was inspired by the evaluation rules of the lambda calculus, and reduces the number of required formal parameters in procedure application. At the interface between independently written program modules, the need to discover and resolve name conflicts makes external references from program modules an unattractive form of interaction. For this reason, we shall adopt as a principle of modular programming, that the only means of communicating data to and from a procedure module is by its formal parameters (and resulting value, if any). Note that this principle rules out "side effects" of the kind observable in *ALGOL 60:* Operation of a module can only affect information explicitly passed to it.

1.4. *SUBSTITUTION*

The names (identifiers) that occur in a representation of a program module can be divided into two groups - *bound* and *free*. By definition, if a name has a free occurrence in the module, it refers to some object bound to the name outside the module. Hence substitution of an alternate name for all instances of the name within the module without rebinding names outside will change the effect of the module. All names that identify primitive operations, constants, etc. of the linguistic level at which the module is expressed are free and have permanently fixed meaning.

Names that are bound in a program module may be uniformly replaced throughout the module without altering its meaning.

If name conflicts occur when two program modules are combined, it is because the same identifier occurs free in both modules, and with different intended meanings. We have seen how such conflicts can arise from function names, subprogram names, and labels for COMMON in *FORTRAN*, and from nonlocal identifiers in *ALGOL 60*. We have noted that name conflicts may be removed by substituting an alternate name for a free name at each appearance as an external reference within a program module. This substitution must be made before the modules to be combined have lost their separate identity, for example before an *ALGOL* program is compiled or before *FORTRAN* subprograms are linked.

There are several difficulties with name substitution as a means of resolving name conflicts. Firtsly, performing the substitution may involve considerable information processing. A program module may itself be a combination of many simpler modules and the substituted name must be chosen so that no new conflicts are generated either inside or outside the program module.

The most important consequence of name substitution is that the possibility of sharing a representation of a program module among users of the module is foreclosed. A substitution required to remove a conflict cannot be made in a representation of a module already in use as part of another modular program. A copy of the module must be made first.

The importance of being able to share representations of program modules is gradually becoming recognized. In Multics [13, 14], the idea has been carried furthest: Every procedure written for operation in the system may be shared by all authorized users without the making of copies. We expect sharing to be increasingly important in future computer systems. Therefore, as a requirement of our concept of program modularity, we adopt the rule that names occurring free in a program module may refer only to fundamental entities of the linguistic level.

1.5   REFERENCES

1. T. O. Barnett, *Modular programming: Proceedings of a National Symposium, Symposium Preprint.* Information and Systems Press, Cambridge, Massachusetts 1968. Out of business .

2. J. M. Sussman and R. V. Goodman, Implementing ICES module management under OS/360. Published in [1], pp 69 - 84.

3. W. E. Boebert, Toward a modular programming system. Published in [1], pp 95 - 111.

4. E. W. Dijkstra, A constructive approach to the problem of program correctness. *BIT* (Nordisk Tidskrift for Informations-behandling), *Vol. 8, No.* 3, 1968, pp 174 - 186.

5. J. B. Dennis, Future trends in time-sharing systems. *Time-Sharing Innovation for Operations Research and Decision-Making,* Washington Operations Research Council, Rockville, Maryland 1969, pp 229-235.

6. J. B. Dennis, Programming generality, parallelism and computer architecture. *Information Processing 68,* North-Holland Publishing Co., Amsterdam 1969, pp 484 - 492.

7. E. W. Dijkstra, Recursive programming. *Numerische Mathematik, Vol.2,*

1960, pp 312 - 318.

8. P. Naur, et al, Report on the algorithimic language *ALGOL 60*. *Comm. of the ACM, Vol.*3 , *No.*5 (May 1960), pp 299 - 314.

9. E. Morenoff and J. B. McLean, Program string structures and modular programming. Published in [1], pp 133 - 143.

10. M. E. Conway, Design of a separable transition-diagram compiler. *Comm. of the ACM, Vol.* 6, *No.* 7 (July 1963), pp 396 - 408.

11. E. W. Dijkstra, Co-operating sequential processes. *Programming Languages*, F. Genuys, Ed., Academic Press, New York 1968. First published as Report EWD 123, Department of Mathematics, Technological University, Eindhoven, The Netherlands, 1965.

12. O. J. Dahl and K. Nygaard, SIMULA -- an *ALGOL*-based simulation language. *Comm. of the ACM, Vol.* 9, *No.* 9 (September 1966), pp 671-678.

13. F. J. Corbato, C. T. Clingen, and J.H. Saltzer, MULTICS -- The first seven years. *AFIPS Conference Proceedings, Vol.* 40, *SJCC*, 1972, pp 571 - 583.

14. R. C. Daley and J. B. Dennis, Vurtual memory, processes, and sharing in MULTICS. *Comm. of the ACM, Vol.* 11, *No.*5 (May 1968), pp 306-312.

2. DATA STRUCTURES IN MODULAR PROGRAMMING

The achievement of program modularity becomes increasingly difficult as
the linguistic requirements for representing program modules move further from the linguistic level defined by the computer system on which
the modules are to be run. In this lecture, we explore issues arising
in the construction of program modules that require the ability to create, extend, and modify structured data. We conclude that, to achieve
modularity, a computer system must define a linguistic level that provides a suitable base representation for structured data, a requirement
not satisfactorily met by conventional computer systems or by implementations of contemporary programming languages.

2.1. ADDRESS SPACE AND MODULARITY

First we note that conventional computer memories and addressing schemes impose a limitation on modular programming. When a program is run on
a contemporary computer system, all procedures and data involved in the
computation must be assigned positions within the address space provided
for the computation by the computer system. If more than a single object
-- whether procedure or data -- is assigned to some area of the address
space, the meanings of addresses must change during the computation.
This violates our principles of modular programming because some program modules will require knowledge of the internal construction of
others in order to determine which objects should occupy the shared areas of address space. Thus the finiteness of address space limits the
size of modular programs. To support modular programming a computer
system must provide an address space of size sufficient to hold all procedures and data structures required for the execution of any modular
program. A more complete presentation of this argument may be found in
[1].

The addressing limitations of finite main memories have been reduced
through the brute force expedient of using larger and larger main' memories. Yet practical main memories are still small in comparison to the
extent of data bases and program libraries we wish to use in constructing modular programs. A more sopnisticated approach to overcoming the
finiteness of main memory is to arrange a computer system to provide a
large virtual address space for each user. In effect, a process is
given a large address space without tying up a corresponding amount of

main memory. As it is currently implemented, the virtual memory idea
also has limitations, for chunks of address space are reassigned from
one physical storage device to another in relatively large units (512-
word pages, for example) and it is difficult for the programmer of a
module to map his data structures into the address space in such a way
that related items will be moved together between physical storage levels.

2.2. *REPRESENTATION OF PROGRAM MODULES*

Other implications of modularity concern features of the linguistic level at which modules are represented for combination into larger units.
We noted earlier that all identifiers occurring in a program module must
be bound within the module unless they refer to primitive constructs of
the linguistic level. Otherwise identifier clashes can occur when independently prepared modules are used together. From this premise it
follows that any information to which a program module requires access
to perform its function must be part of the module itself, or must be
passed to the module by means of formal parameters of the calling statement. Any information created or modified by the module and intended
for use outside must be passed to the caller through formal parameters.

Since the objective of modularity is that any program may be used as
a program module, it must be possible to treat any entity to which reference may be made by a program module as an actual input or output
parameter of the module. A program module that implements a certain
algorithm should be applicable to any input data to which the algorithm
applies. It is possible to design algorithms that work effectively for
a wide range of inputs as, for example, a procedure for matrix inversion
or one for constructing the parse of a sentence according to a formal
grammar. The representation of such program modules requires linguistic
primitives for building and altering data structures of extent not
known until the time of execution.

In summary, we have three requirements to be met by a linguistic level
intended as a foundation for modular programming:

1. Any data structure may occur as a component of another data structure.

2. Any data structure may be passed (by reference) to or from a program module as an actual parameter.

3. A program module may build data structures of arbitrary complexity.

The linguistic levels defined by conventionally organized computer systems have a linear address space as their fundamental notion of data
structure, and indexing as their fundamental means of data access. Such
a level is not an acceptable foundation for modular programming because
the primitive constructs do not provide for altering one data structure
without interfering with the representations of others. To enlarge
one structure may require rearrangement of other structures in address
space and cannot be done without knowledge of their scheme of representation.

There are three ways in which a satisfactory linguistic level for modular programming can be realized starting from a host level H defined by
some computer system:

1. Use a "standard" programming language L with an available translator
to level H and having an adequate class of data structures and primitive
operations.

2. Extend a programming language L' that does not offer an adequate
class of data structures, to realize a new linguistic level L that is
adequate.

3. Design and implement a new language L by constructing either
a. A translator from L to H.
b. An interpreter of L that runs at level H.

Suppose the host level H is defined by a conventional computer which
provides the user with a linear address space. Whichever of the above
means is used to realize the desired linguistic level L, the data
structures of L must be mapped into the linear address space of H in
such a way that the primitive operations of L can be implemented effectively in terms of the primitives of H. The difference between means
(1) above and means (2) or (3) is that in (1) in the language L is
standard and the mapping of L into H is uniform over all program modules expressed in L; in cases (2) and (3) the mapping of structures in
L into the linear address space of H is chosen independently by the

designer of each program module and the same choice is unlikely to be made for any pair of modules.

To be more specific, suppose the designer of a program module is using the second approach. Let the language L' be a language (*FORTRAN* or *ALGOL 60*, for example) that does not provide adequate primitives for manipulating structured data. To implement the program module, the designer must extend L' by adding a *memory*. He does this by setting aside some portion M of the linear address space of H to hold representations of data structures of L as they are created and operated upon during operation of the program module. The memory may be viewed as a pair (M, C) where M is a one-dimensional array, and C is a collection of procedures that implement the primitive data structure operations of L. If L' is *FORTRAN*, the memory array M may be allocated within a block of COMMON storage and the procedures of C may be realized as a group of subprograms. If L' is *ALGOL 60*, the memory array and the procedures of C would be declared within the outermost block of the program module.

There are serious problems with an approach in which the memory is separately implemented in independent program modules. Suppose A and B are two such modules. Then:

1. Either the base linguistic level H includes an allocation mechanism for units of address space, or arbitrarily chosen areas of address space must be set aside as the memory arrays for modules A and B.

2. A structure created by module A cannot be directly accessed from within module B, for the primitives of A are not used within B.

Partitioning the address space into separate areas for each module requires that each area be large enough to hold any structure that could be created. The idea of segmentation [1] is a way of meeting this requirement. If the host level H provides a facility for management of address space, then introducing a second layer of memory management mechanism aggravates the inefficiency of program execution.

The problem of communicating data structures between program modules expressed in different representations may be discussed in terms of Figure 2. Modules A and B are expressed in different extensions L_A and L_B of a host linguistic level H. Sets S_A and S_B represent the classes of data structure representations in L_A and L_B. The maps f_A and f_B

(which may be relations) relate representations in L_A and L_B to corresponding representations at the host level H.

If the linguistic levels L_A and L_B are different, then a data structure produced by module A cannot be directly accessed by module B. Nevertheless, modules A and B may be used together if no data structures are exchanged between them, or if we can prepare routines t and t^{-1} at the host level H which convert structures from their representation in L_A to their representations in L_B and vice versa. Of course, the need to write these routines is a violation of modularity since knowledge of how the data structures of L_A and L_B are represented at H is required, and this knowledge concerns the internal construction of modules A and B.

We have discussed Figure 2 assuming modules A and B include the definitions of L_A and L_B as internal components. The same picture holds if modules A and B are expressed in "standard" languages L_A and L_B that define primitive operations on data structures by two different extensions of a host level H. If L_A and L_B are "standard" languages, then knowledge of the mappings f_A and f_B does not involve internal knowledge of modules A and B. Thus the construction of the conversion routines t and t^{-1} depends on knowledge of the implementations of L_A and L_B rather than the workings of the modules. However, now these routines are subject to invalidation if the implementation of either L_A or L_B is changed.

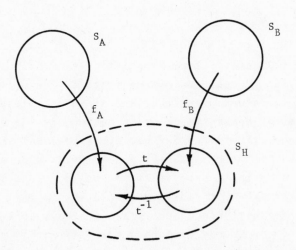

Figure 2. Exchange of data structures between program modules.

If the host level H defines a linear address space, construction of the conversion routines can prove difficult. This is because level H lacks notions that would save the programmer from the need for complete knowledge of the data structures being transformed. A data structure represented in a linear address space is referenced by an *address*, but there is no uniform rule for locating all items in the address space that are parts of the data structure. Also there is no uniform convention regarding how individual data structures may be combined into a single object.

That two program modules are represented at the same linguistic level L does not ensure that consistent representations are used for objects dealt with by the algorithms of the modules. For example, there are many ways in which a directed graph may be represented by a vector of integers. If a community of users interested in sharing program modules that manipulate directed graphs can agree on a standard representation in L for directed graphs, then programs contributed by the community may be used together without difficulty. Otherwise conversion routines are required. Nevertheless, if the representation of a directed graph is to be passed as an argument or result of computation by a module, the scheme of representation in L must be given as part of the functional specification of the module. The necessary conversion routines can be written in L from the module specification. Without adequate data structure primitives in the common language L, the conversion routine would be difficult, if not impossible, to write.

2.3.   *LINGUISTIC LEVELS FOR MODULAR PROGRAMMING*

We have argued that a satisfactory linguistic level for modular programming must provide adequate primitive features for building and transforming data structures, and that the linguistic levels defined by computer systems of conventional organization are inadequate. Next we examine the linguistic levels defined by several well-known programming languages for their suitability to modular programming, particularly in regard to their provisions for building and transforming data structures. The two most familiar languages, *FORTRAN* and *ALGOL 60*, are inadequate by default, since arrays are the only sort of data structure provided, the bounds of arrays are inflexible once storage has been allocated, and the dimensionality of arrays is fixed by the program text. The languages PL/I, *ALGOL 68*, and *LISP* are considered in the following paragraphs.

2.3.1. PL/I

In PL/I [2] the principal data types that may be used to represent and
manipulate structured data are arrays, structures, based variables and
pointers. Arrays in PL/I are subject to similar limitations as arrays
in *FORTRAN* or *ALGOL 60:* an array identifier may only name arrays of
the declared dimensionality; subscript bounds cannot be changed once
storage for an array is allocated; all elements of an array must be of
the same data type. These limitations are imposed so that a permanent
assignment of array elements to a contiguous portion of address space
is possible, and the efficient indexing access mechanism of present
day computers may be used.

In PL/I structures, components are accessed by means of a sequence of
symbolic names called *selectors;* the length of the selector sequence
is the *depth* of the component in the structure. Components of a structure may be further structures, arrays, etc. So that each generation
of a structure may be permanently assigned to a contiguous portion of
address space, each component of a structure is restricted to a size
stated in the structure declaration. Structures (all satisfying the
same declaration) may occur as elements of arrays.

Structures as in PL/I do not meet the requirements of modular programming. It is not possible during a computation to make an arbitrary
structure a component of another structure -- the entire form of a
structure must be specified before any of its components may be given
a value. Furthermore, since the depth of a structure is implicit in
the program text, there is no way of representing data structures of
arbitrary extent as PL/I structures.

Use of PL/I pointer variables, the *addr* primitive, and variables, arrays and structures declared *based* permits the construction of arbitrarily complex address-linked storage structures. The only correct
interpretation of PL/I pointer values is as locations within a linear
address space. Pointer values may occur as elements of arrays and as
components of structures as well as values of simple variables declared
as pointer variables. A pointer value is created either by applying
the primitive function *addr* to a name, or by explicitly allocating

storage for a variable declared to be *based*, the pointer value returned being the origin of the allocated region of address space.

Although PL/I pointers provide a very general facility for building representations of data structures, the needs of modular programming are not met. A pointer value cannot be regarded as a reference to a data structure because PL/I provides no cenvention for identifying the set of elements belonging to the structure referenced by a pointer value. There is no built-in concept of one linked structure being a component of another. There is no guarantee that an element pointed to has the data type intended by the programmer. Further, deletion of elements must be done by explicit *free* statements; an element disconnected from a linked structure through reassignment of pointer values remains in existence until its storage is explicitly released.

Each programmer is forced to adopt his own conventions regarding extent of data structures, a notion of component, and when storage may be reclaimed. Hence the use of PL/I linked structures for communication between independent program modules offers no advantage over a bare machine having a linear address space.

Unsuitability of the data structure facilities is not the only problem PL/I presents for modular programming. Since PL/I refers to "external" procedures and data sets in the same manner as *FORTRAN*, and since procedures may have nonlocal identifiers, name clashes are possible whether one choses the PL/I program or the PL/I procedure as the form of program module. In addition, the introduction of new language features such as tasking has not considered the requirements of modularity.

2.3.2. *ALGOL 68*

In an *ALGOL 68* program [3,4] , each occurrence of an identifier has an associated *mode* that determines the set of values permitted for the named variable. The modes that provide representations for data structures are *multiple values* and *structures*. Multiple values are similar to PL/I arrays and, in themselves, do not provide an adequate foundation for modular programming.

A structure mode declaration in *ALGOL 68* specifies that any value of the mode being declared is an object having a fixed number of component objects identified by *field selectors*, each component being an object of specified mode. Through use of several mode declarations one may define a class of objects having graphs that are trees. Each node of such a tree has an associated mode and is the origin for a fixed number of arcs, each bearing a field selector as specified in the mode declaration.

Since recursive mode declarations are permitted, the objects of a given mode may be of unbounded depth, as for example, the class of binary trees. Yet no *ALGOL 68* structure mode permits values that range over all *ALGOL 68* data structures. Thus there is no means for substituting an arbitrary structure for some component of an existing structure. Specifically, it is not possible to write an *ALGOL 68* procedure that obtains a data structure from one program module and gives it to another module without knowing enough about the data structure to specify its mode. Also, a program module expressed in *ALGOL 68* cannot build an arbitrary *ALGOL 68* data structure because a finite set of mode declarations is insufficient to describe the complete class of *ALGOL 68* objects.

Since *ALGOL 68* includes suitable conventions for delineating the extent of data structures, and has satisfactory provisions for building and accessing complex structures, the data structure primitives of *ALGOL 68* are superior to those of PL/I as a foundation for modular programming. However, the requirement that the mode of every variable be explicit is an unfortunate limitation.

Other limitations of *ALGOL 68* for modular programming stem from the design of the language primarily as a means for one programmer to write a complete program for a computation of interest to himself. A prime example is the concept of coersions by which conversion of values from one data type to another is implicit in many circumstances. A consequence of coersion is that a scan of an entire *ALGOL 68* program may be necessary to fix the meaning of statements in a deeply nested procedure.

2.3.3. *LISP*

In Lisp [5,6] data structures are represented as *lists*. A region of a linear address space (the *memory*) is reserved for *cells* from which lists are built to represent data structures. Each cell has two fields which may contain addresses (called *pointers*) of other cells in the memory.

A list is specified by the address of a cell and consists of all cells that can be reached by tracing pointers from the starting cell. Thus a list is essentially a rooted, directed graph in which each node is the origin of at most two arcs that define the left and right sublists for the corresponding cell. In most applications, lists containing directed cycles do not occur, and lists have the form of a binary tree with shared subtrees.

Lisp includes primitive operations for building lists, for obtaining the left or right component sublist of any list, for testing whether two lists are equal or are the same list, and for making one list the new left or right sublist of an existing list.

The leaf cells of lists are called *atoms* and have associated named values called *properties*. A property of an atom may be an elementary object such as a character string, an integer or a real number, or may be an arbitrary list. Lisp includes basic functions for performing operations on property values. It is easy to devise ways in which lists may be used to represent any of the commonly used data structures in programming practice.

Since any list may occur as an actual parameter of a Lisp function application, and Lisp has primitives for building, disecting and rearranging specified lists without disturbing the meaning of other lists sharing the memory, Lisp meets our fundamental requirements for modular programming with respect to data structures. The principal weakness of Lisp for modular programming arises from its inability to exploit indexing as an efficient access mechanism for arrays. For applications where an array is a natural representation for a data structure, many representations as lists have been designed to yield efficient operation for a variety of different expected patterns of access. Because these representations are generally in conflict, conversion of data structures is often required to combine independently written Lisp functions, where conversion would not be required if the modules were expressed in a language offering arrays as a basic data type.

Lisp also shares with the other languages we have discussed the failing of having a global level of nomenclature. Programmer defined functions and constants are given names that are global in a Lisp program. There is no provision for ensuring freedom from name conflicts when independently written Lisp programs are combined.

2.3.4. DISCUSSION

On one hand, Lisp is superior to PL/I and *ALGOL 68* as a foundation for modular programming because PL/I and *ALGOL 68* fail to provide an adequate foundation for representing and manipulating data structures. The limitations of PL/I and *ALGOL 68* can be traced to the desire of the designers of these languages to make efficient implementations possible for conventional computers that implement a linear address space. Thus it was considered essential that arrays be included as a fundamental data type and that arrays be implemented using the indexing hardware of contemporary machines. On the other hand, Lisp has achieved a more satisfactory concept of data structure by giving up the array as a fundamental notion and ignoring the use of indexing. By making these concessions, the address space may be divided uniformly into list cells so that the allocation and deallocation of cells become trivial operations. In this way a powerful language for expressing computations on symbolic data has been realized.

Is there a way to combine the best aspects of these three languages? In the final section of these notes we explore the definition of a base linguistic level for modular programming using a concept of data structure that yields natural representations for a wide variety of data structures commonly applied in programming practice, including lists, arrays, and structures. Although this concept may prove impractical to implement for general use on computers of conventional organization, it should prove valuable as a standard of achievement, and as a guide for the design of computer systems intended to advance the prospects for modular programming.

2.4. REFERENCES

1. J. B. Dennis, Segmentation and the design of multiprogrammed computer systems. *J. of the ACM, Vol.* 12, *No.* 4 (October 1965), pp 589-602.

2. S. V. Pollack and T. D. Sterling, *A Guide to PL/I*. Holt, Rinehart and Winston, Inc., 1969.

3. A. van Wijngaarden, Ed., Report on the algorithmic language *ALGOL 68*. *Numerische Mathematik, Vol.* 14, *No.*79 (1969), pp 79-218.

4. J. E. L. Peck, *An ALGOL 68 Companion*. Department of Computer Science, University of British Columbia, Vancouver, B.D., Canada, October 1971 (preliminary edition).

5. M. I. T. Computation Center, *LISP 1.5 Programmer's Manual*. Computation Center and Research Laboratory of Electronics, Massachusetts Institute of Technology, Cambridge, Mass., August 1962.

6. E. C. Berkeley and D. G. Bobrow, Eds., *The Programming Language LISP: Its Operation and Applications*. Information International, Inc., Cambridge, Mass. 1964.

3.   *MODULARITY IN MULTICS*

We have seen that most contemporary computer systems and programming
languages do not support a very general form of modular programming. Yet
one advanced computer system comes significantly closer to defining a
linguistic level suitable for modular programming. A major objective
of the development of Multics at Project MAC [1] has been to create an
environment within which programs developed independently and expressed in different source languages may be combined with minimum difficulty. In this lecture we shall study how well this objective has been
achieved.

First, we present a model for those aspects of Multics that must be
understood to discuss modularity from the viewpoint of the Multics user.
Then we discuss the achievements and limitations of Multics for modular
programming in terms of the model. The model consists of a representation for the states of Multics processes as an augmented class of objects, and an informal discussion of certain state transitions that
occur during execution of procedures by Multics processes. We do not
attempt to model the mechanisms of Multics for protection, access, control, and interprocess communication.

3.1.   *THE MODEL*

3.1.1.   *THE FILE SYSTEM*

The file system of Multics [2] retains the programs and data of all
Multics users in the form of a hierarchical structure of *directories*
and *segments*. We represent a directory by an object as in Figure 3. A
directory has arbitrarily many components, each of which may be a
directory entry, a *segment entry*, or a *link* - an example of each type
is shown. The selectors for the entries and links of a directory are
called *entry names*, and are character strings. Each entry name in a
directory must be unique. A directory or segment entry has an 'attr'-
component that gives attributes such as access rights, date of last
change, etc. The second component is an object that represents either
another directory, or a segment. A link is a *pathname* composed of a
sequence of entry names. The Multics *file system* is an object that represents a particular directory called the *root directory*. Each item
(directory or segment) in the file system is specified by the unique

sequence of entry names by which the item may be reached from the root of the directory tree. The sequence of entry names is a *pathname* of the directory or segment.

A *segment* in Multics is a linear address space of 2^{18} addresses which may hold either data or one or more procedures. A segment is represented by an object having elementary components selected by the integers 0, 1, ...

In the root directory of the file system, the entry names are *user names* and the entries are *user directories*. A user is the *owner* of all directories and segments that are entries in his user directory, and is the owner of directories and segments that are entries in owned directories.

We will simplify the representation of the file system state by omitting attribute components and omitting the branches labelled 'directory' or 'segment'. This simplified form is illustrated in Figure 4. Entry names of links are distinguished by an asterisk. The link shown is to the item having pathname 'b.b.a'.

3.1.2. PROCESSES AND ADDRESS SPACES

When a Multics user begins a console session, a *process* is created for him. By typing commands at the console, the user causes the process to execute procedures. The execution of commands results in changes in the file system state. Normally a user process ceases to exist when his console session is terminated, and the changes to the file system are the only record retained in Multics of the user's activity.

For our purposes a state of Multics may be represented as an object having a component for the file system, and one component for each process in existence. In Figure 5 we have identified each process by a distinct user name.

The state of process is an object having components as follows (Figure 6):

1. 'memory'   process address space
2. 'stack'   stack segment and pointer

153

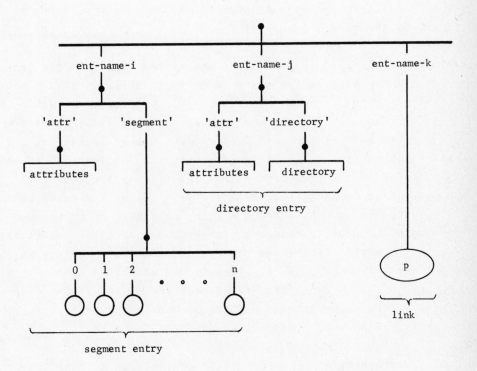

Figure 3. Model for the Multics file system.

3. 'kst'   known segment table
4. 'link'   linkage segment and pointer
5. 'w.dir'   working directory

In fact, components of the process state are implemented as segments in the Multics file system which are accessible to system procedures. We choose to model them as separate objects for ease in discussing their function from the user's viewpoint.

The 'memory'-component of a process state is the address space implemented by the hardware and software of Multics for each Multics process. The object that models the address space of a process is shown in Figure 7. It is a two-level tree. The selectors at the first level are integers called *segment numbers*. Each segment number identifies a segment which may contain up to 2^{18} words. Since the segments of an address space are not distinct from segments of the file system, the nodes selected by segment numbers are, in fact, identical with segment nodes of the file system state. The address spaces of Multics processes are implemented by a complex arrangement of hardware-accessed tables in core memory, a small associative memory, and auxiliary storage devices (drum and disc) to hold pages of segments not allocated space in the core memory [3, 4]. A two-component address consisting of a segment number and a word number, that specifies a word in the address space of a process, is called a *generalized address*.

The 'stack'-component of a process state consists of a segment (for our purposes not part of the file system) and a pointer variable. Variables assigned by the programmer to "automatic" storage are accessed by addresses relative to the stack pointer. On procedure entry the pointer is advanced to the end of the stack area used by the calling procedure; on procedure exit the stack pointer is returned to its value before entry. In this way, all Multics procedures that use the standard call and return conventions may be used recursively.

3.1.3.   *MAKING A SEGMENT KNOWN TO A PROCESS*

The assignment of a segment from the Multics file system to the address space of a process is called *making the segment known to the process*. This action occurs when the process, in executing a procedure, encounters

155

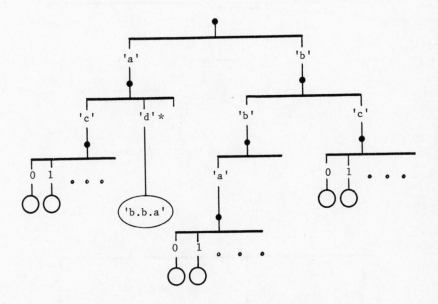

Figure 4. Simplified model for the file system.

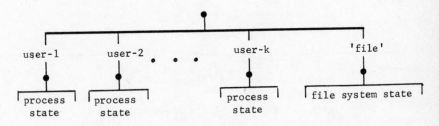

Figure 5. Model for a state of Multics.

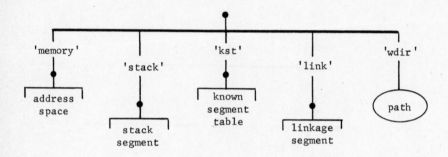

Figure 6. Model of a Multics process.

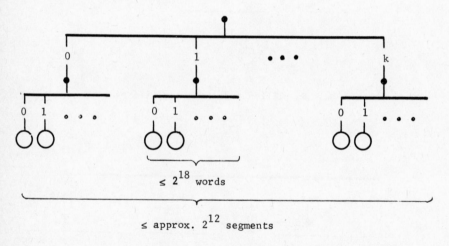

Figure 7. Model for the address space of a process.

a symbolic reference to a segment. The symbolic name used in the code of the procedure segment is called a *reference name*. The path name of the segment in the file system to which a reference name refers is found by a system procedure directed by a set of *search rules* in a manner to be discussed later. A segment known to a process has an associated segment number; segment numbers are assigned to segments sequentially as they become known to the process.

The associations between segment numbers, reference names and path names for all segments known to a process are held in a data structure called the *known segment table* which is the 'kst'-component of the process state. The known segment table is modelled as an object in Figure 8. For example, the figure shows that segment number i of this process has the path name 'x.y.a' and the reference names 'a' and 'b' have been used to refer to the segment during operation of the process. The 'n'-component of the known segment table is the highest integer in use as the segment number of a segment known to the process. It is given the initial value 0 when the process is created, and is incremented by 1 for each segment made known to the process.

An illustration of the state transition that occurs when a segment is made known to a process is shown in Figure 9. The value i of the 'n'-component of the known segment table is incremented and used as the selector for a new entry in the known segment table. The new entry contains the reference name 'a' used by the procedure in execution and the path name 'x.y.a' obtained by system routines directed by the search rules. Segment i+1 of the address space of the process is identified with the segment having pathname 'x.y.a' in the file system.

3.1.4. DYNAMIC LINKING

For a segment S to be made known to a process, reference to S by means of a reference name must occur from within some procedure segment P. Once segment S is known to the process, references to it should use the hardware-implemented addressing mechanism provided for generalized addresses. The Multics state transition that realizes this objective is called *linking*. Linking a site of reference in segment P to segment S cannot involve any change in the content of segment P, because procedure segments in Multics are shared among processes. The scheme used is to implement references to other segments from segment P by indirect ad-

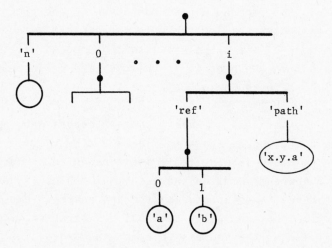

Figure 8. Model for the known segment table.

159

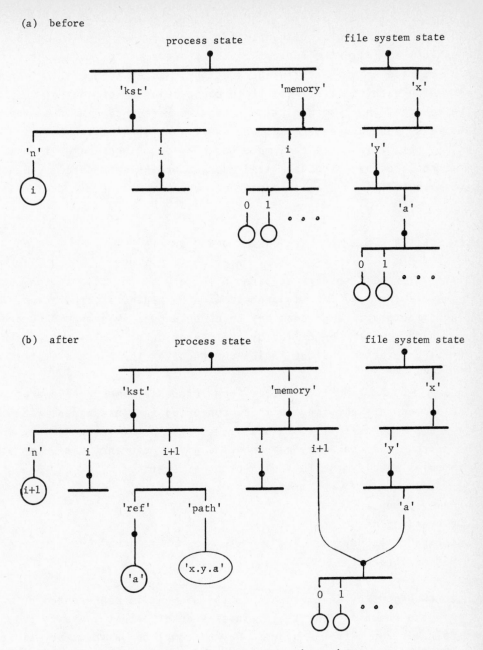

Figure 9. Making segment 'a' with pathname 'x.y.a' known to a process.

dressing through items called *links* that make up a *linkage section* for segment P. The linkage sections for all procedure segments known to a process form the 'link' component of the process state. When a procedure segment is made known, its linkage section is added to the 'link'-component, with each of its links set to cause transfer of control to a system routine. The system routine reads the reference name from the procedure segment and determines whether the referenced segment is known. If not, this segment is made known as described above. Then the link is replaced by the generalized address of the referenced segment. The details of this mechanism have been published [4].

3.1.5. SEARCH RULES AND THE WORKING DIRECTORY

A Multics user must specify an owned directory of the file system as the *working directory* for his process when he begins a computation. The working directory of a process may be changed by a system command procedure which may also be called by the user's program. The pathname of the working directory is the 'wdir'-component of the process state.

The *search rules* of Multics specify how reference names encountered during procedure execution are to be converted into pathnames. The searc rules are stated as a list of data structures in the sequence they are to be searched for an entry named by the given reference name. The usual search rules specify the following order of search:

1. known segments
2. referencing directory
3. working directory
4. system libraries

The search begins by testing whether the segment is represented by an entry in the known segment table. This is done so that links to segments already known to the process may be completed without any directory searching, which consumes significant processing time. If the reference is not to a segment already known, a search is made of the "referencing directory" -- the directory from which access to the procedure currently in execution was obtained. This search rule supposes that procedures that form a subsystem are grouped together in directories, and gives preference to such a related procedure over a procedure of the same name in the user's working directory.

A program expressed in *FORTRAN* or PL/I for execution by Multics normally references its user-owned procedure and data segments in the working directory, and accesses library procedures in the system libraries directory.

3.2. *ACCOMPLISHMENTS*

Multics has realized a number of significant advances in computer system design, and has made them available to a large community of users for the first time. These unique characteristics of Multics include some features of major importance for modular programming.

1. A large virtual address space (approximately 2^{30} elements) is provided for each user.

2. All user information is accessed through his virtual address space. No separate access mechanism is provided for particular sorts of data such as files.

3. Any procedure activation can acquire an amount of working space limited only by the number of free segments in the user's address space.

4. Any procedure may be shared by many processes without the need of making copies.

5. Every procedure written in standard Multics user languages (*FORTRAN*, PL/I and others) may be activated multiply through recursion or concurrency.

6. A common target representation is used by the compilers of two major source languages -- PL/I and *FORTRAN*.

These achievements are major contributions toward simplifying the design and implementation of large software systems. They were made possible by building the Multics software on a machine expressly organized for the realization of a large virtual memory and shared access to data and procedure segments [5].

3.3. UNRESOLVED ISSUES

The ease of modular programming in Multics is limited by certain design problems that remain unresolved issues. One problem Multics shares with all computer systems in which data structures must be mapped into a linear address space. As observed earlier in these notes, each author of a program module must adopt his own private conventions for introducing the concepts of "the extent of a data structure" and "component of a data structure" for no conventions are established by the Multics virtual machine nor by the standard user languages of Multics. This problem can be solved only through the adoption of a more suitable model for structured data as the basis for computer system design. A model having the essential attributes is discussed in the final section of these notes.

3.3.1. TREATMENT OF REFERENCE NAMES

Another problem for modular programming in Multics concerns the treatment of reference names. Basically, reference names are identifiers that occur free in the text of Multics procedures. Since reference names occur not only as identifiers of fixed elements of the Multics linguistic level, absence of name conflicts cannot be ensured when a user attempts to combine independently written procedures. The following discussion of the issue is based in part on a study by Clingen [5].

The set of search rules given earlier for determining the pathname of a segment specified by a reference name is an attempt to avoid the undesired consequences of name conflicts. To see how the set of search rules evolved to this form, we first consider the problems of modular programming with the search rules

1. working directory
2. system libraries

This combination of search rules is appropriate where a user has defined a collection of procedure and data segments and entered them in an owned directory. By making this directory the working directory of his process, all reference names designating members of the user's collection of segments will be associated with the correct segment, and so will references to library procedures so long as their reference names are not duplicated in the working directory.

The possibility of clashes between reference names chosen by the user and reference names of library procedures is not the only difficulty with this choice of search rules. If two programming languages are implemented independently for use in Multics, the sets of reference names used to access the run-time procedure libraries for the two implementations may include duplicate names with conflicting meanings. These names should identify entries in separate directories, but this is not provided for by the search rules. One could let the user, specify one of several library directories in the second search rule, but this would not provide for programs that combined procedures expressed in the two source languages. Alternatively one could use a set of search rules such as

1.   Working directory
2.   Run time library A
3.   Run time library B

but duplicated names would be misinterpreted if they were intended to reference segments in run time library B.

Another difficulty is that a mistake in use of a reference name may lead to successful search and linking to a strange procedure in a library directory, whereas one would prefer to have such mistakes produce an error response by the system.

In Multics, the natural form for a program module is a collection of procedure and data segments entered in a common private directory of the file system. If a user wishes to use two such modules together, some arrangement must be made so that reference names occurring in either module will be interpreted correctly. One scheme is to arrange that the working directory is always the directory containing the procedure in execution. This requires that the working directory be changed whenever control passes from procedures in one module to a procedure in the other module. Since changing the working directory of a process is an expensive task, this solution is not attractive, especially if control transfers between modules occur frequently. Also, this arrangement requires different call and return conventions (the inclusion of a command to change the working directory) for calls on procedures of other modules. This requirement conflicts with the concept that one should be able to apply a program module simply by using its name in a *call* statement.

The difficulty of making the working directory concept work satisfactorily led to addition of the "referencing directory" search rule:

1. referencing directory
2. working directory
3. system libraries .

The referencing directory rule directs search for a reference name to the directory in which the procedure segment in execution was found. This is accomplished by using the segment number of the procedure in execution to locate its entry in the known segment table. The 'path'-component of the entry provides unambiguous identification of its directory. With this rule in effect, calling any procedure of a program module automatically makes the directory of that module the first directory to be searched for all reference names encountered during execution of procedures that are part of the module.

The "known segments" search rule was added to the set of search rules to reduce the time spent performing searches in directories of the file system, thereby improving system efficiency. This search is performed in such a way that it has the same effect as the referencing directory search rule. An entry in the known segment table is located that has the given reference name in its 'ref'-component. Then the 'path'-component of the entry is tested to verify that the entry is for a segment found in the same directory as the segment in execution. If the test fails, the entry is rejected and search for other entries having the given reference name is continued.

Thus the search rules of Multics implement the correct context for reference names occurring in procedures of program modules. Yet several difficulties remain:

1. Mistakes in use of reference names may lead to unsuspected linkage to library or system procedures.

2. Implementers of programming language subsystems must avoid name conflicts among their libraries.

3. No suitable means is provided for representing references among the
data segments of a large data base. This is a problem because no mechanism has been implemented for creating links from uses of reference
names in data segments.

In the final section of these notes, we present a conceptual basis for
a computer system in which these issues of modular programming are resolved by providing the appropriate context for each use of a name.

3.4. REFERENCES

1. F. J. Corbato, C. T. Clingen, and J.H. Saltzer, MULTICS -- the first
    seven years. *AFIPS Conference Proceedings, Vol.* 40, *SJCC,* 1972,
    pp 571-583.

2. R. C. Daley and P. G. Neuman, A general-purpose file system for
    secondary storage. *AFIPS Conference Proceedings, Vol.* 27, *Part* 1,
    FJCC, 1965, pp 213-229.

3. A Bensoussan, C. T. Clingen, and R. C. Daley, The Multics virtual
    memory. *Proceedings of the Second Symposium on Operating Systems
    Principles.* ACM, October 1969, pp 30-42.

4. R. C. Daley and J. B. Dennis, Virtual memory, processes, and sharing
    in MULTICS. *Comm. of the ACM, Vol.* 11, *No.* 5 (May 1968), pp 306-312.

5. E. L. Glaser, J. F. Couleur and G. A. Oliver, System design of a
    computer for time sharing applications. *AFIPS Conference Proceedings,
    Vol.* 27, *FJCC,* 1965, pp 197-202.

6. C. T. Clingen, unpublished memorandum prepared for the NATO
    Conference on Software Engineering Techniques, Rome, 1969.

4. A BASE LINGUISTIC LEVEL FOR MODULAR PROGRAMMING

In this lecture, we present informally the semantic concepts of a linguistic level (a *common base language*) that could serve as a common representation for program modules expressed in a variety of source programming languages. The objective is to describe a linguistic level such that the issues of modular programming raised in the preceding presentations have a satisfactory resolution. It is hoped that this material will serve as a guide or standard of capability for computer system designers so future computer systems will better serve as foundations for modular programming.

Our work toward the specification of a common base language [1] uses methods closely related to the formal methods developed at the IBM Vienna Laboratory [2, 3] and which derive from the ideas of McCarthy [4, 5] and Landin [6, 7].

4.1. OBJECTS

For the formal semantics of programming languages a general model is required for the data on which programs act. We regard data as consisting of *elementary objects*, and *compound objects* formed by combining elementary objects into data structures.

Elementary objects are data items whose structure in terms of simpler objects is not relevant to the description of algorithms. For the present discussion, the class E of elementary objects is

$$E = Z \cup R \cup W$$

where

```
Z  = the class of integers
R  = a set of representations for real numbers
W  = the set of all strings on some alphabet
```

Data structures are often represented by directed graphs in which elementary objects are associated with nodes, and each arc is labelled by a member of a set S of selectors. In the class of objects used by the Vienna group, the graphs are restricted to be trees, and elementary

objects are associated only with leaf nodes. We prefer a less restricted
class so an object may have distinct component objects that share some
third object as a common component. The reader will see that this possibility of sharing is essential to the formulation of the base language
and interpreter presented here. Our class of objects is defined as
follows:

Let E be a class of *elementary objects*, and let S be a class of *selectors*.
An *object* is a directed acyclic graph having a single root node from
which all other nodes may be reached over directed paths. Each arc is
labelled with one selector in S, and an elementary object in E may be
associated with each leaf node.

We use integers and strings as selectors:

$$S = Z \cup W$$

Figure 10 gives an example of an object. Leaf nodes having associated
elementary objects are represented by circles with the element of E
written inside; integers are represented by numerals, strings are enclosed in single quotes, and reals have decimal points. Other nodes
are represented by solid dots, with a horizontal bar if there is more
than one emanating arc.

The node of an object reached by traversing an arc emanating from its
root node is itself the root node of an object called a *component* of
the original object. The component object consists of all nodes and arcs
that can be reached by directed paths from its root node.

4.2. *STRUCTURE OF A BASE LANGUAGE INTERPRETER*

Figure 11 shows how source languages would be defined in terms of a
common base language. A single class of abstract programs constitutes
the base language. Concrete programs in source languages (L1 and L2 in
the figure) are defined by translators into the base language. The structure of abstract programs cannot reflect the peculiarities of any particular source language, but must provide a set of fundamental linguistic
constructs in terms of which the features of these source languages may
be realized. The translators themselves should be specified in terms
of the base language, probably by means of a specialized source language.

168

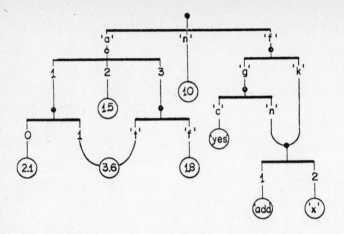

Figure 10. An example of an object.

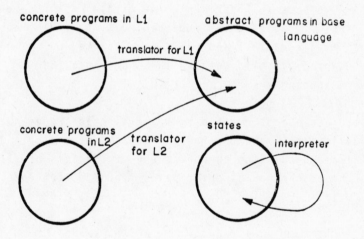

Figure 11. Language definition in terms
of a common base language.

The semantics of abstract programs of the base language are specified by an interpreter which is a nondeterministic state-transition system, as in the work of the Vienna group. Formally, abstract programs in the base language, and states of the interpreter are elements of the class of objects defined above.

The structure of states of the interpreter for the base language is shown in Figure 12. Since we regard the interpreter for the base language as a complete specification for the functional operation of a computer system, a state of the interpeter represents the totality of programs, data, and control information present in the computer system. In Figure 12 the *universe* is an object that represents all information present in the computer system when the system is idle -- that is, when no computation is in progress. The universe has *data structures* and *procedure structures* as constituent objects. Any object is a legitimate data structure; for example, a data structure may have components that are procedure structures. A procedure structure is an object that represents a procedure expressed in the base language. It has components which are *instructions* of the base language, data structures, or other procedure structures. So that multiple activations of procedures may be accommodated, a procedure structure remains unaltered during its interpretation.

The *local structure* of an interpreter state contains a local structure for each current activation of each base language procedure. Each local structure has as components the local structures of all procedure activations initiated within it. Thus the hierarchy of local structures represents the dynamic relationship of procedure activations. One may think of the root local structure as the nucleus of an operating system that initiates independent, concurrent computations on behalf of system users as they request activation of procedures from the system files (the universe).

The local structure of a procedure activation has a component object for each variable of the base language procedure. The selector of each component is its identifier in the instructions of the procedure. These objects may be elementary or compound objects and may be common with objects within the universe or within local structures of other procedure activations.

The *control* component of an interpreter state is an unordered set of *sites of activity*. A typical site of activity is represented in Figure 4 by an asterisk at an instruction of procedure P and an arrow to the local structure L for some activation of P. This is analogous to the "instruction pointer/environment pointer" combination that represents a site of activity in Johnston's contour model [8]. Since several activations of a procedure may exist concurrently, there may be two or more sites of activity involving the same instruction of some procedure, but designating different local structures. Also, within one activation of a procedure, several instructions may be active concurrently; thus asterisks on different instructions of a procedure may have arrows to the same local structure.

Each state transition of the interpreter executes one instruction for some procedure activation, at a site of activity selected arbitrarily from the control of the current state. Thus the interpreter is a nondeterministic transition system. In the state resulting from a transition, the chosen site of activity is replaced according to the sequencing rules of the base language.

4.3. STATE TRANSITIONS OF THE INTERPRETER

Next we show how typical instructions of a rudimentary base language would be implemented by state transitions of an interpreter. This will put the concepts expressed above into more concrete form. For illustration, we will use a representation for procedures that employs conventional instruction sequencing. The instructions of a procedure are objects selected by successive integers, with 0 being the selector of the initial instruction.

The effect of representative instructions on the interpreter state is shown in Figures 13 through 19 in the form of before/after pictures of relevant state components. In these figures, P marks the root of the procedure structure containing an instruction under consideration as its i-component, and L(P) is the root of the local structure for the relevant activation of P.

The *add* instruction is typical of instructions that apply binary operations to elementary objects. The instruction

add 'u', 'v', 'w'

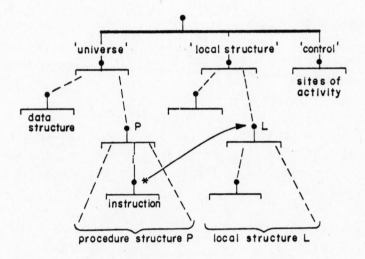

Figure 12. Structure of objects representing states
of the base language interpreter.

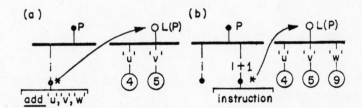

Figure 13. Interpretation of an instruction specifying a binary operation.

is an object having as components the four elementary objects 'add', 'u', 'v', and 'w'. These are interpreted as an operation code and three "address fields" used as selectors for operands and result in the local structure L(P). The state transition is shown in Figure 13. Note that the site of activity advances sequentially to the i+1-component of P.

Let us say that a procedure activation has *direct access* to a data structure if the data structure is the s-component of the local structure for some selector s. The instruction

$$select\ 'p',\ 'n',\ 'q'$$

is used to gain direct access to the 'n'-component of a data structure to which direct access exists. This instruction makes the object that is the 'p'. 'n'-component of L(P) also the 'q'-component of L(P), as shown by Figure 14.

Literal values are retrieved from the procedure structure by *const* instructions such as

$$const\ 1.5,\ 'x'$$

which makes the elemantary object 1.5 the 'x'-component of L(P). *Select* and *const* instructions may be used to build arbitraty data structures as illustrated in Figure 15. Note that execution of *select* 'p', 'n', 'x' implies creation of an 'n'-component of the object selected by 'p' if none already exists.

Figure 16 shows how the instruction

$$link\ 'p',\ 'n',\ 'q'$$

establishes an arc between two objects (the 'p'- and 'q'-components of L(P)) to which direct access exists. Execution of this instruction makes the 'q'-component of L(P) also the 'p'. 'n'-component of L(P). The *link* instruction is the means for establishing sharing -- making one object a common component of two distinct objects.

The instruction

$$delete\ 'p',\ 'n'$$

173

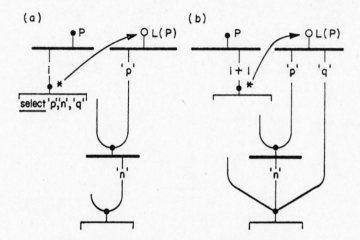

Figure 14. Interpretation of a __select__ instruction.

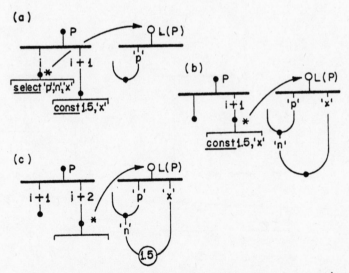

Figure 15. Structure building using __select__ and __const__ instructions.

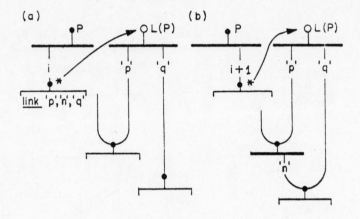

Figure 16. Insertion of an arc by a link instruction.

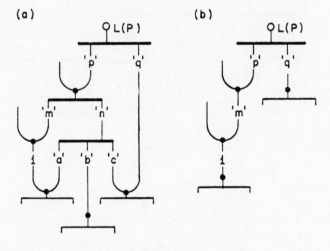

Figure 17. The effect of executing a delete instruction.

erases the arc labelled 'n' emanating from the root of the 'p'-component
of L(P). Any nodes and arcs that are unrooted after the erasure cease
to be part of the interpreterstate, as shown in Figure 17.

Although we have not mentioned them in this brief summary, the base
language will include appropriate instructions for implementing conditional and iteration statements, and for testing the presence and type
of a component of an object.

Activation of a new procedure is accomplished by the instruction

$$apply \text{ 'f', 'a'}$$

where the 'f'-component of L(P) is the procedure structure F of the
procedure to be activated, and the 'a'-component of L(P) is an object
(an *argument structure*) that contains as components all data required
by the procedure (e.g., actual parameter values) to perform its function..Execution of the *apply* instruction causes the state transition
illustrated in Figure 18: A root node L(F) is created for the local
structure of the new activation; the argument structure is made the
A-component of L(F); a new site of activity is denoted by an asterisk
on the O-component of F and an arrow to L(F); and the original site of
activity is advanced to the i+1-instruction of P and made dormant as
indicated by the parantheses.

A procedure activation is terminated by the instruction

$$return$$

which causes the state transition displayed in Figure 19. The root node
L(F) is erased, deleting all parts of the local structure of F that
are not linked to the argument structure; the site of activity at the
return instruction disppears; and the dormant site of activity in the
activating procedure is activated. Note that the entire effect of executing procedure F is conveyed to the activation of P by way of the
argument structure.

176

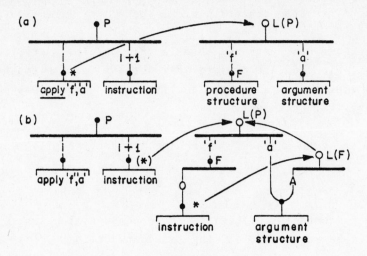

Figure 18.   Initiation of a procedure activation
by an apply instruction.

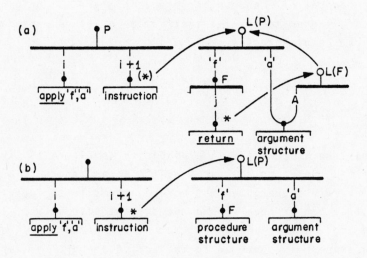

Figure 19.   Termination of a procedure activation
by a return instruction.

4.4. REPRESENTATION OF MODULAR PROGRAMS

With the foregoing introduction to base language concepts we may study
how well the base language could serve the needs of modular programming.
First we consider the adequacy of the base language for representing
and transforming data structures.

The data types of many practical programming languages have natural representations as objects that are strictly trees (have no shared substructures). These include vectors, arrays, directories, symbol tables,
and hierarchical data bases (files). Some data management systems employ
representations that provide for sharing of substructures. Also, most
data structures occurring in Lisp programs have the form of binary trees
with shared subtrees. These structures are directly modelled as objects
having shared component objects.

Some important languages, including PL/I, *ALGOL 68*, and Lisp, permit the
programmer to build data structures containing directed cycles. Such
structures do not have direct representations as objects of the base
language. It is not yet clear to what extent use of cycles is an essential part of modelling real world semantic constructs in contrast to
use of cycles as an implementation technique through which, for example,
objects may be represented and efficiently manipulated as lists.

The primitive constructs of the base language provide a general facility
for building and manipulating objects. Any object may be constructed by
a base language procedure through repeated use of *select* and *const* instructions. Through use of *link* instructions, objects may be made shared
components of several objects, and argument structures may be assembled
from any finite set of arbitrary objects. In contrast to linguistic levels (such as defined by PL/I) closely tired to the concept of linear
address space, passing an object to a base language procedure gives the
procedure the ability to transform the object in any way without the
possibility of affecting objects not passed to the procedure as part of
the argument structure.

In the paragraphs below we show how the use of objects as the fundamental
notion of data structure yields natural solutions to a number of issues
of language implementation and modular programming.

Recursion: Recursion occurs when a procedure makes application of itself in order to perform its function. In the base language interpreter outlined above, there is no way, without introducing cycles, to make a procedure structure a component of itself so it may be applied recursively. However, as shown in Figure 20, the procedure P that makes the initial application of a recursive procedure F may include the procedure structure of F as a component of the argument structure for its call of F. In this way F may make F a component of its local structure and creat recursive activations.

Block structure: Implementation of free variables in procedures require the ability to access variables by means of nonlocal references, and is essential for many programming languages derived from *ALGOL 60*. Although nonlocal references are not permitted in the base language, we may include as part of the argument structure for a procedure application an object having as a component each object to which execution of the procedure may require access because of nonlocal references in the source language program (see Figure 21). In this way, block-structured programs can be translated into base language procedure structures and interpreted correctly. Further details are given in [1].

Procedure variables: Some advanced languages permit assignment of procedure values to variables. In a block-structured language, correct implementation of procedure-valued variables requires use of the notion of the closure of a procedure. In the base language a closure may be represented by an object having two components as shown in Figure 22. The T-component is the text of the procedure and the E-component is an objec that contains as components values of the variables that have free occurrences in the procedure text. A closure serves as the value of a procedure variable.

Context: In the base language the correct context for interpretation of names is provided by objects. Each identifier encountered during execution of a procedure is interpreted as the selector of a component of some specific object. The object is the local structure for the procedur activation or some part of the procedure structure itself, if the identifier was chosen by the author of the procedure. Otherwise the object is part of the argument structure. In this way all usual sources of name conflicts are avoided, and mistakes in use of names lead to error report rather than unsuspected bindings.

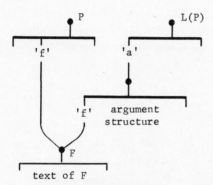

Figure 20.   Implementation of a recursive
             procedure in the base language.

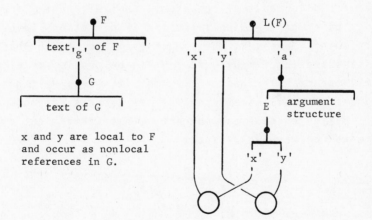

x and y are local to F
and occur as nonlocal
references in G.

Figure 21.   Principle used to translate block-
             structued programs.

Run-time libraries: Access to library procedures of the implementation of a particular programming language is readily handled in the base language. Each procedure structure resulting from translation of a program in source language A has as its 'lib'-component an object that represents the directory of run-time procedures for language A, as illustrated in Figure 23. This directory is a shared component of all procedure structures produced by translation of programs in language A. Procedures expressed in a different source language B become procedure structures sharing a separate directory of run-time procedures.

4.5. USE OF THE MODEL

The base language is founded on objects as the underlying notion of memory instead of the linear address space. Hence, it may turn out that radically new concepts of computer architecture [9] are required to bring the promised advantages into general practice. Nevertheless, the base language concepts presented here should be valuable to computer system designers interested in producing systems and languages that better serve the needs of modular programming. These ideas may be applied in several ways: They may serve as a guide for those proposing and evaluating advanced concepts of computer organization, and they may help the evolution of programming languages in directions favorable to modular programming. Moreover, the linguistic level of the base language can serve as a standard of achievement -- to be equaled or exceeded by the designer of practical computer systems. It should help designers better understand the true limitations of their systems for modular programming and where design changes can correct defects that might otherwise plague users for many years after.

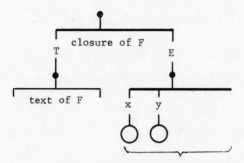

values for free variables of F

Figure 22. Base language representation for the
closure of a procedure.

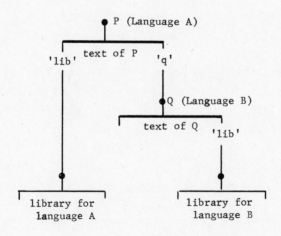

Figure 23. Providing separate libraries
for two languages.

5. REFERENCES

1. J. B. Dennis, On the design and implementation of a common base language. *Proceedings of the Symposium on Computers and Automata. Vol.XXI , MRI Symposia Series*. Polytechnik Press of the Polytechnic Institute of Brooklyn, Brooklyn, N.Y., 1971.

2. P. Lauer, *Formal Definition of ALGOL 60*. Technical Report TR 25.088, IBM Laboratory, Vienna, December 1968.

3. P. Lucas and K. Walk, On the formal description of PL/I. *Annual Review in Automatic Programming, Vol.6 , Part* 3, Pergamon Press 1959, pp 105-182.

4. J. McCarthy, Towards a mathematical science of computation. *Information Processing 62*, North-Holland, Amsterdam 1963, pp 21-28.

5. J. McCarthy, A formal description of a subset of *ALGOL*. *Formal Language Description Languages for Computer Programming*. North-Holland, Amsterdam 1966, pp 1-12.

6. P. J. Landin, The mechanical evaluation of expressions. *The Computer Journal, Vol. 6, No. 4* (January 1964), pp 308-320.

7. P. J. Landin, Correspondence between *ALGOL 60* and Church's lambda-notation (Parts I and II). Part I: *Comm. of the ACM, Vol. 8, No. 2* (February 1965), pp 89-101. Part II: *Comm. of the ACM, Vol. 8, No.3* (March 1965), pp 158-165.

8. J. B. Johnston, The contour model of block structured processes. *Proceedings of a Symposium on Data Structures in Programming Languages. SIGPLAN NOtices Vol. 6, No. 2*, ACM, February 1971, pp 55-82.

9. J. B. Dennis, Programming generality, parallelism and computer architecture. *Information Processing 68*, North-Holland, Amsterdam 1969, pp 484-492.

CHAPTER 3.B.

P O R T A B I L I T Y   and   A D A P T A B I L T Y

P. C. POOLE   W. M. WAITE

Culham Laboratory   University of Colorado
Abingdon, Berkshire   Dept. of El. Engineering
GREAT BRITAIN   BOULDER, COLORADO, USA

1.   *INTRODUCTION*

Portability is a measure of the ease with which a program can be transferred from one environment to another : If the effort required to move
the program is much less than that required to implement it initially,
then we say that it is highly portable. Adaptability is a measure of
the ease with which a program can be altered to fit differing user images and system constraints. The major distinction between the two concepts is that adaptability is concerned with changes in the structure
of the algorithm, whereas portability is concerned with changes in the
environment.

An obvious reason for enhancing the portability of a program is to ease
the transition to a new computer. An installation whose programs are
highly portable is not tightly bound to a particular computer or manu-

facturer. Because of this, the installation has a more flexible position when bargaining for a new machine. Manufacturers whose software is
portable can provide working programs more quickly when bringing out
new hardware. Academic and research people can move to other installations easily and can exchange programs to avoid wasteful duplication.

We have often heard the argument that programs should not be portable
because they can be improved if they are rewritten. We believe the
question here is one of resource allocation : if a program is portable,
one has the freedom to decide whether to allocate resources to improve
it or doing another project. Even if a decision is made to rewrite,
the portable version can be made available during the period of rewriting.

The main argument for enhancing adaptability is the need to satisfy a
broad range of user requirements with a single program. Such requirements are often neither nested nor disjoint. It is necessary to delete
portions of the program so that particular users are not burdened with
facilities which they do not use and cannot afford.

High adaptability also enhances portability, because it enables the
implementor to delete features if necessary in order to meet memory
and system constraints. There are other ways in which a program could
be restructured in response to such requirements. In some cases it is
difficult to classify these techniques as increasing adaptability or
increasing portability. For example, we shall show how the translation
rules can be varied on the basis of the frequency of execution of various parts of the program. Such techniques do not usually make it easier to move a program, but certainly make it easier to improve the
program's performance. Is this increased portability or increased adaptability ?

1.1.   *THE BASIC PRINCIPLES*

Let us consider the normal approach to creating a program.First we examine the problem and determine an appropriate set of basic operations

and data types. We then build an algorithm, which uses the operations to manipulate data. The algorithm simply provides a particular flow of control, tying the basic operations together in a particular way. It says nothing about how the data types are represented, nor how the operations obtain their results. In other words, the algorithm is independent of any particular realization of the operations and data types.

We should point out here that the relative efficiency of two different algorithms for solving the same problem may depend heavily upon the realization of their respective operations and data types. In such a case, the choice of algorithm would depend upon the particular realization available.

An algorithm may be realized on any computer by realizing its basic operations and data types. Because of the considerations noted in the previous paragraph, a more efficient algorithm might be possible. Nevertheless, the original algorithm will work correctly. This is the basic principle used to enhance a program's portability.

To enhance the adaptability of a program, we must make it easy to alter the algorithm in a systematic way. The key is to avoid the necessity of recoding, a process which almost invariably produces errors. In later sections we shall show several techniques and examples of adaptable programs. Unfortunately, however, we cannot state a basic principle of adaptability at this time. Our techniques will only allow adaptation of the algorithm in ways forseen by the designer.

1.2.   WHAT WE CAN EXPECT TO ACHIEVE

The techniques which we will discuss in these lectures can be used to achieve dramatic increases in software portability. When a programmer sets out to transfer an algorithm to a new computer, he must first choose a representation of the basic operations and data types for the problem. Having done this, he must express the algorithm in terms of his representation. Our techniques eliminate the second step entirely.

As an example of the savings, consider the implementation of a *SNOBOL4* compiler/interpreter [1,2]. This program is expressed in terms of 131 macros, which realize the basic operations and data types required by the algorithm. The program consists of roughly 6ooo lines of code, each of which is a call on one of these macros. Approximately one week is required to code the macros, and another four weeks to debug them. Each macro involves the order of 5 lines of assembly language. Making an order of magnitude calculation, we can assume that an assembly language programmer is capable of producing 25oo lines of debugged code per year [3]. Hence the effort involved in implementing *SNOBOL4* by reconstructing the algorithm in assembly code would be about 12 man-years; roughly 2.5 man-years would be required if the implementor made heavy use of macros.

Another example, illustrating the ease with which the characteristics of a program can be altered, is the implementation of the *MITEM* text manipulator [4] on the *ICL 4/70*. Like *SNOBOL4*, the *MITEM* program is expressed in terms of macro calls. Approximately 4ooo lines of code are involved. For the first version each macro was defined by a sequence of machine code instructions. Roughly two man-weeks of effort were required to complete this implementation. No additional effort is required to generate subsets of *MITEM* : The user simply specifies a level number and re-translates the program. Each line of code carries a key which causes the translator to ignore it if it is not relevant to the desired level.

The first version of *MITEM* did not satisfy the memory constraints for interactive programs on the 4/70. A further two man-weeks were spent coding an interpreter and altering the macros to produce a data structure for it. This second version used only 40 % of the memory required for the first version, but the execution time increased by a factor of 10. A third version was running after three more man-weeks. It was a hybrid, with critical parts of the program translated into executable code and the remainder interpreted. The interpreter was changed to pack code efficiently at the expense of slower interpretation. Total memory requirements were still 40 % of those for version 1, but the execution time increased by only 10 % over that of version 1.

2.   PORTABILITY   THROUGH   HIGH   LEVEL   LANGUAGE   CODING

The traditional method of increasing program portability is to use a
language sch as *FORTRAN*, *ALGOL* or *COBOL*. This is a perfectly valid
approach, provided that certain conditions are satisfied :

-   The basic operations and data types required by the
    problem are available in the chosen language.

-   The chosen language has a standard definition, and
    this standard definition is widely implemented.

-   Care is taken to avoid constructions which are accepted
    in the local dialect, but prohibited by the standard.

These conditions are satisfied by a large majority of the programs
which solve scientific problems, and many which solve the standard business problems.

Since adaptability is a property of the coding of the algorithm rather
than its realization, use of a high level language does not automatically make a program highly adaptable. Few high level languages have built-
in mechanisms to select portions of the source text while ignoring others. This effect can be achieved, however, through the use of a separate text editor. A more important weakness of most translators for
high level languages is their inability to vary the code which they generate. In Section 1.2. we indicated that improvements in overall performance could be achieved by using entirely different code generation
strategies for different parts of the program.

2.1.   THE NEED FOR EXTENSIONS

The first of the three conditions stated above is the most difficult
to satisfy. Many problems have several basic operations and data types
which are not available in the chosen language. These basic operations
and data types can usually be realized by combinations of basic operations and data types which *a r e* available in the language, but the
resulting program may be inadequate in several ways.

A high level language must be realized on a computer. It may be that,
although the language does not provide a particular data type, that data type can be easily realized on the given computer. For example,
ANSI FORTRAN [5] provides neither a string data type nor the basic

string operations. The *IBM SYSTEM/360* computers however, do provide these facilities. Character strings may be realized as integer arrays in *ANSI FORTRAN*, but then the translator will not take advantage of the more efficient realization possible on *IBM SYSTEM/360*. If we could extend the *ANSI FORTRAN* language to include a string data type, then the efficiency of the resulting program for *IBM SYSTEM/360* could be improved.

There is another advantage which can be gained by extending the language : improved program documentation. It may not be clear that a certain sequence of operations on integer arrays is, in fact, intended to move a string. If the same sequence is expressed as a move operation with string arguments, the significance is immediately clear.

Several languages provide extension mechanisms which permit the user to define new operations and data types in terms of those which already exist [6,7]. Such mechanisms provide the improved documentation, but do not increase efficiency. Conceptually, they operate on the extended source text to produce normal text. (The practical implementation may not involve such a transformation explicitly.) A mechanism which permits the extensions to be defined in terms of the target computer must involve the code generation procedures of the translator. Such mechanisms have been proposed and are available in some languages [8].

An extension in terms of existing operations and data types has no implications for portability, unless the extension facilities are not part of the standard language. Extensions defined in terms of the target computer, however, reduce the portability : The implementor must make an additional effort to specify the modification of the code generation procedures for the new target machine.

In later sections we shall discuss ways of adapting a translator so that a particular extension may be made either in terms of existing operations and data types, or in terms of the target computer. The former method preserves the portability of the program, while the latter permits increased efficiency at the cost of increased effort.

2.2.   *EXTENSION BY EMBEDDING*

If a language permits separate translation of procedures, then it is possible to make an extension in terms of the target computer by providing procedures written in machine code. This technique is called *embedding*, and is frequently used to extend *FORTRAN*. The *host* language is the one being extended, and the machine code procedures are called *primitives*. Embedding avoids the need for modification of the host language translator, but may involve heavy time penalties for calls on the primitives.

As we indicated in Section 2.1., the reason for extending a language is to improve the efficiency and/or documentation of algorithms which solve certain classes of problems. These goals are totally independent of portability considerations. When creating an extension by embedding, the designer must usually make a definite decision about the balance he desires between portability and efficiency. The remainder of this section is devoted to a case study which illustrates the principles involved.

SLIP [9] is an extension to *FORTRAN* which provides list processing capability. One new data type, the *SLIP* cell (Figure 2.1.), was provided. The basic operations were embodied in the ten primitives of Table 2.1. A complete description of the primitives may be found in reference 3; we shall note their relevant properties as necessary for our discussion.

ID	LNKL	LNKR
(2 bits)	(Address)	(Address)

Figure 2.1.

A SLIP CELL

1.   Immediate operation :   *MADOV(A)*

2.   Direct operations
          2.1. Selectors :   *ID(CELL)*
                                        LNKL(CELL)
                                        LNKR(CELL)
          2.2. Constructors :   *SETDIR(ID,LNKL,LNKR,CELL)*
                                        STRDIR(DATUM,CELL)

3.   Indirect operations

          3.1. Selectors :   *CONT(A)*
                                        INHALT(A)
          3.2. Constructors :   *SETIND(ID,LNKL,LNKR,A)*
                                        STRIND(DATUM,A)

Table 2.1.

The *SLIP* Primitives

When a language is extended by embedding, the new data types do not achieve any status as far as the language is concerned. In our example, supplying the primitives of Table 2.1. does not cause the *FORTRAN* compiler to recognize *SLIP* cells as valid data objects in their own right. The compiler still only knows about integers, reals, etc. Every variable known to the compiler must have one of these types. If the contents of a *SLIP* cell is to be placed into a named variable, we must be able to guarantee that the compiler has reserved sufficient space for that variable to hold the contents of a *SLIP* cell.

ANSI FORTRAN does not specify the relationship between addresses and integers or addresses and real numbers. Hence there is no way to guarantee that a variable of either type will have enough room to hold the contents of a *SLIP* word. For example, the *CDC 3200* has 15 bit addresses and the *FORTRAN* integer variable is only 24 bits long. The real variable occupies 48 bits on this machine, so that it would be sufficiently large. On *SYSTEM/ 360*, however, addresses are 24 bits. *SLIP* was originally implemented on the *IBM 7090*, a machine with 15 bit addresses and 36 bits devoted to each variable, regardless of type.

At this point in the design, a decision on the importance of portability is required. If the program is to be portable, then the entire contents of a *SLIP* cell must never be stored in a *FORTRAN* variable. Let us examine the consequences of such a decision. Since the *SLIP* cell is a structured object, we must have a primitive which accesses each of the component fields. The arguments of these primitives cannot be the contents of *SLIP* cells, since the *FORTRAN* compiler will reserve space only for arguments whose types it knows. Hence the argument of each selector must be the *address* of the *SLIP* cell. (We assume here that an integer variable is large enough to hold an address.) The direct selectors in Table 2.1. all take *CELL*, the contents of a *SLIP* cell, as their argument. They therefore avoid one memory reference, sacrificing portability to efficiency.

The two constructors *STRDIR* and *STRIND* illustrate another potential hazard. These primitives store the contents of a *FORTRAN* variable into a *SLIP* cell. Since the implementor of the primitives presumably has control over the size of the *SLIP* cell, there is no difficulty in ensuring that it is large enough to hold any *FORTRAN* data type. However, neither *STRDIR* nor *STRIND* specifies the type of its first argument. Hence each must act as though that type is the one which occupies the most space. Consider, however, a computer (such as the *CDC 3200*) in which an integer occupies one word and a real occupies two. Suppose further that the first argument of the primitive is an integer variable which is stored in the last word of the user's allocated space. If the primitive accesses two successive words, the program crashes with a bounds fault ! Different primitives, one for each data type to be stored, are required to avoid this problem and preserve portability. Note that these primitives might be realized by exactly the same machine code routine in a given implementation. The important point is that they can be distinguished if necessary.

A set of primitives which handle *SLIP* cells while preserving the portability of the program is shown in Table 2.2. All operations involving the full contents of a *SLIP* cell are indirect, and there are separate constructors for integer and real arguments. (We assume that double, complex and logical values will not be stored in *SLIP* cells. If this assumption is false, the modification should be obvious.)

Table 2.2. contains one primtive, *MEMORY*, which has no analog in Table 2.1. *MEMORY* is an environment inquiry. It permits the initialization to discover the limits of the memory available for *SLIP* cells,

and the size of a cell in address units. The argument *NUM* is provided
by the user, and its exact interpretation depends upon the implementation : If the memory is in a *COMMON* block declared by the user, or if
the memory should be requested from the system, then *NUM* is the number of *SLIP* cells in the memory. If the user will be given all memory
not occupied by his program, then *NUM* is the minimum number of cells
which he is prepared to accept. (*MEMORY* will terminate execution if
there are fewer than *NUM* cells available.)

1.	Environment inquiry :	*MEMORY(NUM,IBOT,ITOP,ISIZE)*
2.	Selectors :	*ID(A)*
		LNKL(A)
		LNKR(A)
		CONT(A)
		INHALT(A)
3.	Constructors :	*SETIND(ID,LNKL,LNKR,A)*
		STRINT(IDATUM,A)
		STREAL(RDATUM,A)

Table 2.2.

Primitives which preserve Portability

Efficiency considerations dictate that primitives should be realized
in machine code if possible. We have already noted that portability
suffers if this is done. It is certainly possible to provide a realization of the primitives in the host language. This will result in more
portable version, which can be used while the more efficient one is being constructed.

3. *PORTABILITY THROUGH ABSTRACT MACHINE MODELLING*

In Section 1.1. we discussed the separation of a problem solution into
a set of basic operations and data types, and an algorithm to manipulate them. Abstract machine modelling is simply a mechanistic interpretation of this separation : The basic operations and data types are used

to define a fictitious computer which is ideally suited to the problem at hand, and the algorithm is then coded in some language for this computer. We call the fictitious computer an *abstract machine* and say that it models the requirements of the problem. To run the program on a real computer, we realize the abstract machine on that computer.

The conceptual distinctions between use of high level languages and use of abstract machine models are trivial, and could even be argued to be nonexistent. Practically, the differences lie in the problems to which the techniques are applied. Use of a high level language implies to us use of an *existing* high level language. An abstract machine model, on the other hand, could be used to construct a *new* high level language. When one selects a particular high level language to solve a problem, one is selecting the abstract machine model specified by the language designer. Extensions to the language are changes in this model to make it more suitable for a given problem.

Selection of a language for expressing a problem solution is not based solely upon the abstract machine which underlies that language. There are other questions which relate to the available translators :

- Are translators available for a sufficiently broad set of computers, or is a highly portable translator available ?

- Are the translators adaptable (i.e. can the language be extended and/or can the code generation strategy be altered) ?

It should be clearly recognized that these are properties of the *translator*, rather than the language or the underlying abstract machine.

Our primary concern is those problems for which no adequate language exists. Available languages may be considered inadequate because of their underlying abstract machines or because of negative answers to the questions in the preceeding paragraph regarding their translators. In any event, the prospective user must become a designer. He must create an abstract machine model for his problem, devise a suitable language to use in programming this machine, and then provide a translator which is both highly portable and adaptable.

3.1.   *BACKGROUND*

When high level languages first became popular, much thought was given

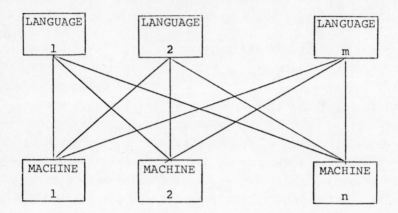

a) The m×n translator problem

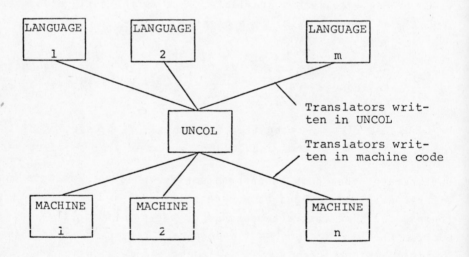

b) A proposed solution

Figure 3.1

UNCOL

to what was known as 'the $m^x n$ translator problem' (Figure 3.1a) : If we wish to run programs written in any one of m languages on any one of n machines, then $m^x n$ translators are required. To reduce this number, it was proposed [10] that a single intermediate language be devised. This language was to be called *UNCOL*. It would then only be necessary to produce m translators written in *UNCOL*, and n translators written in machine code (Figure 3.1b). The total number of translators required was therefore $m^+ n$, a substantial savings if m and n are large.

One of the main reasons that this scheme was never put into practice was the difficulty of specifying *UNCOL*. This should not be surprising, since *UNCOL* must be based on an abstract machine suitable for every problem. One needs only to consider the operators and data types for *ALGOL*, *LISP* and *SNOBOL* to appreciate the problems involved. It seems obvious to us that a single abstract machine will probably never be adequate to support all languages, and hence the *UNCOL* model is too simplistic. We shall point out, however, that there *are* operations and data types common to most problems. There is no need for these to be redesigned for every abstract machine. Our approach is thus quite similar to that of *UNCOL*, but avoiding its major pitfall.

Another early attempt to provide enhanced portability in this way was *SLANG* [11]. This project was never fully described in the open literature, but apparently it used a common core set of operations and data types which were extended to meet the needs of a particular problem. The realization techniques were also similar to those we shall discuss.

The first step in producing a piece of software by abstract machine modelling is to design the abstract machine model. Three considerations must be kept in mind when designing this model :

- The relationship between the model and existing computers.
- The realtionship between the model and the problem being solved.
- The tools available for the realization.

Overall efficiency depends primarily upon the first two considerations, while the third determines the complexity of the model.

Some care is needed in balancing the first two considerations. An extremly simple model results in a highly portable program since the model is easy to realize. If the problem requires relatively complex operations, however, these must be coded in terms of the simple model. Often it turns out that certain machines have hardware to realize these complex operations. Since the algorithm has been coded in terms of the simple operations, it must be changed to take advantage of the more sophisticated hardware. Conversely, if the algorithm is coded in terms of the sophisticated operations, its portability suffers because of the difficulty of realizing those operations on simple hardware.

The solution to this problem is to design a hierarchy of abstract machines. At the top of the hierarchy is an abstract machine which provides all of the complex operations required by the problem. This machine is then realized in terms of a simpler one. There may be several levels involved, with the lowest providing only very simple operations. Only the realization of this lowest machine *must* be carried out in terms of the real hardware; however, operations of any machine in the hierarchy *may* be so realized. We shall discuss this technique in more detail in Section 7.

3.2.   *RELATING THE MODEL TO EXISTING COMPUTERS*

It is not sufficient to consider a single real computer when designing the abstract machine model. In order to maintain portability, the design must take into account the characteristics of a wide class of computers. The major features of interest are the register organization, memory organization, mechanisms for addressing data aggregates, and I/O facilities. We shall attempt to classify existing computers according to these features.

Let us review the major register/processor organizations which we are likely to encounter. This classification should not be considered exhaustive. For each category, we shall note several typical computers which belong to that category :

- No programmable registers. All instructions take their operands from memory and leave their results in memory. (*IBM 1400* series, *IBM 1620*)

- A single arithmetic register. This register often has an extension, which does not have the full capabilities of the major register. (*IBM 7040, 7090, CDC 3000* series, many minicomputers)

- Multiple arithmetic registers. Arithmetic instructions may take their operands from registers or memory; some registers may be related, but all have essentially the same capabilities, (*IBM System/360*)

- Register file. Operands for arithmetic instructions must be in registers. There are multiple registers, all of which have essentially the same capabilities. (*CDC 6000, 7000*)

- Stack. Operands for arithmetic instructions are found in fixed positions in the stack. (*ICL KDF9, BURROUGHS 5000, 5500*)

The major effect of the organization is on the programmer's storage. Intermediate results must be explicily stored if only a single arithmetic register is available; they are automatically preserved by stack hardware. Explicit storage is only required in multiple register and register file machines if the number of simultaneous intermediate results become too large. The register used for computation must be varied, however.

In view of these differences, it would be reasonable to design a model in which temporary storage need not be explicitly referenced by the programmer. This applies not only to temporaries which a compiler would generate in the course of translating an expression, but also to those normally provided by the programmer (e.g. the extra location used to interchange words during a sort).

There are three major kinds of memory organizations which we are likely to encounter :

- Linear address space. The memory consists of a series of locations, consecutively numbered. (*IBM System/360, CDC 6000, 7000*)

- Piecewise-linear address space. The memory either consists of a number of modules with independent, linear address spaces, or the addressing mechanism imposes such an organization. (Many minicomputers, *BURROUGHS 5500*)

- Memory Hierarchy. There are several independently-addressed memories of varying speeds, with data transfer between levels explicitly controlled by the programmer. (Some minicomputers, *CDC 6000* with extended core)

Any of these organizations may have either bytes or words as the smallest addressable unit.

Differences in memory organization usually appear as size limitations.
In a piecewise-linear memory, for example, there is a large increase in
the cost of an array reference if the size of the array exceeds the size
of one module. This is because every index must be explicitly divided
into two parts - a module address and the address of a location within
the module. If the size of the array is less than the size of the module, then the module address can be supplied by the translator. (We consider a paged memory to provide a linear address space if the paging
is transparent to the user.)

It is unreasonable to design a model in which the maximum size of an array is limited to some fixed value. Whatever value is chosen will be
incorrect for the majority of computers. A better course is to simply
make the programmer aware that large arrays will be expensive on some
computers, and then generate the best code possible for each case. The
language design should avoid any implicit relationship among separately
declared arrays (such as exists in *FORTRAN COMMON*) which assumes a
linear address space.

References to constants and simple variables can be completely specified
by the translator. References to data aggregates, however, may be left
partially unspecified until the program is executed. There are three
common mechanisms for providing the information to complete the specification :

- Program modification. The actual address is pre-computed
  by the program and placed in an instruction which is
  then executed. (*IBM 1400* series, *IBM 1620*)

- Indirect addressing. The actual address is pre-computed
  by the program and placed in some location. The instruction references that location and the hardware interprets its contents as an address (*IBM 1620*)

- Index modification. The actual address is computed by
  the hardware at the time the reference is made. Part
  of the data required to compute the address is supplied
  by the referencing instruction, the remainder comes from
  a register specified by the referencing instruction.
  (*IBM System/360, CDC 3000, 6000, 7000* series)

There are many variants of index modification, but the central point is
the computation of the effective address by the hardware.

Components of data aggregates are accessed frequently, and these accesses often occur inside loops. In fact, the only purpose of an inner loop in most programs is to sequence through some data aggregate and perform operations upon its components. Measurements show the timing of the inner loops usually controls the execution time of the program. Hence the way in which data aggregates are accessed will have a significant effect upon the execution of most programs.

If a model assumes a particular mechanism for accessing data aggregates, then the programer can use particular coding techniques to improve the performacne of the algorithm. Unfortunately, the techniques are different for the different mechanisms. This is a case in which the algorithm does depend on the model, and large penalties can accrue on certain computers from the use of an inappropriate model. The best escape from the dilemma seems to be to model the most probable mechanism (index modification) and try to avoid inefficiencies by direct encoding of higher-level constructs, as illustrated in Section 7.

A procedure call involves two distinct actions - parameter passing and status saving. The realization of the former is closely linked to the model for accessing data aggregates; we shall discuss the possible alternatives in Section 6.1. There are four common hardware mechanisms for realizing the latter :

- Relevant status is placed on a stack by the hardware when a subroutine jump instruction is executed. (*ICL KDF9, BURROUGHS 5500*)

- Relevant status is placed in a register by the hardware when a subroutine jump instruction is executed. (*IBM 7040, 7090, System/360*)

- Relevant status is placed in memory by the hardware when a subroutine jump instruction is executed. The memory location bears some fixed relationship to the target of the subroutine jump *(CDC 6000 and 7000 series, IBM 7040)*.

- A separate instruction is provided for saving the relevant status *(GE 645)*.

The makeup of the 'relevant status' depends entirely upon the computer. At the least, it is the return address.

The actual realization of a procedure call depends not only upon the hardware, but also upon the operating system of the target computer. A standard procedure calling sequence is mandatory if the system is to have a common base language (see Dennis B.). As in the case of data aggregate addressing, the detailed coding of a procedure call would necessarily depend upon the model assumed. We must therefore use a high level model, simply stating that a procedure is to be called.

In some cases the procedure call mechanism provided by the hardware is such that there is no difference in cost between recursive and non-recursive calls. Unfortunately this is not true in general. For example recursion using the third mechanism described above requires that the procedure retrieves the status from the memory and places it on a stack. (Alternatively, all calls could be set up to simulate the first mechanism in software.) Most modular programs employ one or more short procedures which are used in inner loops to perform some simple task (such as obtaining a character from an input string). These procedures are never used recursively. Because of the frequent calls, the overhead required for recursion builds rapidly. In view of this, we strongly advocate *two* procedure call operations - recursive and nonrecursive.

Existing computers communicate with a wide range of peripheral devices. In spite of this diversity, efficient modelling of input/output operations is easier than efficient modelling of references to data aggregates because the time scale is much longer. There is no need to split microseconds to initiate a transfer which requires milliseconds to complete. It is immaterial whether the program is I/O bound or compute bound, or wether the data transfers are overlapped or not. If the time which the model requires to initiate an I/O operation is a small fraction of the time required to complete it, then the overall execution speed of the program would not change even if the initiation time vanished completely. A satisfactory model is therefore one which avoids *gross* inefficiencies and provides a simple user image.

An abstract machine model is connected to a number of abstract peripheral devices. Each of these devices has a model which describes its characteristics and defines its behavior when it is presented with certain operation codes. The abstract machine has a single instruction which it uses to communicate with all of its peripheral devices. Control information is passed in both directions, and information transfer may occur as a side effect. A I/O request is defined by specifying the following :

- The peripheral to be used (logical unit number).

- The operation to be performed (operation code).

- If the operation involves data transmission, the
  memory to be used.

A peripheral device returns a completion code which defines the results of the operation. Each model may require different codes, but the following three are common to all :

- The operation was completed normally.

- The operation was not completed because of an end condition on the peripheral device (e.g. endfile, disc full).
- The operation was not completed because it requested an action which is illegal on the peripheral device.

The existence of a completion code does not imply that the possibility of overlapped operations is being ignored. There are two major device classes : sequential and random. A random device can be reset at any time to any arbitrary position; a sequential device can be reset only to some specified initial position. (It also may be possible to back space a sequential device.) Note that this classification depends only on the use made of the device in the abstract machine program, not on the particular realization of the device.

Suppose that a user is accessing a sequential device. At each request the position of the next record to be read or written is known. This means that standard double- or multiple-buffering techniques can be used in the realization of the device if they are not provided by the operating system of the target machine. The maximum possible overlap can be obtained by this strategy, and hence there is never any need to use overlap in the abstract machine program for sequential devices.

The sequence of requests for information from a random access device is not well defined. Thus the overlap cannot be handled in the realization of the device, but must be built into the abstract machine program. One way of doing this is to double the number of permissible I/O requests. The new requests simply 'advise' that the corresponding operation will be issued at some future time. 'Advice' requests give exactly the same information as normal requests. A specified buffer may be filled (or emptied) at any time after the 'advice', but the transfer must be completed before the corresponding normal request returns.

I/O operations can be divided into three categories :

- Read. Operations which transfer information from a
  device to memory.

- Write. Operations which transfer information from
  memory to a device.

- Control. Operations which do not transfer information
  between a device and memory.

There may be many operations in each category, not all of which are possible on a particular device.

Occasionally it is difficult to classify a given instruction. For example, consider the plotter operation 'draw a line from the current position to X,Y'. This should be a write operation - after all, a line is drawn. The operation 'move the pen from the current position to X,Y without drawing a line' should be a control operation. If, however, we examine the way most pen plotters actually work, the distinction is not as clear. Both operations use the plotter hardware command 'move pen'. When the line is drawn, this command is preceeded by a 'pen down' command.

Such conflicts can usually be resolved by adhering to the conception of an abstract model. How the plotter goes about producing the line is irrelevant. The program is simply instructing the model of the plotter to produce a line (clearly a write operation) or reposition its writing mechanism (clearly a control operation).

The classification of I/O operations is useful because it reflects the general capabilities of devices and the structure of their realizations. Most devices with limited capabilities cannot perform *any* operations in a given class. If requests for such operations are presented to the operating system of the target computer, they often result in fatal errors and a complete loss of control by the abstract machine model. By having the realization of the abstract machine's I/O request make a few simple checks, most of these catastrophes can be avoided.

3.3.   *RELATING THE MODEL TO THE PROBLEM*

As we have noted, each problem requires a certain set of basic operations and data types. Some of these may represent high level of abstraction, in the sense that a great deal of code is necessary to realize them on many computers. Particular computers may, however, provide hardware which realizes them directly. The character string data type, with its basic operations concatenation and lexical comparison, provides an excellent example for this type. A significant amount of code is required to realize concatenation and lexical comparison on word oriented computers which have no field selection hardware. (Remember that, in general, the operand strings will have different offsets within a machine word. Hence words must be shifted and spliced together during the operation.) On *SYSTEM/360* the same operations can be performed using only a few instructions.

We have already noted the importance of including high level operations and data types in the model. They permit the user to provide more information about *what* he expects to happen. The decision about how to achieve the desired results can then be deferred until we know what tools are available.

It would be possible to construct an abstract machine model which had one instruction : solve the problem. Such a model is not interesting because it does not in any way reduce the labor of realizing the solution. One might therefore ask questions about the level of abstraction which is appropriate for a model. These questions are virtually impossible to answer in general. The answers depend upon the algorithm, the designer and the current state of the hardware art. They represent an engineering compromise. Unfortunately, it has been our experience that the proper model only becomes clear *after* the algorithm has been coded for the abstract machine and then realized on several computers.

The design process begins with the selection of some operators and data types which seem appropriate. As the coding of the algorithm progresses, this original choice becomes 'obviously' less appropriate. Sometimes minor modifications are indicated, but to often a drastic revision is necessary. Most drastic revisions invalidate large portions of the code already written. The need for rewriting and respecifying results in co-

ding times which are significantly longer than those required to implement equivalent software using an existing language which permits no
extensions.

When the designer begins by selecting operators and data types which he
believes are suitable for the problem at hand, he is adrift in a vast
sea of possibilities. There is no fixed point which he can use to guide
himself in his design. These are the conditions under which the coding
requires the greatest amount of time. To provide a fixed point, we need
to recognize a common core of operations and data types which are applicable to virtually all problems [12].

People with different backgrounds and experience may well specify somewhat different common sets of operations and data types. At the time of
writing, we propose the following :

- Integers and integer arithmetic

- Tests for equality and relative magnitude

- Input/output of character information

The most common extensions to this list would be :

- Reals and real arithmetic

- Strings; concatenation, selection and lexical
  comparison

- Input/output of memory images

Neither list is to be considered gospel. We reserve the right to change
our minds at any time.

In addition to a common set of operations and data types, one can specify a common set 'organizational' features of the model. These are features which permit the programmer to order the execution of basic operations, specify that certain variables have certain types, form and reference data aggregates, and break the algorithm into intercommunicating
parts. We would place the following constructs in this category :

- Labels and transfers of control

- Declarations

- Arrays and records

- Conditional and repetitive statements

- Procedures and blocks

4. *REALIZATION OF ABSTRACT MACHINE MODELS*

An abstract machine model is realized by defining its basic operations
and data types in terms of the target computer. The algorithm, which
was written in terms of the model, is then translated mechanically.
Hence the major tool required for the ralization is a translator.

4.1. *TRANSLATOR CHARACTERISTICS*

The most important characteristic of the translator is its portability.
If a language is to be useful for constructing portable programs, then
its translator must be widely available. If the translator is not portable, then two problems must be overcome :

- Lack of resources for constructing a translator on
  the desired target machine. (This may be due to an
  inadequate selling effort by the user)

- The tendency to produce incompatible local dialects.
  (This may be due to misunderstandings on the part of the
  implementor or to a misplaced desire for efficiency.)

Our experience has been that these problems are virtually insurmounta-
ble for languages other than *ANSI FORTRAN*. This may be a poor comment
on the state of the art, but it is something which we must recognize as
being true at the moment. The user of any other language must be prepared to implement it himself from material in his possession, with little or no aid from the staff of the installation.

A translator differs from most portable programs because the desired
results depend strongly upon the target computer. Hence a portable
translator must also be adaptable - it must be easy to alter the code
generation algorithm to fit the target machine. This characteristic re-
lates to the techniques used to achieve portability in the translator.
We shall discuss these techniques in some detail in Section 4.2.

Translation may be divided into two subtasks : recognition of source
language constructs and code generation. The recognition process depends
only upon the source language, and hence could conceivably be different
for every abstract machine. We have, however, already noted a common
core of organizational features, basic operations and data types which
seem applicable to most problems. A framework for language design can
be based on this common core, and a uniform recognition algorithm built.

Such a framework will be presented in Section 6.

Our experience has been that the interface between the recognition and code generation tasks must also be adaptable, even if a common framework is used for designing abstract machine languages. The level at which constructs in the source language are recognized often depends upon how code for them is to be generated. Section 7.3. illustrates this point with examples from *MITEM*.

One important characteristic of a translator is its complexity. By increasing the complexity of the translator it is possible to make the source language more convenient for the user, to perform more complex optimization and to provide better diagnostics. At the same time (with the current state of the art) one makes the translator more difficult to adapt and less accessible to small computers. We have taken a deliberate decision, based upon our perception of today's needs and our own limitations, to concentrate on simple translators. As the methods for achieving adaptability in more complex translators become clear, they can be written in terms of abstract machine languages processed by the simpler translators.

A conventional compiler is obviously unsuited to our purposes. There are some compilers, such as that for *BCPL* [12], which are realtively portable and have code generators which can be adapted. The source language may or may mot be extensible. It is generally difficult to change the linkage between the recognizer and code generator. Usually the code generator is coded into the compiler, which is written in its own source language. A thorough knowledge of the internal structure of the compiler is necessary to adapt it. Such translators are only marginally useful for our application.

Syntax-directed compilers [13] and translators produced by compiler generators [14] can be modified to accept different source languages. Unfortunately, most recognition algorithms depend upon context-free grammars. This means that a particular construct is always parsed in exactly the same way. For example, the arguments of a procedure call may always be recognized before the entire call is recognized. When using a hierarchy of abstract machines, we would probably represent high level operations by procedure calls. Suppose that our target computer provided some, but not all, of these high level operations. it would be convenient to be able to recognize the procedure calls which were directly translatable as single units, while processing the others in the normal way.

This difficulty is avoided by systems which allow the user to embed 'semantic actions' in the syntax specification [15]. These are simply procedure calls, possibly with parameters, which can perform any arbitrary actions. They may return a value in some systems. The value is often restricted to 'success' or 'failure', with a failure return causing the recognizer to backtrack. If a more general output is allowed, it is interpreted as an element which must be recognized at the current position of the input string (see reference 1 for examples). Care must be taken with semantic actions if the recognizer is permitted to backtrack over them [16].

Most syntax-directed compiler designs are slanted toward the recogniton phase. Code generations facilities are primitive, or are written into the compiler. The coupling between recognizer and code generator is usually well-defined, and can be changed only by changing the syntax of the source language or making extensive modifications to the compiler. The final blow is the apparent lack of portability of these systems, despite claims to the contrary.

At the current state of the art, the most suitable translators for our purpose seem to be those which perform both recognition and code generation interpretively. The translation rules are supplied with the program to be translated, and can easily be modified to meet particular requirements. In effect, these processors provide a language expressly suited to compiler writing. The important primitives (such as dictionary lookup, code conversion and lexical scanning) are built into the interpreter and can be called upon by simple constructs in the translation rules. When the user defines his translation rules he is, in effect, writing a compiler for his source language/machine pair. In some cases the system allows the user to 'freeze' a set of translation rules, compiling them into the system [17]. These rules can then be used as primitives for constructing other rules. If such a feature is provided, it is also useful to be able to excise some of the frozen rules [18].

Processors of this type are normally presented either as syntax-directed compilers [19,20] or as general purpose macro processors [21-23]. The main variations seem to be in the recognizer. Programs like *TMG* [19] use a formal syntax, possibly with embedded semantic actions. Macro processors use either keywords or a general pattern matching scheme. Each technique has advantages and disadvantages which we shall not pursue here. Our choice of *STAGE2* [23] as our basic implementation tool was determined almost entirely by its portability. *STAGE2* can be made available on a new computer with an effort ranging from one man-day to two man-weeks. It has been implemented on 25 different computers ranging from the *IBM 1130* and *DEC PDP-11* to the *CONTROL DATA 7600* and *STAR*. The term 'macro processor' may be misinterpreted by some people to imply simple text replacement. In his classic paper [24], McIlroy pointed out that a macro processor should be capable of performing at translation time any action which could be performed at run time by a normal program. This says, in effect, that a macro processor is an interpreter for a general programming language. Since that language is to be used for a particular purpose, translation, it should be provided with high level operations which are useful in constructing translators.

STAGE2 interprets a low level language designed expressly for string manipulation. Since the portability of *STAGE2* itself was the primary design criterion, the language has no frills. It might be considered almost equivalent to absolute machine code in structure. Some people have critized *STAGE2* on this basis. (Our experience has been that such criticism usually comes from those who are primarily oriented to programming in a high level language. Assembly language programmers seem to find *STAGE2* quite acceptable.) The design can be defended only on the basis of intended use : *STAGE2* is a basic tool for obtaining portable systems programs. It is not to be considered a general translator for casual use. Such a general translator could be written for a suitable abstract machine and realized using *STAGE2*.

Many of the examples in the following sections will use *STAGE2* macros to illustrate methods of achieving portability and adaptability. Any detailed characteristics of the macro language which are required to understand those examples will be discussed at the time. We shall close this section with a brief overview of the processor to provide the necessary background.

Each macro has a *template* and a *code body*. The template is a sequence of literal characters and parameter flags. A template is matched to a string by a left-to-right scan which compares literal characters of the string. Each parameter flag can match any substring of the given string (including a null string) which is balanced with respect to parentheses. The match must account for all of the characters in the string. There may be several templates which match a given string. This ambiguity is resolved in a standard way which does not depend upon the order in which the macros were defined.

When a template is matched to a string, the corresponding code body is effectively a procedure in the language interpreted by *STAGE2*. Its parameters (called by value) are substrings which matched the parameter flags of the template. The purpose of the code body is to construct strings. A constructed string may be matched against the set of templates, output to some device, stored in an internal memory location, or split according to a set of break characters. Strings may be built from literal characters supplied by the code body, parameter strings, strings extracted from the internal memory, or constructed strings which have been transformed in some way (e.g. evaluated as arithmetic expressions). A complete description of the facilities of *STAGE2* may be found in reference 25 .

4.2. *OBTAINING THE TRANSLATOR*

In Section 4 1. we advocated a highly portable translator to insure that a particular abstract machine program was portable. But all of our argument has been based upon a translator as the basic tool for realizing an abstract machine. Since infinite recursion is not permitted, we must have some other way of realizing the first translator.

Let us denote the translator which we wish to implement by T, and the abstract machine for which it is coded by A. The new computer is N, and a running version of T is already available on computer M. No matter what implementation strategy is used, A must be defined in terms of N. This definition is subject to the usual errors which seem to creep into even the most carefully constructed code.

One implementation strategy [26], known as *half bootstrapping,* is to use the version of T which is running on M to produce code for N. The basic difficulty with this strategy is one of communication. We have heard a great deal about the difficulties of data interchange : lack of common peripherals, incompatible file formats, incompatible character sets, etc. All of these must be surmounted if M is to produce code for N. The problem is further aggravated by the errors mentioned in the previous paragraph. Several iterations will be necessary before a definition of A in terms of N is obtained. On each iteration the communication difficulties must be surmounted. No wonder a half bootstrap is sometimes beyond the patience of mortal man !

Full bootstrapping [27] avoids the iterative aspect of the communication problem, at the expense of some additional hand coding. A very simple translator is implemented by hand on N and then used to realize

lize *A*. The effort involved in hand coding is small - one suitable translator [28] can be expressed by fewer than 100 simple *FORTRAN* statements. The main disadvantage lies in the limitations placed on the language of *A* by the simple translator. These limitations may restrict the power of *T* to an inacceptable degree.

Certain basic software on the target computer is necessary for either of the methods : An input/output package is part of the definition of *A*, and is a univeral requirement. The simple translator can easily be arranged to use the same I/O conventions. *T* would normally produce assembly code for the target computer, and hence an assembler is needed to process *T's* output. Since *T* does most of the work, the complexity of the assembler is minimal. Its primary function is to provide the interface between a character stream and the relocatable object code of the target computer.

There is a third strategy, which has characteristics of both those menmentioned above. The design of the abstract machine *A* is carried to the point of specifying an absolute object code. The result is a block of numbers which could be loaded into the memory of *A* (if such hardware existed). A simulator for *A* is now written for *N*. The block of numbers which form the absolute object program *T* can be executed by this interpreter.

This strategy is like the full bootstrap in that it avoids the communication problems of the half bootstrap at the expense of additional hand coding (the interpreter). The translation of *T* to absolute object code need only be done once; it can then be used to realize *T* on any number of computers.

The version of *T* which is interpreted is only used to translate *T* for *N*. In that respect this strategy is a half bootstrap - *T* is being run on the *simulated* machine *A* to produce code for *N*. All communication problems are avoided because the simulated *A* has exactly the same peripherals and character set as *N*, and is at the same locaton.
Our experience has been that if *A* meets the constraints imposed by the simple translator of reference [28], then an interpreter for *A* could be built with approximately the same amount of effort. In fact, it appears that the most burdensome restrictions necessary for the simple translator could be lifted without increasing the cost of the interpreter. Hence we conclude that the third strategy is the one to use.

5.   *A CASE STUDY OF SOME EARLY ABSTRACT MACHINES*

In Section 3, we ennunciated a number of principles forconstructing
portable and adaptable software. We must stress that we have not arrived at these principles just by processes of abstract thought; rather,
they are based on the results of a number of experiments on abstract
machine models which we have carried out over the last few years. It
is now our intention to consider two of these early models in some
detail, pointing out where they were successful, where they failed
and how they have influenced our current thinking. By considering the
design and implementation of some actual models, we hope to set the
principles of abstract machine modelling in a more concrete framework
and demonstrate how they can be used to produce working software. In
this way, we will attempt to evaluate the principles against not just
what might be achieved, but what has been achieved. In particular, we
will consider:

(a)   *FLUB,* a machine designed specifically for the
        task of constructing *STAGE 2;*

(b)   *TEXED*, a machine used to implement *MITEM*   a
        program for text manipulation.

5.1.   *MACHINE AND LANGUAGE DESIGN*

In Section 3.1, we noted that in designing abstract machine models,
we had to bear in mind not only the relationship of the model to the
problem but also its relationship to the structure of real machines.
In our early approaches to abstract machine modelling, we tended to
emphasize the former at the expense of the latter. Our assumption was
that if the model adequately reflected the characteristics of the
problem, then encoding the algorithm in terms of the basic operations
and data types of the abstract machine is equivalent to programming
the problem for the actual computer once the abstract machine has
been realized. Obviously, we kept a wary eye on the structure of real
computers but the requirements of the problem tended to dominate the
design process. Now in principle, it should be possible to construct
the correct model just by considering the characteristics of the problem alone with little or no regard for the way real machines operate;
in practice, this can make an efficient implementation of the abstract
machine difficult or even impossible to obtain. In presenting these
case studies, we will attempt to point out where our emphasis of the
                                              model to the

ADDRESS	FLG	VAL	PTR	
100	0	C	107	(Root of the tree)
101	0	A	104	
102	0	T	0	
103	1			(End of CAT)
104	0	O	0	(Continuation of COT)
105	0	T	0	
106	1			(End of COT)
107	0	D	0	(Beginning of DOT)
108	0	O	0	
109	0	T	0	
110	1			(End of DOT)

Figure 5.1.

Representation of a Tree

problem has created difficulties.

STAGE2 deals with three data types : trees, strings and integers; in *MITEM*, only the last two are used. Since the tree is the most complex of these structures and a very fundamental one in the *STAGE2* algorithm our early design strategy dictated that the abstract machine should at least be well suited to manipulating this data structure. The representation of a tree was therefore a key factor in determining the composition of the *FLUB* word. Figure 5.1. illustrates a tree containing the strings *CAT*, *COT* and *DOT* set up in a sequentially addressed store. Each word is divided into 3 fields : the flag field (*FLG*) contains indicator bits; the value field (*VAL*) stores one character and the pointer field (*PTR*) is used to hold a link address.

Given such a structure for the *FLUB* word, the next question that was asked was whether it was also suitable for specifying strings and integers. Clearly, economy in data structures should also lead to economy in basic operations. It was noted that a string could readily be represented as a linked list of words with the *VAL* field of each word containing a character of the string and the *PTR* field addressing the word containing the next character. Substrings of a string as required for *STAGE2* could also be set up by specifying a word whose *PTR* field addresses the first character of the substring and whose *VAL* field contains the length of a substring. The *FLG* field again stores indicator bits denoting a substring header. When we came to design *TEXED* after the design of *FLUB* had been completed, we decided that this structure for a string would also be quite convenient for implementing such editing operations as insertions and deletions. Figure 5.2. illustrates how the string *CAT* can be changed to *COAT* by storing the character "*O*" in the next available free space and adjusting various links in the pointer fields.

With the representation of trees and strings fixed, there only remained the problem of deciding how to represent integers. They could be allocated a full word but again on the grounds of economy, it seemed sensible to examine the possibility of storing an integer in one of the three fields. *FLG* was obviously too small since it was only used for indicators and no arithmetic operations would be required. Addition and subtraction operations at least would be needed for the *VAL* field since it was to be used for storing string lengths. However it would still be too small to hold integers of a useful size since it was not expected that the programs would be manipulating very long strings. Similarly, the use of a *VAL* field to hold a character only implied the ability to

ADDRESS	FLG	VAL	PTR
1ØØ	Ø	C	1Ø4
1Ø1	Ø	A	1Ø2
1Ø2	Ø	T	1Ø3
1Ø3	1		
1Ø4	Ø	O	1Ø1
1Ø5			
1Ø6			

Figure 5.2.

The string COAT

FIELD	CONTENTS	OPERATIONS
FLG	indicator bits	assignment test for equality
VAL	character length of a string	integer addition and subtraction test for equality
PTR	address integer	integer arithmetic test for equality test for relative magnitude

Figure 5.3.

Use of fields in the FLUE word

store quite small integers. On the other hand, the *PTR* field was already large enough to contain an address, and the operations of addition, subtraction and a test for equality would be required to sequence through a tree of the type shown on Figure 5.1. Thus the decision was taken to store integers in the *PTR* field since only multiplication, division and a test for relative magnitude had to be added to those already required. This is to be contrasted with any decision to represent an integer by a full word which would have required a complete set of arithmetic and conditional operations. Hence the size of the pointer field determines the range of integers allowed in any implementation.

With the format of the basic data structure decided, the design of the abstract machine had reached the situation summarized in Figure 5.3. The main emphasis so far had been on the requirements of the problem. However, some thought had to be given to the way such a design might be mapped onto actual machines. The operations required were almost universally available and it was not expected that there would be any problem in realizing them. However, the data structures were another matter and the match between abstract machines and real computers was poor. It was unlikely that a real computer would be found whose words were partitioned into the three fields making up the *FLUB* word. Methods for implementing such a structure had to be considered in more detail.

There were two obvious ways in which the data structure could be mapped onto a real machine. Either the fields of the *FLUB* words could be packed into one or more words of the target machine or each field could be allocated a full target computer word. The first approach conserves memory but results in large overheads for the packing and unpacking; the second enables efficient access to be made to each field but is expensive on space. The situation was resolved by providing *FLUB* with a small set of *registers*, on which almost all operations take place, and a mechanism for transferring information between the registers and memory. The fields could then be packed in the memory to conserve space and the registers implemented with one target computer word per field for efficient execution. Since the number of registers was small (36 for reasons given later), the amount of space required for such an implementation was not prohibitive. The fields would still have to be packed and unpacked for transfer to and from the memory, but the overheads would be small since memory would not be accessed by most operations. The memory-register transfer operations take two registers as operands. One either receives or transmits information while the *PTR* fields of the other specifies the memory location. Hence all access to memory is indirect. This required some decisions about how the address stored in a *PTR* field was to be interpreted - as an abstract address or a real address. The latter was chosen for reasons of efficiency but a program had to be given access to the number of target machine address units per abstract word so that actual addresses could be computed. For example, on *System/360*, if 1 *FLUB* word is mapped onto 8 bytes, then 8 must be added to any address to compute the address of the next *FLUB* word. This problem of address mapping has already been discussed in Goos B. The mapping factor together with actual addresses defining the upper and lower limits of the *FLUB* memory were provided as preset quantities in three *PTR* fields.

Apart from input-output, the models still lacked a number of essential features, for example, a method of handling subroutines. The common hardware mechanisms for this operation have been summarised in Section 3.2. The method chosen for *FLUB* was to transmit the return address in the *PTR* field of a register and to specify a register on exit. This does not require a store operation into the program area and is therefore applicable to a wide class of computers. In *TEXED*, subroutine calls and exits do not specify a register explicitly and may therefore take advantage of whatever hardware mechanisms are available on the target machine. At this point, it is also appropriate to consider the other differences between *FLUB* and *TEXED*. These were mainly additional *hardware* features required for the implementation of *MITEM*. In designing *TEXED* as an extension of *FLUB*, we had some doubt whether there would be sufficient registers to implement the program. Rather than add extra registers, we incorporated a stack to serve as a temporary store. This could also be used for the transmission of parameters in procedure calls. We also noted that, under certain circumstances, *MITEM* needed to be able to interrogate its environment in order to choose between alternative courses of action. For example, if the program is running interactively and an error is detected, then it must inform the user and wait for him to respond; on the other hand, in batch mode its only course of action is to terminate processing since the execution of further commands could corrupt the text. We therefore added a *BATCH-MODE* flip-flop to allow the program to make such a decision. Similarly an *INTERRUPT* flip-flop allowed the on-line user to regain control and cancel a complex search process. This feature could be difficult or even impossible to implement in some systems and hence we made it an optional one which could be adapted out.

Before going on to consider the design of the I/O system, it will be useful at this point to pause for a moment and examine how the models we have described actually performed in practice. As expected, none of the basic operations have proved difficult to realize on actual machines. However, the data structure is another matter. Although it is relatively easy to implement, it does result in *STAGE2* having a voracious appetite for memory. Thus, while the program performs quite adequately on medium and large machines, it very often cannot be used effectively on small machines. The trouble lies with the design decision to use the word structure required to store a tree for the other data types as well. Although we attempted to justify this on the grounds of economy of concepts, there is really no valid reason for this decision. In *STAGE2*, strings are handled in a predictable way and occupy contiguous blocks of storage. There is thus no need for any explicit linkage. The length of each string is known and no flag is required to denote the end. When integers are stored in memory, *FLG* and *VAL* fields rarely contain useful information. We might therefore save considerable space by having three data types (tree nodes, characters, integers). We would of course require distinct operations to transmit the various data types between registers and the memory, but once in a register, all the data could be treated uniformly. Thus only set of arithmetic and conditional operations would be required, and our economy of concepts would be retained.

In *TEXED*, the problem created by using the *FLUB* word structure is not one of space but of speed. *MITEM* needs only a small amount of memory of a fixed size and the fact that the *FLG* field is not really necessary is largely immaterial. However, although the storage of strings as linked lists is quite convenient for the process of insertion and deletion, it does preclude us from making use of special hardware instructions available on some machines for the manipulation of characters. For example on *SYSTEM/360*, to locate the position of a character in a string, we would use a *TRANSLATE AND TEST* instruction if the string is set up as a contiguous sequence of bytes. This is much faster than any programmed search on a list structure. Since the text editor can spend a great deal of its time searching for specified character strings, we could improve its performance considerably on some machines if we could make use of any special hardware facilities available. Even on machines without such instructions, we would probably lose very little if we discarded the list structure entirely and stored a string as an array of characters. Insertion and deletion could then be carried out during the process of copying the string from one buffer to another.

Thus, in practice, both abstract machines have revealed design deficiencies which we believe were due to emphasizing the relationship of the
model to the problem and not paying sufficient attention to the structure of real machines. As our goals are efficiency as well as portability, in future, we will have to place more weight in the design process on the facilities available on actual computers.

Now let us consider the problem of designing an input-output system for
these abstract machines. From an external view, both $STAGE2$ and MI-
TEM process lines of input text to produce lines of output text. Internally however, they manipulate linked lists of characters. Hence the
simplest view of the I/O was one in which both input and output are
treated as streams of characters divided into lines by an end-of-line
symbol. The first system designed for $FLUB$ provided character-by-character operations only with the VAL field receiving and transmitting
a character. Internally, characters were represented by non-negative
integers apart from the end-of-line symbol which was assigned the value
-1. Input consisting of the macro definitions and text to be processed
was read from one stream and output could be sent to two streams; the
first received the generated text in a machine readable form so that it
could be re-input to the computer for further processing;the second was
used for error and diagnostic messages.

After some experience in using $STAGE2$, we came to the conclusion that
the character I/O system, although easy to implement, was not flexible enough. In particular, we did not wish to restrict $STAGE2$ to a
fixed set of I/O devices. About this time, $TEXED$ was being designed
for the implementation of $MITEM$ and it was evident that a much more
complex I/O system would be needed.

In its simplest mode of operation, $MITEM$ accepts lines of text from
a $READ$ stream, edits them according to commands issued on a $CONTROL$
stream and outputs the modified lines to the $WRITE$ stream; success or
failure of the editing process is reported on the $PRINT$ stream. Thus
we already needed one more I/O channel than was required for $STAGE2$.
Character-by-character I/O operations were sufficient if a line from
the $READ$ stream had to be scanned or modified since it must be placed
in the $TEXED$ memory. However, in a simple copying operation from one
file to another, considerations of efficiency dictated that, at least,
the line is the basic unit and the operation must be performed outside
the memory of the abstract machine. Hence some form of record I/O operations was required for reading and writing lines. For more complex

editing operations, it was also clear that a number of control functions would be needed. For example, to move a block of text from one position in a file to another, we could first delete it with respect to the WRITE stream and copy it to a DELETE stream. Subsequent lines could then be copied from the READ to the WRITE streams until the new position was located. If the file containing the *deleted* information were now connected to the READ stream, the block of text could be copied to the WRITE stream in its new position. We could then reconnect the original file to the READ stream to continue processing. This operation would require at least write endfile and rewind. Notice it also implied that we must be able to disconnect a file from a stream and still recover the current line when it is reconnected.

Given that both record and character I/O operations were needed, we next considered how such a system might be implemented on real machines and what interfaces to the abstract machines would be required. Record operations presented no great problems since the I/O systems of most computers transmit records to and from peripheral devices. Character I/O on the other hand would have to be implemented by routines which pack and unpack buffers. If characters can be directed to a number of devices, each character I/O operation must specify a device number which can be used by the buffering routine to select the appropriate buffer. We avoided this overhead by noting that both STAGE2 and MITEM actually process lines and do not switch from one I/O device to another during transmission of a line to or from the memory. We therefore included a line buffer which is loaded or unloaded by character I/O operations. The record I/O operations transmit information between the line buffer and the external devices via *channel buffers* (see Figure 5.4.). These enabled the switching of channels as required for MITEM to be carried out. The current line can be recovered via record operations, which merely move information between a channel buffer and the line buffer, without affecting the external device.

Any I/O request to a peripheral device must specify the device number. Since STAGE2 permitted the use of up to 9 channels and MITEM up to 32, we made use of the VAL field to specify the channel number. The FLG field of the same word was used to hold the completion code which reflects what happened to the operation (see Section 3.2.). Character I/O operations also set the FLG field, either to indicate that an end of line symbol has been read on input, or to inform the program that the line buffer is full during output of an overlength line.

In designing this I/O package [29] to satisfy the requirements of both *STAGE2* and *MITEM*, we anticipated that we might be able to use it for a wider range of abstract machines. Since the I/O environment must be recoded for any actual computer, the use of a generalized package would permit the implementation effort to be spread over a number of abstract machines, thereby reducing the cost of obtaining a particular piece of portable software. In practice this has not turned out to be the case. The package has too rigid a structure, particularly with regard to its organisation of buffers, to qualify as a general system. Again we have got into difficulties by placing too much emphasis on the needs of a particular problem, in this case *MITEM*. Even for *STAGE2*, we find that the system imposes some unnecessary inefficiencies, for example, the channel buffers are not really required by this program. Further, the effort required to obtain an efficient implementation on some systems has proved larger than we anticipated. For these reasons, a new version of the I/O system [30,31] has been designed which is more in keeping with the principles outlined in Section 3.2. In this version, the boundary between the abstract machine and the environment has been greatly simplified, and its only function now is to control the flow of information to and from the channels. It is simpler to realize on actual machines and efficient versions are more readily obtainable.

In the foregoing sections, we have discussed the design of the abstract machines in relation to the requirements of the problem and the structure of real machines. Now we must consider what limitations were imposed by the tools used to realize the models. The first abstract machine, *FLUB*, was created for the purpose of implementing *STAGE2*, the tool to be used for realising other abstract machines. Since *STAGE2* was not available, a much simpler macro processor was used to realize *FLUB* and initiate the bootstrap sequence. It recognized templates in a somewhat similar manner to *STAGE2* but the parameters could only be single characters. Hence the operands of *FLUB* statements were restricted to single characters or fixed length strings of characters. Two types of operands were required : register names and program labels. Hence *FLUB* was provided with 36 registers named A-Z and 0-9. All program labels consisted of 2 digits. e.g. the *FLUB* statement

$$TO \quad 67 \quad IF \quad FLG \quad A = B$$

transfers control to label *67* if the *FLG* field of register *A* is equal to the *FLG* field of register *B*. The corresponding template is

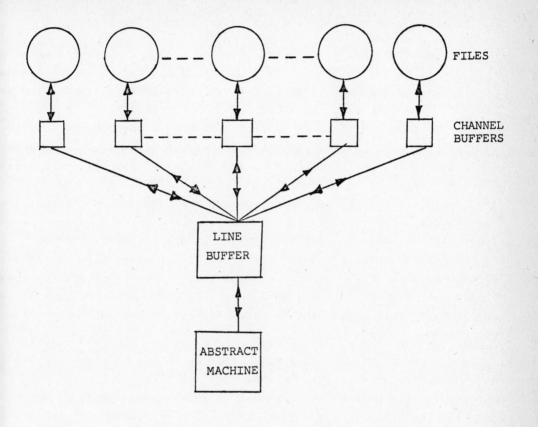

Figure 5.4.

Input-Output System

```
TO '' IF FLG ' = '
```

where the apostrophe represents a single character parameter.

Once *FLUB* was realized on an actual machine, *STAGE2* became available and the simple macro processor could be discarded. *TEXED* was therefore the first abstract machine whose design was based on the use of *STAGE2* and we were able to provide ourselves with a more convenient language for programming *MITEM* than we had for *STAGE2*. We removed the restrictions on *FLUB* operands and permitted the use of strings, for example, as identifiers for manifest and character constants. The register/memory transfer operations also differed from those in *FLUB* since they reflec ted the fact that the *TEXED* memory can be divided into an arbitrary number of arrays by declarations. The format for labels was changed so that identifiers could be used instead of 2 digit integers. Also, pseudo operations were introduced to delimit procedures with a procedure heading consisting of an identifier and a list of formal parameters specifying register fields. A call on a procedure could also include a list of actual parameters comprising register fields and manifest oR character constants.

A complete list of *TEXED* statements is given in Figure 5.5. Statements marked with an asterisk are those available in *FLUB*. The single apostrophe is used to mark the position of a parameter. When *STAGE2* matches a source text line against one of these templates, it will assign a character string to each parameter, which can then be used to control the process of generating code.

5.2.   *PORTING AND ADAPTING*

The first stage in the process of implementing a piece of portable software involves realizing the underlying abstract machine by expressing its basic operations and data types in terms of the basic operations and data types of the target computer. The essentials of this process have been outlined in section 4. Now let us consider in more detail how *FLUB* and *TEXED* can be mapped onto existing machines.

Since the data structure described in the last section is fundamental to the design of these machines, the first question that must be asked is how much space will be required to represent each field. This depends on the information to be stored in each field which, for *FLUB*, may be

1. Data Transfer Operations

(a) Register to Register

* FLG ' = '
  VAL ' = '
  PTR ' = '
  REG ' = '
* VAL ' = PTR '
* PTR ' = VAL '

(b) Register to Memory

* GET ' = '
* STO ' = '
  SET ' = '(')
  SET '(') = '
  ARRAY ' = Ø

(c) Register to stack

PUSH ' ON '
POP ' FROM '
EMPTY ' STACK

2. Integer Arithmetic

(a) VAL field arithmetic

* VAL ' = ' + '
* VAL ' = ' - '

(b) PTR field arithmetic

* PTR ' = ' + '
* PTR ' = ' - '
* PTR ' = ' * '
* PTR ' = ' / '

3. Control operations

a) Unconditional

* STOP
* TO '
  CALL '(')
* TO ' BY '
  RETURN
* RETURN BY

(b) Conditional

* TO ' IF FLG ' = '   * TO ' IF PTR ' = '
* TO ' IF FLG ' NE '   * TO ' IF PTR ' NE '
* TO ' IF VAL ' = '   TO ' IF PTR ' GT '
* TO ' IF VAL ' NE '   * TO ' IF PTR ' GE '
  TO ' IF VAL ' GT '
  TO ' IF VAL ' GE '

4. Input Output Operations

(a) Character I/O

* VAL ' = CHAR
* CHAR = VAL '
  LOAD MESSAGE '

(b) Line I/O

FORWARD SKIP '   WRITE CURRENT '
READ CURRENT '   * WRITE NEXT '
* READ NEXT '   WRITE ENDFILE '
                     * REWIND '
                       BACKSPACE '
                     * MESSAGE ' TO '

5. Declarations

CONSTANT ' = '   PROC'(')
DECLARE ARRAY'(')   * LOC '
DECLARE STACK (')   COMMENT
MESSAGE'(')   END COMMENT

Figure 5.5.

TEXED Machine Instruction

*(Instructions preceded by an * are those also
available on the FLUB machine)*

summarized as follows :

>   FLG -   0, 1, 2, 3
>   VAL -   non-negative integers representing characters
>   or string lengths, - 1
>   PTR -   address in memory or program,value of an inte-
>   ger arithmetic expression constructed by the
>   user.

Clearly the space required for some of these quantities will best be
determined by the characteristics of the target machine. However, let
us first enquire what is the minimum number of bits needed to represent
a FLUB word. Only 2 are required for FLG; for the VAL field,
6 would be sufficient if we restrict ourselves to a character set consisting of upper case characters, digits and a few control symbols.
(This would require the user of STAGE2 to avoid constructing strings
of length greater than 64 characters). With 10 bits allocated to
the PTR field, we might therefore expect to be able to map the FLUB
word directly onto an 18 bit machine. (Program addresses could be
handled by storing an index to a table of addresses rather than the address itself). Unfortunately,experience has shown us that 1024 words
of FLUB memory are insufficient for other than the most trivial of
problems. We need about 4K words before useful problems can be solved.
This sets the minimum limit to 20 bits.

Economical use of bits is not the only factor which determines how we
map the word of the abstract machine. This could be classed as optimization for space; the other side of the coin, optimization for speed,
is also important. We have already paid some attention to this during
the design of the machines by providing the registers, to save packing
or unpacking the fields at every operation. However, some consideration
must be given to the way the memory access instruction will operate
when one is deciding how to lay out the fields. For example, there would
be little point in choosing a representation which optimized the space
required if no instructions were available to extract information from
the various fields.

Another factor which can affect the decision is the representaion of a
character on the target machine. The implementor is free to choose the
internal representation subject to the constraint that the characters
0-9 are represented by successive integers. Although he may be satisfied with a restricted character set requiring only 6 bits, he may
not wish to incur conversion overheads in the I/O to transform the

hardware representation to the internal one. Thus, on a byte oriented machine with characters represented by integers in the range 0-255, he may choose to assign 8 bits to the *VAL* field.

Having fixed a representation for the data structures we must next enquire how the registers will be implemented. In section 5.1., we pointed out that the cost of allocating one target computer word to each field was not prohibitive (108 words). Further, a uniform representation simplifies the translation process. Most instructions operate on one field of a register independently of other fields in the same register. We can therefore consider a register as consisting of three separate entities. The field rather than the register is the basic unit of information in most operations. This means that the number of instructions to be implemented can be decreased. For example, we no longer need to consider the addition of *VAL* fields and the addition of *PTR* fields as separate instructions. Both are simply instances of an instruction which adds one field to another and leave the result in the third field. A uniform representation of the fields is therefore the logical first choice. However, it can be worthwhile paying some attention to the way the hardware registers are organized on the target machine.

In section 3.2.,we categorized various register/processor organizations. For machines with no programmable registers or a single arithmetic register, the only course of action is to map the registers of the abstract machine into memory in a uniform way. However, for machines with multiple arithmetic registers or a register file, it may be possible to map some or all of the abstract registers directly onto hardware registers. This could result in a considerable increase in execution speed at the cost of a more complicated translation process. We will describe one such application in more detail later in this section.

Let us now consider how these general principles have been applied in practice. On a 16 bit Modular One with a single arithmetic register, two words were required for each *FLUB* word. The first was used to hold the *PTR* field and the two bytes in the second word were assigned to the *FLG* and *VAL* fields respectively. The register fields were mapped uniformly into core. On a 24 bit machine, one might expect to use only one word to hold the data structure. However, on a *32K* machine, we will need 16 bits for the *PTR* field in order to access any location in memory. This leaves 6 bits for the *VAL* field. Although this is sufficient, in practice, it is not very convenient since

STAGE2 could not be used to process normal card input if any line contained more than 64 characters. Hence on a machine like the *CDC 3200*, we have it found it best to use two 24-bit words to hold the 3 fields.

Moving now to 32-bit machines, we can take as an example *System/360*. If we use the hardware representation for character, we need 10 bits for the *FLG* and *VAL* fields. This leaves 22 bits for *PTR* which, at first sight, may not appear to be sufficient to hold the 24-bit address used on this machine. We might therefore conclude that again we must allocate two words for the three fields. However, here is a situation where a trade-off between space and speed is possible. An implementation can be made which saves space at the cost of some additional complexity in the generated code.

If we pack the three fields into one word, 21 bits are available for storing an address, since 1 bit must be reserved for a sign. This address may be increased to an effective 23 bits by arranging that the start of each *FLUB* word corresponds to a full word boundary. This can be done by suitable choice of origin. Each address then ends in two zeros which carry no information and may be discarded. Either of the operations which access memory must now calculate the actual address from the contents of the *PTR* field before using it. Notice also that the memory mapping factor must be changed. Although the number of target address units/abstract word is 4, we only need to add 1 to the contents of a *PTR* field to obtain the address of the next abstract word. Effectively, the *PTR* field contains an abstract address rather than an actual one.

By restricting the *PTR* field to 22 bits, only one half of the possible address space on *System/360* is available to the program. In practice, this has not proved to be a serious limitation. If we increase the size of the *PTR* field to store more address bits, then we will have to use two words for each abstract word, thereby also halving the available memory space. We may be prepared to incur this penalty, if the speed of the program can be increased. If a double word is also used to implement each register with the *FLG*, *VAL* and *PTR* fields represented respectively by 1, 2 and 4 bytes, then we can avoid the overheads of packing and unpacking. Memory/registers transfers can now be implemented as *MOVE CHARACTER* or *LOAD* and *STORE MULTIPLE* operations. The choice of how the abstract machine will be represented rests with the implementor and will depend on which characteristics of the program he wishes to optimize.

For machines with a word size larger than 32 bits, one word is usually sufficient to hold the three fields. The allocation of bits will depend on what instructions are available to pack and unpack the fields.

In section 5.1., we have already made some mention of the problems we
have encountered implementing the I/O system for these abstract machines and the steps that have been taken to improve the situation. We do
not propose to go into any great detail here. The system is implemented
as a collection of subroutines with integer arguments. A version exists
in *ANSI FORTRAN* which serves both as a document describing the logic of
of the package and a means for implementing the system quickly on any
machine which has a *FORTRAN* compiler. Our experience has been that
the *FORTRAN* version is very slow and assembly code versions are needed
for efficient operations. One of the difficulties is that all I/O requests, even character-only operations, are via subroutine calls. This
imposes severe overheads. In the new version, record I/O operations
remain as routine calls but a character operation can be implemented as
in line code. This operates on the line buffer as a simple fetch or store and improves the efficiency of the package considerably.

Now let us return again to the problem of realizing abstract machines
on actual computers and consider ways in which this could be improved
for the two machines we are studying. Our objective will be to increase
the *efficiency* of the generated code, where the term *efficiency* has
implications with respect to both space and speed. Clearly this is a
very necessary objective if one is producing portable software since it
is of little value to port a program and then find it is too slow to
use or too large to fit in the memory. It may be argued that the techniques we will describe are best classified under the heading of *optimization*. However, this term conventionally refers to those processes
used by high level language compilers to improve the efficiency of the
generated object code. Such improvements are usually carried out only
on the basis of a static analysis of the program and do not take into
account any of its dynamic characteristics. Further the programmer is
unable to control the way the optimization takes place, For instance,
he cannot choose to reduce the size of the program at the cost of a higher *CPU* utilization. As we will demonstrate, the techniques we use take into account both the static and dynamic characteristics of a program
to improve the mapping of the abstract machine on the real one. We can
also readily control the balance between space and speed. Thus we are
able to *adapt* a program to satisfy various constraints imposed by the
                                                              system

or hardware of the target machine. Earlier we defined *adaptability* as the property of a program which allows it to be altered to fit differing user images and system constraints, and suggested that it is largely concerned with changes in the structure of the algorithm. In the following examples, the transformation of the program will not involve changes in the sequence of instructions; rather, it will only affect the way the program is realized on the target machines. However, a key factor will be the ease with which we can change the code generation of the translator. It is for this reason that we choose to discuss the techniques under the heading of *adaptibility*. We will describe three experiments which illustrate how the following objectives were achieved :

(a)   minimization of *CPU* utilization

(b)   minimization of core occupancy

(c)   balancing space versus speed.

The first experiment was carried out for both *FLUB* and *TEXED* on the *ICL KDF9*. This is a 48-bit machine which has 15 registers called Q-stores and two stacks, one for arithmetic operations and the other for subroutine linkage. Each register is divided into three 16-bit fields and there are arithmetic and conditional instructions which operate on these fields. The match between the abstract machines and the real one is very good but fortuitous. As we have described, the design of *FLUB* and *TEXED* were based on the requirements of the problems and not on ease of mapping onto the *KDF9*. The choice of a representation for the abstract word in terms of the real one was straightforward. The machine has *32K* words of memory and 16 bits are therefore sufficient for the *PTR* field. Since information may be transferred between memory and the registers via the stack, the other fields were also allocated 16 bits each. The choice of a representation for the abstract registers was not so obvious. We wished to make use of as many of the real registers as possible but the problem was to decide which of the 36 registers of the abstract machine should be mapped directly onto the hardware. We first made a naive realization in which each of the register fields was allocated one machine word. Once the program was running, we altered the macros so that extra code was generated to gather statistics. The resulting program was then run on a comprehensive set of data to measure which registers were used most frequently. This data was combined with the results of a static analysis of register usage and used to allocate Q-stores to the registers of the abstract machine.

The macros were then rewritten to generate code sequences which depended on which registers were involved in the operation. At the same time, other forms of optimization were introduced (use of immediate operands 0 and 1 etc). Subsequent measuremants showed that the optimized programs were about twice as fast as the unoptimized ones. It is important to realize that because of the ease with which one can change the code generators in *STAGE2*, only a few man-days of effort were required to to produce the optimized versions.

The degree of optimization achieved in this experiment was of course largely due to the similarity between the real and abstract machines. However, the question of optimizing the use of hardware registers has also arisen on other machines. For example on *ATLAS* with 128 registers, there was no question as to how the abstract registers should be implemented. On the other hand, for *System/360*, this approach is of little value since so many registers are already required for accumulators, base register, subroutine linkage etc.

In the second experiment, the objective was to reduce the size of *MITEM* on an *ICL 4/7o* a machine with an architecture similar to that of *System/360*. At the time, core was limited and we wanted to fit *MITEM* into a small interactive partition to continue testing. We already had a version in assembly code with one word mapped onto 8 bytes and optimized to use immediate operands wherever possible. However, it would only run in a batch partition. The approach taken to cut down the amount of core required by the program was to realize *TEXED* as an interpreter.

The form of the code to be interpreted reflects the structure of the abstract machine and the characteristics of the program itself. *TEXED* accesses 108 register fields and permits the use of an unspecified number of constants. *MITEM* only uses about 100 constants so that the total number of operands is less than 256. Only 1 byte is therefore required to address an operand in a global array of register fields and constants. Although there are more than 256 labels in the entire program, there are less than this number in any one procedure. Further, since *MITEM* contains no direct jumps into or out of any procedure, labels are strictly local.This means that any label can also be specified by a single byte which is used to access an array of local addresses associated with each procedure. Since there are less than 256 procedures in the program, procedure addresses can be stored on a global array and indexed by a 1-byte operand of a procedure call. An examination of the remaining instructions shows that all other operands can also be represented by a single byte.

With a uniform representation of the register fields, we found that 28 instructions were required to implement the interpreter. Since the number of operands in an instruction varies between 0 and 3, we could either arrange for operators to take a variable number of operands or use a fixed format. In this version of the interpreter, we chose the latter course. Each instruction is 4 bytes long and consists of an operation code and up to 3 operands. This representation wastes some space but simplifies the interpreter and speeds up its inner loop.

With the design of the interpreter complete, we then rewrote the macros to translate *TEXED* into the interpretive code. This required only a few man weeks of effort, again because of the ease with which we could adapt *STAGE2*. The resultant program occupied *16K* bytes (excluding I/O) which is 40 % of the size of the optimized assembly code version. *1K* bytes were required to implement the interpreter itself. We estimate that the interpretive version is about an order of magnitude more expensive with respect to *CPU* utilization than the directly executable one. We have saved space and paid for it in speed.

Any decision to use a fully interpretive version of a piece of portable software will obviously rest on how important it is to have that program available in a particular installation. An implementation which is expensive on *CPU* time may be better than no program at all. However, the two cases we have considered so far represent extreme positions. In the first example, we were optimizing for speed and in the second, for space. One is therefore tempted to ask whether it is possible to produce a version of the program in which these two resources are balanced to suit the needs of a particular environment. This is what we have attempted to answer in the third experiment.

Once an interpretive version of the program is available, then it is a relatively simple matter to obtain a frequency histogram showing the number of times each instruction is obeyed when the program is processing a standard set of test data, The necessary code to gather statistics can be inserted into the main loop of the interpreter and the *STOP* routine modified to output the histogram. For convenience,this can refer not to individual instructions but to sequences of instructions between one label and the next. When this operation was carried out for *MITEM* running under the interpreter described in the last example, we found that the program was spending a major portion of its time in small localized areas. These were the routines to set up the current line as a list and the one to search a line for a particular pattern. It was clear that if these routines could be executed directly rather than interpretively while the remainder of the program was left in the interpretive form, then we could speed up the program considerably with only a marginal increase in size. We therefore set out to produce a hybrid version of the program.

The first stage was to rewrite the interpreter so that operators took a variable number of operands. This increased overheads for interpretation but reduced the size of the interpretive code still further. At the same time, the number of operators was increased to enable more space to be saved by optimizing instructions which contained frequently used constants. The net result was that although the amount of space required by the interpreter increased to 1700 bytes, the size of the interpretive code was reduced by 30 %. We then altered the macros which generated this interpretive code to produce directly executable code as well. Before translation commences, label pairs are read in to define the areas of the program which are to be translated into directly executable code. The normal generation mode is interpretive but a switch to the other mode takes place when a label is encountered which matches the first label in one of the pairs. Reversion to normal mode occurs when the second label is detected. Thus the generation process is completely parameterized and the form of the program can readily be altered by reading in a new set of label pairs.

We have produced a hybrid version of *MITEM* with the routines which use up most of the *CPU* time translated into directly executable code.The resultant program is still the same size as the fully interpretive version produced in the second experiment; that is, the reduction in the space required for the interpretive code has compensated for the extra space needed for the directly executable code. However, the program is now only 10 % slower than the optimized assembly code version. This figure can easily be reduced at the expense of using more core. Thus an installation could select the appropriate balance between space and speed to suit their own particular requirements.

The results of these experiments suggest that these techniques could be very powerful ones for tailoring a piece of software to meet differing criteria for optimality. For example when constructing an operating system, one could proceed with the writing of a module and defer any decision about its final form until after it has been integrated with the remainder of the system and the appropriate measurements made. Infre-

quently used modules could operate interpretively to minimize core and
backing store occupancy; critical sections could be optimized for speed
to maintain throughput and response; other modules could exist in a hybrid form. However, there still remains the problem of what to do with
a program which has been compressed in size as far as possible, yet is
still too large to satisfy some constraint on space. The only solution
here appears to be to construct the program in the first place so that
it is adaptable. By automatically changing the algorithm, it may then be
be possible to reduce its demands for space. Unfortunately, this is
not something that can be done as an afterthought. It must be built into
the design of the program in the first place. Again, we will use *MITEM*
to illustrate an approach to the problem of constructing adaptable software.

A text editor is a fairly common module which one would expect to find
on most online systems. They vary from simple editors which merely insert and delete lines on the basis of an associated line number to programs which can locate a position in a file of text by searching for a
complex pattern. In writing a portable text editor, we had to plan to
satisfy a wide range of user requirements. If the problem contains too
many facilities, it might be too large to include in some systems; too
few facilities, on the other hand, might result in the program not being adopted on the grounds that it was not powerful enough. Further,
some facilities, for example the interrupt flip-flop, might be impossible to implement on a particular system. Our approach was to include
many facilities and allow an installation to select those which it wished to make available to its users. *MITEM* contains 6 versions and
a number of options incorporated within the one body of text. Before generation, the user declares which version and what options he wants and
STAGE2 then adapts the input text accordingly. Routines and declarations not required for the version and options requested are ignored.
Since *STAGE2* is line oriented, it is also possible to change code sequences within a routine by prefixing statements with appropriate headers. Such lines may then be selectively included or ignored according
to the initial declarations. The resultant programs vary from *MITEM 1*
(a simple context editor operating on 4 streams and channels) up to
MITEM 6 (which manipulates up to 8 streams and 32 channels). Excluding I/O, the size of *MITEM 6* is 3 times that of *MITEM 1*. Typically, one might expect to make *MITEM 2* or *3* available for everyday
use and only use *MITEM 6* when more esoteric text manipulation facilities are required. The choice is up to the installation and depends on
what core is available and what facilities it decides should be made

available to the users.

5.3.   *REVIEW AND EVALUATION*

We have described two abstract machine models used to produce portable
and adaptable software. We have noted that the programs based on these
models have been moved easily from one machine to another and modified
to meet a variety of user requirements and system constraints. The implementations have resulted in usable software of reasonable efficiency.
Typical implementation times have been of the order of 1-4 man weeks
regardless of the software of the target computer but assuming reasonable access to the machine and a good turn around. We estimate that at
least one order of magnitude more effort would be required to recode the
programs for a new machine and achieve comparable efficiency and reliability.

However, as we have noted in our discussion, the approach is not without
its problems. A major difficulty lies in the design of the abstract machine itself. This is not an easy task since the design is intimately
linked with the algorithm and may not be clearly visible until after the
algorithm has been encoded. For each of our models, we have noted design
deficiencies which have become apparent through implementing the programs on a number of machines. We believe that these deficiencies were
caused by our emphasing the relationship of the model to the problem
and not taking sufficient account of the structure of real machines.
Since our objective is to produce software for today's machines, our models must be influenced by the current architecture. We hope that this
will not preclude us from moving the programs onto the next generation
of computers but, if there are marked changes in the structure of machines, then we will have to accept some degree of inefficiency. However,
we suggest that it is better to have working software, albeit inefficient than no software at all.

Another major problem with the approach is that it leads to a diversity
of language and hence to an increase in the cost of realizing many abstract machines. Although each machine is easy to realize, we can rarely make use of the macros developed for one abstract machine when we come to implement another one. Although this is not strictly true for
FLUB and *TEXED* because of the close similarity between the two machines, it becomes very apparent when one compares them with *AIMI*, a machine developed to implement an interpretive *BASIC* system [32].Yet when

we examine a number of different designs we find that there is a common
set of basic operations and data types. This suggests that the way ahead
lies in creating a *general purpose* abstract machine model which embo-
dies this common set, yet which is still capable of being extended to reflect the characteristics of a particular problem. This model can serve
as a starting point for the design of special purpose abstract machines
and ensure that the resulting programs are both portable and inexpensive
to implement. We shall pursue this theme in more detail in the subsequent sections.

6. LOW LEVEL LANGUAGES FOR ABSTRACT MACHINES

In Section 5. we presented two examples of early abstract machines
which were designed on an individual basis. We have pointed out the inadequacy of this process and the need for a uniform framework which em-
bodies the common set of basic operations, data types and organizational
features discussed in Section 3.2. To build this framework, we shall
reason from the properties of real computers summarised in Section 3.1.
This approach differs from the one taken by Goos in his discussion of
language characteristics (Goos B), which was based primarily upon convenience for the programmer.

We do not mean to imply that programmer convenience should be ignored.
It must, however, be evaluated in conjunction with such constraints as
translator complexity, object code efficiency and portability. The balance to be struck depends upon the intended applications of the software. We are firmly committed to the belief that portable software must
be based on the full bootstrap implementation technique. In Section 4.
we explained how *STAGE2* could be made available on the target computer. The next step is a more complex translator, say for a language such
as that disussed by Goos. This translator must be expressed in a language which can be translated by *STAGE2*, the only tool guaranted to be
available.

6.1. THE BASIC HARDWARE MODEL

Figure 6.1. shows the register/processor organisation on which we
shall base our low level language framework. The picture is mainly intended to provide a concrete peg upon which to hang our concept of evaluation. We shall explain below how we can relate this model of evalu-

235

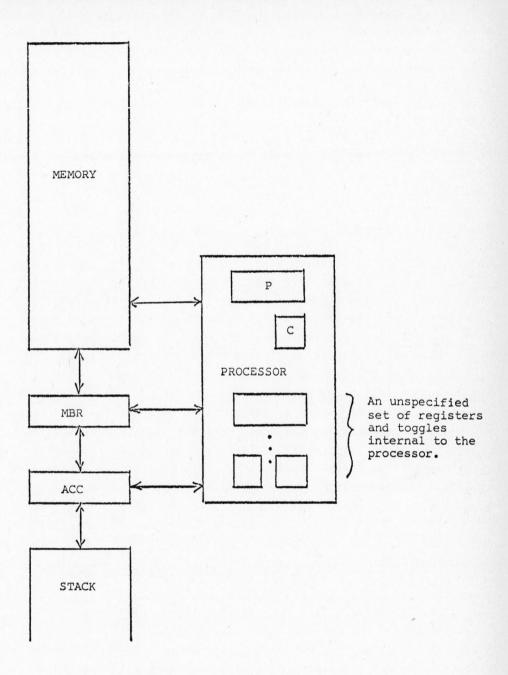

Figure 6.1.

The Basic Hardware Model

ation to the major register/processor organisation summarized in Section 3.2. In order to discuss the model, we shall assume that the processor is capable of performing integer arithmetic. *This should be construed to mean that it is incapable of other operations or, in fact, that it is necessarily capable od integer arithmetic.*

The processor accepts two operands, one from the accumulator (*ACC*) and the other from the memory buffer register (*MBR*). It returns any result to the accumulator. If the operation is not commutative (for example, a subtraction), then the left operand is assumed to be in *ACC* and the right operand in *MBR*. The single operand for a monadic operator is taken from *ACC*.

Each operator corresponds to a single instruction. If the operator is monadic, the instruction does not specify an operand. If the operator is dyadic, then the instruction specifies an operand. The operand may be a constant, the contents of a memory location, or the contents of the top location of the stack. In the last two cases the operand is placed in *MBR* and the operation is executed. In the third case the contents of *ACC* are transferred to *MBR*, the operand is placed in *ACC* and the stack is popped up. Then the operation is executed.

A set of load operations is also provided. A load instruction always specifies an operand as above. It replaces the contents of *ACC* with its operand, after modifying the operand in some way. For example, a *load negative* instruction would replace the contents of *ACC* with the negative of its operand. There is one load instruction which does not modify its operand.

There is one store instruction. It specifies either a memory location or the top of the stack. The contents of the accumulator are stored in the specified memory location or pushed onto the top of the stack. The contents of the accumulator are not altered by a store operation.

We assert that an acceptably efficient realization of this model is possible for any of the register/processor organizations discussed in Section 3.2. Moreover, we assert that the conversion of abstract machine code to target computer instructions can be carried out by a simple processor.

Stack-organized computers fit the model almost exactly. The only mismatch is in the load and store operations : usually a load instruction on a stack machine pushes down the stack, saving the contents. In our model, the load operation destroys the previous contents of *ACC*. conversely, the store operation of a stack machine usually pops up the stack. This means that the value is lost, whereas in our model the contents of *ACC* is preserved.

These differences provide no serious obstacles. Stack machines have instructions for duplicating the top element and erasing it. Our load operation could then be realized by erasing the top element before loading, and our store by duplicating before storing. We would not actually generate the duplicate and store until we had looked ahead to the next instruction. If it is a load, then both the duplicate and erase can be omitted.

The match is also quite good for a computer with a single arithmetic register. Here the only problem is the stack, which must be simulated in memory. There is no need to simulate the detailed movement of the stack pointer at run time, since the translator can easily keep track of most of the changes. We shall say more about this below, in connection with procedures.

An instruction specifiing a non-commutative operator is a bit tedious if its operand is the top of the stack. Unless the target computer permits, say, a *subtract from memory* operation, the contents of the arithmetic register must be stored, and then the register loaded with the operand from the stack before the operation can take place.

The remaining three organizations are essentially variants of the single arithmetic register. All of them require more complex optimization to make best use of their facilities. The basic technique is to simulate the single register computer, but allow the register or storage location which simulates *ACC* to vary with time. For example, in the case of a computer with no registers, we would look ahead to the next store instruction. That instruction specifies some memory location (which may be a simulated entry in the stack). Simply translate all intervening instructions, using the operand of the store operation as *ACC*, and then omit the store operation. Optimization for multiple registers or a register file is similar : one register is selected to simulate *ACC*. A store instruction whose operand is the stack is ignored, and another register selected to simulate *ACC*. If too many temporary registers are required, then one is freed by actually storing contents.

There is evidence [33,34] to indicate that complex optimization facilities do not pay their way in improved code. Similar results may well apply to the three cases discussed above. Only measurements on actual code could answer this question, and we feel that we must at least indicate what sort of optimisation is possible.

We need not specify a memory organization for the basic model. Different memory organizations can be accommodated by the additional registers and toggles internal to the processor. These could be base registers, toggles which determine the level of memory addresses, etc. Remember that this model is simply a framework within which to design abstract machines; it is not a particular abstract machine, since it specifies only the core discussed in Section 3.3.

An operand may be a constant, a reference to the top entry in the stack, or a reference to memory. References to memory may involve data aggregates. We use index modification as the data aggregate access mechanism, for the reasons discussed in Section 3.2. Instructions which reference single items have a different form than instructions which reference data aggregates. A modifier is attached to the normal instruction. This modifier specifies a memory location and a signed integer. The contents of the specified memory location (which is assumed to be a signed integer) is added to the normal operand of the instruction to provide the effective address. After the operation has been completed, the contents of the memory location used as an index is altered by adding to it the signed integer from the modifier.

Such a data aggregate reference can be realized in a straightforward way using any of the mechanisms summarized in Section 3.2. In each of the first two cases, the computation is carried out and the result placed in the proper location. If the target computer actually employs index modification, then an index register is loaded from the memory location specified by the modifier. Since any alteration of the index is specified by the same instruction, this modification can be carried out while the value is still in the index register. It is therefore possible to use any target machine instructions which increment or decrement index registers. The normal optimizations can be applied if the target computer has multiple index registers.

In Section 3.2. we argued that a high level model should be used for a procedure call. This is done by permitting a procedure with arguments as an operand in any instruction except store. The value of the

operand is the value left in *ACC* by the procedure. If the operator
is not a load, then a procedure operand implies that the contents of
ACC is pushed into the stack before the procedure is called. When
the procedure returns, leaving a value in *ACC*, the operation continues as though the operand had specified the top entry of the stack.

Our model has one I/O instruction [31]. The value of the operand is
the memory address of an area which contains the full specification of
the operation. This specification consists of five integers. The
first two are the operation code and logical unit number, while the
interpretation of the last three depends upon the particular request.
For data transmission requests, they define the participating memory
area by giving the base address and indices of the first and last word.

We did not discuss transfers of control in Section 3.2. A transfer of
control is an instruction whose operand specifies the target location.
The value of the operand replaces the contents of the program counter
(*P*). Any number of transfer operations could be definded. Our basic
model only *requires* three :

- Transfer unconditionally.
- Transfer if the condition code (*C*) is *true*.
- Transfer if the condition code is *false*.

The condition code is set by some operations, and left undisturbed by
the rest. Our model makes no explicit assumptions about which operations affect the condition code or how they affect it.

6.2.   *A FRAMEWORK FOR LOW LEVEL LANGUAGES*

The basic hardware model presented in Section 6.1. is only a skeleton. In order to design an abstract machine for a particular problem,
this skeleton must be *fleshed out* by specifying a set of operators
and data types appropriate to the problem. There is a framework for
designing low level languages which corresponds to the skeleton hardware. It too must be *fleshed out* to produce a particular language.
We call this framework *Janus*, because it looks both to the programmer and to the machine.

Janus is *line-oriented*. It is possible to translate languages based upon *Janus* by considering one line of input text at a time. Input lines are divided into two classes :

- Declarations. The first four characters of a declaration line are either DCL⊔ or END⊔ . A declaration line provides information for the translator, informing it about the program structure, the operators and the types of variables.

- Executable lines. Any line which is not a declaration is an executable line. An executable line is to be translated into a sequence of machine instructions.

Particular languages based on *Janus* may provide different conventions for recognizing declarations. For example, DCL might be omitted, and keywords denoting type (e.g. INTEGER) used instead. In general, however, the DCL is required. We would not know which words to reserve because we do not know what data types will be required. Remember that our hardware model does not specify any data types, and hence *Janus* must not.

In our hardware model, an instruction is an *action* which changes the state of the machine in some way. We conceive of these actions as occuring in some well defined order, which is significant in determining the result. Since the order is significant, it must be reflected in *Janus*.

Let us consider an instruction which adds an integer from memory to the contents of the accumulator. Like most instructions, it specifies an operand. One way of writing such an instruction would be :

        ADD   B

Here the operator is 'ADD' and the operand is the contents of the memory location called 'B'. The instruction could also have been written with a plus as the operator :

                + B

There is really no change of meaning here, but we must tread carefully. This construction does not have quite the same connotations as the conventional mathematical notation. There + serves to combine two values, whereas here it is an imperative command to operate upon one value with another.

Suppose now that we wish to combine several instructions in order to place the sum of two integers into a memory location. Such a sequence of instructions could be expressed by :

```
    LOAD  A                              A
    ADD   B           or               + B
    STORE C                            → C
```

Again, the instructions on the right are identical in meaning to those on the left. I am simply using different codes for the operations.

Placing the sum of two integers into a memory location is often an atomic action when one thinks in terms of an entire algorithm. Thus it would be more convenient to gather the three instructions of the previous paragraph into a single line of executable code :

$$A + B → C$$

It is extremely important to recognize that nothing had been changed by this rewrite. Each operator performs an action, and the actions are taken in a well-defined sequence. We simply choose to write all three operations on one line because they happen to be related.

When the contents of ACC is stored into memory, it is not altered. Thus we may operate upon it further, storing the modified value in some other place :

$$A + B → C + D → E$$

There is no limit to this process.

The   *current expression* is the *Janus* analog of ACC.   Each dyadic operator takes the current expression as its left operand. There is no precedence of operators, and evaluation is strictly from left to right. These conventions arise directly from the development sketched in the previous paragraphs. A *Janus* expression is a means of expressing a sequence of instructions which performs some atomic action in the program. It is not an expression in the classical sence of mathematics, where the operators represent ways of combining their operands.

It can be argued that if one is going to write sequences of symbols which look like normal arithmetic expressions, then one should make them them act like such expressions by adhering to normal precedence conventions. There is merit in these arguments if the expressions are going to be used by mathematicians to solve mathematical problems. However, we are not in that position. We are specifying algorithms which are fundamentally non-numeric, and we must control the sequence of operations at a basic level. In any case, *normal* precedence conventions deal only with the common arithmetic and logical operators. We do not have well-established rules for all operators which we may encounter in designing an abstract machine.

Operator precedence permits us to write expressions whose evaluation requires temporary storage, without forcing us to mention this storage explcitly. Remember that in section 3.2. we argued the need for avoiding explicit references to temporary storage. We must therefore provide an alternate mechanism, the *deferred expression*.

A deferred expression in *Janus* corresponds to the stack. When an expression is deferred, it means that the contents of ACC is pushed onto the stack. Any number of expressions may be deferred. To indicate that the current expression is to be deferred, the user simply writes a left parenthesis and begins the new current expression. The deferred expression is popped from the stack when the matching right parenthesis is encountered. Several examples of deferred expressions are givem in Figure 6.2. If an operator precedes the left parenthesis, then the deferred expression is its left operand and the new current expression is its right operand. In Figure 6.2a., for example, the left operand of + is the value of $A*B$ and the right operand is the value of $C*D$. Figure 6.2b. shows a situation where there is no operator before the left parenthesis. In this case, the value of the deferred expression is simply reloaded into ACC. The value of the expression within the parenthesis is lost.

The contents of ACC does not change when an expression is deferred. Figure 6.2c. shows how the translator can be informed not to reload ACC after the expression has been deferred. (This sequence is the classic method of multiplying a number by 10 on a binary machine without multiplying). *LEFT* is a shift operator whose right operand is the number of places *ACC* is to be shifted left.

$$A * B + (C * D)$$

(a)   Deferring one operand while evaluating another

$$X (Y \rightarrow X) \rightarrow Y$$

(b)   Exchanging two variables

$$P \quad LEFT \quad 1 + (() \quad LEFT \quad 2)$$

(c)   Avoiding an unwanted load instruction.

Figure 6.2.

Deferred Expressions

Our hardware model provides only a single index for a reference to a data aggregate. Hence only singly-dimensioned arrays are allowed in *Janus*. The syntax of an array reference mirrors the structure of the operand exactly :

$$W (J + 17) D3$$

W is the name of the array in this example, J is the index variable and $D3$ indicates that the index is to be decremented by 3 following the reference.

Professor Goos has discussed the problem of array elements which occupy more than one storage location, and we have mentioned it in connection with the implementation of $FLUB$ (see section 5.1.). This problem affects the translation of an array reference. Let us suppose, for example, that W is an array of $FLUB$ words as realised on $System/360$. Each element of W thus occupies 8 storage locations.

According to our abstract machine model, the actual numbers in the instruction must be stated in terms of storage locations. From the programmer's point of view, however, the numbers 17 and 3 in the reference above are considered to be indices. That is to say, he is referencing the 17th element of W beyond that addressed by J. After the reference takes place, J should be modified to address the 3rd element of W before that currently addressed.

The translator performs the adjustment of 17 and 3 on the basis of information contained in the declaration of W. Thus it will produce a base address of $W + 136$ and an index increment of -24. J is assumed to contain the proper number at the time the reference takes place. It is this last assumption which provides the major motivation for combining the index increment with the array reference. If the incrementing were done with a separate assignment, then the translator would have difficulty associating it with the proper array element length.

There is another way of associating an index with a particular array element size : it could be declared as type $reference\ to\ (say)\ FLUB$ $word$. This brings us to the whole question of data types and why they are necessary.

The main reason for assigning types is not the abstract machine, but the computer on which it is realized. There are radical differences, for example, between integer and real arithmetic on $System/360$. The $Burroughs\ 5500,$ on the other hand, treats the two identically. Storage economies are also possible on many computers, as we pointed out in section 5.2.

If data is typed, then the problems of type conversion (or $coercion$)

must be faced. Coercions may be implicit or explicit. We reject the former, unless it can be done at compile time. The reason is that the effect of a coercion on the state of the target computer depends strongly upon that computer. By forcing the user to request the coercion explicitly, we are making him aware of its (possibly) expensive consequences.

A procedure with parameters can also be used as an operand. The normal explanation of procedure calling involves a *copying* process : the procedure is represented by a lambda expression, which specifies a bound variable list and a procedure body. A copy of the procedure body is substituted for the procedure call, with the bound variables replaced by (some transformation of) the corresponding arguments. Although such copying is never done in practice, it is instructive to investigate various possible transformations of the arguments :

- Each occurrence of a bound variable is replaced by
  a new variable which does not appear elsewhere in
  the program. The procedure is augmented by preceding it with a series of assignments which set the
  values of these new variables equal to the values
  of the call. (*Algol* call-by-value).

- As above, however, the procedure is also augmented
  by following it with a series of assignments which
  reset the values of the arguments to the values of
  the new variables. These following assignments can
  only be made to arguments which are of type *reference to* -. It is assumed that all argument expressions which yield a reference (such as subscripted
  variables) are evaluated before the procedure call.
  (Copy/restore).

- Each bound variable is replaced by a reference to
  the value of the corresponding argument. If an argument has no reference (for example if the argument were the number 3.5.), then the call is augmented by preceding it with an assignment, making
  that argument the value of a new variable which does
  not appear elsewhere in the program. Similarly, if
  an argument expression yields a reference, then that
  expression is evaluated before the call. (Call-by-reference).

       - Each bound variable is replaced by the corres-
        ponding argument. (*ALGOL* call-by-name).

Note that no pair of transformations yield identical results for all
procedures. *ALGOL* call-by-value is obviously different from the rest
because assignments to the bound variables do not affect the calling
program. Figure 6.3. gives counter examples for the conjecture that
other pairs are equivalent.

Janus does not specify the precise form of a procedure call, nor does
it specify how the arguments are to be interpreted and passed to the
procedure. The choice depends upon the needs of the abstract machine
designer and the addressing facilities available on the target computer.
We shall present one example in section 6.3.; further discussion can
be found in the lectures by Goos, Griffiths and Dennis.

A deferred expression in *Janus* represents a change in storage allocation. This change might be made at compile time (when the stack is
being simulated in memory) or at run time (when the stack is in hardware). If there are no run-time changes in storage allocation over a
particular region, then arbitrary transfers of control within that region can be permitted. For transfers between such regions, some action
of the storage allocation mechanism is required. The main justification for complex control structures (conditionals, case statements,
etc.) is simply this problem. By providing such structures we relieve
the programmer of the need to specify local transfers of control explicitly, and hence we relieve the compiler of the need to check their
destinations.

Again, our interpretation of a conditional is drawn directly from our
basic hardware model. The condition is not considered to be a Boolean
expression, but simply a sequence of operations which sets C at some
point. THEN (or THEF) is translated into an instruction which
transfers on C *false*. The value of the current expression is unchanged by the transfer.

When an expression is deferred, one temporary storage location is created. An *Algol* block allows the user to create as much temporary storage as he needs, simply by declaration. This storage must be freed
when control leaves the block. Since it is possible to leave the block
by a simple transfer, the cost of freeing storage is not made apparent
to the user. The user is also not aware of the high penalties for ac-

247

```
                FUNCTION F(X,Y)
                X=X+1
                Y=Y+1
                F=X+Y
                RETURN
                END
                A=1
                B=F(A,A)
                PRINT 100, B
        100     FORMAT (1H, I5)
                END
```

(a) Different results from copy/restore and call-by-reference.

<u>begin</u>

    <u>procedure</u> SWAP(i,j); <u>integer</u> i,j;
      <u>begin</u> <u>integer</u> t; t:=i; i:=j; j:=t <u>end</u>;
    <u>integer</u> k; <u>integer</u> <u>array</u> A[1:2];

    k:=1; A[1]:=2; A[2]:=3; SWAP(k,A[k]);
    print(k); print(A[1]); print(A[2]) <u>end</u>;

(b) Different results from call-by-reference and call-by-name.

Figure 6.3.

Examples of Argument Substitution

cessing temporary arrays on some computers. We prefer to make these costs explicit by requiring the user to manage his own dynamic storage.

The preceding paragraph should not be construed to mean that an abstract machine design cannot include operations which allocate stack storage and reference it. Such a design would certainly be indicated for, say, a machine which was to run *Algol* programs [35].

Modularity is definitely an important property of any program. *Janus* has the concept of a procedure, and these procedures may contain local variables. The way in which storage is allocated for these local variables is left unspecified. A stack could be used, or space could be permanently associated with the procedure. It is also possible for the abstract machine designer to provide a declaration which allows the user to select the type of allocation when he writes the program.

A program written in a language based on *Janus* consists of a sequence of operators and operands. The recognition phase of the translator must extract and identify these tokens, constructing operator-operand pairs. Each operator-operand pair is then considered to be an abstract machine instruction, which is passed to the code generation phase for realization. There must be rules by which the recognizer extracts tokens from the input string, and a dictionary which provides information about each token. The same recognizer can be used for any language which obeys the same extraction rules.

We have a set of recognition rules coded as macros for *STAGE2*. These rules accept code in a free format, and produce macro calls in a rigid format (Figure 6.4.). The recognition rules use a dictionary which is set up by other macros which the user provides. They are thus able to break down any language based upon *Janus* into a series of abstract machine instructions.

The code generator is constructed by writing definitions for all of the possible macros of the forms shown in Figure 6.4. Actually, this is not as burdensome as it might seem. For most machines, it is possible to translate operators and operands separately. Thus it is not necessary to provide a macro definition for each possible combination of operator and operand format.

Remember that the macro definitions are simply code generation routines which will be executed interpretively by *STAGE2*. They may be very

```
.EC  op constant
.ES  op simple variable
.EA  op data aggregate reference
.EP  op procedure call
.ET  op                        (operation involving the stack)
.EN  op                        (monadic operator)
```

(a) Executable instructions

```
.DS  type symbol declaration
.DA  type data aggregate declaration
.DP  type procedure declaration
.DO  type operator declaration
.DM                            (main program entry)
.T   name                      (end of procedure "name")
.T                             (end of text)
.C   comment
```

(b) Declarations

Figure 6.4.

Output of the Recognition Phase

simple, depending upon the circumstances. We have written a set of macros which produces absolute object code for one computer, thus simulating a complete assembler. It is easier to produce assembly code for
the target computer and then process it normally, but sometimes this is
not possible. (For example, if one wishes to provide portability via
an interpreter as discussed in section 4.2.).

6.3.   *AN EXAMPLE OF A LOW LEVEL LANGUAGE*

In section 6.2., we presented a framework for designing a low level
language based on an underlying model of the hardware. We will now consider a specific example of such a language constructed in the *Janus*
style. The obje tive in developing this language which is called *LSD*
(Language for System Development) [36] was to provide systems programmers with some of the facilities of high level languages whilst, at the
same ti e, encouraging the production of efficient programs. The programmer is made aware of the underlying machine and has access to a
number of facilities which enable him to organize his program so that
it can readily be optimized.

In assessing the merits or otherwise of this language, the reader must
be careful not to form his judgements just by comparing the facilities
it provides with those in other languages. The design was carried out
by looking upwards from the machine, not downwards from the programmer.
The main goals were object code efficiency and portability. The latter
depends on the existence of a translator which is itself highly portable
the former implies that the code generation algorithm of the translator
must be readily adaptable. The only translater available at the moment
which seems to satisfy both of these requirements is *STAGE2*. This fact
was taken into account during the design of *LSD*. Some features of
high level languages which might prove difficult to translate or which
might result in unacceptable inefficiencies were omitted even though one
could readily have justified their inclusion on the grounds of programmer
convenience. This does not mean that this factor was ignored. Rather it
implies that any decision to incorporate a particular facility was also
influenced by considerations of object code efficiency, portability and
the facilities available in *STAGE2*.

Another imporatnt factor which influenced the design of *LSD* was its projected use as a language for implementing software for small machines used in data acquisition and the online control of experiments. Such programs would be written by the physicists running the experiments rather than by systems programmers. We therefore needed to create a convenient environmant for compiling testing and debugging programs written in the language. We planned to provide this via an interactive test bed running on the *ICL 4/70*. A program could then be checked out in this environmant on the large machine before being transferred to the small machine and put into service. This raised the problem of what compiler should be provided for the test bed. Since *LSD* was designed to be translated by *STAGE2*, we could implement the translator for the test bed by constructing a set of macros to provide good error checking facilities and a comprehensive set of diagnostic messages. However, as the complexity of a set of macro definitions increases, the processing speed of *STAGE2* decreases. Further, we have already noted that this program is expensive in its use of store. Diagnostic messages would have to be stored as one character per abstract word and we could easily produce a translator which was unacceptably large. *STAGE2* is a very useful program for moving portable software from one machine to another, but it has its limitations when viewed as a tool for producing software, particularly in such an environment. We therefore concluded that the test bed should be equipped with a more conventional compiler. We proposed to produce such a compiler with the aid of *SID* [15], a program which automatically generates a syntax analyser from a syntactical description of a language. Thus an important design criterion for *LSD* was that the syntax should be capable of being one-tracked and therefore acceptable as input to *SID*. No feature was added to the language without first ensuring that this condition remainded true. Some of the characteristics of the language have been determined by these constraints and are not essential if the only translator used is *STAGE2*.

We shall now present a brief overview of the main features of the language indicating how they fit into the *Janus* framework. This will also give some measure of the complexity of a language that may be tramslated by *STAGE2*. For a complete description of the language, the reader should read reference 37.

LSD is line oriented, where a line is either an executable statement or a declaration. The former are translated into a sequence of machine instructions; the latter provide information to the translator about the structure of the program and its data. Central to the design of *LSD* is the form of an expression which differs in several respects from that found in many existing high level languages. An expression is constructed in the *Janus* style and consists of a linear sequence of operands and operators which is evaluated, as described in section 6.2., strictly from left to right without any operator precedence. After each operation is completed the current value of the expression so far is available in the *accumulator*. A dyadic operator takes the current value in the accumulator as its left operand and combines this with the next operand to the right; a monadic operator references only the operand to its right. There is no concept of an assignment command in *LSD*. The assignment operator is treated just like any other and causes the current value of the accumulator to be stored in the location specified by the next operand. Assignment is simply part of the expression and may be placed in any statement which contains an expression. If an expression does not include an assignment operator, then the effect is simply to set the value of the expression in the accumulator. The only situation which causes the normal left to right evaluation to be interrupted is the occurrence of parentheses. This is the *deferred expression* concept discussed in section 6.2. At the end of any executable statement, the accumulator contains a current value. This is retained between statements and may be referenced at the start of the next statement by means of the symbols ().

A table illustrating the operators and operands available in *LSD* is given in Figure 6.5a. The operators *SRL* and *SLL* shift the accumulator right or left a number of places specified by the right hand operand. The operators *INDEX* and *ORDNL* are used to optimise array accesses and will be described in more detail later. Figure 6.5b. gives a number of simple examples of *LSD* expressions.

The usual conventions hold for the structure of identifiers and constants and we shall not consider them any further except to note in passing that character, string and manifest constants are permitted. Let us consider the problem of accessing data aggregates. As we have already noted, the way in which this is carried out can have considerable influence on program efficiency. In keeping with the *Janus* framework, *LSD* permits only one dimensional arrays. These are declared and dimensioned by the appropriate type statements which reserve a block of consecutive storage locations. An element of an array can be accesssed by a subscripted array name where the subscript is any valid *LSD* expression which yields an integer value between 0 and the maximum al-

OPERATORS	OPERANDS
+ plus	constant
− minus	identifiers
* times	array elements
/ divide	pointer variables
** exponentiate	function calls
& and	address references
| inclusive or	current value of accumulator
$\Rightarrow$ assign	
SRL shift right logically	
SLL shift left logically	
INDEX convert integer to index	
ORDNL convert index to integer	

Figure 6.5a

Operators and Operands in LSD

PATTERN SRL 2|255$\Rightarrow$PATTERN

1$\Rightarrow$A $\Rightarrow$B $\Rightarrow$C+1$\Rightarrow$D$\Rightarrow$E

( )+A $\Rightarrow$B

Figure 6.5b.

LSD Expressions

lowed subscript of the array. We will now examine in more detail what
happens when an array element is referenced.

When an array is declared in *LSD*, two actions take place :

> (a) the appropriate number of consecutive storage
>   locations are reserved;
>
> (b) a global or local variable of the same mame
>   as the array is set up and loaded with the
>   address of the first of these locations, that
>   is, the base address of the array.

The process is illustrated diagrammatically in Figure 6.6a. for an
array *A* of 5 elements. Notice that since the base address has been
loaded into a variable, it can always be referenced by writing the array name without a subscript. Although this facility is quite useful
and can be developed in a natural way to provide the concept of pointer variables discussed later in this section, it can create certain
problems. Since the program can reference a base address, it can easily change it at run time. Let us consider, in terms of the basic hardware model of section 6.1., what effect this has on the code required
to effect an array access. Remember that the model permits a modifier
to be attached to a normal instruction and assumes that the effective
address is computed by adding the contents of the modifier operand.
With these facilities, the following operations would be required to
handle the general case :

> (a) Evaluate the subscript expression;
> (b) Multiply the result by the memory mapping
>   factor if something other than 1;
> (c) Add in the base address;
> (d) Store the result in a modifier and make the
>   access.

This sequence could result in unacceptable inefficiencies, particularly
if it occurs inside a loop.

We could improve this situation if we restricted ourselves to subscript
expressions of the form

$$variable \pm constant$$

255

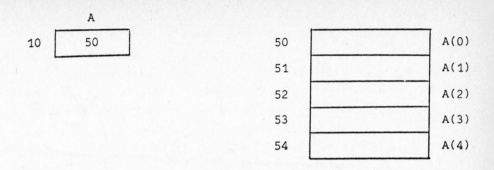

Figure 6.6(a)

Structure of an Array

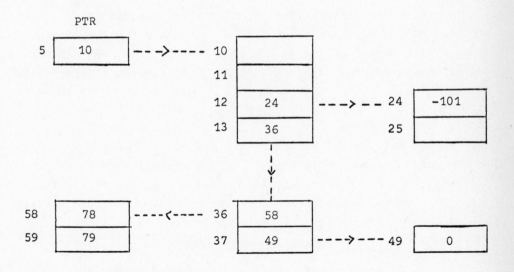

Figure 6.4.

Output of the Recognition Phase

and at translate time, had available the base address of the array. Optimisation of the array reference would then be possible providing the
program does not change the base address at run time. In terms of the
instructions of the basic model, the modifier contains the current value
of the variable and the normal operand address is just the base address
of the array incremented or decremented by the constant. We could gain
even more if once a variable is loaded into the modifier, it could be
left there for say the duration of a loop and incremented or decremented in situ. *LSD* provides for this situation by allowing the programmer to declare index registers.

The declaration of type   *IREG*   allows one or more variables to be declared as index registers. Efficient access to an array element can
then be achieved by restricting subscripts to the form

> index register $\pm$ constant

providing the variable declared to be a register contains a value adjusted for the memory mapping factor. This can be effected via the
special operator *INDEX* which multiplies the current value of the expression by the number of target computer address units per element of
the array whose name is the next operand. For example, the expression

> $J \quad INDEX \quad A \quad \Rightarrow \quad J$

multiplies the integer *J* by the memory mapping factor for array *A*
and stores the resultant index back in *J*. The array name is specified
to allow for possible differences in the memory mapping factor for different array types. The reverse operation is provided by the operator
ORDNL which converts an index back to an integer by dividing the appropriate memory mapping factor.

If a subscript of an array reference is restricted to the form described above, then *LSD* provides a mechanism for incrementing or decre-
menting the index register after the access has been performed. The
notation follows that outlined for *Janus*. The programmer can append
a *D* or an *I* followed by a constant to the array reference depending
on whether he wants the index register decremented or incremented. If
no constant is specified, then *1* is assumed. Since the array name
is available at translate time, the specified increment or decrement
can be adjusted for the memory mapping factor. Thus the following
LSD statement :

$$A(J)I+A(J)I+A(J)I=>SUM$$

would add three successive elements of an array. After each array access, the index register J would be incremented by the memory mapping factor required for A. Note , however, that the following would be a more efficient way of achieving the same effect :

$$A(J)+A(J+1)+A(J+2)I3=>SUM$$

In this case, only one set of instructions is required to increment the index register.

Earlier we noted that the manner in which array references were handled in LSD could be developed quite naturally to provide the concept of a pointer variable, a necessary feature in any systems programming language. This facility is obtained quite simply by allowing the subscripting of scalar variables.

In our discussion of array references, we noted that in the general case the effective address was calculated by adding the value of the subscript to the contents of the variable associated with the arrayname. If we extend this mechanism to permit scalars to be subscripted, then it is easy to see that if X is a scalar variable containing a valid address, $X(O)$ will reference the word pointed to by X, $X(1)$ the following word and so on. An obvious extension to this facility is to allow the use of pointers to any depth. Compound data structures of any complexity can then be constructed. The process is illustrated in Figure 6.6(b).

In the diagram, PTR is a scalar variable which points to location 10. Location 12 points to location 24, 13 to 36, 36 to 58 and so on. Hence $PTR(2)$ references location 12 and accesses the value 24; if $PTR(2)$ is now itself subscripted, one more level of indirection will be specified. Hence $PTR(2)(O)$ references location 24 and accesses the value -101. Similarly $PTR(3)(O)(1)$ accesses the value 79 in location 59, $PTR(3)(1)(O)$, the value 0 in location 49. In its general form, a pointer variable consists of an identifier followed by any number of subscripts. The identifier may be a scalar variable or an arrayname; any valid LSD expression may be used as a subscript.

In order to create the structures accessed by pointer variables in the manner just described, we must be able to specify and manipulate addresses. *LSD* therefore permits access to the addresses of variables, array elements, pointer variables, procedures, functions or labels. Angle brackets are used to denote the address. Thus

<FRED>   is the address of the variable   *FRED*

<A(10)>   is the address of element   *10*   of array   *A*.

Some care must be exercised by the programmer when using this facility since again there may be problems connected with the mapping of addresses. Thus the expression

<A(3)>+1

does not necessarily produce the address of the array element   *A(4)*. To remedy this situation in   *LSD,*   we can use a manifest constant. Thus the expression

<A(3)>+MMF

will produce the correct result if the value of the memory mapping factor for the particular machine is assigned to the manifest constant *MMF* before translation of the program is carried out.

Of the operands listed in Figure   6.5(a)., we have only function calls to consider. Instead, let us examine the whole question of how procedures and functions are implemented in   *LSD*. As noted in section   6.2., the   *Janus*   framework does not explicitly define the form of a procedure call nor the manner in which arguments are to be transmitted to the procedure itself. The choice is left to the designer of the abstract machine.

An   *LSD*   program consists of a sequence of one or more procedures each of which must be preceded by a declaration of the form

PROCEDURE   identifier   (formal input parameters) (formal output parameters)

Either or both of the formal parameters may be omitted. A procedure body consists of local type declarations   (if any)   followed by executable statements some or all of which may reference the formal parameters. The procedure must contain at least one   *RETURN*   statement to return control to the point from which it was called. The textual end of the procedure body is indicated by means of an *END* statement.

Every *LSD* procedure returns a value in the accumulator and hence procedure calls may be used as operands in an expression. The conventional distinction between procedures and functions does not apply. However, as a documentation aid, a programmer may use *FUNCTION* as a synonym for *PROCEDURE* in a declaration and a *CALL* statement is also provided. However, the only action really required to activate a procedure is to write an operand of the form

    identifier (actual input parameters) (actual output parameters)

where identifier is the name of the called procedure. Again either or both of the parameter lists may be omitted but the format of the call must correspond to that of the declaration. Actual parameters are passed to a procedure by value. The actual input parameter corresponding to any formal input parameter may be any valid *LSD* expression. On the other hand, an actual output parameter can only specify the address of a storage location into which the corresponding output value is stored, i.e. it is restricted to an identifier, an array element or a pointer variable.

The mechanism used in *LSD* for passing parameters is copy/restore via a stack. (Recursion is allowed in *LSD*). When a procedure call is encountered, the current value of the accumulator is stacked and the actual parameters evaluated.

In turn these are placed on the stack and a return jump to the procedure is executed. On entry to the procedure, the link is preserved and the stack base adjusted so that both the input parameters and locations reserved for output are effectively within the local work space of the routine. All instructions in the routine which reference this space do so relative to the current value of the stack pointer. Before exit, the link is retrieved and the stack base reset. A return to the calling sequence is then executed. The output values are extracted from the stack and stored in the locations addressed by the actual output parameters. The value of the procedure returned in the accumulator then becomes the right hand operand for the pending operator and the evaluation of the current expression is resumed.

This mechanism is quite a straightforward one and relatively easy to

implement. However, it does raise some problems particularly with regard to array references. We cannot use the techniques described earlier for optimising such references unless the array in question is a
global one. For local arrays or for arrays passed as parameters, we
must compute the address of an element even for the restricted form of
a subscript unless the actual hardware allows an instruction to specify
two modifiers as well as an offset. Few machines provide such a facility and it is at variance with our basic hardware model. Hence the
accessing of data aggregates in a loop in a procedure could be in source of ineffeciency in a *LSD* program.

Of the remaining features of the language , we will consider briefly
only the declarations and a few of the executable statements. We noted
in section 6.2 that although *Janus* specifies that a declaration
should be introduced by the characters *DCL*, particular languages constructed in the *Janus* framework could use a different convention.
In *LSD*, keywords are used to denote type, e.g. *INTEGER, CHARACTER*
etc. To allow a programmer to introduce new types into the language,
the *TYPE* declaration is provided. A declaration line in *LSD* consists of a keyword followed by a list of variable and array declarations. A variable may be preset to a constant in a global declaration
but arrays may only be initialized by means of a *DATA* statement which
is placed at the end of the declaration but before the first executable
statement. The function of the declaration is mainly to supply information to the translator so that it can allocate storage space and construct the correct access mechanisms. Different translators may behave in different ways. Thus, the *LSD* compiler merely allocates one
word to each quantity irrespective of type; the macros, on the other
hand, produce optimized code and take cognisance of the fact that some
data types require less space than others, for example, that a number
of characters could be packed into one word of the target machine.

The remaining executable statements of interest are those concerned basically with transfer of control-jumps, conditionals, loop control and
switch. The *GOTO* statement provides local transfer of control to a
label in the same procedure. Variations on the simple form of the statement are *GOINDTO* and *GOTOVIA*. The former allows an indirect transfer of control to an address contained in the location specified by the
operand; the latter allows control to be transferred indirectly to a
given address whilst at the same time preserving the return address.
Conditionals follow the *Janus* framework. A relational operator com-

pares its right hand operand with the current value of the accumulator and sets a condition code accordingly. This is inspected when the appropriate operator is encountered. Thus : (which is a shorthand form for *THEN*) is translated into a jump-if-false instruction as is the operation *AND*. *OR* is translated into a jump-if-true. The current value of the accumumlator is not changed by these tests or transfers. Note that optimization which depends on the statement following the operator which inspects the condition code is possible. Thus the *LSD* statement

$$IF \quad A \quad LT \quad 2 \quad : \quad GOTO \quad B$$

would be translated into a jump-if-true to label *B*. Note that the *IF* is an optional keyword.

The *LOOP* statement in *LSD* has two forms. The first indicates that the loop is to be executed a specified number of times; the second performs a controlled iteration incrementing a counter by a specified amount each time from a starting value to a final value. The statements performed within the loop are delimited by an *ENDLOOP* statement. Loops may be nested to any depth. The *SWITCH* statement as expected transfers control to one of several labels depending on the value of the operand.

To date, *LSD* has been implemented via *STAGE2* on two machines, the 4/70 and the Modular One. On the basis of these implementations, we estimate that about one man month of effort would be required to implement 95 % of the language on a new machine. This would include all the common and most frequntly used facilities. The remaining 5 % would require another man month of effort. These estimates assume that the programmer making the implementation is experienced in the use of *STAGE2*. We have attempted to obtain some estimate of the efficiency of *LSD* by comparing the size of a program written in *LSD* with the size of the same program written in assembly code. We have found that a typical *LSD* program is 5 % larger than the equivalent hand coded version. Currently we are using *LSD* to implement, amongst other things, the *LSD* compiler/test bed, an operating system for a small machine and a data acquisition system. Both systems programmers and scientific users alike are finding the language convenient and easy to use. We expect that it will prove to be a useful addition to our kit of Software Engineering tools.

7.   A HIERARCHY OF ABSTRACT MACHINES

Mention has already been made in this course of the concept of a hierarchy. Dennis had referred to it in discussing the representation of
programs and systems; Goos has considered in some detail the whole
question of hierarchical ordering, illustrating its use as a design
methodology and its relationship to language; in his discussion on the
problem of protection, Tsichritzis has shown how protection hierarchies
can be used in the implementation of a system. In this section of the
course, we are concerned with the development of techniques for producing portable and adaptable software based on the concept of abstract
machine modelling. We shall now show again how the concept of a hierarchy can be of great value in achieving these goals. In particular,
we will consider how a hierarchy of abstract machines can be used to
achieve the correct balance between the first two principles of abstract machine modelling enunciated in section 3.1. As we have already
dy noted, if we emphasize the requirements of the problem with little
or no regard to the structure of real machines, then we can easily
create a model which, although providing a convenient language for describing the problem, can be very difficult to implement. On the other
hand, a simple model, designed with the structure of real machines in
mind, will be easy to move but may not adequately reflect the characteristic of the problem. Complex operations required to solve the problem will have to be coded in terms of the simple operations of the
model. If the program is moved to a machine which incorporates such
operations directly in the hardware, then no advantage can be taken of
these features, unless the algorithm is broken. Thus efficiency suffers. Achieving the correct balance between portability and efficiency is very much a software engineering task and one in which we suggest
the concept of a hierarchy will be of great assistance.

7.1.   NEED FOR THE HIERARCHY

The need for the hierarchy has been amply demonstrated by some of the
results presented in earlier sections. Both *FLUB* and *TEXED*, designed with emphasis on the requirements of the problem, gave rise to some
degree of inefficiency when implemented on real machines. Yet each was
highly portable because of the simplicity of the model. We would expect
that a person not familiar in any way with the techniques to achieve

an implementation with a few weeks of effort. As our emphasis in the
design process has shifted to take more account of the structure of
real machines, our model has become more complex, at least as seen by
the implementor. To realize a program written in *LSD*, he will have
to handle a variety of data types as well as provide mechanisms for storage management, parameter passing, loop control etc. This will require a fairly complicated set of macros, certainly a much more complex set
than the 28 simple macros required to implement *FLUB*. We have already noted that we expect an experienced user of *STAGE2* will take about
a month to implement most of *LSD*. An inexperienced user will take considerably longer and require some knowledge of the fundamentals of compiler construction. This is not in keeping with our objective of
cook-book implementation. As we have already pointed out, we are firmly committed to the concept of a full-bootstrap and this implies that
an implementor of a piece of portable software should be able to obtain
a running version merely by following a set of instructions which guides him through the bootstrap sequence. He should not require any specialized knowledge, nor should he have to refer back to the originator
of the program for assistance. The question therefore that we must ask
and answer is : how can we distribute a program written in a language
like *LSD* and guarantee that it can be implemented on any machine in a
reasonable period of time by someone without special skills. The solution seems to be to create a hierarchy of abstract machines. Let us
see how this could be achieved.

Suppose the program which we wish to construct is a compiler for *ALGOL*.
We can postulate that there exists an abstract machine which is well
suited to solving this problem and that it has one instruction, *COM-
PILE ALGOL*. To realize this abstract machine on a real computer, we
would have to write the whole compiler in assembly code. We would not
have produced a very portable program. However, we can also postulate
that below the first machine, there exists a second abstract machine
with a few more high level instructions which could conveniently be used
to encode the algorithm. Again, considerable effort would be required
to map any one of these *instructions* onto a real machine and we would
still be a long way from attaining portability. However, if we continue this process down through a number of levels, eventually we might
reach a machine with instructions like *LOAD, STORE, ADD* etc. which
could readily be implemented on a number of real machines. If we code
the compiler in this language, then we will have achieved portability -
at a price. Although we could move the program easily from one machine

to another, it is unlikely to be very efficient.

The hierarchy of abstract machines we have postulated possesses the following structure. Machines near the top of the hierarchy reflect the characteristics of the problem and provide convenient languages for encoding the algorithm. The resultant programs are efficient but not very portable. Conversely, the machines near the bottom are designed to take account of the structure of real computers. The languages are low level and produce programs which are highly portable but not very efficient. This suggests that we might be able to find an abstract machine somewhere between the two extremes which will provide a reasonable balance between portability, efficiency and convenience. Further, if we can connect the hierarchy together in such a way that an abstract machine at one level can be mapped onto the machine at the next level down in an automatic and machine independent manner, then we may not have to rely on the properties of one machine alone to control the quality of the software. A convenient problem-oriented language could be obtained from a machine high in the hierarchy; lower level machines would then be used to ensure that the software was both portable and efficient.

To illustrate how this can be achieved, consider the hierarchy of abstract machines A_1, A_2, ... A_i, ... A_n structured such that machine A_{i+1} is defined in terms of A_i for all values of i such that $1 \leq i < n$. Such a hierarchy is shown in Figure 7.1. The machine at the top of the hierarchy, A_n, provides the language in which the problem is expressed. A_1 at the bottom of the hierarchy provides the link to the outside world. It can easily be implemented on a variety of actual computers. If the definition of $A_i (i \neq 1)$ in terms of A_{i-1} does not depend on the characteristics of real machines, then realizing A_1 on a particular computer effectively implements each machine in the hierarchy. Thus any program written for A_n is portable. However, it is unlikely to be very efficient when realized via A_1 since this machine (by virtue of its position in the hierarchy) is a fairly simple model whose structure is an intersection of those of real machines. Thus the part played by A_1 in the hierarchy is to guarantee high portability. As we have already noted, A_n provides the convenient language. It is the function of one of the intermediate machines to ensure that an efficient implementation can be obtained.

As we move up the hierarchy, each machine will tend to reflect more a and more the characteristic of the problem to be solved embodied in the

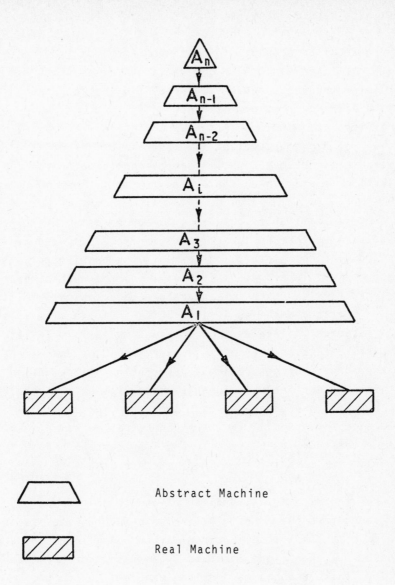

Figure 7.1.

Hierarchy of Abstract Machines

higher level operations. In general, to realize these operations on
the target machine will require more effort than is required to implement the operations of A_1 . However, this should result in a more efficient program since account can be taken of the particular characteristics of the target machine, e.g. special hardware features, similarities in data structures between the real and abstract machines etc.
Hence if the hierarchy is organized correctly, the more work we expend,
the more efficient an implementation we will obtain. Notice, however,
that we have not given up portability to achieve this efficiency. While the exercise to optimize the implementation is being carried out, a
running version is available for use on the target machine.

There is a marked similarity between this approach to the implementation of software and the design strategy, commonly referred to as *top-
down*. In applying this method, one expands the problem to be solved
through a number of levels of design until one reaches the appropriate
logical elements which can be expanded into code. Each level in the
hierarchy of abstract machines is in a sense equivalent to a level in
the design sequence. Since we can construct rules to translate one
abstract machine into another at the lower level, we can effectively
automate the process of generating a description of the design at a given level from an earlier one. Changes in design at any one level can
therefore be used to produce the corresponding changes at lower levels
in an automatic way. Similarly, they can be reflected automatically
in the generated code so that design and implementation do not diverge
as so often is the case in the current state of the art.

Returning now to our original problem of how to distribute a program
in *LSD*, we propose that the solution is to incorporate *LSD* into
such a hierarchy. The actual program may be coded in a language above
LSD with special operations and data types determined by the needs of
the problem. This language may include many of the features of *LSD*
so that it fulfills its role in providing the common organizational statements required to solve any problem. However, transformation rules
will be available so that the entire program can be translated automatically into *LSD* if required. Languages beneath *LSD* will look more
towards the machine than to the programmer. We have already noted that
there exists a set of recognition rules coded as macros for *STAGE2*
which are able to break down any languages designed in the *Janus* style into a series of abstract machine instructions. These can either be
mapped onto the real machine or translated into instructions of an even

simpler abstract machine at a lower level. Thus the problem of obtaining a program written in LSD to the problem of realizing one of these
simple abstract machines - a much less burdensome task.

We have noted what influence the use of a hierarchy has on portability;
we must also examine briefly how it affects adaptability Changes in
the behaviour of the algorithm are still something for which the programmer must plan in his original design. However, they do not necessarily have to be incorporated in the original text. For example, the
way in which an operation at one level is expanded into those of the
next level could be controlled by declarations made before translation
starts and the algorithm modified accordingly. As far as altering the
way an algorithm is realized, the use of a hierarchy offers many possibilities. The techniques discussed in section 5.2. could be applied
at any of the levels, thereby allowing the implementor a great deal of
freedom in choosing the final form of the program.

7.2.   A STANDARD BASE FOR THE HIERARCHY

From the discussion in the previous section, it is clear that the design of the machine A_1 at the base of the hierarchy has little to do
with the characteristics of the problem being solved. Its function is
merely to ensure that the program is highly portable. This suggests
that it may be possible to make A_1 common to a number of hierarchies.
In fact, there could be a number of machines above A_1 which exist in
various hierarchies and one is led to suggest the possibility of setting up a tree structured hierarchy of abstract machines as shown in
Figure 7.2. The machine at the base of this tree is called SELEAC
(Standard Elementary Abstract Computer). Once the rules describing
SELEAC in terms of the target machine have been developed, then any
piece of software constructed for a higher level machine could readily
be made available. We have already noted in section 3.1. the similarity between our techniques and the UNCOL proposal. The similarity
is even more marked when one postulates the existence of an abstract
machine into which all other abstract machines can be translated in a
machine independent way. However, remember that the function of SE-
LEAC is to ensure that the software is portable; it makes no guarantees about efficiency. Further, the user is always free to by-pass
any number of the lower levels and map a specific abstract machine directly onto the hardware to obtain more efficient implementation. Thus

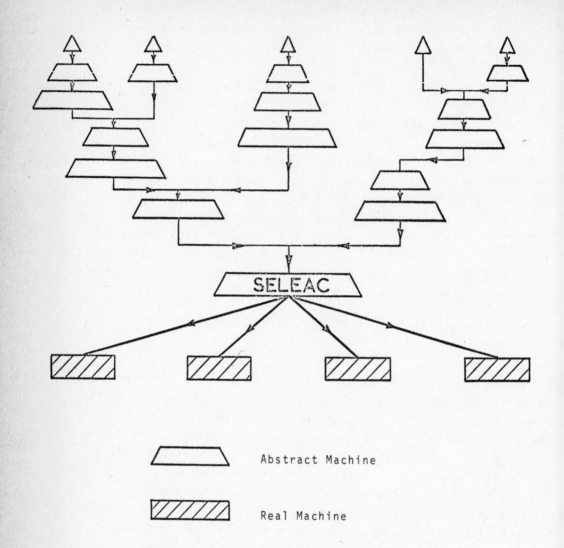

Figure 7.2.

*Tree-structured Hierarchy
of Abstract Machines*

the inflexibility of the *UNCOL* proposals have been avoided.

In creating the design of the *SELEAC* machine, we must take account of the following factors.:

      (a)   *SELEAC* must be simple enough so that it can be quickly and easily implemented on a wide variety of current machines. On the other hand it must not be so simple that the resulting implementations are unusable.

      (b)   *SELEAC* must be extendable. It must be possible to add new facilities to the machine if they cannot easily be expressed in terms of existing facilities. Thus the inclusion of a new high level abstract machine in the hierarchy can produce an extension in the design of the base machine if its particular needs cannot be satisfied.

Our starting point for the design of *SELEAC* is the basic hardware model discussed in section 6.1. We have indicated how it could be realized with an acceptable degree of efficiency on any of the register/processor organizations described in section 3.2. Remember, however, that the model left certain things unspecified since it is merely a framework within which to design abstract machines. For example, it said nothing about the way the memory is to be organized. *SELEAC*, being an abstract machine within this framework, must specify such details explicitly.

SELEAC is a single address machine with two registers - an accumulator and an index register. The integer arithmetic operations of addition, subtraction, multiplication and division can be performed on the accumulator; only addition and subtraction operations are available for the index register. The stack which formed part of the basic model has not been included specifically since it can be simulated in memory.

The *SELEAC* memory is divided into two main areas. The first which may be addressed both directly or indirectly is a static memory which holds both instructions and data. Nothing is specified about the size of a word except to note that it must be large enough to hold the elementary data types used in the higher level machines. In general, we

would expect it to be 16 bits or larger.The second area is a dynamic
data memory which can only be addressed indirectly and which could, in
some implementations, be mapped onto backing store. The address for
either memory is constructed from the operand address and the contents
of the index register (if specified). Thus the index register ful-
fils the function of the modifier discussed in connection with the basic model and is used in addressing elements of a data aggregate.
The selection between static and dynamic memory is made on the basis of
the operation code. Only fetch and store to and from the accumulator
is permitted for the dymamic memory. Instructions which access the
static memory include memory/register transfers and the arithmetic operations.

Another factor which influenced the design of *SELEAC* was the possibility of using it to start the bootstrap sequence. As we noted to Section 4.2., *STAGE2* could be distributed expressed in the object code
of a simple abstract machine. All that would then be required to obtain a running version of the program would be an interpreter for this
simple machine. Subsequently we could use this interpretive version
to obtain a more efficient version by translating *STAGE2* expressed
in the language of a higher level abstract machine directly into the
instructions of the target computer. If the simple machine used was
SELEAC, then we would only need to construct this interpreter once
for a given computer. Any item of portable software expressed in *SE-
LEAC* could then be examined with minimum effort before any decision
was taken to expend further effort to produce an optimized version. If
SELEAC is to be capable of supporting *STAGE2*, then some attention
must be paid to the problem of storing and manipulating characters. For
this reason, we have added instructions to *SELEAC* which allow characters to be packed into or unpacked from the accumulator. The number of
characters which can be stored in a word is only specified via a manifest constant.

Both conditional and unconditional transfers of control are provided.
In keeping with the basic model,there is a test register which may be
set by an instruction which compares its operand with the contents of
the accumulator. This is then inspected by the conditional transfer of
control operations to determine whether a branch is required or not.
The comparison instruction does not alter the current contents of the
accumulator. Operations to effect entry to or exit from subroutines
are included in the instruction set. The exact mechanism is left unspecified and depends on the particular implementation. For example,

in an interpreter constructed for *SELEAC*, the return address is stored in the first location of the called routine. Input/output in *SE-
LEAC* is handled by one instruction which interfaces the machine to the
standard I/O package. Its operand specifies the address of a list
of parameters required by the operation.

The assembly code provided for the machine consists of declarative
and executable statements, Each instruction is made up of a mnemonic
operation code and a single operand. The general form of the operand
is

n(m)t

where n is an identifier unique to the whole of the program. It may
stand for an array, a label or a procedure. As noted later, a single
valued variable is just regarded as an array of one element. m is an
arithmetic expression whose evaluation results in an integer which may
be positive or negative. The expression may contain integers, manifest
constants and character constants. t is the operand type which is
null for an ordinary address and X if the contents of the index register is to be used in forming the final address. This is evaluated
as follows :

(i)   determine the address associated with the
        name n. If n is null then this address
        is taken to be 0.

(ii)   evaluate m and add the resulting integer
        to the address of n.

(iii)   if indexing is specified, add in the con-
        tents of the index register.

There are 24 operations specified for the basic *SELEAC* machine,
16 of which may be extended to indicate that the operand is to be interpreted as immediate, e.g.

    LDA CELL(N)X - load *contents* of (N+x)th element
                    of the array *CELL* into the accumulator

    LDAI CELL(N)X- load *address* of (N+x)th element of
                    the array *CELL* into the accumulator

All identifiers used in a *SELEAC* program must be declared. This includes labels, procedures and arrays. Only one dimensional arrays are
provided and an array declaration specifies how much space is to be
allocated. A variable is treated as an array of one element. Array
elements may be initialized to the value of an integer arithmetic expression which obeys the same rules as m described above. Each array is
assumed to be a linear sequence of words but nothing is specified about
the contiguity of different arrays.

Our intention in presenting this brief description of the structure of
SELEAC is to give the reader some indication of our current thinking
about the characteristics of an abstract machine which could serve as a
standard base of the hierarchy. Obviously, what we have described is
merely the core of this machine. It will need to be extended considerably if it is to be capable of supporting operations widely available
on current machines, e.g. shifts, floating point etc. The design is
an ongoing process and the final form will depend on a series of experiments to determine the ease with which it can be mapped onto actual machines and its suitability as a target language into which higher level
language may be translated.

7.3.   *A CASE STUDY*

Finally, let us consider briefly a case study which involves the construction of a piece of portable software via a hierarchy of abstract
machines. We have already tested out some of the ideas on our early
abstract machine models [32, 37] and these experiments have indicated
that the approach is a feasible one. The program we will examine is a
new version of the text editor *MITEM* which is being constructed in a
hierarchy that includes *LSD*.

In section 5.1., we noted that the basic data types required for *MI-
TEM* were strings and integers. Instead of choosing a representation
for a string as we did in *TEXED*, let us first enquire what characte-
rizes a string and what operations on strings we might need to implement the *MITEM* algorithm.

A string is an ordered sequence of characters which may be completely
specified in a machine by the address of the first character (*BASE*)

and the number of characters in the string (*LENGTH*). During the process of editing, *MITEM* moves a cursor along the string being scanned. We therefore need to maintain a pointer to the current position of the cursor and this can be held as an offset from the first character (*HEAD*). If we assume (as the algorithm permits) that there is a maximum size for any string and dynamic storage allocation is not required, then in order to check for possible overflow, we will need to have this quantitiy available (*LIMIT*). These four quantities are sufficient to define the state of a string at any instant and together with the actual string of characters itself, constitute the data type *STRING* in the abstract machine model. Since we may wish to reference these quantities independently of the character string, we will refer to them collectively via the data type *STRING REGISTER*. Thus the declaration of a string results in the creation of a string register and the reservation of sufficient space to hold the maximum size allowed for the string. In *LSD*, these would be represented by an integer array of four elements and an array of type *CHARACTER*.

The basic operations required to manipulate these data types are determined partly by the needs of the algorithm and partly by the instructions we might expect to find on some machines. The format of the operation is chosen with a view to simplifying its recognition by *STAGE2* and its translation into *LSD*. Thus the operation

```
        SEARCH  STRING ' FOR ' CHARACTER : '
```

scans the string named by the first parameter for the character named in the second parameter. If the search fails, control is transferred to the label given as the third parameter. If the search is successful then *HEAD* in the string register associated with the string is set to point to the required character. Clearly the operation can readily be translated into the *LSD* conditional statement

```
        IF  SEARCH (' , ') LT ∅ : GOTO '
```

providing the corresponding *LSD* procedure returns a - 1 in the accumulator if the search fails. It could also be translated into an online code sequence containing a *TRANSLATE AND TEST* instruction if such is available on the target machine.

The language in which the program is being written is a mixture of the special operations in the form described above and LSD. In order to distinguish between the procedures which implement the algorithm and those which provide the LSD equivalents of the special operations, the latter are declared as OPERATIONS. Thus, the operation SEARCH described above would be declared as

OPERATION : SEARCH STRING ' FOR ' CHARACTER

which could readily be translated into the equivalent LSD procedure declaration. By distinguishing operations in this way, we can easily arrange to replace the LSD by a more efficient routine in assembly code or delete it entirely if the call itself is replaced by an inline code sequence. The macros which perform the translation from the special language to LSD may be combined with those which convert LSD to SELEAC and are effectively a pre-pass. The implementor is therefore free to come in at any level to carry out optimization.

The development of this new version of MITEM is still underway and, as yet, we have no measurements to assess the efficiency of this process or otherwise, However, some work carried out by Brown on the macro processor ML/1 [38] supports the view that the use of a hierarchy improves portability without resulting in an unacceptable loss in efficiency. ML/1 is a program constructed for an abstract machine called L. The language is quite high level and experience in a number of implementations has shown that about 3 man months of effort are required to realize L on a new machine via a half bootstrap, using an existing version of ML/1 on another computer. In an effort to reduce this figure, Brown first created a machine called LOWL [39] which is simpler than L and whose structure is more oriented towards that of real machines. He then used ML/1 to convert the source text of ML/1 from L to LOWL. The form of LOWL is such that any of the common macro processors (e.g. 360 macro assembler, STAGE2) can be used to implement the program on a new machine. The effort required to do this is now about 2 man-weeks. However, measurements on the efficiency of ML/1 generated from LOWL indicate that it is only 5 % slower than the optimized version. Thus the portability of the program has been considerably increased at virtually no cost in efficiency.

8. R E F E R E N C E S

1   Griswold, R.E., Poage, J.F., Polonsky, I.P. *The SNOBOL4 Pro-gramming language.* Prentice-Hall, Englewood Cliffs, N.J.,1969

2   Griswold, R.E. *The Macro Implementation of SNOBOL4.* W.H. Freeman & Co., San Francisco, 1972.

3   Harr, J.A. *The design and production of real-time software for electronic switching systems.* Quoted in Software Engineering, Naur, P., Randell, B. (Eds.), NATO Science Comm., Jan. 1969,27.

4   Poole, P.C., Waite, W.M. *A Machine Independent Program for the Manipulation of Text.* Tech. Rept. 69-4, Computing Center, University of Colorado, 1969.

5   American National Standards Institute. *FORTRAN,* X3.9-1966.

6   Galler, B.A., Perlis, A.J. *A Proposal for Definition in ALGOL.* CACM, $\underline{10}$ (April, 1967) 204-219.

7   van Wijngaarden, A. (Ed.), Mailloux, B.J., Peck, J.E.L., Koster, C.H.A. *Report on the Algorithmic Language ALGOL 68.* Numerische Mathematik, $\underline{14}$ (1969) 79-218.

8   Newey, M.C. *An Efficient system for User Extendible Languages.* Proc. AFIPS. FJCC, $\underline{33}$ (1968) 1339-1347.

9   Weizenbaum, J. *Symmetric List Processor.* CACM, $\underline{6}$ (September 1969) 524-544.

10   SHARE Ad-Hoc Committee on Universal Languages. *The Problem of Programming Communication with Changing Machines : A Proposed Solution.* CACM, $\underline{1}$ (1968) 12-15.

11   Sibley, R.A. *The SLANG System.* CACM, $\underline{4}$ (Jan., 1961) 75-84.

12   Richards, M. *BCPL : A Tool for Compiler Writing and System Programming.* Proc. AFIPS. SJCC, $\underline{34}$ (1969) 557-566.

13   Irons, E.T. *A Syntax Directed Compiler for ALGOL 60.* CACM, $\underline{4}$ (1961) 51-55.

14. McKeeman, W.M., Horning, J.J., Wortman, D.B. *A Compiler Generator*. Prentice-Hall, Englewood Cliffs, N.J., 1970.

15   Foster, J.M. *A Syntax Improving Program*. Computer J., 11 (May, 1968) 31-34.

16   Waite, W.M. *Implementing Software for Non-Numeric Applications*. Prentice-Hall, Englewood Cliffs, N.J., 1973.

17   Irons, E.T. *Experience with an Extensible Language*.   CACM, 13 (January, 1970) 31-40.

18   Yezerski, A. *Extendible Contractible Translators*.   Ph.D. Thesis, University of New South Wales, Sydney, Australia, 1972.

19   McClure, R.M. *TMG - A Syntax Directed Compiler*.   Proc. ACM 20th National Conference, 1965, 262-274.

20   Brooker, R.A., Morris, D. *Some Proposals for the Realization of a Certain Assembly Program*.   Computer J., 3 (1961) 220-224.

21   Waite, W.M. *A Language Independent Macro Processor*.   CACM, 10 (July, 1967) 433-440.

22   Brown, P. J. *The ML/I Macro Processor*.   CACM, 10 (October, 1967) 618-623.

23   Waite, W.M. *The Mobile Programming system : STAGE2*.   CACM, 13 (July, 1970) 415-421.

24   McIlroy, M.D. *Macro Instruction Extensions of Compiler Languages*.   CACM, 3 (April, 1960) 214-220.

25   Waite, W.M. *The STAGE2 Macro Processor*.   Tech. Rept. 69-3-B. Computing Center, Universiy of Colorado, 1969.

26   Halstead, M.H. *Machine Independent Computer Programming*.   Spartan Books, Washington, D.C., 1962.

27   Waite, W.M. *Building a Mobile Programming System*.   Computer J., 13 (February, 1970) 28-31.

28   Orgass, R.J., Waite, W.M. *A Base for a Mobile Programming System.* CACM. 12 (September, 1969) 507-510.

29   Poole, P. C., Waite, W.M. *Input/Output for a Mobile Programming System.* Software Engineering, Vol. 1, Tou, J.T. (Ed.) Academic Press (1970).

30   Waite, W.M. *A New Input/Output Package for the Mobile Programming System.* Department of Information Science, Monash University, Clayton, Victoria, Australia (1970).

31   Waite, W. M. *Input/Output Conventions for Abstract Machines.* Proc. Culham Symposium on Software Engineering (April 1971).

32   Newey, M.C., Poole, P.C., Waite, W. M. *Abstract Machine Modelling to Produce Portable Software - a Review and Evaluation.* Software, 2 (1972) 1o7-136.

33   Knuth, D.E. *An Empirical Study of FORTRAN Programs.* Software, 1 (1971) 105-133.

34   Wirth, N. *The design of a Pascal Compiler.* Software, 1 (1971) 309-333.

35   See reference 31.

36   Randell, B., Russell, L. J. *ALGOL 60 Implementation.* Academic Press (1964).

37   Calderbank, V.J., Calderbank, M. *LSD Manual.* CLM-PDN 9/71, Culham Laboratory UKAEA, Abingdon, Berkshire (1971).

38   Poole, P.C. *Hierarchical Abstract Machines.* Proc. Culham Symposium on Software Engineering (April 1971).

39   See reference 22.

40   Brown, P.J. *Levels of Language for Portable Software.* CACM, (to be published).

CHAPTER 3.C.

DEBUGGING AND TESTING

P. C. Poole

Culham Laboratory, Abingdon, Berkshire

Great Britain

1.   INTRODUCTION

When a programmer looks at the output from his latest run
and finds that the computer has kindly sent him a message

UNRECOVERABLE ERROR DUE TO UNKNOWN CAUSE

then, although he may not realise it at the time, he is about
to move from the testing to the debugging phase of software
production. Testing has demonstrated the presence of a "bug";
debugging must now be used to identify what caused it. Too
often, the starting point for this process is the 50 or so
pages of hexadecimal dumps that the computer appends to the
above message to help clarify its lucid comment. However, there
are alternatives and an important function of software engineering is to ensure that powerful tools and techniques for testing
and debugging are readily available and widely used.

Now it seems to be the nature of things, at least within
the current state of the art, that programmers make, and will
continue to make mistakes. Whether these are due to faults in
the design, misunderstandings of the design specifications or
just plain coding errors, there is a tendency to refer to such
mistakes as bugs, almost as if to attribute their existence to
some external agency. It has been suggested (cynically, I hope)
that is is only through such a transference of responsibility

that programmers are able to preserve their own sanity - considering the rate at which they seem capable of generating such errors.
Now there is no doubt at all in my mind that the best way of
reducing the number of bugs in a program is to prevent them ever
occurring in the first place. Many of the topics discussed in
this course have been aimed at just this objective - the use of
high level languages, structured programming, portability,
modularity etc. However, although such techniques can reduce
the probability of bugs occurring, they cannot guarantee that
it will be zero. The programmer must still face the task of
demonstrating that the program he has constructed will operate
correctly, at least to his own satisfaction. It may be possible
some time in the future to effect this by means of a formal
proof. The question of the correctness of programs is currently
evoking a great deal of interest in the computer field and a
number of significant advances have been made. Noteworthy is
the work of the Vienna group who were able to demonstrate an
error in an IBM PL/1 compiler by formal methods [1]. However
such techniques are still a long way from being generally applicable to the wide range of software we are currently required
to produce. As good software engineers, we must remain aware
of such developments and make use of them when and where we can;
but, in the meantime, the task of proving the program by more
conventional means still remains. We must therefore plan for a
testing and a debugging phase in the software production
sequence. If there is an underlying theme to these lectures,
then it is the importance of planning well ahead of time for
these phases. I shall return to consider this point in more
detail in Section 2.

Testing and debugging must not be viewed in isolation from
the other phases of software production. Once design and implementation have been completed, the programmer commences testing
and attempts to demonstrate the presence of bugs by exercising
the program with a suitable set of test data. It is important

to remember that testing can never show the absence of bugs, only their presence. Once an error has been detected, the programmer hopefully makes use of various debugging tools and techniques in order to determine why it occurred. In turn, this may lead him back either to the design or the implementation phase to correct the error in the light of what he has discovered. Once the correction has been made, the testing sequence is re-entered. This cycling through the phases continues until the programmer is satisfied the program is working correctly (which unfortunately too often means merely that there are no obvious errors). The next phase in the life of the program depends on whether it is part of a larger system (in which case it will be integrated with other modules and the testing/debugging phase re-entered) or whether it is a product to be made available to a customer. Experience has shown that it is not good sense to allow a piece of software to move directly from the developer to the customer without carrying out further tests. These checks are performed in the validation and certification phases. The former is similar to testing except that the test data is prepared by persons other than the developer of the program. Usually such people belong to the same organisation, i.e. the supplier of the software. Certification, on the other hand, is the responsibility of the customer and again involves testing the program to see that it meets its design specifications and performs satisfactorily under local conditions. HELMS will have more to say about these phases in his lectures. I have mentioned them here for completeness since each involves testing in one form or another. Planning for the testing phase must take account of the existence of these subsequent phases and make special provision for them.

In presenting these lectures, I must make it very clear at the outset that I am not proposing some new and revolutionary approach to the processes of testing and debugging. Many of the techniques I will discuss should already be familiar to you, at least I hope they are. Yet one cannot help noticing that the programmers continue over and over again to make the same mistakes when producing software. In some cases, the techniques are not well documented and are part of the folklore of programming. They are often only learnt in the hard school of experience. The new programmer quickly discovers that writing programs is easy; it takes him some time to realise that engineering reliable software can be difficult. Only then is he prepared to pay more attention to the problems of testing and debugging and consider how they could be solved more effectively. For these reasons, two main points I want to stress in these lectures are:

(a) the importance of planning for the testing and debugging phases;

(b) the use of testing and debugging aids.

In concentrating on these points, I am of course assuming that sensible decisions have already been made about such factors as language, structure, modularity etc.

2. PLANNING FOR THE TESTING AND DEBUGGING PHASES

Forward planning is of paramount importance if testing and debugging are to be carried out effectively and efficiently; lack of it will almost certainly guarantee that the phases are long and costly ones. The planning should form an integral part of the design process; it cannot sensibly be carried out after the software has been written. Let us examine what factors we should consider and what influence they might have on testing and debugging.

2.1 DOCUMENTATION

The need for and importance of high standards in documentation have already been stressed in this course by GOOS. Documentation has a fundamental role to play in ensuring that the testing and debugging phases can be successfully carried out. Lack of good documentation usually means that testing is not performed as thoroughly as it should be and debugging is that much more complicated.

It has been suggested that computer programs should be written and documented in such a way that they could be published [2]. An analogy is drawn between a computer program and a text book and it is proposed that many of the specific techniques used to make a book attractive and readable should be adopted in order to remove difficulties that people encounter when trying to understand programs. Particular attention should be paid to techniques for improving the readability of the program by people; it should not just be considered as input to a machine. Thus every variable used should be annotated, every subroutine accompanied by a description of what it is intended to do and what algorithm it uses. Any listing of the program should be paginated so that a table of contents can be set up to show where every subroutine or module occurs. There should also be an index which shows where every routine and variable is referenced. In creating such documentation, the programmer must take as his goal the need to ensure that someone other than himself can understand the program and how it should behave. The effort required to document a program to this standard will pay handsome dividends in the testing and debugging phases.

Other useful pieces of information which could be recorded in the commentary are any conditions which should be true

at particular points in the program. For example, if an integer
input parameter to a procedure should lie within a given range,
then this fact should be recorded in the comments associated
with the procedure. Such information is useful for debugging and
invaluable for maintenance and enhancement. Too often, when a
working program is modified, it stops working because some
implicit restriction has been broken by the modifications. If
the condition is not specifically checked in the code, then the
comment will at least warn the person making the change of any
restriction that should apply.

Documentation should also be used by the programmer to
remind himself of what actions need to be carried out during
testing. He is much more aware of the problems that may arise
from using a particular algorithm and the special cases that
need to be checked while he is writing a particular routine
than he will be when the whole program is completed. If he
includes such information as comments in the program, he is much
more likely to remember to make the appropriate checks when testing is being carried out. The whole question of documenting
test procedures is one that requires considerable attention.
It is just as important as the documentation of the program
itself, particularly if the program is one which will be maintained
and enhanced by other people. There is a tendency on the part
of programmers to ignore this aspect of program development and
to treat test data as something to be discarded once the program
is thought to be working satisfactorily. The correct approach
is one in which a well-documented set of test procedures and data
is built up and retained throughout the life of the program.
Whenever the program is modified, it should be exercised on the
test data in an attempt to reveal any interference between the
modifications and the original code. Any change made to a

program should be reflected in corresponding changes to the test procedures and data. Remember that such testing is no guarantee that interference has not occurred; it merely indicates that the test data can be processed correctly.

2.2   DEBUGGING CODE

The obvious step from the provision of comments which describe what the program should do is the inclusion of code to enable the programmer to inspect what it is actually doing. The idea of inserting code into a program specifically for the purposes of debugging has been around as long as people have been writing programs [3].

"It is good to plan to include extra printing of
the kind described here in all new programs when
they are first drawn up rather than to wait until
the program has been tried and found to fail"

(Wilkes et al, 1951).

Unfortunately, in spite of such advice and the great wealth of subsequent experience which supports it, there are still far too many programs written today which do not include adequate provision for the testing and debugging phases. Too often the necessary code is only added as an afterthought in an attempt to meet the needs as they arise. It usually results in large quantities of output but little understanding of the problem. Undoubtedly, the most effective debugging aids are those built into the program from the very beginning. They can lead to substantial increases in the productivity of programmers. Let us consider in general what type of information could be useful and how it might be obtained. Whether or not a programmer

has explicitly to include the code himself will depend on
what debugging aids are available in the system. We will discuss these in more detail in Section 3.

The simplest action a programmer can take is to include a
number of print statements which allow him to monitor the
execution of the program. These might output intermediate
results, current values of variables or just markers to indicate
that a particular label has been passed or a subroutine entered.
The statements produce output similar to that of the trace
debugging aid described in Section 3.1. However, they can be made
much more selective since the programmer knows which statements
should be monitored and what variables examined.

Another function that can be performed by debugging code
is to improve the usefulness of post mortem dumps. The evidence
that can be obtained from a dump is often not sufficient to
locate an error unless steps have been taken to ensure that
more information has been placed in the memory than is actually
required to solve the problem. For example, on entry to a
subroutine one might arrange to store the following:

(a) name of the calling routine;
(b) location in the routine from which the call was made;
(c) value of any input parameters;
(d) value of any global variables altered by the routine;
(e) contents of registers (for assembly code programs);
(f) a count of the number of times the routine has been
    entered.

If this information is placed in a cyclic buffer, then it can
be extracted from the dump for the last n entries to the
routine where n is determined by the size of the buffer.
Application of this technique need not be restricted to routine

entry points but may be used at any point in the program where the programmer wishes to preserve some current information before it is changed. The main advantage it has over simple print statements is that the amount of diagnostic output can be reduced. If the point of interest is inside a loop, then the technique provides the programmer with the last n values before the program is terminated rather than m values where m is the number of times control has passed through the inspection point. In many circumstances, m could be very much larger than n. Its main disadvantage is that the programmer may have to learn how to interpret the dumps produced by the machine. We will return to consider this point in more detail in Section 3.

Earlier we noted the possibility of including comments describing conditions and restrictions which should apply at various points in the program. Such comments could be supplemented by code which actually checks that the condition holds true, e.g. that an input parameter to a routine does indeed lie within a specified range. The action taken by the program on detecting that a condition is false may simply be to initiate a dump; other possibilities include entering a diagnostic routine or even ignoring the failure (after printing a message) so that testing can continue.

Normally one expects to remove debugging code once the program has passed through the testing phase. However, in some circumstances, we have found it advantageous to leave instances of such code in programs even when they have been put into service. This is particularly true for real time systems in which input cannot be reproduced exactly. Under such circumstances, it can be a very difficult task to determine the exact cause of a failure. When a fault occurs, it may initiate a long sequence of events which eventually produces the final

collapse. The reconstruction of this sequence can be very
difficult since much of the evidence may be of a transitory
nature. In such situations, the use of what we have termed
"guard code" [4] can pay handsome dividends. This code can be
used to apply consistency checks, to test that restrictions
have not been violated or to preserve useful information.
Effectively one is using the principle of redundancy to improve
the reliability of the software in the sense that an attempt is
made to ensure that errors do not go undetected. We made
extensive use of the guard code technique during the development
of the COTAN multi-access system on the ICL KDF9. It contributed
very significantly to the rate at which errors could be located
and corrected when the system was put into service.

2.3   GENERATION OF DEBUGGING CODE

The use of debugging code can sometimes lead to difficulties
when the time comes to remove it from the source text. One often
finds that a program which appears to be working satisfactorily
suddenly starts to fail when the debugging code is taken out.
This situation is more likely to occur when the code is deleted
manually. An alternative approach is to make the debugging
code a permanent feature of the source text and generate the
actual machine instructions as and when required. An added
advantage is that the debugging code can be reactivated at any
time even after the program has been put into service. Unfortunately, high level language compilers rarely provide facilities
which enable a programmer to control whether code is generated
from a particular statement or not. In some implementations,
he may be able to request that extra code be generated to help
with debugging and we will consider this in more detail in
Section 3. However, language designers do not, as yet, seem

to have recognised the value of including constructions in a
language which may either be treated as a comment or used to
produce code depending on the setting of a compiler parameter.
For this reason, a macro processor can be a very useful tool
to control the generation of debugging code.

The technique is applicable both to assembly code and
high level languages particularly with the availability of such
language-independent macro processors as STAGE2 [5] or ML/1 [6].
The programmer is free to introduce extra statements into the
language providing he defines a set of rules which allows the
macro processor to translate these into a sequence of legal
operations. This translation is usually carried out in a pre-
pass before the source text is input to the compiler. By
redefining the rules or parameterising the generation so that
one of a number of translation rules can be selected, the
programmer can easily arrange that a particular statement or
class of statements is ignored. These extra statements therefore
form part of the source text but do not result in the production
of any code unless it has been specifically requested.

There is no need to restrict this approach to special
statements created by the programmer. If the macro processor
is powerful enough to recognise constructs which are legal in
the language, then these could be used to direct the generation
of debugging code. For example, one could use STAGE2 to detect
a function declaration in FORTRAN and generate code to monitor
entries to the routine; assignment to a particular variable
could be used to produce code to preserve the current value.
How far one can use this technique will depend on the facilities
in the macro processor and the language in which the program is
written.

Earlier, it was pointed out that debugging code could be

used to supplement comments describing some condition which
should apply at a particular point in a program. By using
a macro processor, it may be possible to actually generate the
code from the comment. Thus instead of merely noting in a
comment that the value of a variable should lie within a given
range, one could introduce a statement of the form

ASSERT RANGE OF ' IS ' TO '

where the first parameter is the name of the variable and the
second and third parameters, the lower and upper limits of the
range respectively. This statement contains as much information
as the comment but could be turned into the appropriate code
via a macro processor. Apart from the economy in writing, an
added advantage is that the writer is encouraged to keep the
comments up to date as changes are made to the program. The
dual role played by the comments can help to ensure that they
do not get out of step with the code as is frequently the case.

2.4   MODULARITY

One of the advantages claimed for a modular approach to
the construction of software is that the problems of testing and
debugging are greatly simplified. Larger systems can be built
up from a number of thoroughly tested modules and a high degree
of reliability should be readily obtainable. However as Dijkstra
has pointed out [7], if the individual modules have a probability
p of being correct, then the probability that the whole program
is correct cannot exceed p^N where N is the number of modules.
For systems where N is large, p must be almost equal to 1 if
the overall probability is to be significantly different from
zero. Hence, although we make every effort to ensure that

individual modules are as correct as possible, we must not overlook the need to test and debug the module aggregate.

In any large system, a module rarely exists as an entity in its own right. It interacts with other modules passing information to and fro across an interface. Since modules which will ultimately coexist in a large system are often constructed in parallel by different programmers, the difficulty that arises is how to test a module in isolation from the other modules on which it depends. A common solution is to construct a test bed which simulates the behaviour of the module's external environment. The module can then be placed in the test bed and suitably exercised.

A major drawback with this approach is the difficulty of ensuring that the test bed correctly simulates the actual environment in which the module will eventually operate. Usually the test bed is created by the person writing the module, and any misunderstanding he has about the other modules and their interfaces will be incorporated into it. When a number of modules tested in this way are combined, the result is often chaos even though each module is claimed by its originator to be working satisfactorily. Unfortunately, what has been tested is the interface between the module and its test bed, not necessarily its true interface to the actual system.

There are a number of ways one might improve this situation. The task of creating the test bed may be assigned to someone other than the programmer constructing the module. It may also be possible, in some cases, to construct a common test environment for a number of modules and the responsibility for doing this should be placed in the hands of the more experienced programmers. Test harnesses and test data generators can sometimes be very useful in reducing the probability that the test bed itself contains errors. At a minimum, the writers of individual modules should make extensive use of the guard code technique discussed earlier and be guided by "the principle of mutual suspicion". This states that a module must not make use of any data passed to it across an interface without first checking on its validity as defined by the specification of the interface. The checks applied should be even more rigorous than one might expect to use, say at a subroutine interface within the module. Again, the question arises as to what action should be taken if an item of data is found to be invalid. In this case, a possible approach would be to organise inter-module communication in such a way that if one module calls another, it must be prepared to have the call rejected. Thus the called module on finding that the input is invalid can return control to the caller indicating which item is at fault. The writer of this module can then take whatever steps he wishes in an attempt to isolate the cause of the error. The extra code required to make these validity checks will be more than justified by the time saved in locating the errors. It can of course be progressively removed via the techniques discussed above as the reliability of the module aggregate increases.

Another problem raised by the concept of modularity is the choice of the test strategy. Obviously, it would not be a sound policy to wait until all the modules were ready and then attempt to test the whole system as a unit. A better approach is to combine a number of modules and test these thoroughly before going on to form larger aggregates. We will refer to this process as "incremental testing". The size of a test increment will vary from one situation to another but should be chosen to obtain a reasonable balance between increase in complexity and the cost of creating the test procedures.

The concept of incremental testing can also be applied
to the construction of individual modules. These usually consist of a number of routines and again one should not wait
until the whole module is formed before starting to test. For
example, in a module consisting of a main routine which organises
calls on a set of subroutines, it may be possible to commence
testing as soon as the main routine and a few of the subroutines
are ready. Dummy routines could be substituted for any routines
not yet available and set up to return values which satisfy
the needs of the main sequence. Thus the overall flow of
control could be tested. Complex subroutines could first be
subjected to a preliminary testing in isolation before being
added to the remainder of the program. In this way, the section
of the program already checked out can be used to provide a test
environment for the new routine.

There are no hard and fast rules about the best way to use
incremental testing. Much will depend on the type of problem
being solved, the structure of the program and the skill of the
programmer. However, experience has shown that there are decided
benefits from using such an approach - reduced costs and more
reliable software. It must therefore be given adequate consideration when the testing phase is being planned.

2.5   PARAMETERISATION

In Section 3.3, we will discuss the technique of extreme
case testing. Some attention must be paid during the construction
of the software to ways of making such an approach feasible.
In particular, the programmer must ensure that the code is well
parameterised so that the appropriate test situation can easily
be created.

To illustrate this process, suppose we are constructing

a dynamic buffer control routine. An area of core will contain
a number of buffers and these may be allocated to processes on
request. If a process asks for a buffer and none is available,
then the control routine will have to move the information from
one of the incore buffers to backing store so that the buffer
becomes free. Subsequently this information will have to be
retrieved once the process to which it belongs is reactivated.
Now, it is clear that the mechanisms for transferring information to and from the backing store will only come into operation once the level of activity has risen to the point where
the demand for buffers is greater than the supply. In order to
check these mechanisms, either we could create a test situation
in which demand is high or we could restrict the supply. The
latter is by far the easier approach providing the number of
incore buffers is a parameter which can readily be altered. If
this is the case, then the first test might be one in which
there is only a single buffer. This number could be gradually
increased as the level of confidence in the reliability of the
various parts of the package rises. When the package is included
in say a real time system and put into service, the number of
buffers required may depend on such factors as the amount of
core available and desired response time. The parameter can be
set accordingly. If at some later stage in the life of the
system, we suspect that an intermittent error is being caused
by the package, then we could reduce the number of buffers
available in an attempt to increase the frequency with which
the error occurs and the probability of locating it. The ability
to control the availability of this resource simply by changing
one parameter has provided us with a powerful method for creating
convenient test situations.

Intelligent use of parameterisation is not as widespread,

in my opinion, as it should be amongst programmers. One still
finds far too many instances in current day systems where
quantities which should be parameters have been built in as an
integral part of the code. It then becomes a very difficult
and expensive task to change them. All languages should include
features which encourage programmers to make use of these
techniques. For example, the manifest constant is a very useful
facility for allowing a programmer to parameterise both declarations and executable statements. A macro processor can be a
useful tool in this context if the language does not provide
the appropriate facilities. A better understanding of the value
of parameterisation could help programmers to improve the quality
of current software, particularly in the areas of reliability
and adaptability.

3.   TESTING AND DEBUGGING TECHNIQUES

Once the testing and debugging phases have been entered, a
programmer must be aware of the tools and techniques that are
available to aid these processes. An important aspect of
Software Engineering is the development of such tools and
techniques since their use can greatly reduce the cost of
producing software and contribute significantly to an increase
in reliability.

Underlying any discussion on the use of testing and debugging aids is the problem of man-machine communication. On the
one hand, the programmer must be able to state conveniently
and succintly what aspects of the behaviour of the program he
wishes to examine and what information he requires to assist
him in locating an error; on the other hand, the machine must
be able to respond with clear and informative diagnostic messages.

A singularly bad feature of many current systems is the lack of
attention that has been paid to these aspects of the man-
machine interface. To use some debugging aid, the programmer
often has to prepare his requests in a coded form which is
difficult to comprehend and construct. Diagnostic messages from
the machine are often unintelligible to the average programmer
or even non-existent [8]. In many cases, the messages which
are produced appear to be the relics of diagnostic output
included by the system programmer for his own purposes. They
are often very cryptic, being composed of numbers and symbols
which, although perhaps of some value to the originator of the
program, are meaningless to the user. It is clear that we will
have to pay considerable attention in the future to obtaining a
better dialogue between man and machine if we wish to improve
the processes of testing and debugging.

3.1 CLASSICAL DEBUGGING TECHNIQUES

We will consider first some of the classical techniques
and examine ways in which they might be improved.

(a) Post-Mortem Dumps

A common sight around any computer room is that of a programmer bearing away a large pile of computer output. As often
as not, it is a system dump. Nowadays most computer systems
provide such a facility, activated either by a call from the
program or in the event of some catastrophic failure. Dumps
can be a very useful debugging aid but their value is often
reduced by the way in which they are implemented. The output
tends to be voluminous and use of octal or hexidecimal characters in the listing can make understanding the dump a difficult

task, particularly for high level language programmers who
often have little knowledge about the structure of the underlying machine. To increase the usefulness of this aid we need
to be able to control the amount of information produced and
make the dump listing more meaningful to the programmer.

At a minimum, the program should be able to notify the system of which areas are to be dumped and in what format the
information should be produced. For example, a FORTRAN program
could request that a certain array be dumped in the event of
a failure and that the format required is integer or floating
point. A further improvement would be to permit the program
to select a particular area as a candidate for dumping and
later cancel this request. Thus as the program executes, it
could notify the system of the areas to be dumped and these can
be accumulated in a dump request list. Subsequently, control
may reach a point at which the programmer knows that the requests
made so far would be of little value if a failure occurred in
the next stage. Thus he could cancel all current requests and
re-initialise the list. New items could then be added and
when the program ultimately fails only those areas currently
of interest will be dumped. If the final instruction clears
the dump request list before the program terminates successfully,
then no dumps will be produced unless the program ends prematurely.
Thus the instructions controlling the state of the dump request
list could advantageously be made a permanent part of the program
so that diagnostic information is produced if some unforeseen
set of circumstances causes the program to fail.

A major increase in the usefulness of a dump can be made
if all the information presented to the user is expressed in
terms of his source program and the language in which it is
written. This implies that the dump routine must have access

to the symbol table. This presents no great problem if the
program is being executed in a test mode in which case the
symbol table could be made available in core. Some difficulties
arise if we wish to retain the facility after the program has
passed through the testing phase into production. In this
situation, one would not wish to waste core to hold the symbol
table and it may have to be retrieved from backing store.

An example of a system which outputs a dump in terms of
the source language is one developed for ALGOL W [9]. The post-
mortem analysis includes frequency information for statements
obeyed and, if termination was abnormal, a dump of the active
storage. A listing of the original source text is produced with
the approximate location of the error clearly indicated. In
the dump of active storage, variables local to each active
procedure or block are displayed. In the case of arrays, the
display is limited to 8 or fewer elements including the first
and last so that array bounds are available. Any variable which
has not been initialised is marked as such in the output. It
is claimed that the system does not impose very large overheads.
The basic compiler generates reasonably compact and efficient
code for the System/360 and the debugging routines (which also
include a tracing facility) increase the size by a factor between
1.2 and 2 depending on what options the user selects.

(b) Snapshots

This is similar to the dump in many respects except that
output occurs as soon as the request is made and execution continues. The user specifies one or more snapshot points and the
information he wants output. The instruction at each such point
is preserved and replaced by a transfer of control to the
snapshot routine. When the program is being executed and control

reaches one of these points, a jump to the snapshot routine
occurs and the required information is output. The original
instruction is then obeyed and execution of the program is
resumed. Obviously some care must be exercised about where
the snapshots points are located - particularly in cases where
the program can modify itself.

The advantage of the snapshot technique is that it obviates
the need to include explicit print statements in the program;
the disadvantage is that it is usually a facility provided at
a low level and the snapshot points may have to be specified
in terms of actual machine addresses. Further, the technique
can result in voluminous output if the snapshot point is
unwisely chosen, for example in the middle of a loop. In some
circumstances, this may be just the point at which the information is required. To handle this situation, it should be
possible to specify three parameters - 1, m and n - when declaring
a snapshot point. 1 is the number of times control is to pass
the point before output commences; thereafter output occurs
every mth time until the total number of passes is greater than
or equal to n.

(c) Trace

When a program is being executed in trace mode, each statement, within the area being traced, causes some information to
be output. What the information is depends on the level at which
the trace is being applied. At the machine code level, it might
include program counter, instruction being obeyed, contents of
accumulator and index registers. In the ALGOL W debugging system,
output consists of the source text line together with the values
of all variables and function procedures required for expression
evaluation; in the appropriate context, the display also contains

any newly assigned values, the outcome of conditional tests, procedure calls and the correspondence between formal and actual parameters.

The problems which arise from using a trace are excessive output and greatly reduced execution speed. The former can be controlled to some extent by arranging that the system imposes an upper limit on the number of times any statement is traced and that the default option for this limit is low. The latter difficulty arises from the fact that tracing is usually done interpretively. Hence it must be possible to arrange that trace mode will only apply to specified areas of the program. Execution of the program in other regions can then proceed at normal speed. This can also help to reduce the amount of trace information produced.

(d) Traceback

The purpose of this debugging aid is to show how control reached a point in the program where an error occurred. It may be used in conjunction with a post-mortem dump or operate in a similar manner to a snapshot. Thus a traceback produced when a FORTRAN program fails might be a record of all the procedure calls and the associated actual parameters that brought control to the failure point. In a similar manner, the traceback feature in STAGE2 outputs the current line which caused the failure, followed by the call on the current macro, the call on the macro that generated that call and so on, back to the original input line. Unless the error is a fatal one, processing is then resumed. Thus the user is free to build diagnostics into a macro without causing premature termination.

(e) Debug Mode

Aids such as post-mortem dumps and tracebacks are often made available for high level languages via a debug option in the compiler. If debug mode is requested, then the compiler generates the extra code and storage required by the various facilities. At the same time, code to check other features of the language may be produced, e.g. that array bounds in ALGOL are not exceeded, that the address used in a FORTRAN assigned goto statement is valid. What checks can be made depend on the structure and facilities of the language. Obviously, there will be some overheads to pay for such run time checks. However, the extra code can be removed once the program has passed through the testing phase by recompiling the program with the debug option off.

(f) Documentation Aids

We have already discussed the importance of good documentation in the testing and debugging phases. Programs which assist users to create, maintain and understand the documentation are therefore useful tools to have available when software is being tested and debugged. The facilities offered by such programs are many and varied [10,11,12]; often they depend on particular features of a programming language. Examples of the actions we might expect to be able to carry out are:

(i) reformat the source text to produce a neater listing in which any underlying structure is displayed, e.g. in ALGOL 60, indentation could be used to make the block structure clearly visible;

(ii) paginate the listing and prepare a table of contents

for all procedures, labels and declarations;

(iii) construct an index to all calls to procedures,
transfers to labels and references to variables;

(iv) systematically change identifiers throughout a
program or in specified procedures;

(v) draw flowcharts from the code or associated comments.
It should be possible to vary the level at which the
flowchart is constructed - from a detailed one for
individual procedures to one which illustrates the
global structure of the whole program.

3.2   ONLINE DEBUGGING

To a user of first generation machines, the tasks of
testing and debugging seemed much less difficult than
they are today in modern batch processing systems. He could
interact very closely with his program under test, controlling
its behaviour from the console of the machine. By setting breakpoints, he could make the program stop on any desired instruction;
he could then examine the contents of any register or memory
location and alter its value if required; by means of the single
shot key, he could cause instructions to be executed one by one
and monitor the effect of individual operations; once detailed
examination of a particular area was complete, he could cause
the program to restart at any point and operate at full speed
until the next breakpoint was encountered. Debugging was a
much more rapid process than it is today, particularly if the
turnaround of the system is poor. The only users who seem to
have convenient debugging facilities are those with small machines,
since again close interaction between man and machine is possible. Many of these small machines are equipped with powerful

debugging systems which make the process even easier than it was before, e.g. DDT on the PDP series. However, with the advent of interactive time sharing systems, the possibility of improving the debugging facilities on large machines becomes a feasible proposition. Because of the resources available on such machines, it should be possible to construct an interactive test bed into which the program can be placed and exercised. The conversational facilities provided by such a system should enable a programmer to interact not only with his own program but with the test bed itself. He can then gain access to convenient mechanisms for monitoring and modifying the behaviour of the program under test. Since resources are not likely to be as limited as they are on small machines, the facilities provided could be such that all requests for information or changes could be directly related to the language in which the program was originally written. The system could then cater for the needs of high level language programmers who constitute the majority of computer users today.

There has been considerable debate in recent years on the virtues or otherwise of conversational debugging techniques [13]. There are those who feel it will tend to make programmers adopt a rather sloppy approach to debugging. Since access is made so easy, it is felt that programmers might substitute interaction for thinking and make only superficial attempts to correct errors instead of searching for the perhaps more fundamental reasons why the faults occurred. Such fears are not unreasonable. However, I feel that a programmer can be trained to make sensible use of conversational debugging facilities, provided he can choose conveniently between using the machine or desk checking the program. Thus, if he can only book a console for a limited period of time, then he may

be tempted to make hurried and superficial corrections. If,
on the other hand, the console is in his own office, he
can choose the method most appropriate to the particular error.
A reasonable approach would be for the programmer to carry out
a short period of desk checking and then return to the console
when he feels more information is needed to solve the problem.
By achieving a correct balance between the two techniques, he
will be able to locate errors more quickly and efficiently.
In contrast to this, when using a batch system, the programmer
must plan his next run carefully in an attempt to obtain the
information he needs. To guard against the possibility of not
getting sufficient evidence, he may err on the side of requesting too much and be faced with the task of sorting through a
large quantity of output. In the conversational system, since
he has immediate access, he need only ask for the next piece
of information he thinks might help to locate the error.
However, there is a word of warning: we must not make it too
easy for a programmer to alter a program which is perhaps part
of a larger system and then immediately make this new version
available to other users. By all means, let him make the
correction as quickly as possible but then ensure that the
appropriate validation procedures are applied to the modified
code before incorporating it with the remainder of the system.
It it all too easy to "correct" a module without fully apprecia-
ting what affect the change could have on other modules in the
system.

　　Let us now consider what type of facilities one might wish
to see in online debugging systems. For the purpose of the
discussion, we will restrict ourselves to systems which support
high level languages rather than ones which handle only assembly
code. The techniques used in both types of systems are very

similar. However, we wish to concern ourselves with systems
which could be of value to a wide class of programmers.
Further, we will consider general-purpose rather than special-
purpose high level languages. Many online systems which
concentrate on specialised areas have been constructed and
equipped with powerful debugging aids [14,15]. Again, however,
our emphasis is on languages which are suitable for a wide
class of problems.

In constructing an online debugging system for a high
level language, one might expect to provide the following:

(a) Commands to set and reset breakpoints on any statement in
the program. When the program reaches a breakpoint, its current
state is "frozen" and control is returned to the online user.
The breakpoint is requested by specifying either a statement
number or a position relative to a label or procedure entry
point. This implies that the debugging system must have access
to the symbol table and the structure of the source text. This is
relatively simple to implement if the program under test is
being interpreted; there may be problems if the program is
being executed directly in machine code since instructions
have to be extracted and jumps to the monitor routine inserted.
An extension to the simple breakpoint is one that associates
a condition. In general, this could be any condition that can
be legally expressed in the language. However, on the grounds
of programmer convenience, it should be possible simply to supply
a number n with a breakpoint request. Exit to the user then
occurs only after the breakpoint has been passed n times.

(b) The ability of the system to return control to the user in
the event of an error in the program, e.g. attempting to take
the square root of a negative number, exceeding the array

bounds in an array reference. The compiler should generate
code in a debug mode similar to that discussed in Section 3.1
so that the execution of the program is monitored as closely
as possible. When an error occurs, a clear diagnostic message
should be output to the console accompanied by any relevant
information needed to pinpoint the faulty source line. This
information should be couched in terms of the original language
e.g. position relative to a label in a particular procedure.
More esoteric error detection is also possible in such a test
bed (particularly if the program is being interpreted) e.g.
attempting to use an uninitialised variable. Further, it
could be useful to be able to mark a variable or a number of
array elements as "protected" so that any error is reported
as soon as any attempt is made to access them. This is a particularly valuable facility if a variable is being altered
illegally, and one cannot see which statement is the culprit.

(c) Facilities for examining and altering any item of data in
a program once it has been frozen and control returned to the
console. This may involve merely executing a simple assignment
or print statement - which implies that the system must be able
to recall the compiler. More complex operations may, for
example, involve executing a loop statement to print the elements
of an array. Unfortunately, it is unlikely that the original
language will be sufficient to couch all the enquiries that a
user may wish to make, e.g. if the language permits recursion,
he may wish to inspect previous values of a variable on the stack.
Hence some extensions to the language will be necessary. This
is also true for other data which could be accumulated by the
debugging system, e.g. the last n sets of actual parameters
supplied to a procedure.

(d) The ability to restart the program not necessarily at the point at which execution was interrupted. It should also be possible to cause statements to be executed one-by-one with control returning to the console between statements without having to set a breakpoint on every one. Trace information could be produced if requested when statements are executed in this manner. However, the ability to obey a section of the program in trace mode is probably not required since it could produce too much output for the console to handle efficiently. Since rapid interaction is possible, the programmer should be encouraged to be selective about what information is to be returned to him.

(e) Facilities for deleting, replacing and inserting lines in the program. Ideally one would like such changes to become effective immediately they are made. Whether this is possible or not depends on how the program is set up in the test bed. Thus in the FORTRAN debugging system [16] for the Berkeley time sharing system, the program is held in a compiled form and no facilities are provided for modifying the code. The only way a user can make any changes is to edit the symbolic version and recompile the whole program. On the other hand, in the QUICKTRAN system [17], the FORTRAN statements are interpreted and the program being debugged may be freely modified. The price that must be paid for this convenience is of course efficiency since interpretation will reduce execution speed considerably. However, providing an optimising compiler capable of accepting the same symbolic text is available, one could use the online test bed for debugging and then recompile the program before it is put into production. This is not a complete answer to the difficulty since it may not be possible to

carry out all the required testing if the program operates too
slowly. A better solution might be one in which the program
in the test bed consists of a mixture of interpretive and
directly executable code. In the lectures on portability and
adaptability (WAITE, POOLE A), we described an experiment in
which such a hybrid program was produced, and pointed out that
the selection of the type of code for a particular area of the
program was parameterised. Thus we could envisage a situation
in which the first time a program is placed in the test bed, it
is set up entirely for interpretation. Once the basic subroutines
have been debugged, they could be compiled into directly executable code in a later test run. In this form, they could be
called from an inner loop in, say, the main routine without
degrading the overall speed of the program. Only those parts
of the program held in the interpretive form would be available
for modification. Finally, the whole of the program would
exist in the compiled form and could be checked out in the
test bed before being placed in production.

Another problem that arises when the user is provided with
facilities for modifying the program in the test bed is that of
updating the source text so that it corresponds to the actual
code. If the test bed does not need to access the source
text once it has been compiled, then any changes could be
saved and edited into the original text once the test run has been
completed. However, the user then has to work from the original
listing which existed when the run commenced. A more convenient (and more expensive) solution is to make any changes to
the source as soon as they are supplied. A user can then
produce an up-to-date listing of his source text at any time
during a test run.

(f) Commands to request statistical information about the behaviour of the program, e.g. the number of times any state-ment has been obeyed, a list of all statements (or routines) which have not been executed, a list of variables which have not been initialised or referenced. This information can often provide insight into the performance of the program as well as indicating possible sources of error.

(g) Convenient methods for initiating any of the foregoing facilities. Particular attention must be paid in the construc-tion of any test bed to ensure that the user has available a powerful and concise language for issuing his requests. A macro facility which enables him to combine frequently used sequences of commands is a very necessary feature of such a system.

Most of the facilities described above have been implemen-ted in one way or another in a number of online debugging systems. The response from users has been one of enthusiasm even when the facilities are quite primitive. In a multi-access system developed at Culham [4], we provided an interpretive ALGOL compiler for use online and an optimising compiler to prepare jobs for production. Modifications in the source text were made via an interactive text editor. With these facilities, users found they could develop programs much more rapidly than was possible in the batch system alone. Undoubtedly, as the use of time sharing systems increases, online debugging will have a larger and larger role to play in the production of software.

Before leaving this topic, I will describe briefly a system in which a somewhat different approach to online debug-ging is taken. One of the drawbacks to the above proposals

is that the test bed is effectively tied to one high level
language. In modern computer systems, there are usually a
number of such languages and the possibility of having a common
test bed becomes an attractive one. EXDAMS [18] is an attempt
to set up such a facility since it provides a single environment
in which the users can easily add new online debugging aids
to the system without modifying the compilers, the test bed or
their own programs. The approach taken is one in which the
program to be debugged is run with an EXDAMS monitor routine
which collects all the necessary information about the program's
behaviour and stores it on a history tape. Subsequently, the
debugging routines extract information from the tape and present
it to the online user. The monitor which prepares the history
tape is language dependent. However, the remainder of the
programs which process the tape are independent of both the
implementation of the source language and the source language
itself. Any debugging and monitoring aids can easily be added
to the system by writing the appropriate file search and for-
matting routines, providing the necessary information is
available. Some efficiency has been sacrificed since scanning
the history tape will involve a large amount of I/O, but it is
claimed that the added flexibility far outweighs any loss.
Output is through a CRT and both static and motion picture
displays can be produced. The former displays information that
is invariant with execution time, e.g. values of variables at
the time an error occurred. The latter displays data which
varies with time, e.g. last n values of a particular variable.
The user can run the motion picture aids both forwards and
backwards at variable speeds and stop at any desired point.
This type of application is just one example of the great
potential displays have in an online debugging system. Since

output can be displayed at a much faster rate than on a
teletype, a user can be provided with more rapid and convenient
ways of scanning the information about his program. Further,
it may be possible to use graphical presentations to aid the
debugging process. If the flowchart of the program is displayed on the screen while the program is being executed,
then the flow of control could be monitored visually. With
such output devices connected into powerful online test beds,
it is not unreasonable to hope that many of the debugging
problems that beset us today may eventually disappear.

3.3   TESTING STRATEGIES AND TECHNIQUES

To this point, we have been mainly concerned with debugging aids and techniques. Now let us turn to consider what
strategies and techniques we might use to improve testing
procedures. Unfortunately the situation is nowhere near as
clear-cut as it is for debugging. Whether or not a program is
well tested will depend on many factors, including the adequacy
of the planning for this phase during the design of the program,
the skill of the programmer and his experience, which should
warn him that insufficient testing means unreliable software.
However, it is not the quantity but the quality of the testing
that is the important factor.

It should not be difficult to prove to oneself that
exhaustive testing, i.e. testing all possible cases, is an
inefficient and time consuming exercise. Yet it seems to be
a common enough approach. Many programmers apparently think
that if they exercise the program on enough test cases, then
all the bugs will be revealed. However, the fact that a program
has worked on many cases does not prove that it will work in
all cases. One must give considerable attention to the way in

which testing is carried out. In particular, if one chooses
the right test cases, then, by induction, one has a fair degree
of confidence in the correctness of the program. There are
no general rules; much depends upon the problem and the algorithm being used. For example, if the program being constructed
is one to calculate the logarithm to base e then at least
one should test it with a negative number, zero, 1,e, and the smallest and largest non-zero positive number that can be represented
in the machine. Even though such choices seem fairly obvious,
one still hears of cases where mathematical subroutines which
have been used for years are suddenly found to be in error.
It is interesting, if not alarming, to conjecture what faith
may have been placed in results which have been incorrectly
computed because of errors in some basic routine supplied by
the system. Far too many users tend to treat computers as
infallible, believing every answer they produce. An important
aspect of testing is the possibility of applying a consistency
check to the output to see if it makes sense, say, in terms of
the physics of the original problem.

Test cases which can pay handsome dividends are tnose in
which extreme conditions apply. Often these may be difficult
to set up and the value of parameterisation to make them
possible has already been discussed. In other cases, it is
merely a matter of experience and knowing what sort of errors
people are likely to make, e.g. forgetting to allow for the
null string [19]. Extreme case testing is also important for
validation and certification. For example in a multi-access
system designed to support 20 consoles, one should arrange a
test in which 20 users login simultaneously. The probability
that this situation will occur in real life is very small
and it might seem an unfair test. However, the load that it

puts on the system might be sufficient to ensure that if
queues are going to overflow, they will; if time dependent
errors exist, then they will be revealed. It is far better to
produce the errors in a controlled test situation than to have
them occur at random when the system is in use, for then they
become far more difficult to locate.

    Testing aids do not seem to be as widespread or as
numerous as debugging aids. Usually they involve systems for
preparing test data in a systematic, convenient and reproducible
manner. Module test packages allow a programmer to take a
module or module aggregate in isolation from the remainder of
the system, submit test data and monitor the execution of the
test run. Most test packages allow the module to be executed
a number of times during one run. Among the capabilities often
included in such packages is that of file simulation in order
to test modules which read input files and write or update
files for output. Testing can then be undertaken without the
need to set up or dump actual physical files, thereby reducing
both programmer and computer time. Test data generators have
a useful role to play in the development of real time systems.
For example, in testing a multi-access system, one might use a
small computer to simulate the behaviour of a number of online
users and create a stream of messages for input to the system.
The form and content of this stream is controllable and reproducible, even down to the time delays between specific messages.
Hence time- or load-dependent errors once revealed can be reproduced during the debugging process. We can contrast this with
a situation in which one is attempting to test the system with
a number of people at consoles. Since we have no control over
the rate at which input is generated, it may not be possible
to cause an error to repeat itself. Locating the error is
then a much more difficult task.

The testing of portable software raises some special problems particularly where a full bootstrap is used to effect an implementation on a new target machine. In such a case, it is unlikely that the implementor will be in close contact with the originator, and therefore not only must the implementor be able to validate the new implementation, but also he must be given some assistance in debugging his implementation if the validation fails. Since one of the aims in producing portable software is to make the implementation procedure a fairly mechanical one, it is also unlikely that he will have any detailed knowledge of the algorithm. The solution we have adopted is to provide "engineering test programs" for the abstract machine [20].

The macros which define an abstract machine are equivalent to the hardware of a real computer. Just as the manufacturer must test for faulty components and wiring errors, so the implementor of an abstract machine must test for coding errors in the macros. To aid this task, the designer must provide a series of test programs. These must be designed very carefully to verify every macro indicating the specific macro in which an error occurs and giving necessary details if possible, e.g.

TO '' IF VAL ' = ' FAILS ON UNEQUAL, OPPOSITE SIGN

The test programs are similar in construction to conventional hardware tests, but rely on the normal I/O mechanisms to report any failures. The first test therefore simply reads and prints one line. (The I/O package itself is provided with a set of test data to assist the implementor to realise it on his machine.) Thereafter, each subsequent test reads a line describing a failure and then checks to see whether the failure has occurred. If so, the line is printed; otherwise the next

test is begun. The designer must select a minimal set of
operations, test these and then use them in the testing of
other operations. Selection of the test sequence and overall
strategy depends upon the organisation of the abstract machine.

Unfortunately the technique has a number of drawbacks:

(a) The test programs are difficult to write and expensive
to produce - we are already using a second set of tests
for FLUB and currently they contain 30% more lines of code
than STAGE2 itself.

(b) It is by no means foolproof - we have recorded instances
where the test programs reported that the macros were
correct but STAGE2 subsequently failed to operate
successfully.

The difficulty lies in the fact that the test programs cannot
be exhaustive. While they can be made to check, say, various
combinations of signs in an arithmetic operation, they cannot
test all possible register combinations. The problem is even
more severe once the implementor begins to adapt the program
to his specific machine. Thus if the operation

$$PTR \ A = B + C$$

is checked by the test program, we can be fairly safe in
assuming that

$$PTR \ X = Y + Z$$

will also function correctly if registers X, Y, Z are mapped
in exactly the same way as A, B, C. However, if X, Y and Z
are mapped, say, onto actual registers of the real machine, while

A, B and C are mapped into core, then the test program will
no longer check the latter operation. A possible solution to
the problem might be to generate a set of test programs from
the actual program itself. It might be possible to construct
a set of machine independent macros which would analyse the
program being implemented and create a test program which,
when combined with a set of basic tests, would check only
those operations actually used. Thus if the operation

$$PTR\ A\ =\ B\ +\ C$$

does not occur in the program, then it is irrelevant whether
it maps correctly or not.

In addition to providing test programs, the designer of
a portable program must also supply some test data to validate
a new implementation at least to the point when the implementor
can use the program with a reasonable degree of confidence.
Both STAGE2 and MITEM are supplied with such data for validation purposes. Again considerable effort is required to produce
such test data since it must be carefully planned to exercise
all parts of the program. For STAGE2, the test data serves
simply to validate the implementation; for MITEM, since there
are no complete test programs for TEXED (other than those
which already exist for FLUB), we attempted to use the test data
to provide debugging information as well. Thus as the editor
processes the test data, it constructs files containing lines
of text which themselves are continually validated. If
at a certain point in the test sequence, we expect a line to
contain a particular character string, we issue a command to
locate that string and then organise the subsequent command so
that the test sequence is only continued if the desired character string is successfully located; if it is not, then the

program stops at this point. By comparing the output produced
so far by this version with the correct output, the implementor
may gain some idea of what is causing the error.

4. REFERENCES

1. Henahpl, W. A proof of correctness of the reference mechanism to automatic variables in the F-Compiler. LN 25.3.048 IBM Vienna Laboratory.

2. Roberts, K.V. The publication of scientific FORTRAN programs, Computer Physics Communications, 1 (1969) 1-9.

3. Wilkes, M.V., Wheeler, D.J., Gill, S. The Preparation of programs for an electronic digital computer. Addison-Wesley (1951).

4. Poole, P.C. Developing a multi-access system online. Software, 1 (1971) 39-51.

5. Waite, W.M. The mobile programming system: STAGE2, CACM, 13 (1970) 415.

6. Brown, P.J. The ML/1 macro processor, CACM, 10 (1967) 618-623.

7. Dijkstra, E.W. Structured programming, Software Engineering Techniques, Report on NATO Conference in Rome (1970) 84-88.

8. Barron, D.W. Programming in Wonderland, The Computer Bulletin, 15 (1971) 153-153.

9. Satterthwaite, E. Debugging tools for high level languages, University of Newcastle upon Tyne Computing Laboratory Technical Report Series no. 29 (1971).

10. Conrow, K., Smith, R.G. NEATER2: A PL/1 source statement reformatter, CACM, 13 (1970) 669-675.

11. Mills, H.D. Syntax directed documentation of PL/360, CACM, 13 (1970) 216-223.

12. Scowen, R.S., Allen, D., Hillman, A.L., Shimell, M. SOAP - a program which documents and edits ALGOL 60 programs, Comp. J., 14 (1971) 133-136.

13. Software Engineering Techniques, Report on NATO Conference in Rome (1970) 23-24.

14. Engelman, C. Mathlab 68, IFIP Congress '68, B 91-95.

15. Sutherland, I.E. Sketchpad: a man machine graphical communication system, Proc. S.J.C.C., Sparton Press, Baltimore, Maryland (1963).

16. Carr, C.S. FORTRAN II Reference Manual, Document No. 30.50.50, University of California, Berkeley (1966).

17. Dunn, T.M., Morrissey, J.H. Remote Computing - an experimental system. Proc. S.J.C.C. (1964).

18. Balzer, R.M. EXDAMS - extendable debugging and monitoring system, Proc. S.J.C.C. (1969) 567-580.

19. Pyle, I.C., McLatchie, R.F., Grandage, B. A second order bug with delayed effects, Software, 1 (1971) 231-235.

20. Newey, M.C., Poole, P.C., Waite, W.M. Abstract machine modelling to produce portable software - a review and evaluation, Software (to be published).

R E L I A B I L I T Y

D. Tsichritzis
University of Toronto
Department of Computer Science
Canada

1.   DESIGN AND CONSTRUCTION OF RELIABLE SOFTWARE

1.1   INTRODUCTION

As computer users become more experienced, mature
and disillusioned the efficiency requirements are usually
replaced by reliability requirements. Many reasons can be
given.

a)   As equipment becomes cheaper and faster the pressure is
     diminishing to drive it "hard".

b)   Unreliable software is worthless no matter how efficient.

c)   For some applications the cost of failure is much higher
     than the cost of the computer system, e.g. process control
     applications.

d)   An inefficient system can be "tuned" with considerable
     success. An unreliable system is much harder to rescue.

e)   Reliability might affect data which are very expensive
     to duplicate.

f)   The result of inefficiency is obvious, one has to wait
     long. Unreliable software can have hidden errors, which
     can violate the system and users data without much warning.
     The results of the error might be discovered much later.
     For instance if a defective airplane were designed due to
     a software bug, it will take many "crashes" to trace the
     bug.

We wholeheartedly agree with the remarks of E. Dijkstra
"Testing can show the presence of errors and not their absence"

and B. Randell "Reliability is not an add-on feature". Reliable software is designed and implemented with care. It just does not happen, because the programmers were good, or careful. There are some fortunate persons who can write small error-free programs, the generalization is not valid. The idea behind software engineering is to develop tools, which enable a person of average competence and intelligence to produce good work. (Real "hero" programmers are few, although many think they are.)

Reliability is often viewed only qualitatively in software. A system is considered reliable, or not. Only on rare occasions such as in Electronic Switching System [1] are reliability requirements quantified. It will be even more appropriate to talk about reliability for a price. There is an inherent extra cost both at the development stage and the running stage of reliable software. The field will be really mature, when a level of reliability can be contracted for a piece of software according to specified cost. By incorporating many run-time interpretive checks one can also think of different versions of functionally the same software system according to desired reliability levels.

We will outline several aspects of software design and production affecting reliability.

1.2 INFLUENCE OF THE LANGUAGE

Programmers do not make the same errors in different programming languages. Certain constructions introduce more frequent errors. Ichbiah calls them characteristic errors [2]. The reasons for characteristic errors might be complexity of the construction, poor definition, unnatural behaviour etc.

We give two simple examples.

Example 1 [3]

MISTAKE = MISTEAK + 1

The intention of the programmer was to increment the variable MISTEAK. In FORTRAN two separate locations will be

assigned to the variables MISTEAK and MISTAKE and the error
will be undetected. In ALGOL, where variables have to be
declared, the error will be pointed out by the compiler.

Example 2 [2]

Consider the CASE construction in ALGOL W, where the
actions A, B, C are taken according to the value of I = 1,2,3.

```
CASE I OF
BEGIN
    A;
    B;
    C;
END
```

Frequent errors arise from the CASE construction, due to ommision
of cases, or rearrangement of the cases.

Consider now the modified version of the CASE
construction

```
SPACE COLOR: (RED,ORANGE,GREEN)
TYPE COLOR LIGHT;
...
CASE LIGHT/COLOR OF
GREEN: A
RED:   B
ORANGE: C
```

In the modified version the numbers associated with
the cases do not have to be known to the programmer. The order
in which the cases are written can be changed easily.

Unfortunately there is very little known about the
behaviour of programs, especially with respect to bugs. It
would be nice to organize a collection agency for frequent characteristic errors. This type of information would be invaluable
to language designers to ensure proper properties of languages.
So far most of the emphasis in language design is concentrated
on efficiency and programming style. Clarity of programs
is a positive influence on reliability, but it is not enough.
Even nice, well structured programs can have bugs [4].

1.3 SEMANTIC CHECKING

The compiler is in a position to do much checking, especially if the language has the proper characteristics. At least the compiler should catch most of the clerical errors e.g. keypunching.

We will give some simple examples.

Example 1 [3]

Suppose a FORTRAN program contains the following statements:

```
Z = <simple arithmetic expression>
(Some statements which make no reference to  Z , do
not have branching instructions and are not targets
of GO TO's)
Z = <a different arithmetic expression>
```

The above program is either wrong or ridiculous, since the value of Z is changed without using at all the previous value. A compiler should do some checking and point out such a discrepancy.

Example 2 [3]

```
DO 100 I = 1,5
DO 100 I = 1,10
      ⋮
100  CONTINUE
```

The above code is syntactically correct, but it does not make any sense. The compiler should point out the discrepancy, because it is probable that an error is present.

The compiler cannot absolutely ensure reliability since some information is only available at run time. When the language has many constraints there is more information to detect errors. This goal is sometimes not compatible with the philosophy of flexible, powerful and natural language constructions.

1.4 PROGRAMMING STYLE

The style of programming can greatly influence reliability. We mention two cases.

P1) Semantic naming. Names in the program should have a direct relation with their intended function. In certain cases elegance should be sacrificed by using long names.

P2) Verification length. Humans can look and grasp a piece of program at a time. As a result paragraphing rules, control statements and clustering of actions are very important. This is one of the arguments against the use of GO TO statements.

The art of computer programming is receiving much attention lately starting with the pioneering work of Dijkstra (THE), Mills (IBM) etc. The goal is to establish a set of conceptual and operational principles for good programming practices. Before a program is written a structure of abstractions should be designed which leads in a natural and well organized way to the final program. This method of structured programming is outlined with an example by GRIFFITHS. Structured programming slows down programming speed but greatly reduces the testing and validation phases. The result is more productivity for programmers and better programs. Structured programming enables the programmer to obtain a global view of the problem and deep understanding of the relations between the different modules. As a result the program is easy to understand and more amenable to proof of its logical correctness. The structure which is superimposed on the program during the design phase provides good documentation of the

program's behaviour. The context of the different variables
and the effect of changes is easier to visualize. As a result the maintenance effort is greatly reduced.

In general structured programming is an elegant and
organized way for writing programs. Recent results have also
proved the method to be practical. It is a first step towards
a programming methodology.

Some ad hoc techniques can also be used. They are
based on redundancy and the incorporation of checking code.
The objective is to detect and isolate errors at runtime.

T1) Cross-checking. The method used by accountants for adding
columns and rows and expecting the partial sums to add up
to the same number.

T2) Range checking. Certain variables in the program can
take values within some range due to their semantic meaning.

T3) Consistency checking. If a program is run frequently,
certain outputs have to be consistent e.g. a telephone bill
cannot be $10 for months and then jump to $2,000 without
cause for alarm.

T4) Unique names. Items in the system are provided with unique
bit patterns, which serve as identification cards. Local
mneumonic oriented names are used for reference, but the
additional unique names serve to avoid ambiguities.

T5) Pointer keys. A bit pattern is associated with every
pointer. The same bit pattern is associated with the item at
which the pointer points. This way when the pointer should
point at "apples", we can detect an error if by following
the pointer we picked "oranges".

T6) <u>Stage processing</u>. Perform the computation in stages.
After every major stage, check the integrity of the programs
and data involved.

T7) <u>Positive checking</u>. If an action has n outcomes
incorporate an extra one for unpredictable behaviour. At
least there is a definite path for the errors, instead of
taking any arbitrary one.

The above mentioned techniques were communicated
to us by other persons, notably B. Randell. We welcome any
additional techniques that programmers are using or have
used to increase reliability. Our intention is to compile
a list of programming techniques which can influence reliability.

1.5 INFLUENCE OF PROTECTION

A protected system is a controlled environment in
which some well-defined boundaries and ground rules exist to
restrict communication. Protection increases reliability
and fault tolerance in a software system in two important
ways.

a) <u>Diagnostic</u> An error in the system usually results in
an attempt to violate the protection mechanism.

b) <u>Error isolation</u> The protection mechanism establishes
firewalls. If an error occurs in one part of the system
it is isolated in such a way that only the particular
part is affected. As a result the system fails gracefully.

We will elaborate later on protection mechanisms and their
implementation.

1.6 PROGRAM CORRECTNESS

A program representing an algorithm can conceivably
be proved to be mathematically correct. Lately there has been
much work in this topic following essentially two approaches.
First to give a conventional manual mathematical proof that

the program is doing what it is supposed to. Second to state the properties of the program in a formal manner using a mathematical model and express the correctness of the program with a formula of the predicate calculus which can then be verified by a mechanical theorem prover.

1.6.1 INFORMAL PROOF [3]

This approach dates back to Von Neumann but it has acquired significant importance through the work of Floyd [6], London [7], and Naur [5]. In principle, it is quite simple. Assume there are points $p_1, \ldots, p_n$ in the program, where the programmer provides assertions of invariant conditions among the variables of the program. There is at least one assertion about the input variables of the program and one assertion about the output variables in connection with the input expressing the intent of the program. The verification procedure takes the following steps.

Assume that p_i is an assertion and p_j is the following assertion in a control path of the program. Prove that the code between p_i and p_j is such that, if p_i is true, p_j is true.

If this verification process is performed for all adjacent pairs of assertions, for all paths of control, then the program is correct assuming it halts. As a result the verification process shows only partial correctness, up to halting, and it should be supplemented by another halting proof. The interested reader can find a simple example of this technique in Elspas [3] or a more elaborate example in London [8].

The following comments are pertinent:

1)   The creative part of the proof is to develop the assertions which can be very hard for fair size programs.

2)   The proofs of programs tend to be very long and tedious. The problem of verification of the proofs is apparent.

3)   Some of the constructions in high level languages are
very powerful and the verification conditions must be developed
to identify the relationships between assertions [6,9].

4)   A proof of this type does not guard against clerical
errors e.g. keypunching, or safeguard a particular program
from hardware or system errors. On the other hand, to view a
whole software system as one program for verification
purposes is unrealistic considering the present state of the
art.

5)   The effort of proving a program correct is of such
magnitude that it precludes the application of the method in
any large scale. If all the mathematicians of the world
would join forces, they could not probably prove the correctness
of a large size Operating System (assuming they can find a
candidate).

     The method of assertions is a very general and
flexible method which can be used heuristically without any
claims for proofs. For instance, in some languages the
programmer can specify assertions which produce checking
code when the compiler is in the debug mode and are inserted
as comments when the compiler is in the regular mode [10].
An interactive program verification system could offer many
advantages [11]. In such an environment a programmer makes
assertions which can be verified or proved erroneous. As
a result he gains a deep understanding of the program
properties.

     To conclude, proving correctness of programs manually
is interesting, and it can be useful for small sensitive
algorithms of a software system. Practical limitations though
will always be present.

1.6.2 FORMAL PROOF [3]

     Much work has been concentrated in expressing the
correctness and general properties of programs within a formal
model, specifically the predicate calculus. Floyd [6] showed

that the partial correctness of programs can be reduced to
proving corresponding theorems in the first order predicate
calculus. Manna [12] demonstrated that total correctness,
including halting, can be reduced to proving theorems in the
first order predicate calculus. The hope is that after
expressing the correctness problem in the formal framework
automatic theorem proving techniques can be used to establish
the correctness of the program. As a result the future of
automatic program verification is closely related to the
advance of theorem proving techniques. The current state of
the art in theorem proving is far from being adequate to
handle the long, well formed formulas associated with the
correctness of programs [13]. The currently used resolution
technique is a semi-decision procedure, but it is inefficient.
Heuristic techniques might provide the answer [22].

In short formal proof techniques give some hope
for the future, but unfortunately they cannot be considered
available tools for current software engineering.

1.7 DESIGN FOR RELIABILITY

During the design phase decisions can be made and
the program structured in such a way which greatly enhance
reliability. Good design increases reliability in a number
of ways.

1) The program structure can allow easier and more complete
testing.

2) The logical correctness of some mechanisms can be proved
informally.

3) Problems of timing can be eliminated by ensuring proper
synchronization and cooperation of the processes.

A very good example of design for reliability is the
level approach [15]. Namely, the system is designed as a
hierarchy of abstract machines. Each level of the hierarchy
is tested exhaustively before the next outer level is implemented.
This type of approach greatly reduces the program states for

testing purposes. The general principle of levels of
abstraction and their usefulness in the design of systems is
discussed in GOOS C. A very nice concise explanation of
their influence for testing and reliability can be found in
Dijkstra's paper in the Rome NATO report [16].

Certain mechanisms or tools used for the design can
be proved informally to be correct. A very good example is
the use of synchronization primitives to provide mutual
exclusion. This type of relation is frequent enough in a
software system that an informal argument of its correctness
should be given. A simple proof is included in Habermann [17]
for the case of P's and V's on semaphores.

Finally there are certain timing considerations
which can introduce problems. Typical examples are the
determinacy and deadlock problems discussed in the concurrency
section DENNIS C. The problem of deadlock and its detection
and prevention has received special attention in the literature [18]

In general during the design phase, attention should
be paid for the logical correctness of the design, together
with its influence for the reliability and ease of maintenance
of the final product. In order to ensure logical correctness,
the design could be described formally using some model of
computation, for example, as discussed in the concurrency
section DENNIS C. The description can then be analyzed using
known theorems about the properties of the model.

1.8   RELIABILITY DURING THE LIFE CYCLE OF THE SOFTWARE

We discussed so far the design and implementation
of reliable software. In actual practice, if we follow any
one or all the techniques outlined, we will still not have
an error free software system. To ensure ultimately reliability, we have to admit our weakness as a fact and anticipate
errors. Each module of the system and the users themselves
should operate defensively. The following steps are
appropriate.

1)   The integrity of information should be preserved using frequent incremental and/or complete dumps.

2)   Key information of the system should not only be safeguarded, but duplicated e.g. directories.

3)   Hardware will malfunction. The software should be designed to cope with and not enhance the disaster.

4)   Good restart facilities can minimize the effect of failures.

Another practical aspect is the maintenance of the produced software. Functional changes and known bugs force new releases of the system. A very interesting study by Belady and Lehman [19] investigates the dynamics of the maintenance function using a model. It is shown that with certain conditions the maintenance effort can increase exponentially with time. When this happens the software system is a candidate for retirement. More about the life cycle of software is discussed in HELMS.

1.9   SUMMARY AND CONCLUSIONS

We will summarize our discussion by giving a set of informal rules for increasing reliability in software.

1)   Design a well structured system which will be easier to test.

2)   Describe the design formally and argue about logical correctness.

3)   Have a powerful protection mechanism.

4)   Prove the correctness of certain key algorithms (if you can).

5)   Choose an appropriate high level programming language for implementation.

6)   Have the compiler do much checking.

7)   Enforce a clean and structured programming style, usually through the language.

8)   Incorporate many run-time checking techniques.

9) Make available many testing and debugging techniques
    (POOLE B).

10) Pay extreme attention to the testing, debugging and
    validation stages (POOLE B).

11) Accept the inevitability of errors and prepare for it.

12) Set up a good maintenance facility.

2. <u>PROTECTION</u>

2.1 INTRODUCTION

  Protection is a general term describing the mechanisms which protect items of a system from their environment. The mechanisms are not the same in different systems and they can also be different for parts of the same system. For instance in some systems, there is a different protection mechanism for the file system, another one for memory protection etc.

  The goal of protection is stopping a malicious or erroneous user from harming other users. We could make the assumption that users are friendly and infallible, but it would be unrealistic. A user can do harm in three different ways.

  a) By destroying his own virtual machine

  b) By destroying another user's virtual machine e.g. by modifying data in an unauthorized way

  c) By degrading the service that all other users are getting with the ultimate degradation being "crashing" the system.

  A good protection mechanism should not allow (b), and (c) and it should provide some tools to the user to safeguard his own virtual machine against himself. Protection provides some extra benefits, for instance support for proprietary programs against unauthorized use. As a side benefit the protection mechanism can be expanded to provide some accurate accounting for measurement and billing purposes.

  In a system all information resides on some storage device. Hence the system is protected if some mechanisms exist to divide the logical address space into parts henceforth called <u>regions</u> and allow information to flow between the regions in a controlled way.

  Each region will have to be protected from attempts by the rest of its environment to:

E1) obtain unauthorized information

E2) provide unwanted information

As a typical example consider a region defined by a particular file. We might want to protect the file from unauthorized read operations (E1) or from somebody trying to overwrite (E2). A more subtle case of (E2) exists if somebody provides information to the region which is superficially welcome but inherently dangerous. To uncover such a potentially dangerous situation requires much checking. A typical case is that of a user passing a seemingly innocent command to the system which causes it eventually to "crach". A protected system should be able to refuse such unwanted information. Two basic problems require solution.

P1)   How we build walls around the regions with specific gates for communication purposes.

P2)   How we police the communication.

2.2   DOMAINS AND OBJECTS

We will develop a set of concepts which can be used for the understanding and design of different protection mechanisms.

The notion of regions is too general to be successful in describing the protection status of a system. Two roles are easily distinguished. In a protected environment there are both passive elements (the victims) and active elements (the aggressors). We will call passive elements objects and active elements, domains [20,21]. Note that these roles might change in the course of time. For instance two processes may very well guard against each other, in which case both are objects alternatively. Files are typical objects.

We will elaborate the notion of domain. Many words have attempted to capture it e.g. protection context, state, or sphere, capability list etc. [21,22].

The simple active element in a system is a procedure activated by an activation record. To indicate that some activated procedures can operate conceptually in parallel we give them separate status and call them processes [23]. Processes cooperate and synchronize each other through the use of basic primitive operations like P and V on semaphores, or by

sending and receiving messages. The units of activity for
concurrency purposes are the processes. In other words processes are candidates for CPU time allocation.

Other resources (e.g. memory), are allocated to the
activated procedures in an Operating System according to some
general guidelines. We will call the unit for purposes of
resource allocation a task. The concept of a task does not
have to be the same as that of a process. In most implementations, however, it is convenient to allocate all resources
to processes. In order to manage the facilities we need a
header (task control block--internal process descriptor).
If we distinguish between tasks and processes we need different
kinds of headers. If all resources are allocated in terms of
processes we only need one kind of header. This is consistent
with treating CPU time allocation in conjunction with general
resource allocation.

For protection purposes the active element can be any
activated procedure not necessarily corresponding to a process and/or task. To make this possible, Lampson introduces
the notion of a domain which is essentially the unit representing a set of access privileges to a set of objects [21].

A process always operates out of a particular domain.
Again it is expedient to identify domains with processes such
that every process corresponds uniquely to a domain. What we
lose is some flexibility. Namely, if we want a particular
activated procedure inside a process to have different protection status we have to make it a different process, although
it is not allowed to operate concurrently.

To summarize, if we choose to consider processes as
the only active unit they serve three distinct functions.
a) concurrency
b) resource allocation
c) protection

2.3   PROTECTION WALLS AND MONITORS

Since regions correspond to parts of logical address space the walls surrounding them must be present in the addressing mechanism. Addresses within the region are immediately executed, while addresses pointing outside the regions go through a specified mechanism which can be considered as a gate. It is very hard to discuss the mechanism for building walls around regions without making reference to specific addressing schemes.

Consider as an example a segmented address space. Segments correspond to regions and are protected. Every time a segment is retrieved from the segment table its protection status must be checked against the privileges of the process generating the command. In the same way, when a process wants to access a file, its request goes through the file system which checks the privileges of the process against the protection status of the file.

In general, every region which must be protected has a monitor that serves as a gate. Every time an access is generated from outside the region (somebody trying to cross the gate) it must go through the monitor in question. The monitor can be in hardware, or software, or a combination of both. For instance the physical keys in /360 machines together with the key in the PSW of the executing process form a hardware monitor, protecting regions of 2K bytes in memory. A purely software monitor is the file system which sits between the files residing in secondary storage and main memory. The file system can be considered as the monitor safeguarding the information on secondary storage.

The monitor can be near the domain generating the access, or near the object it guards, or inbetween. The main requirement is that it sit somewhere in the linking path from the domain to the object and interupt the access attempts. Note that many linking paths can share the same monitor as it is the case of the file system.

Another way of providing logical blocking walls is to
keep the linking path secret. That is, the object is not protected but its location is not known except by the right processes. Any process can use an internal name to address the
object but the linking path to the object will be only revealed
to privileged processes. Such a mechanism does not usually provide
adequate protection. The malicious user can search all memory
trying to locate the object. This is not always easy. To
begin with, in a virtual memory environment the very size of
the address space makes it very difficult.

Another technique which can be used is encoding [24].
Namely the information is there, but it is encoded and in
order to decode it one needs a special code key provided only
to privileged processes. A middle of the road approach might
by to link parts of the object in a linked list with encoded
pointers. This implies that if the object is split in n
parts the malicious process has to work n times as hard to
locate the different parts.

2.4   IDENTITY CARDS AND CAPABILITIES

Before we can talk about any checking going on at
the gates we must identify the different domains, objects and
privileges using unique names. The names used internally
are not necessarily unique. We will use unique numbers called
magnums (magic numbers) to serve as identity cards in the
system. A magnum identifies an item and will ensure a unique
name with global validity for any item in the system. A
bit pattern of 64 bits can provide by simple addition a different
magnum every μ sec for 10^7 years. If magnums are not provided by hardware we will assume that a high-privileged process issues them according to the needs of the system. In case
we need numbers which are not absolutely unique, but relative
to a particular application we will name them using the name
of the application e.g. process magnums for magnums which

identify uniquely processes.

Privileges of domains over objects will be identified with capabilities [21,22].In order to be able to pass capabilities around we have to identify them using magnums. Capabilities will also have an indication if they are local, or can be copied, or passed around.

Capabilities are checked by the monitor which sits on the linking path between regions. Note that capabilities provide protection without any specific reference to the internal nature of the regions or the contents of the messages being passed. It is assumed that a capability is enough recommendation for the privileges of the domain.The monitor could ask for the identification card (magnum) of the process trying to access the object either for some checking purpose or for reference if something anomalous happens.

The way we have talked so far about capabilities they are strictly boolean and represent authorization for an access privilege. They are like "passes" which are used to traverse a linking path between regions. Another way to view capabilities is as "tickets" which are consumed when they are used. This introduces some elementary form of memory in the capabilities.

Recalling capabilities is an issue. Some feel that once a process has certain capabilities nobody should be able to take them away. We subscribe to the other view that the agent issuing the capabilities should certainly have the right of recall. The resource manager of a particular resource should, for instance, be able to invalidate all or part of the tickets used to request that resource. This can be done easily by changing the capability magnum, in which case the old ones automatically become invalid. The process can demand the right to be protected either by making a capability inviolate à la Lampson or registering a complaint for the action and demanding the new capability.

An interesting problem arises if we want to limit
the number of accesses. Suppose we want to give a process
the privilege of accessing an object only n times. Such
an ability is important to safeguard a data base from information through correlation (Lampson) or for accounting purposes.
There are many distinct ways we can solve the problem.
a) With boolean capabilities ("passes") we can still give
    the pass but introduce some memory in the monitor which
    counts up to n . After we reach n we change the
    capability's magnum and the passes become invalid.
b) With the ticket system, we issue n tickets. This en-
    sures that only n accesses are possible.
c) It will be useful to introduce some memory in the capability
    itself. Every time it is used the count decreases and
    the capability becomes invalid when the count becomes
    zero. This type of capability is like a "ticket book"
    or "cash".
d) An indirect capability can be used as a pointer to a
    specific place where a count is kept. The monitor uses
    the pointer and the capability to decrease the count.
    This type of operation is like a "checking account".
2.5   POLICING
We have now the necessary items to police communications between sections. We could have local police, that is,
every object with its own monitor checking for capabilities.
This has two main disadvantages.
1) It is very inefficient since the guiderules are generally
    the same for some   large class of objects. For
    instance, it would be highly inefficient if each file
    had its own mechanism to check capabilities.
2) Local police can be very restrictive. There must be a
    higher control authority which can overrule its decision.
    For instance, if a file locks itself out completely there
    must be some way of remedying the situation.

There can be a central police policing all communications and checking all capabilities. This is conseptually acceptable
but it becomes cumbersome for every access to go through the
same central authority.

The best solution is to have policing in groups with
monitors which serve as gates between a large class of
domains and objects. A typical example is the file system
which has its own ground rules about the use of capabilities
to police all accesses from processes to files.

So far we made no reference to the data involved in
such communications. It follows that a simple capability-
oriented protection mechanism does not check for corrupt data which
can cause harm to the receiver. It is obvious that the policing
should include:

1) Some identity checking
2) Some data checking

The rules for data checking can be frozen, or better,
they can be specified to the monitor and updated regularly.
What we propose is to incorporate a data-checking process in
the monitor which can change dynamically.

The treatment of violators is an interesting question.
What do we do with intruders in most systems? We simply refuse unauthorized access. But if identifications are provided one
could conceivalby keep track of violations. If nothing else, somebody has to pay for the policing so it may as well be the
attempting violators (yes, we are suggesting fines).

One of the most difficult problems is the communication
between two mutually suspicious processes. Each one will try
to restrict the accesses generated from the other and closely
supervise the data which goes back and forth. What we propose in such a case is that the two processes come to an
understanding on their communication requirements and establish
a third independent process, which is the monitor and policeman. Note that this is a typical case of a contract. That is,
once the processes agree about the supervision and set up

the policeman they can't change it unless they appeal to
higher authority. This appeal to higher authority is always
present in the system, with the final "supreme" authority the
operator himself. After all, he can stop the machine.

   We talked about capabilities, magnums, monitors,
policemen, etc. All these protection mechanisms have to be
protected, especially if they are in software. Their protection can be ensured by having a protection mechanism safeguarding them, whose protection status is frozen either in software (a key has to be present which can only come from the
operator) or in hardware. For instance, all the file protection mechanisms checking file manipulation capabilities are
highly protected. Only one process, the file manager, can
talk to them and must do so in a restrictive manner. This
capability of file manager is locked in his capability list
and even he can't change it. Finally the capability list can be
protected through a different hardware protection key.

   A final problem is unauthorized use of information [26].
For instance, consider the communications between a proprie-
tory tax package program and its input process. The pro-
prietory package will certainly not want to reveal its secrets,
but on the other hand we don't want the package to retain
information about Mr. Ive's taxes. This type of problem cannot be solved by considering the processes as black boxes and
looking only at their interaction and messages, we have to
look inside them. It then becomes a problem of program
certification and security.

2.6   DESCRIBING THE PROTECTION STATUS OF A SYSTEM

   It is advantageous to use the concepts outlined in the
previous paragraphs to describe the protection status of the
system. At any point of time the protection status can be
represented by the set of privileges that each domain has. We
can view this information as a matrix with rows the domains
and columns the objects of the system [21]. Each entry of the
matrix will define the privileges of the domain corresponding

to the row over the object corresponding to the column of
the matrix. These privileges will be capabilities expressed
with access attributes like read, modify etc. The matrix is
very sparse since a domain has on the average privileges on
very few of the system's objects.

The matrix representation as described so far does
not give a mechanism for changing privileges of domains. We
could consider it as a solution only if there is a central
facility which manipulates the matrix. The central facility
can change the entries of the matrix according to well defined
rules. The disadvantages of such a centralized scheme are
rigidity and the problem of storing the large sparse matrix.

If we want to allow the domain privileges to be
changed in a flexible manner we have to consider the domains
as objects. They need protection from unauthorized access.
It is implied that the matrix columns should be augmented with
more entries corresponding to domains. Consider the following
scheme for controlling the changing of the domain privileges [21,22].
We have an access matrix A(i,j) with domains d as rows
and domains d and objects u as columns. The entries of
the matrix are access attributes plus certain special attributes.
The special attributes are "owner" and a copy flag which can
be set or not for every access attribute. "Owner" attribute
of a domain d for another domain d' or an object u
implies that d has complete control over d' or u as
the case may be.

We give now the following rules for changing the
protection status of the system.
1) A domain d can remove access attributes from A(d',x)
    if it has "owner" access to d' .
2) A domain d can copy an access attribute to A(d',x) if
    it has the copy flag set for this particular access attribute.
3) A domain d can add access attributes to A(d',x) with
    or without the copy flag set if it has "owner" access to x .

The above rules do not give the opportunity for recalling capabilities. In order to give a domain the ability
for a recall we introduce the following rule.

4) A domain d can remove access attributes from A(d',x)
   if d has "owner" access to x , provided d' does not
   have "protected" access to x .

Note that the scheme does not provide for the relation of
processes to domains and the mechanism by which a process can
change domains. Also no mention was made about the mechanism
of creating a new domain, or deleting a superfluous object or
domain from the protection status description. The idea of
a protection matrix is very useful as an abstraction in which
context we can understand and visualize different protection
mechanisms of systems.

2.7   IMPLEMENTATION

The protection status can be represented in many
different ways in a computer. The simplest way is to provide
a description of the matrix using triplets [domain, object,
access attributes] in a table T . This global table is
searched whenever the value of A(d,x) is required. This
representation is usually impractical for the following
reasons [21].

1) Memory protection is not usually provided with respect
   to T by the hardware.

2) The table will be quite large. It will be unrealistic
   to store it all in core memory. A way must be found to
   keep only relevant portions in core memory.

3) Objects or domains may be grouped in certain ways which
   make T very wasteful in terms of storage e.g. a public
   file.

4) It is usually necessary to obtain all objects that a
   domain has certain access to e.g. all objects for which
   a domain is owning and paying.

Another implementation is to group all the objects to which a domain has access in a list and attach it to the domain. This list is usually called a capability list. The entries [x,A(d,x)] are capabilities representing the access privileges of domain d on object x . Most hardware does not provide read-only arrays which can be used by the supervisor to store the capability lists. It can be simulated though by keeping all capability lists in the same storage area highly protected by a separate storage key and being accessed only by a highly privileged monitor. Linking paths to the objects can be stored in the same area together with the capabilities.

To facilitate implementation domains could also be structural in levels or using a tree hiererchy. This enables a more efficient implementation of the capability lists at the expense of some flexibility [27] .

A third Implementation is to group all the domains having access to a particular object in a list and attach it to the object. The entries of the list are of the form [d,A(d,x)] and they give the access attributes for every domain which has access privileges to the object x . There is a procedure provided by the owner of the object which checks the domains attempting to access the object. This implementation is similar to the access control list such as used in Multics. The domains still need a way of connecting to the object. We could take the approach of providing the linking paths to everybody upon request by the system, without any checking, or leave it to the domains to keep information about the linking paths to the objects on which they have access.

A fourth implementation is using unique numbers (magnums) as locks and keys. In every domain there is a list of objects together with a unique number for every object which serves as an identification of the access method. In the object there is a list of unique numbers together with associated meaning in terms of access privileges for each one.

A domain accessing the object transfers to the appropriate monitor safeguarding the object the unique number which corresponds to an access privilege. The monitor interprets the unique number according to the list in the object and grants or refuses the access depending on the access method requested.

This idea of giving capabilities special status by providing them with some unique identification is very important. The capabilities can be passed around without any reference to their meaning. When the owner of an object wants to recall or change certain capabilities, he can make the old ones obsolete by changing the list of access methods associated with the object. We will outline the use of capabilities by giving an example of a file system.

2.8   A CAPABILITY BASED FILE SYSTEM

2.8.1   INTRODUCTION

We will describe the design of a basic file system which uses the capability concepts. The design is associated with the SUE project in the University of Toronto [28]. The file system is intended for implementation in IBM /360 hardware and it has to take into account some of the hardware characteristics.

We will not use a separate notion of domain; processes will correspond to domains. Each process has a capability list of all its privileges   as part of the internal process description, together with other information relevant to the operation of the process e.g. its father and sons, mailboxes it owns for communication etc. We assume an environment where processes form a tree structure and communicate using ports and mailboxes very similar to RC 4000 [29].

Processes are ephemeral; they are created and deleted. On the other hand we need a permanent entity which contains information about a particular user account, its file information etc. We will call such an entity a sponsor [28]. Sponsors have descriptions residing permanently on

secondary storage. When a user logs in a system process obtains information about his sponsor and initiatesthe first
process corresponding to the user. When a user logs-out all
of his generated processes are destroyed and information about their
capabilities generated, accounting etc. are transcribed to the user's
sponsor. Capabilities sit inactive as data in a user sponsor,
when he is not active. When he becomes active the capabilities
should be reactivated. For instance when a user creates a new
capability e.g. by creating a new file, this mechanism ensures
that the capability is retained after he logs-out.

The file system will utilize capabilities to
monitor the access of files. Capabilities will be used mainly
for:

a) Protection for authorized access of the files
b) Accounting of the use of the file manipulating facilities

Capabilities are of two basic types:

1) Boolean capabilities mainly used for authorization
   purposes
2) Numeric capabilities used mainly for accounting purposes.
   (We will sometimes refer to them as financial capabilities
   since their presence signifies ultimately ability to pay
   for an operation.)

In addition capabilities can be distinguished to
many (up to 2^8) different types according to their use.

2.8.2   CAPABILITY FORMAT

A capability is a double word (64 bits) with the
following fields.

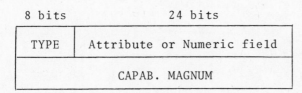

8 bits   24 bits

TYPE	Attribute or Numeric field
CAPAB. MAGNUM	

32 bits

TYPE is a codeword signifying the use of the
capability.   For example TYPE = 0...10 might imply
that the capability is an ownership capability for a file.
The TYPE will also indicate if it is a boolean or numeric
capability.

In case of a boolean capability 24 bits are used
for control and attributes in the following way. The first
8 bits are used to control the passing of capability e.g.
PASS, COPY, SEND and to indicate if the attribute field can
be changed. The next 16 bits are used for access attributes.
This enables the same capability (same type and Magnum) to
be used for many purposes according to the turned on bits on
the attribute field e.g., READ attribute bit on, but WRITE
off in case of a file manipulation capability.

In case of a numeric capability the 24 bits are
used to hold the numeric value of the capability. A numeric
capability can always be divided, or decreased by anybody
holding an indirect capability for it. It can always be sent
but not copied. Hence we don't need the 8 bits for control
and can devote all the 24 bits for the numeric value.

The capability magnum is a number which is unique
for capabilities. Namely two different capabilities (created
at different times) cannot have the same magnum. A process
naming magnum can be the same as a capability naming magnum,
which is acceptable since they are used differently. We also assume
that processes and sponsors will have 32 bit identification
magnums. The 32 bits are enough to generate one capability
per second for at least ten years.

The system creates capabilities according to the
specifications in the create primitive.

2.8.3   PACKING CAPABILITIES

Capabilities will proliferate in the system
unless we use indirection and/or some encoding. Conceptually
it is useful   to think of all these capabilities passed

around, each process having its own copy, and used as passes
or tickets. We feel that a simple scheme like this is workable
but even after reducing the size of the capabilities to a
double word we still can't afford the proliferation.

Two encodings can be used at two different levels.

1) The attribute field of a boolean capability enables the
   encoding of up to 16 different access attributes in the
   same capability.

2) Instead of having a capability we have a pointer (which
   must be a capability in itself) pointing to the right
   capability. One use for instance is use of boolean capabilities for the ability to decrease indirectly numeric
   capabilities. We extend further the notion of an indirect capability to enable encoding of combinations of
   capabilities.

For that purpose we have at least two different
TYPES: "Indirect to process", "Indirect to sponsor". This
type of capability is boolean and it points to a particular
sponsor or process. The magnum of the process or sponsor
takes the place of the capability magnum.*

The first 8 bits of the attribute field are used
for control of passing purposes. The other 16 bits are
divided in two fields of 8 bits. The first 8 bits indicate
the relative number of an 8-size block of the capability list.
The second 8 bits specify which capabilities are pointed at
within the 8-size block.

TYPE	PASS CONTROL	A	Mask
MAGNUM pointing to process or sponsor			

---

* Note that this implies that an indirect capability may
  have the same magnum as another direct capability, but
  it is permitted since the types are different.

For instance if A = 13, Mask = 01010000, it is implied that the capability points to the second and fourth
capability of the 13th block in the capability list of the
process or sponsor specified by the magnum.

This mechanism enables us to have indirection, to cut
down a capability list by a factor of eight and to pick any
consecutive block of capabilities we need. The mechanism
can accomodate any capability list up to 2^8 x 8 entries.

2.8.4   KERNEL SYSTEM FACILITIES

The following is a list of facilities needed to manipulate capabilities.

1) CREATE. Create a capability according to specifications.
    Capabilities of certain types can only be created
    by specific processes, e.g. file capabilities. The
    created capability is boolean or numeric.

2) DESTROY. We must have the ability to delete a capability
    from a capability list. This is especially useful
    when we want to save some of the capabilities in the
    sponsors, or when a capability becomes obsolete
    e.g. owner's capability in the deletion of a file.
    The capability can be boolean or numeric. We make
    the assumption that a numeric capability does not
    get destroyed automatically when it becomes zero,
    but explicitly with a DESTROY command.

3) DECREASE. Applicable to both boolean and numeric
    capabilities but with very different effects. The
    numeric capability gets decreased (this command can
    also be indirect). The boolean capability loses
    some of the "on" bits on the attribute mask.

4) INSPECT. Copy a capability in core to inspect it. The
    capability gets copied, except for its magnum. The index
    of the capability in the capability list is an argument.

5) MOUNT. Some privileged processes should have the ability
    to mount a capability from their core to a capability list.

This is true for the process which picks up the
authorization capabilities from the sponsor (sitting
there as data) and initiates the first user process
      The highest process with respect to
father-son relation, which has the same sponsor will be
called a patriarch of the lower processes.

6) COPY. Applicable only to boolean capabilities. The
   corresponding numeric capability facility is SPLIT
   capability. A check is made for the ability to copy.

7) SPLIT. Applicable to numeric capabilities. The numeric
   value is divided into parts.New capabilities with
   the same magnum are generated and obtain as values the
   parts of the numeric capability.

8) SEND. Facility to send capability from one capability
   list to another.

9) WAIT. Wait for the reception of a capability.

10) PACK. Create a new capability which points indirectly
    to a block of 8 capabilities in a capability list.

11) EXPAND. Substitute an indirect capability with the
    capabilities it points to. One bit in the passing
    control indicates the ability to expand. In some
    instances of numeric capabilities we might like the
    indirection to remain.

2.8.5   PASSING CAPABILITIES

      One of the main problems we have to face is the passing
of capabilities from the sponsor structure, where they sit
inactive as data, to the logical resource, e.g. the file
system, through the family of processes. We divide the problem
into three distinct parts. We need one mechanism to transfer
capabilities from the sponsor to the patriarch (process with
a different sponsor than his father). We need to pass capabilities between processes. Finally we need to pass the
pertinent capability to the module providing the logical resource e.g. file system.

Capabilities are passed between processes as special purpose messages [28]. This provides a solution for Parts 2 and 3. We only have to be careful to pack capabilities and use indirection, so they don't proliferate in the capability lists of the processes.

For Part 1 we need a special process called the Sponsor manager providing the interface between sponsors and processes. When the patriarch is initiated, he gets in his core a list of capabilities he can use, together with some explanation of what they mean e.g. capability #7 on the sponsor list has to do with ownership of file FILENAME. The patriarch can then choose the capabilities he will need and he requests the sponsor manager to mount them for him (recreate them as capabilities). The sponsor manager is one of the few processes having the ability to pick an image of a capability from its core and reactivate it as a capability.

The second problem we have is how to pass a capability from the process structure to the sponsor. When the file system creates a capability for the manipulation of a file it can do three different things.

a)   Pass the capability only to the process P_n issuing the command.

b)   Pass the capability to both P_n and its sponsor

c)   Pass the capability to both P_n and its patriarch.

As part of the command the process P_n can specify which option it needs. Note that if we take (b) or (c) as standard we don't need to do anything for these capabilities when P_n is deleted.

Suppose we take option (a). Then we have to have a mechanism to prevent the capabilities from being lost when P_n terminates. P_n might require different action for the capabilities i_1 created when it terminates, Namely :

a')   Some capabilities to be transferred directly to the sponsor.

b')   Some capabilities to be transferred to its father.

c')   Some capabilities to be transferred to its patriarch.

When a patriarch terminates all of its capabilities are transferred to its sponsor.

We favour the solution (a) combined with options (a'),(b'),(c') specified by the type of capability created by the logical resource in this case the file system. P_n passes an indication about the option (a'),(b'),(c'). Note that when P_n terminates there are some bookkeeping operations with respect to capabilities.

2.8.6   OUTLINE OF THE FILE SYSTEM

The basic file system has as goals:
1)   A complete set of instructions which can be used to implement more user-oriented commands.
2)   A structural design which will allow the introduction of new processes to accommodate extra facilities e.g. different sponsor directories and space allocation schemes.
3)   Adequate facilities for the development of an Operating System nucleus and the implementation of an interactive service.

A rigid assumption is made:

All files consist of an integer number of fixed size blocks.

2.8.7   FACILITIES OF THE FILE SYSTEM

The following commands can be executed directly by the file system.
1)   REQUEST (VOLUME NAME, SPECS)

The process issuing the command (henceforth called the process) asks for the allocation of an extra volume named VOLUME NAME. SPECS include: a)   Capability for requesting volume;   b) Sponsor of the process issuing the command; c) Pointer to the internal process descriptor (i.p.d.) of the process.
2)   RELEASE (VOLUME NAME, SPECS)

The process wants to release a volume it owns for other uses.   SPECS include: a) Capability of ownerhsip of this volume;

b)   Sponsor; c)   Pointer to i.p.d. of the process.

3)   ATTACH (VOLUME NAME, SPECS)

The process wants to mount a volume it can use on a
logical drive. SPECS include: a) Capability for using the
volume VOLUME NAME; b) Capability of issuing ATTACH command
(financial); c) Capability of ownership of a logical drive
(optional); d) Sponsor; e) Pointer to the i.p.d. of the process.

4)   DETACH (VOLUME NAME, SPECS)

The process wants to dismount the volume VOLUME NAME from
the logical drive it was mounted and get back the logical drive
if it owned it. SPECS include: a) Capability of detaching
the particular volume; b) Sponsor; c) Pointer to i.p.d. of
process.

5)   CREATE (FILE NAME, SIZE, VOLUME NAME-optional,SPECS)

The process wants to create a file FILE NAME. If a
VOLUME NAME is specified it wants the file to be in the
particular volume. SPECS include: a) Capability for creating
files (financial); b) Capability for using the specified
volume (optional); c) Sponsor; d) Pointer to the i.p.d. of
process.

6)   DELETE (FILE NAME, SPECS)

The process wants to delete the file FILE NAME.   SPECS
include: a) Capability of ownership for the file; b) Sponsor;
c) Pointer to the i.p.d. of the process.

7)   OPEN (FILE NAME, SPECS)

The process wants to open (link to) a file FILE NAME.
SPECS include: a) Capability for opening files (financial);
b) Capability of opening of the file; c) Sponsor; d) Pointer
to the i.p.d. of the process.

8)   CLOSE (FILE NAME, SPECS)

The process wants to close and disconnect from the file.
SPECS include: a) Capability of closing file; b) Sponsor;
c) Pointer to the i.p.d of the process.

9)   READ (FILE NAME, NFILE, MPROCESS, COUNT, SPECS)

The process wants to read from FILE NAME a number of

blocks specified by COUNT starting from the NFILE block of
the file consecutively and to deposit them at memory consecutively starting from MPROCESS block. SPECS include: a) Capability of issuing read-commands (financial); b) Capability
for reading the file; c) Capability for writing on the MPROCESS
to MPROCESS + COUNT - 1 on memory; d) Sponsor; e) Pointer to
the i.p.d. of process.

10) WRITE (FILE NAME, NFILE, MPROCESS, COUNT SPECS)

The process wants to write a number of blocks specified
by COUNT from the FILE NAME starting from the NFILE file block
to the main memory starting from the MPROCESS block of the
process. SPECS include: a) Capability of issuing write
commands (financial); b) Capability for writing the file;
c) Capability for reading from the MPROCESS to MPROCESS + COUNT
- 1; d) Sponsor; e) Pointer to the i.p.d. of the process.

11) SWITCH (FILE NAME, SPECS)

The process wants to change the capability of use for
a particular file. This will not affect the processes which
have the file open but from now on nobody will have access
to the file unless he produces the new capability. The same
way the process can change the financial capability. SPECS
include: a) Capability of ownership of the file; AND/OR
b) Capability for creating files (financial); c) Sponsor;
d) Pointer to the i.p.d. of process.

Each command will have many associated actions. Consider as an
example the CREATE command which has the following results.

1) The file FILE NAME has been created. Here is the
    capability of ownership of the file.
2) Your financial capability is no good.
3) The name FILE NAME is in conflict. Please change it.
4) The capability you specify for the volume is no good.
5) VOLUME NAME cannot be found.
6) VOLUME is not mounted. Please arrange to be mounted.
7) Volume or file system is loaded. Your file cannot be
    created.

8) Really sorry, but something went wrong.

2.8.8. ORGANIZATION OF THE FILE SYSTEM

Files have entries in a sponsor directory.
A tree structured sponsor directory is implemented corresponding to the sponsor structure. The entries in the sponsor
directory simply point to the appropriate entries in the Master
directory. We will allow both sharing and the ability to use
local names for files.

For every file there is a unique entry in the Master
directory. The entry will be of the following form:

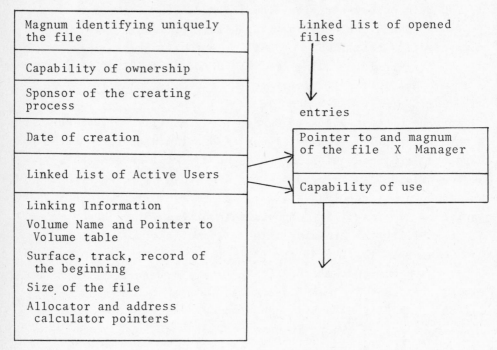

For every successful execution of an open command in
the file system a process is created to manage the read and
write operations for the particular file. Pointers to the
processes are kept in the Master directory to ensure that
the processes do not change the file concurrently.

The file system manages two sets of volumes. Regular
volumes belonging to the file system where it allocates space
for regular files. Special volumes belonging to other owners
in the system which are managed by the file system. A volume
table is kept containing the current status of all volumes.
The entries contain:

a)   Volume unique identifier.
b)   Logical drive and capability if the volume is mounted.
     Flagged if the volume is not mounted.
c)   Count of currently open files.
d)   Pointer and magnum of volume's allocator.
e)   Capability of ownership.
f)   Date of creation.

Note that the entries are of fixed size.

Attached is a diagram of all the processes related or
belonging to the file system and their communication lines.
We hope that their names provide a hint for their function.

We do not claim any particular functional or performance
properties for the file system outlined in comparison with
existing file systems. It was described mainly as an example
for the use of the protection concepts discussed in this section.

FILE SYSTEM STRUCTURE

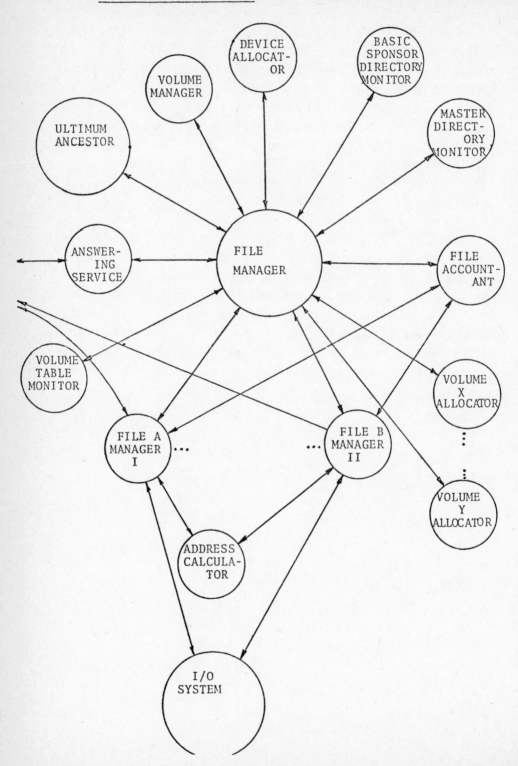

3. SECURITY

3.1 INTRODUCTION

Lately there has been much discussion on the control of access of privileged information stored in large scale data banks [24,30,31]. The issues can be separated into three major categories [24].

Information privacy "involves issues of law, ethics and judgement" [24] controlling the access of information by individuals.

Information confidentiality involves rules of access to data.

Information security involves the means and mechanisms to ensure that privacy decisions are enforceable.

We share as individuals the concern of citizens for information privacy, but our main concern as computer professionals involves questions of information security. We must warn the public about the difficulties involved with control of access privileges and develop the techniques for implementing confidentiality decisions in systems and data banks in a cost effective manner.

We propose the following distinction between protection and security.

Protection deals with the control of information access within the operating system without consideration of the nature of information. That is, protection mechanisms use labels, locks, keys etc. to ensure that an information block can only be accessed by privileged active units in the system.

Information security differs from protection mainly in two ways.

1) The whole information system is considered rather than the system operating on the computer. The active elements are people. For example user identification is assumed correct for protection purposes but it is of prime importance in security enforcement.

2)   The nature and content of data play an important role for
the access privileges. The security mechanism can base its
decisions on the contents of a file, or perform data checking
during transmission, or insist on certifying the properties
of a program.

It is implied that a secure system must be protected
but that is not enough. We discussed in the previous section
protection mechanisms. In this section we will concentrate on
approaches to achieve security in addition to protection.

The following example gives an indication of
potential security requirements imposed by selective privacy
of information [24]. Consider an employee personnel/payroll
file for a large industrial concern. The file might include
data structures named NAME, SALARY HISTORY, CURRENT SALARY,
PERFORMANCE EVALUATION, DEPARTMENT, MEDICAL HISTORY, and
SOCIAL SECURITY NUMBER. The following could be conceivably
the privacy decisions concerning the access of the file by
individuals.

R1. He has complete access of file.
R2. He has no access of file.
R3. He may see any portion of the file, but change none of
     its contents.
R4. He may see exactly one record and may change only some
     fields of the record.
R5. He may see only the NAME and MEDICAL HISTORY and alter
     only the MEDICAL HISTORY.
R6. He may alter only "financial" portions of each record
     but only at specific times of day from specific terminals.
R7. He may see and modify only "financial" records with
     CURRENT SALARY below $15,000.
R8. He may see "financial" information but only in an aggregate
     way and not individual records.
R9. He may see PERFORMANCE EVALUATION but only for certain
     DEPARTMENT.

The protection mechanisms which were discussed in
the previous section can very easily handle R1, R2, R3, R4.

As a matter of fact they can conceivably handle all requirements but in a rather inelegant manner. In addition we might ask the following embarrassing questions:

Q1) How can we ensure the identification of the individual?

Q2) What measures are taken against wiretapping?

Q3) What control is exercised over the discs or tapes when they are off line?

Q4) What happens when the system is not working properly due to malfunction of hardware or software?

A good security environment should attempt to provide solutions to the above mentioned problems. It is almost impossible to design an "unbreakable" system and maybe needless in a commercial environment. It is important to make the security mechanism very difficult and very expensive to bypass.

3.2 INFORMATION SYSTEM APPROACH

We will take an information system approach to the problem of security. It should be kept in mind that a breach in security will happen in the weakest link of the protection chain, which is not necessarily associated with the most complex or technically advanced operation.

3.2.1 INTEGRITY OF PERSONNEL

One of the most direct methods to break a security system is through the trust of a privileged user. This problem is well known and methods are similar to manual data systems. Personnel are investigated, high penalties for breach of security are established, accidental disclosure is minimized by labelling of information. A common method in banks is the authorization in pairs. It takes two persons to perform a sensitive operation. Both persons have to agree for a malpractice. In the same way functions of individuals should be separated. For instance, an operator who is also a systems programmer can violate security easier. The presence of a security guard is not beneficial unless he understands the operation sufficiently.

As a general rule both privileged access and information about the operation of the system should be disclosed to as few persons as possible. The "need to know" serves as a criterion.

3.2.2 AUTHENTICATION OF USERS IDENTITY

Users are traditionally identified with passwords. This procedure is not always adequate [30]. Three more elaborate identification means are outlined.

A1) The user is provided with a unique number every time he logs out. He uses this as a password to log-in. If another person impersonates him in the meantime by producing the password the user will at least be able to detect that his environment was violated.

A2) The user identifies himself at log-in. The system provides a pseudo-random number x. The user performs a simple transformation $T(x)$ and sends the result back. The system has the transformation stored in a highly secure area and is able to check the identity of the user [30]. Note that x and $T(x)$ provide very little information for identification of T, assuming the transmission line was tapped.

A3) Some point out that one-time passwords are not adequate against infiltrators who attach a terminal to a legitimate user's line [30]. They propose identifying the messages with unique numbers implemented by hardware in the terminal and possibly in the central processor.

The problem of user identification is also related to the security of the physical location of the terminals and transmission lines.

3.2.3 PROTECTION OF DATA OFF LINE AND IN TRANSMISSION

Data in hard copy, removable discs, or tapes should be adequately protected off line. This type of security is common among manual systems, and is handled by security

guards, vaults, etc. Care should be taken for data which can
be considered useless, but can provide a breach of security
e.g. old tapes, core images. It is customary to leave core
and tapes "dirty" after their use. They should be cleared
by overwriting zeros to erase the information. Another
processing restriction important for security is the mounting
of removable volumes on drives which must be authenticated
before access. Special care should be taken for adequate
back-up facilities for integrity purposes without undue
proliferation of copies. Some of the data are so valuable
that it is not a question of security but of survival for the
organization.

During transmission there is the potential danger
through wiretapping, especially if common carriers are used.
Sensitive data should be encrypted. We will discuss in the
next section encrypting methods.

3.2.4 THREAT MONITORING [30]

Any password protection scheme can be violated
assuming that the infiltrator has enough resources and patience.
Thus, monitoring of the system must take place. Petersen
and Turn [32] give a description of threat monitoring. "Threat
monitoring concerns detection of attempted or actual penetrations
of the system or files, either to provide real time response
(e.g. invoking job cancellation, or starting tracing procedures)
or to permit post facto analysis".

Threat monitoring enables the system to respond to and
enforce penalties for attempted violations. Periodic reports
on file activities can serve for performance evaluation and
tuning of the system in addition to an indication of misuse
or tampering. Without any threat monitoring a malicious
process can, in addition, slow down the system by attempting
different unauthorized accesses.

Audit logs of the operations enable detection
of security violations off-line. Audit logs are hard to

interpret, but they provide an audit trail and evidence of breaches of security. As such, they serve as a deterrent to malpractices.

3.3 DATA DEPENDENCE AND DATA TRANSFORMATIONS

While discussing protection data were protected without any reference to their content. A good security system has sometimes to revert to both data transformation and/or investigation of data or program properties to ensure careful monitoring of access.

3.3.1 DATA TRANSFORMATIONS

Reversible encodings of sensitive data can be used to conceal the information. They can protect against transmission wiretapping, unauthorized access to data files etc. They are especially useful if a highly secure system needs to be attached as a subsystem to a system with marginal security e.g. ASAP on O.S./360 [24]. Substitution of character strings, transposition of characters, and addition of key characters are three common types of transformations which can be combined to increase the work factor associated with breaking the code. The work factor depends (among others) on the following criteria [30,33].

a) Length of the key. Keys require protection, storage, transmission and often memorization. It seems that a short key is desirable; on the other hand, better protection can be obtained by long keys.

b) Transformation space. Sufficient transformations should be available to discourage "trial and error" approaches. Transformations are user dependent and possibly time dependent.

c) Complexity. The work factor is related to the complexity of the hardware, software and processing time involved in the security system.

d) Error sensitivity. Enough redundancy should be provided
to make decoding possible in the presence of errors.

Encryption by data transformation is discussed in
[32,34]. Good theoretical studies are also available. Certain
machine instructions can be used to make the transformation efficient.

3.3.2 DATA DEPENDENT ACCESS

It is sometimes desirable to control the access of
data not only on the file level, according to the user or
process privileges, but at the record level according to the
data accessed. This approach avoids duplication of data
proliferation of capabilities, especially in a shared information
environment. Hoffman points out the inadequacies of a
capability scheme when he discusses a particular case [30,35].
In the example of a personnel/payroll file as discussed at
the beginning [24] and assuming we do not duplicate data,
we cannot restrict a file user from seeing SALARY items
above $15,000 in access R7 without taking into account the
value of the data in the field SALARY. Data dependent access
decisions can be made interpretively by invoking a procedure
in the monitor associated with a particular access as
represented by a password. It should be pointed out that a
procedure related to a capability provides a very general
form of protection, for instance, it can provide memory,
policy decisions etc. The interpretive nature of the
operation implies a certain amount of overhead, and it
should be used only when needed [24]. For an example of
a security mechanism based on procedures, consult Hoffman [36].

3.3.3 PROGRAM CERTIFICATION

The security mechanism could involve the verification
of certain program properties which falls under the general
area of program certification. We mention a few instances:

1) Consider the case where we would like to prohibit a program
from retaining statistical information about the data on which

it is operating. There is no other way that a security
mechanism can enforce such a condition, unless the program
is shown to demonstrate the proper behaviour by analyzing
its structure.

2)   In order to decrease overhead, sometimes we would like
the compiler to test the accesses at compile time as compared
with the protection status of the system. In such a case
we have to trust the compiler that it will not willingly
or erroneously provide the wrong access.

3)   In most cases the security mechanism is implemented with
software. It is important that the procedures providing the
security be both protected and certified.

3.4   SUMMARY OF CURRENT PRACTICES

Some security measures on existing systems are
outlined [31]. For a general overview a table of "Counter-
measures to Threats to Information Privacy" is very interesting
as appears in [30,32]. Cost can be an overriding criterion.
For example Hoffman [30] gives an example of a dial-up user
identification which was marketed without much success due to
cost.

	System	ATS -- text editor for /360
S I G N O N - S I G N O F F	Identification	account number; changeable password
	Authentication	none
	User options	none
	Accounting	duration of use; (needed for billing anyway)
F I L E U S A G E	Determination of file names	files in account listed on request
	User identification	five character passwords for another account's files
	User options	none
	Accounting	date last stored
	Types of capabilities	read-only, delete-only (separate passwords)
	Determination of capabilities	available through passwords
	Security scope	file
	Cryptography	none
P R O T E C T I O N	Separation from data	kept in separate directory
	Integrity considerations	no user programs
	Protection from concurrent systems	very poor -- directory may be erased
	Back-up	separate working storage
	Residual information protection	password of file made unmatchable after delete
V I O L A - T I O N S	Standard response	messages only
	Non-standard responses	disconnected for error in signon
	Comments	information obtained from U of Toronto Computer Centre

	System	CPS -- time sharing for /360
S I G N O N - S I G N O F F	Identification	account number; fixed password
	Authentication	none
	User options	none
	Accounting	duration of use; (needed for billing anyway)
F I L E **U S A G E**	Determination of file names	able to find all file names in system
	User identification	six character password
	User options	none
	Accounting	date last stored; date last accessed
	Types of capabilities	read-only
	Determination of capabilities	available through password
	Security scope	file
	Cryptography	none
P R O T E C T I O N	Separation from data	password kept in file directory
	Integrity considerations	poor -- open to all OS trap-doors; uses separate storage keys and designated disks
	Protection from concurrent systems	none
	Back-up	user explicitly saves files
	Residual informa-tion protection	zeros core used
V I O L A - T I O N S	Standard response	messages only
	Non-standard responses	two signon errors result in disconnection; some errors abend CPS
	Comments	information obtained from U of Toronto Computer Centre

	System	APL-Plus time sharing --/360
S I G N O N - S I G N O F F	Identification	account number; changeable password
	Authentication	none
	User Options	none
	Accounting	duration of use; (needed for billing anyway)
F I L E U S A G E	Determination of filfile names	files to which some access is allowed are listed on request
	User identification	password (integer) for a file; unlockable seals for functions
	User options	able to use integer password to allow own checking fcn.
	Accounting	date and time last stored; who stored it; amount of storage used
	Types of capabilities	read-only, append, read-write etc.
	Determination of capabilities	matrix of user numbers vs. capabilities stored with file
	Security scope	file
	Cryptography	mnemonic passwords encrypted
P R O T E C T I O N	Separation from data	access matrix separated from file; entry in care also separate
	Integrity considerations	good -- no remote job entry; there exist batch programs to examine and alter files
	Protection from concurrent systems	good -- uses DOS protect features
	Back-up	every file update written directly onto disk file
	Residual information protection	nothing on disk readable before writing;
V I O L A - T I O N S	Standard response	error in function gives msg. and haltsfile error logged
	Non-standard	a particular error in array subscripting disconnects user and makes workspace open to system
	Comments	information obtained from I.P. Sharp and Assoc. Ltd.

		System	PDP/10 time sharing
S I G N O N - S I G N O F F		Identification	project number; programmer number; fixed password
		Authentication	terminal number can be read but it's not used
		User options	none
		Accounting	duration of use; (needed for billing anyway); core usage
F I L E U S A G E		Determination of file names	able to find all file names in system
		User identification	password
		User options	none
		Accounting	date last used; date and time created
		Types of capabilities	read-only, execute, append, write, etc.; by programmer number, project number,
		Determination of capabilities	list of user passwords stored with file
		Security scope	file (field added at UofWOnt)
		Cryptography	none
P R O T E C T I O N		Separation from data	none
		Integrity considerations	good -- nobody able to get into EXEX state
		Protection from concurrent systems	
		Back-up	user explicitly saves files
		Residual information protection	core zeroed; deleted file erased on disk
V I O L A -	**T I O N S**	Standard response	messages only
		Non-standard responses	none
		Comments	information obtained from University of Western Ontario

System	MTS time sharing for /360
SIGNON-SIGNOFF Identification	account number; changeable password
Authentication	none
User options	none
Accounting	duration of use (needed for billing anyway); date of last signon; resource usage
FILE USAGE Determination of file names	files in account listed on request; others provided by user
User identification	none
User options	a program file can check the user identification
Accounting	date last used; location and size of file; date created
Types of capabilities	read-only for all shared files (including own access)
Determination of capabilities	not applicable
Security scope	file
Cryptography	none
PROTECTION Separation from data	kept in directory
Integrity considerations	poor -- privileged users can read all files and find all passwords; not all usages tagged
Protection from concurrent systems	none -- other jobs under UMMI PS can access all files
Back-up	file editor uses explicit saves
Residual information protection	nothing on disk readable before a write
VIOLATIONS Standard response	messages only
Non-standard responses	three signon errors result in disconnection; some return codes abend a terminal
Comments	new version is currently being prepared

System	CP operating system for /360
SIGNON-SIGNOFF	
Identification	account number; fixed password
Authentication	none
User options	changeable signon procedure
Accounting	duration of use (needed for billing anyway); user identification
FILE USAGE	
Determination of file names	files in account listed on request
User identification	none
User options	none
Accounting	date last stored
Types of capabilities	all capabilities on own "machine"; read-only on other
Determination of capabilities	not applicable
Security scope	file
Cryptography	none
PROTECTION	
Separation from data	
Integrity considerations	good -- no user can access CP core (only "virtual")
Protection from concurrent systems	not applicable
Back-up	user explicitly saves files
Residual information protection	core zeroed at signon; virtual "mini-disk" have volume labels erased at sign-off
VIOLATIONS	
Standard response	messages only; some errors will deadlock a "machine"
Non-standard responses	three signon errors result in disconnection; some severe line errors cause CP abend
Comments	information obtained from Brown U. Computer Center

371

4. REFERENCES

1) NATO Report on SOFTWARE ENGINEERING, Garmish, Oct. 1968. Available through NATO, Dr. H. Arnth-Jensen, Scientific Affairs Division, OTAN/NATO, 1110 Bruxelles, Belgium.

2) Ichbiah, J. Compagnie Internationale pour l' Informatique private communications.

3) Elspas, B. et al "Software Reliability", IEEE COMPUTER, Vol. 1, No. 1, Jan. 1971.

4) Henderson, P. and Snowden R. "An experiment in structured programming", Technical Report 18, Computer Laboratory, University of Newcastle upon Tyne, 1971.

5) Naur, P. "Proof of Algorithms by General Snapshots", BIT, Vol. 6, No. 4, pp. 310-316, 1966.

6) Floyd, R.W. "Assigning Meanings to Programs", Proceedings of a Symposium in Applied Mathematics, Mathematical Aspects of Computer Science, Vol. 19, pp. 19-32, J.T. Schwartz (Ed.), American Mathematical Society, Providence, Rhode Island, 1967.

7) London, R.L. "Computer Programs can be Proved Correct", Proceedings of the Fourth Systems Symposium - Formal Systems and Non-Numerical Problem Solving by Computers, held at Case-Western Reserve University, 1968.

8) London, R.L. "Certification of the Algorithm Treesort", Communications of the ACM, Vol. 13, No. 6, pp. 371-373, 1970.

9) Hoare, C.A.R. "An Axiomatic Basis for Computer Programming", Communications of the ACM, Vol. 12, No. 10, 1969.

10) Clark, B. and Horning, J. "The system language for project SUE", SIGPLAN Symposium for Languages for Systems Implementation, 1971.

11) Snowden, R. "PEARL: An interactive system for the preparation and validation of structured programs", Technical Report 28, Computer Laboratory, University of Newcastle upon Tyne, 1971.

12) Manna, Z. and Pnueli, A. "Formalization of Properties of Recursively Defined Functions", ACM Symposium of Theory of Computing, pp. 201-210, 1969.

13) Luckman, D. "The Resolution Principle in Theorem Proving", Machine Intelligence 1, Collins and Michie (Eds.), American Elsevier, Inc., New York 1967.

14) King, J. C. and Floyd, R. W. "Interpretation Oriented
     Theorem Prover Over Integers", Second Annual ACM
     Symposium on Theory of Computing, pp. 169-179, 1970.

15) Dijkstra, E. W. "The Structure of THE Multiprogramming
     System. CACM 11, 5, May 1968, 341-346.

16) NATO Report on SOFTWARE ENGINEERING, Rome, Oct. 1969.
     Available through NATO, Dr. H. Arnth-Jensen,
     Scientific Affairs Division, OTAN/NATO, 1110
     Bruxelles, Belgium.

17) Habermann, N. "Synchronization of Communicating Processes",
     Third Symposium on Operating Systems Principles, Palo
     Alto, 1971.

18) Coffman, E. et al "System deadlocks", ACM Computing
     Surveys, Vol. 3, No. 2, June 1971.

19) Belady, L. and Lehmann, M. "Programming System Dynamics"
     IBM Report RC 3546, September 1971.

20) Lampson, B. W. "Dynamic Protection Structures", Proc. AFIPS
     Conf. 35, 1969 FJCC.

21) Lampson, B. "Protection", Proceedings of the Fifth
     Annual Princeton Conference on Information Sciences
     and Systems, March 1971, p. 437-443.

22) Graham, S. and Denning, P. "Protection: Principles and
     Practice", Tech. Report No. 101, Princeton University
     Electrical Engineering Dept. to appear in SJCC 1972.

23) Dijkstra, E. W. "Cooperating Sequential Processes" in
     Programming Languages (F. Genuys ed.) Academic
     Press 1968 p. 43-112.

24) Conway, R. W. et al "Security and Privacy in Information
     Systems - A Functional Model" Tech. Report No. 133,
     Dept. of Operations Research, Cornell University,
     June 1971, to appear in CACM.

25) "COSINE Report on Operating Systems", available through
     Commission on Education, National Academy of
     Engineering, 2101 Constitution Avenue, Washington,
     D.C. 20418.

26) Schroeder, M. and Saltzer, J. "A Hardware Architecture
     for Implementing Protection Rings", Proceedings of
     the Third Symposium on Operating Systems Principles,
     October 18-20, p. 42-54.

27) Graham, R. M. "Protection in an Informations Processing
     Utility", CACM 11, 5, May 1968.

373

28) Project SUE internal documentation workbook. Computer Systems Research Group, University of Toronto.

29) Brinch, Hansen P. "The Nucleus of a Multiprogramming System", CACM 13, April 1970.

30) Hoffman, L. "Computers and Privacy", ACM Computing Surveys, Vol. 1, No. 2, June 1969.

31) Gotlieb, C. C. and Hume, P. "Systems Capacity for Data Security". Draft report for study 6 of Privacy and Computers Task Force.

32) Petersen, H. E. and Turn, R. "System implications of information privacy". Proc. AFIPS 1967 Spring Joint Comput. Conf., Vol. 30, Thompson Book Co., Washington, D.C., pp. 291-300.

33) Shannon, C. E. "Communication theory of secrecy systems", Bell Syste. Tech. J. 28, 4, Oct. 1949, 656-715.

34) Baran, P. On distributed communications: IX. Security, secrecy and tamper-free considerations. Doc. RM-3765-PR Rand Corp., Santa Monica, Calif., August 1964.

35) Hsiao, D. K. "A File System for a Problem Solving Facility". Ph.D. Diss. in Electrical Engineering, U. of Pennsylvania, Philadelphia, Pa., 1968.

36) Hoffman, L. "The formulary model for access control and privacy in computer systems", SLAC Rept. No. 117, Stanford University, May 1970.

37) Beardsley C. "Is your computer insecure". IEEE Spectrum, January 1972.

CHAPTER 4.A.

P R O J E C T   M A N A G E M E N T

D. Tsichritzis
University of Toronto
Department of Computer Science, Canada

1.   INTRODUCTION

To say that software is usually not produced within the specified cost
and time constraints while demonstrating the proper performance requirements is probably an understatement. Past experience has shown
that considerable delays and cost overruns are so often present that
they are almost accepted as a fact of life in software production. One
could always multiply the estimates by a large safety factor and let
the project participants fill up the time with irrelevant activities.
This approach can hardly be considered engineering.

The reasons for the difficulties in managing software projects can be
divided according to two schools of thought.

a) *Poor management.* Due to the gap between manager and computer science
education, there are very few persons with adequate technical and
managerial skills. As a result software projects are managed either by
good technical people with limited managerial talent, or by good managers
who do not really understand and communicate with the software engineers.

b) *Random activity.* The production of software is not a deterministic
activity. Product specifications are liable to be shifted. Personnel
changes are frequent and painful. Planning tools are lacking. In general
in order to manage software one has to use very different techniques,
which take into account the natureof the project. It must be accepted
from the beginning that the final product will be very different than
the originally proposed.

We will outline some facts of life which give nightmares to managers
of software projects.

1) Programmers tend to be "devious". They consider themselves artists and they demonstrate their artistic style and raw intelligence in many disastrous ways.

2) Documentation is not usually up to date. As a result the progress of the project is very sensitive to the continuous availability of certain project members. As a matter of fact a shrewd project member can make himself indispensable due to lack of documentation.

3) The really precious resource in software projects is designers time. In view of the limited availability and use of software tools designers have to be very talented. Talent is limited in any occupation.

4) When a bridge engineer designs successfully a bridge, he is expected to go on and design another bridge. When a software engineer is successful in designing a software system, he usually moves to a more complicated and different system, or to a managerial position, or to an academic environment. As a result most project members are new to the project activity and they obtain concurrently training and education.

5) Due to the informal description of the software product at the early phases, it is easy to hide and postpone problems right down to the implementation phase. Sometimes major decisions are left to inexperienced hands.

6) Performance requirements force rewriting and redesign of some product modules.

7) The marketing people can come right in the middle and shift the groundrules.

In general the goal of project management should be:

To produce the desired product within the stated design goals, specifications and available resources.

In order to achieve the goal the manager has to maximize "happiness" among the project members. Realistically, the resources are provided to produce the system and not to make anybody "happy". Unfortunately, the production of software according to specifications and within stated constraints is a question which can only be answered right at the end.

Until that time of "reckoning" we should concentrate on keeping the project progressing at full speed.

2. *PROJECT COMMUNICATION, ORGANIZATION AND CONTROL*

I/ Team communication. The initial problem is to find a common dialect
of natural language for communication purposes. Unfortunately the terms
in the area of software do not always convey the same meaning to everybody. Our suggestion is to adopt an easily readable (!) manual of an
existing similar system as a preliminary term dictionary. We propose
as an example the RC 4000 manual for an Operating System's project [2].
Project members read the manual which provides the first iteration of
the language spoken and written during the lifetime of the project.

If the team is *small* (5-10 persons so they can get together around a
table), two or three meetings per week of all the members is desirable.
One meeting should be more technical and one very informal. Frequent
informal conversations should be encouraged. Parnas suggests that too
much communication between the members might negatively affect modularity [13]. Persons could use informal information to bypass standard
interfaces. This is a risk one should take.

If the project team is large, communication is almost hopeless. We
don't have any clever suggestions except to ask: Why is it so large?
Couldn't it be smaller? There are the usual mechanisms of memos. but
one should realize that much of the talent in the project will be ex-
pended on communications.

Proper documentation is important. In the SUE project now underway in
the University of Toronto we use a workbook [15]. Every project member
carries a copy which is updated regularly (3 to 5 new write-ups per
week). Every major decision reached, working and technical papers, minutes of meetings, everything which is judged important to the project
goes in the workbook. One team member is responsible for the updating.
Material is condensed periodically. Old versions go in a special section in the back. The workbook gives not only the current status of the
project, but a complete history as well. We expect the workbook to form
the basis of adequate documentation; it will also enable us to perform
an anatomy of the project after its completion.

II/ Team organization. According to "Conway's Law" [10] systems resemble the organizations which produce them. If we split the system
into its different functions and give separate pieces to separate groups,
the interfaces will be as good or bad as the interfaces between the
groups. If the team is small there is adequate communication and project
members get involved in the design of more than one function. This has
three immediate advantages.

a) There is at least one person (preferably two) who has the complete
design in his head. This person can't be the project manager, since no
manager can both manage the project and keep all the design details
under control. The "walking documentation" of the system should be
freed from other time-consuming tasks, so he can devote most of his
time as a sounding board for the ideas of all other designers.

b) Members take part in more than one design and they begin to view the
system globally. They do not try to optimize locally with the obvious
disastrous effects.

c) There is less need for formal lines of management. Democracy works
in small enough numbers. The project manager should keep the final
strings, but he should not impose his will, especially on technical
matters. Project members should feel free to make decisions, which is
very desirable.

If the team is large (more than 10 persons), then a management structure
must be developed. As a result many of the man-hours go into management.
In some cases it is inevitable, but before one hires many persons one
should ask the obvious questions. Do we need that many? How many designers
and how many managers are needed? a good programmer and/or designer does
not make a good manager.

III/ Control Checkpoints should be carefully followed and accompanied
by checkpoint reports. Checkpoint reports should not be regarded as a
burden for the project; they should provide some real benefits and
feedback. The following comments are pertinent.

a) Checkpoint reports should be realistic. If the need arises for an
"optimistic" checkpoint report for political reasons, the "bare" report should be distributed internally. The optimistic tone can then be
added before the report goes out.

b) Checkpoint reports should not be apologetic, or gloomy. If there
are real problems then reasons and solutions should be offered. If no
reasons for the delays exist, then the project is not well managed. If
there are no solutions to the problems, then an attempt should be made
to change the groundrules.

c) Projects are very seldom discontinued as a result of checkpoint repor
The implication may be that checkpoint reports try to cover up the real
problems. If this is the case, then they should not qualify as checkpoint reports, they exist mainly for political reasons. Every checkpoint
report should always go as far back as the original objectives, specifications and benefits of the proposed project. If the need arises for
a modified proposal, then it should be written.

d) Checkpoint reports can get out of hand. A specific short allotment
of time should be made for the report. After all, the purpose of the
project is to design a system and not to write checkpoint reports.

3. *PROJECT PHASES*

An outline will be given of the different stages, constituting a software project.

3.1. Proposal

We believe strongly that a detailed proposal should be the first step
of any serious effort. This is true irrespective of the financing
sources of the project. The proposal serves as much (maybe more) for
internal documentation purposes as a presentation of the project's objectives to the outside world.

The proposal should include:

1. Project objectives. Different goals should be discussed, among them
generality, efficiency,desired reliability level, etc. In case of trade-
offs, the relative weights and priorities should be given. A method of
testing the product should be outlined with respect to the stated objectives and acceptance criteria. System specifications should be given,
for instance functional facilities, internal organization, etc.

2. *Resources*. Time and cost requirements should be proposed. Personnel requirements should be clearly stated taking a realistic view of the state-of-the art within the organization and the availability of outside persons. A schedule should be prepared with frequent checkpoints. A team organization should be outlined.

3. *Benefits*. This might seem superfluous at first, especially if the decision to initiate the project is reached for other, mostly marketing and political reasons. For psychological reasons though, people like to think that they are participating in something important and exciting. Benefits for the organization and for the general community should be emphasized.

The proposal should be widely circulated both among the project members and within the organization. Interested or important persons should be asked to comment on the contents until a specific date. It should be emphasized to everybody that no response is equivalent to approval. In the case of outside financing the proposal serves the real purpose of obtaining the resources. Many iterations might be necessary. The proposal should be written with the participation of all key project members. They should take personal interest in the project from the beginning. We take the stand that money is not enough to ensure the loyalty of the participants. They should take pride in what they are doing.

3.2. *Survey phase*

During this phase the literature is surveyed for appropriate information. Use of past experience should be made whenever feasible. A general design technique is chosen. Finally tools for the production are imported or generated.

We will illustrate this phase for the particular case of the design and construction of an Operation System [15].

First by a survey of the literature we identified several design approaches [16].

I/ *Level-approach*. The best example is the "THE" system produced by Dijkstra et al [4]. Starting from the bare machine the system is built in levels. Each level uses only the facilities provided by the lower (closer to the machine) levels as logical resources. The final level is the system itself. The advantages of such an approach are mainly elegance, nice structure and reliability.

II/ *Top-down* [14]. Starting with the outer layer (Job Control Language, or other formal description of the system), one obtains the system by gradual refinement towards the actual machine. In the beginning the system is simulated. As the simulation becomes more refined by breaking into modules and substituting real code, the simulation finally meets the hardware and it becomes the system.

III/ *Nucleus-extension* [2,3]. Start by isolating the basic facilities of the system. Good candidates are process generation, message communication, CPU allocation, capability manipulation etc. Generate a small nucleus of a system which provides these facilities. The nucleus may or may not be structured. From the nucleus, different Operating Systems can be obtained by extension, preferably using a level approach.

IV/ *Modules-Interfaces*. The system is broken into modules usually based on the different functions to be performed e.g. file system, I/O system etc. The modules are designed independently and then interfaced together. Problems may arise from incomplete specification of the interfaces.

We chose as a design approach a combination of the different techniques and methodologies. We adopted the nucleus approach (III) using levels (I). Starting from a kernel (small nucleus) the nucleus is obtained using the level approach. The system is obtained from the nucleus again using a level approach for every system or subsystem attached. The outer facilities of the system are always kept in mind and simulation is used whenever appropriate (II).

Second we surveyed system programming languages. We decided to design and implement our own by borrowing many ideas from other different languages, notably PASCAL [15].

Third we generated the facility by which we can run and test our programs under an existing system, in the particular case OS/360.

In view of the fact that designer's time is the critical resource in the development of a software system it is surprising to see how few design tools are available. For description purposes flowcharts are not adequate, since they do not provide the ability to describe concurrent operations. Many description models are available such as Petri nets, Program schemata etc. [8,9]. Unfortunately they are more appropriate for theoretical results than description and analysis of systems. Models tend to be rather primitive to facilitate theory and they grow to tremendous proportions when used in practice.

Simulation is very helpful, but time-consuming. If the system is to be implemented in a high level language, extensive simulation may be as difficult to implement as the system itself. Queuing theoretical and probabilistic analysis tools can be very useful for insight, but when we move to multiple resource and multiple queue models, they usually become intractable.

There are efforts to produce an environment for Computer Aided Design of software systems [7,11]. This type of approach has tremendous implications in the development of systems. One such environment, AED, originally developed in MIT is now a commercial venture.

3.3. *Design and implementation phase*

We will not attempt to describe this phase in any detail, since most of our colleagues already talked about it. It involves among others:

1) Conceptual design
2) Structural design
3) Detailed design
4) Programming
5) Testing and debugging
6) Validation

In some projects where a "turn-key" product is desirable, there is the final stage of actually implementing the system in the users environment. The project is only complete and successful after the product is certified by the user.

We will mention two mistaken approaches which could prove disastrous in the design and implementation phase.

a) Deadline approach. The system has to be ready by a certain date, or at least it has to "look" ready from a terminal. Without proper design the programmers are rushed on in the implementation. The system "almost" works and it "almost" meets the deadline. From then on, it is a continuous battle against unfavourable odds to make the system work at any time. We do not imply that deadlines are not important; the designers should have enough foresight and courage to change them or change the project (or job).

b) Million monkey approach. Untrained, or at best not properly trained persons are hired in numbers. They are given desks, pencils, paper, a machine and the specs and they are expected hopefully to produce the system. It usually does not work. System designers are needed with particular skills and sheer numbers cannot be a substitute. As a result whatever talent is in the project is probably wasted on management of the vast numbers of staff.

4. MANAGING "LARGE" PROJECTS

A "large" software project is usually defined as one with more than 25 members, or with at least two levels of management. The problems of managing "large" projects are outlined in the two NATO reports [11,12]. We feel that the state of the art for the management of such projects has not advanced significantly, since the time of the discussions in Garmisch and Rome. There is rather a tendency to eliminate the necessity of "large" software projects. Instead of hiring enormous numbers of people, a few persons are selected and they are given good tools to produce the same product. For instance, it seems that only three experienced persons are used to produce the initial software for the CDC Star computer. One is responsible for the microprogramming, the other for the compilers and the third for the Operating System. This is quite a departure from the 5,000 people used for O.S/360.

It seems that the productivity and joint intellectual output increases as more people get involved, it reaches a plateau and then it starts decreasing rapidly. The point of diminishing returns varies between ten and twenty-five members according to the managerial talent in the project. The inherent reason is that above 5-7 members a managerial structure is needed.

We will outline the historical cases as presented in the Rome NATO report.

a) In 1950 a small group of people with very limited equipment produced an aircraft surveillance system. Judging from their success the SAGE system went underway with 1,000 people recruited from undertakers to school teachers according to aptitude tests. The result was one year delay and considerable cost overrun.

b) In 1961 a small well-knit group of people in MIT produced a very successful time sharing system, CTSS, on equipment which can at best be described "extraordinary". The MULTICS project was launched as a follow-up and although it is a successful running system now, it overran its estimates by 100 %.

In short to manage a "large" software project, managers are needed which are "skilled, flexible, tolerant, informed, extremely tactful and unfortunately rare" [12]. Such people may exist, but to think that they are readily available for managing software projects is an illusion.

One can always argue that "large" projects are necessary because with much parallelism they can shorten the production time. We will counteract this argument by a quote due to an unknown software soldier "You can't have a baby in one month by impregnating nine women".

5. REFERENCES

1. Belady, L. and Lehmann, M, *Programming System Dynamics* IBM Report RC 3546, September 1971.

2. Brinch Hansen, P. (ed.) *RC 4000 Software Multiprogramming System,* A/S Regnecentralen, April 1969, Falkoner, Copenhagen F. Denmark.

3. Brinch Hansen, P. "The Nucleus of a Multiprogramming System", *CACM* 13 (April 1970), 238.

4. Dijkstra, E. W. "The Structure of THE Multiprogramming System", *CACM 11,* 5 (May 1968), 341-346.

5. Dijkstra, E. W. "Structured programming" in the second NATO Report

11 , p. 84-88.

6. Dijkstra, E.W. *Notes on Structured Programming*
Technological D. Eindhoven, The Netherlands, August 1969.

7. Glaser et al. *Project LOGOS*. Distributed material. Project LOGOS
conference. Case Western Reserve University. October 1971.

8. Holt, A. and Commoner, F. "Systemics" in *Proceedings of Project
MAC Conference on Concorrent System and Parallel Computations*.
Woods Hole, Mass., June 1970.

9. Karp, R. and Miller, R. "Parallel Program Schemata", *Journal of
Computer and System Sciences* 3.2, May 1969.

10. Mealy, G. "The System Design Cycle" *Second Symposium on Operating
Systems Principles*, October 1969, Princeton University.

11. NATO Report on *SOFTWARE ENGINEERING*, Garmisch, Oct. 1968.
Available through NATO, Dr. H. Arnth-Jensen, Scientific Affairs
Division, OTAN/NATO, 1110 Bruxelles, Belgium

12. NATO Report on *SOFTWARE ENGINEERING TECHNIQUES*, Rome, Oct. 1969.
Available through NATO, Dr. H. Arnth-Jensen, Scientific Affairs
Division, OTAN/NATO, 1110 Bruxelles, Belgium.

13. Parnas, D. "Information Distribution aspects of Design Methodology",
IFIP Congress 1971, COMPUTER SOFTWARE, pp. 26-30.

14. Zurcher, F. and Randell, B. "Iterative Multi-Level Modelling.
A Methodology for Computer System". *IFIP Congress 68*.
Edinburgh, Scotland, (Aug. 1968).

15. *SUE project development workbook*. Computer Systems Research Group,
University of Toronto.

16. *COSINE Report on Operating Systems*, available through the
Commission on Education, National Academy of Engineering,
2101 Constitution Ave., Washington, D.C.

CHAPTER 4.B.

D O C U M E N T A T I O N

Gerhard Goos
University of Karlsruhe, Germany

0. INTRODUCTION

Documentation is the information about a program available in writing.
The creation of a program is accompanied by documenting the different
phases of development. There exist therefore different documentations
describing the state of the program at different stages. These different
documentations are used by different sets of people and for different
purposes.

Documentation must be available. Not any sheet of paper on the desk of
some programer can be considered part of the documentation. There must
be some standards stating which information is considered part of which
documentation. These standards prescribe also the form in which the
information has to be presented; without such rules it will be very
difficult to retrieve the information. Lastly documentation standards
allow for checking the completeness of the documentation, i.e. they
guarantee that all relevant aspects are covered.

Documentation must be valid. There is no interest in knowing which algorithms are thought yesterday to solve a problem if they are different
from those which are implemented today. Guaranteeing the validity of the
documentation if many people are involved is no easy undertaking. The
best way to achieve validity is the use of an automated documentation
system.

There are many thick handbooks defining different standards for documentation to every detail. It is not thought the topic of this lecture
to give lengthy listings about which detail should be described how. We
try to overview the different needs for documentation and to give an introduction into some crucial problems.

1. THE NEEDS FOR DOCUMENTATION

Documentation has to answer different questions:

(1) How to use a program?

(2) What is the state of the project?

(3) What are the overall specifications of the project?

(4) Which models are used to subdivide the program and to interface
    different modules?

(5) Which basic models are used for the modules?

(6) Flow of control and flow of data through the program.

(7) Detailed description of data.

(8) What is the meaning of the error-messages?

These questions must be answered by different documentations at
different times.

We distinguish

(a) the user's guide (ad 1,8)

(b) the conceptual description (ad 2, 3, 4, 5)

(c) the design documentation (ad 2, 3, 4, 5)

(d) the product documentation (ad 2, 6, 7, 8)

The user's guide is at least conceptually initiated first but finished
last. It must be independent from the other descriptions.

The conceptual description is developed as the project proceeds. It
serves as an introduction, overview and specification of the project.
It contains references to the design and product documentation.
The design documentation describes the current state of the project
during the design phase. It defines the input for the construction phase.

The product documentation describes the current state of the project
during the construction and maintenance phase. The program itself is
part of the product documentation. It is the basis for writing the
user's guide.

All these documentations are subject to the following conditions:

- Any question about details must be answered using a very small amount
  of time. For instance there could be a tree-like ordering imposed
  allowing for tracing easily from the root to every detail found at a
  terminal node of the tree.

- The answers must be complete. They must reference related details which
  the reader has not asked for because he did not know that they exist
  or that they are related.

Many projects have died because these conditions were not fulfilled by
the design and product documentation. Programming is a creative task;
nobody can fulfil this if it takes him too long a time to inform himself
about the basis of his work. If programmers cannot get a clear understanding how their work is related to the work of others they must fail
because they usually start from wrong assumptions about their environment.

1.1. THE USER'S GUIDE

The user's guide is subdivided into two or if necessary three parts:

- introductory manual

- the reference manual

- the operator's guide (if there is any activity of an operator implied).

The introductory manual serves three goals:

It gives an informal introduction and overview about what problems can
be attacked by the program and what the limitations are. It is that part
of the user's guide which should be drafted before the design of the program starts because it specifies the objectives of the program. But note
that the final version of the introduction describes the objectives one
has achieved, not those one was trying to achieve when one started! The
introductory manual mostly forms the descriptional basis for advertising
and selling the program.

Secondly the introductory manual describes the "standard use" of the
program. It is very useful to separate this part of the introductory
manual from all other parts and to make it as short as possible because

every user is expected to know these informations by heart or has them in his pocket. It eases the job of the user if he has not to select these basic informations from different parts of the introductory manual. A "cookbook" must be given describing the commonly used job control cards with only a few number of options; layout and order of input and output data are described mostly by examples. E.g., for an ALGOL 60-compiler the following information is given:

- Command for starting the compiler with listing of source text and standard core size.

- Command for starting the translated program using standard core size.

- Advice how to punch special characters ("(/" instead of "[" etc.)

- Rules for punching input data (separation of numbers by two blanks etc.)

- How to use the available test facilities.

- Explanation of commonly occurring error messages.

Nothing is said about language restrictions or extensions.

Thirdly the introductory manual describes all possible applications of the program, informally and in common terms. The main difference between this description and the corresponding description in the reference manual consists in that this description should be readable by every user of the program. Previous programming experience or formal training of the user can be requested only if the objectives of the program require it. In such cases, however, the informal description is superfluous and must not be supplied. E.g., an informal description of the interface between operating systems and assembly programs is not needed; the informal description of a compiler contains an informal description of the language as implemented. "Informal" means that sometimes a compromise must be made between readability and the rigidity required for describing *all* exceptional cases. The reference manual assumes that the reader has some familiarity with related publications and with the current state of the art how to solve a given problem. The informal description does not assume this. It therefore should provide the user with some background information motivating him for the best usage of the program and telling him which cases can be handled particularly efficiently.

The user's reference manual supplies complete information how to use the program. The formal level of the description must be such that clarity and completeness of the description can be achieved. In addition to the description of commands, format and content of input, output and error messages the following information is needed:

- How to install the program (minimal configuration required, operating system required, permanent files and other resources exclusively used, how to read the delivered tape etc.)

- Time and space estimates as a function of input data.

- List of programs which might be useful for ameloriating the performance of the given one or for solving related problems.

- Possible changes or extensions for increasing the availability, robustness, range of applicability etc.

The operator's guide is needed whenever operator's intervention is required by the program either for mounting devices or for reacting at the console. The operator's guide must describe the input stream (job control cards, data, tape files, disc filed), the output stream (tape files, disc files, punched cards, printer-output and its preparation) and the operation at the console, in particular for handling abnormal conditions.

1.2. THE CONCEPTUAL DESCRIPTION

The first version of the conceptual description is that paper from which the design starts from. The overview belonging to the user's guide describes the objectives of the program from the user's point of view; the conceptual description specifies them in technical terms. Especially it specifies the constraints (minimal configuration, estimates for amount and properties of usual input data, exceptional cases yet to be handled efficiently) to which the creation of the program is subjected. Whenever possible it must specify a lower bound for the requested performance.

During the design of the program the conceptual description extends to a description of the basic concepts and models underlying the design. It describes the decomposition of the program into modules and the basic concepts and objectives of each module.

Ideally the conceptual description should be stable when the design is finished. In practice this happens very seldom. Too often there are changes afterwards, e.g. because during production or maintenance the objectives could not be met or because the design was changed later or because the objectives have changed due to market conditions.

1.3. DESIGN AND PRODUCT DOCUMENTATION

The design and the product documentation have many properties in common:

- They will never be produced if there is no authority who insists on that.

- They are the working documents by which the designers and the pro- grammers respectively report on their work. They provide the means of communication in the design and production group.

- Both should be subdivided by the same scheme so that explicit cross- referencing is minimized since every reader of the product documenta- tion knows where to search in the design documentation and vice versa. The subdivision corresponds to the subdivision of the program into modules.

- The information for each module is hierarchically ordered. First we get the basic information how it works including the interface descrip- tion to the outside. Then there follow the details about the internal structure, data and algorithms.

It is very important that the classification scheme of the documentation is created very early in the design. It may be revised later. The early existence of the classification allows to control that every design decision is really documented and does not remain in the air or on some- body's desk.

The design documentation contains a detailed description of the models underlying each module. This includes the specification of the formal description how the module works as well as a description of the basic data structures. All functions provided and requested by the module are specified. Diagrams specifying the flow of data and control through the program as a whole and through each module are given. Lastly the design documentation should record the history of the design. One often comes back revising an earlier decision. To this end it is useful to preserve the results of earlier discussions for reuse.

The product documentation consists of a detailed description of all

module-interfaces, data, data formats and algorithms. This description
is crossreferenced to the source program which itself belongs to the
product documentation. The source program contains comments which in
most cases should allow for local understanding of the meaning of the
program without going back to the description.

Special care must be taken to describe all kinds of error-handling very
extensively. It is this information from which the maintainers of the
program have to start for searching errors and correcting them. Error
messages are useless if it is impossible to trace them back to their
source.

There is no program which is stable forever. Either the base system or
the objectives change sometimes. To adapt the program it is crucial that
the product documentation describes clearly the program points where
additional activities can be inserted and that it distinguishes between
the goals to be achieved by certain algorithms and the particular way
by which this is done. Very often non-adaptability is a consequence of
a bad documentation. The people involved must make experiments for reconstructing the essentials of an algorithm or a data structure instead
of reading this information in the documentation.

2. SPECIAL PROBLEMS

2.1. DESCRIPTION OF DATA AND ALGORITHMS

Data belong to different classes:

- Data on permanent files

- Auxiliary files (scratch files)

- Tables accessed by many program-modules

- Parameters of calls of program-modules

- Local tables of a program module

- "State variables"

- Auxiliary variables

To describe data on files the record-structure and the methods of accessing them must be specified. In case of permanent files it is described to which purpose the data are or can be used by other programs (e.g. updating, gathering statistics). If this may happen the synchronization in case of multiple access is described.

The description of files, tables accessed by many modules and parameters are part of the interface-description between modules. It must be indicated to which extent the consistency and validity of these data is checked by the modules using them.

The distinction between state variables and auxiliary variables depends on the problem. A boolean variable can be a state variable or itcan be an auxiliary variable if it is used only for the purpose of abbreviation. In describing the meaning of the variable it is, however, important to say which class the variable belongs to. Auxiliary variables have meaning only in a restricted part of a module and sometimes in different parts they are used for different purpose. This must be indicated clearly

In all cases it is necessary to state not only the possible range of values but also the meaning of the values in terms of the problem to be solved.

The description of the algorithms may be given by flow charts. This, however, is not recommended when using a programming language which includes a rich set of control structures (nesting, loops, conditional expressions etc.). In this case it is more appropriate to describe the program-modules by "pseudo-programs" which preserve the structure of the original program but replace detailed constructions by explanations in plain English.

2.2. CROSSREFERENCING BETWEEN DOCUMENTATION AND PROGRAM

In many cases procedures and local data can be described by comments in the source program. Otherwise appropriate means must be established for finding the description given a piece of source text and vice versa. Four problems are involved:

- The searching problem. There must be listings which allow for specifying the corresponding section of the description to each part of the program and vice versa. The program part can be specified by (module name, data name) or (module name, procedure name) in the documentation.

The program should specify the documentation section by a comment containing a pointer to the index of the documentation. Additionally a table of contents of the program must be established specifying the line numbers in the source text for each procedure etc. Moreover, there should be automatic means for finding all program points where a given identifier occurs.

- The naming problem. To each identifier occurring in the description or in the source program an algorithm must exist for finding the declaration and the corresponding description. This is difficult when the same identifier is used many times for different purposes. A solution is given by establishing the following conventions:

Every program component has a unique name. Every other identifier is either local to a certain component or it is global and then it starts by the name of the component which contains its declaration:Component&globname. A "component" in this context means a unit small enough to be searched in reasonable time in the documentation or in the program for a certain information.

- The interface problem. There must be listings telling which functions of a module can be called by other modules and which outgoing calls reference which other modules.

- The unnamed data problems. This is the most serious problem in cross-referencing. There must be a guarantee that to every identifier naming a certain variable or value in the documentation the use of these data can be found in the program and vice versa. This causes trouble when the data are allocated dynamically or when they are packed into one word and the program contains the access algorithm explicitly instead of naming the data by identifier. In this case the source program must everywhere contain at least comments such as "access to <identifier as given by the description>". However, the better solution is the use of a programming language which allows for describing the access to packed data by qualified names.

2.3. *MAINTAINING THE DOCUMENTATION*

The design and product documentation must be complete, up to date, accessible to every member of the team and it should not contain information which is out of date.

The first goal is achieved by having a good table of contents in advance which allows for controlling the completeness. To update a documentation and to guarantee accessibility mechanic aids for establishing the documentation are recommended. A text-editing system in a time-sharing environment solves a lot of trouble: It allows each programmer to update the documentation most easily (so he will be more inclined to do the job), it saves clerical work in writing and distributing material, it guarantees that not only the one copy of the documentation in the archive is up to date.

To delete outdated information appropriate rules must be set up to decide which information is no longer needed. At least during design it is better to hold information too long than to destroy it too early. A very trivial rule should be recalled in this context: Never enter any document or make any change without adding the date.

PERFORMANCE PREDICTION

R. M. GRAHAM[*]

DEPARTMENT OF COMPUTER SCIENCE

UNIVERSITY OF CALIFORNIA

BERKELEY, CALIFORNIA, USA

PERFORMANCE PREDICTION

In the following sections we will consider the problem of predicting the performance of a proposed, but not yet implemented, computer system. Because of the need to limit the scope of our subject we will focus our discussion around operating systems, even though we consider the hardware to be an important part of any computer system. Most of our discussion is also valid for any complex software, especially other types of computer systems, such as, a management information system or an airline reservation system. We have elected to focus on operating systems in our discussion and examples since operating systems are probably more well known to software engineers than any other type of software.

Our discussion begins by considering the meaning of performance, the problems encountered when trying to measure it, and the limitations which bound the attainment of specific performance goals. We then consider the modelling of systems, which is an essential part of any performance analysis, and how these models are used in predicting performance. Since simulation is the most powerful of all the tools for predicting performance we explore this topic in more depth. Finally, we conclude our discussion by exploring the integration of performance prediction with the design and implementation of software systems.

[*]Present Address: Dept of Computer Sciences, The City College, New York, New York, USA

1. PERFORMANCE: DEFINITION, MEASUREMENT, AND LIMITATIONS

A well formulated set of design goals for a proposed system will include some explicit performance goals which the final implemented system should satisfy. Even if the design goals do not contain any explicit performance goals, some minimal performance goals are certainly implicit, for example, an implementation which takes an infinite amount of time to perform its functions is generally unacceptable. The basic problem in performance prediction is: given the design goals and given the specification of a particular design determine whether the performance of the proposed design satisfies the design goals. Before we can discuss how this can be done we must have a clear understanding of what performance means, how it can be measured, and what limitations exist which may prevent the attainment of arbitrarily selected performance goals.

1.1. WHAT IS PERFORMANCE?

Performance, in the present context, is the effectiveness with which the resources of the host computer system are utilized toward meeting the objectives of the software system. That is, how well does it do the job it was designed to do? Thus, performance has to do with the minimization or maximization of certain parameters in a system. For example, "minimum response time" and "maximum throughput" are phrases often used in discussing the performance of a system. Two levels of performance are important in any discussion of the subject: minimum acceptable performance and optimal performance.

Minimum acceptable performance is specified by a set of constraints on performance which an implementation must satisfy to be an acceptable implementation. These constraints may be explicitly stated as part of the design goals. For example, it may be specified that for a certain class of jobs the throughput must be more than a specified number of jobs per hour or that the response time for a certain class of requests is less than a specified number of seconds. Another type of constraint which is often explicitly stated is the maximum amount of primary memory which the operating system may use at various times. If these constraints are not explicitly stated then they must be derived from the design goals. For example, if no constraint on response time is specified for an interactive system, then some reasonable constraint is assumed. Five seconds is probably reasonable for a trivial request while five minutes is quite unreasonable.

In general the system designer attempts to produce a system which

achieves optimal performance. There are many system designs which satisfy the
minimum acceptable performance constraints. Some subset of these designs, which
is usually small, contains all those designs which are "best" in some sense.
It is difficult to define "best" precisely and this problem is discussed in the
next two sections. A "best" design is one in which the values of certain parameters are maximized or minimized. We say that the implementation of such a
design is a system which achieves optimal performance. The design goals may explicitly call for optimal performance in addition to specifying the minimum
acceptable performance. For example, the design goals for an interactive system may explicitly call for minimal response time while the design goals for
a non-interactive system might specify maximum throughput.

The performance of any particular system must always be related to the
purpose and goals of that system. No universal set of system parameters can be
used to define performance, since the significance of parameters depend on the
particular objectives of the system. In fact, it is possible that the performance of two quite similar systems, each designed for a different purpose,
will be defined in terms of two nearly disjoint sets of system parameters. In
a sense, the performance of a particular system is a characterization of how
well that system does the job that it was designed to do. Thus, any discussion
of the performance of a particular system must always be relative to the purpose for which the system was designed.

1.2. MEASUREMENT OF PERFORMANCE

In the preceding section we used words like "optimal" and "minimization"
in discussing the meaning of performance. Use of these words implies that
performance, or at least some aspect of it, is quantitatively measurable.
There are two significant problems in connection with the measurement of
performance: selection of an adequate metric and the variability of performance as a function of the input to the system.

1.2.1. PERFORMANCE AS A FUNCTION OF INPUT

It is clear that performance is a function of the inputs to the system,
that is, it is variable and depends on the characteristics of the jobs
or requests which are submitted to the system. For example, in an interactive system if every request takes one hour of computing time and the
system contains only one computational unit (processor) then the average
response time cannot possibly be five seconds. A computer system has at
its disposal a finite amount of a number of different resources, such as,
processors, primary memory, secondary memory (disks, drums, ...), input-

output devices (tape units, printers, card readers, communication lines,...), and input-output channels (or processors). The system uses these resources to process the jobs or requests submitted to the system.

The characteristics of a job (or request) which are significant in performance measurement can be specified in terms of the sequence in which a job demands the use of various resources and the amount of these demands. It is usual to consider types of jobs rather than individual jobs. A job type is a class of jobs all of which have similar sequences of resource demands. There are clearly an infinite number of different job types. Fortunately many of the jobs encountered in real systems seem to belong to one of a relatively small number of different types. For example, one common job type consists of a sequence of more or less evenly spaced requests for input-output with a relatively small amount of computation between each request. The term input-output limited is often used to characterize this type of job. Many data processing jobs are of this type, especially file maintenance. Another common job type is a short sequence of input requests followed by a long computation and terminated by a sequence of output requests. Many scientific computations are jobs of this type. Even though the number of different job types commonly encountered in real systems is relatively small there are a number of open problems in this area. For example, it is not clear how much difference is acceptable between the resource demand sequence of two jobs of the same type. Also, the common job types have not all been identified and precisely characterized.

1.2.2. METRICS

Since the performance of a system must always be related to the purpose for which the system was designed, there is no single metric for the measurement of system performance which is clearly superior to all others. For example, in an airline reservation system the performance might be measured by the sum of the average response time and its standard deviation. Thus, for the performance of the system to be optimal both the average response time and its deviation must be small (but not necessarily minimal). On the other hand, in a multiprogramming batch system the performance might be adequately measured by the inverse of the fraction of time that the central processor is not in use. Thus, optimal performance is obtained when the percent of processor idle time is almost zero.

Performance requirements which are contained in the design goals are usually specified in terms of user oriented system parameters, such as, throughput or response time. These parameters are usually not basic variables of the system and are thus often difficult to work with or measure. If we view the system as mainly concerned with resource management then its basic variables are those things having to do with resource management. A number of different variables are relevant for each system resource, for example, the percent of the resource currently in use, the number of requests for the resource which are currently queued, and various statistical properties of the preceding two variables, such as, the average and maximum queue length, the average and maximum time a request stays in a queue, and the average and maximum amount of the resource used.

Use of user oriented parameters in the design goals is natural and reasonable since they describe the performance goals in terms which are meaningful to the user. When considering the purpose of a system and its performance requirements, parameters like throughput and response time are meaningful, while the basic system variables like average queue length are practically useless. However, the opposite is true when the system designer is attempting to produce an optimal design. The system designer is concerned with the internal workings of the system. Thus, he is dealing with things such as queues and resource allocation algorithms. Knowledge of the average response time is of little use to the designer since his problem is to design allocation and scheduling algorithms which will achieve optimal performance. In analyzing the performance of the system he is interested in the way that a job's resource demand sequence, interacting with his allocation algorithms, affects such variables as average and maximum queue length and the average percent of unused resources.

Of course the system designer is attempting to ultimately minimize or maximize the parameters specified in the design goals, however, knowledge of their values often gives him no other information than whether or not he has succeeded. What he needs is some information about where the problem lies, that is, where the system design needs to be changed in order to improve its performance. When he makes a change in the design the values of the basic system variables are directly affected, while parameters like response time are only indirectly affected. The values of these higher level parameters are functions of the values of the basic system variables. These functions are usually quite complex. We have now uncovered the fundamental problem in performance analysis, that of finding and expressing the relationship between parameters such as, throughput and response time, and the basic system variables. This process is called modeling and the expression of this relationship for a specific system is called a model of that system. The problem of modeling systems is discussed in a later section.

The problem is further complicated by the fact that the basic system variables are not necessarily mutually independent. If these variables are not mutually independent, then changes in the system design which affect one variable may also cause unwanted affects in other basic variables. This makes it more difficult to figure out what changes in the system will cause the desired change of behavior. Another complication arises if the basic variables are not all relevant, that is, some of the variables may be such that changes in their values have little or no affect on the performance of the system.

1.2.3. STEADY STATE, TRANSIENT, AND OVERLOAD BEHAVIOR

When measurement of performance is considered it is important to recognize the difference between the steady state behavior of a system and its behavior during transients or under overload conditions. The system will normally spend most of its time in a steady state condition. We are most interested in the performance of the system when it is operating in this normal, steady state condition. When measuring a system's performance we must make certain that we are measuring the steady state performance. Generally, the performance of the system in the steady state is some reasonable function of the input, thus, the change in its performance due to a change in the input is easily predictable. This is frequently not true for transient or overload behavior. For example, if the input changes from jobs of one type to jobs of a quite different type there may be a short period of quite erratic and unpredictable behavior until the system settles down to a steady state behavior which is a function of the new job type. An overload condition will usually result in similar unpredictable behavior, as for example, when an interactive system which can give good service to only N terminals is operated with 2N terminals.

Even though the steady state performance of a system is the system designer's major interest, it is important that transient and overload behavior be studied. There are two reasons for this. The ideal design is one in which the erratic affects of transient and overload behavior are minimal. Study of performance under these conditions should help the designer in achieving this ideal design. Since the erratic behavior under transients and especially overload conditions can never be completely eliminated it is important to know under what conditions such behavior occurs and what affects it has on the system performance. This knowledge is needed so that during normal operation of the system these conditions can be avoided, or when they occur, their occurrence recognized and corrective action initiated.

1.3. LIMITATIONS OF PERFORMANCE

It is important that we recognize that there are limitations on performance, that is for any proposed system there exist performance criteria such that no possible design can satisfy the criteria. These limitations can be divided into two classes, inherent and economic. Inherent limitations are limits which are theoretically impossible to overcome. Economic limitations are limits which are possible to overcome in theory but not in practice, that is, the cost of overcoming the limit is unreasonable. The following discussion is intended to be suggestive of the types of limitations which exist and is not an exhaustive list.

1.3.1. INHERENT LIMITATIONS

Since all operational computing systems use physical devices, the laws of physics are an obvious inherent limitation. These laws limit the speed of signal (information) transmission. This ultimately limits the speed at which a given task can be accomplished. The larger a computing system is, the more serious this problem becomes. For example, there is a lower bound on the time it takes to add together two numbers which is certainly not smaller than the time it takes to transmit the two numbers to the computer's adder unit and their sum back to memory (the working registers of a computer are a form of memory). Thus, no matter what technique is used for addition, the minimum time is limited by the laws of physics. A similar limitation exists in interactive systems where the minimum response time is limited by the transmission time of the request from the terminal to the computer and the reply from the computer to the terminal.

Another inherent limitation results from conflicting objectives. Whenever the performance goals include constraints on more than one variable it may be impossible to design a system which satisfies all of the constraints if the variables are not mutually independent. The oldest and most well known example of this conflict is the time-space trade off. For example, it is well known that the fastest method of computing a value for a common mathematical function, such as the cosine, is by use of a table of values where the argument of the function is used as an index. However, this speed is obtained at the expense of a large amount of memory space. On the other hand a method for computing the cosine which uses a minimum of memory space is considerably slower. This difference is even more pronounced for more complicated functions. Thus, we can minimize memory space or computation time, but not both simultaneously. In principle the minimization of a set of variables can be accomplished by linear programming methods. However, in practice the designer is usually unable to formulate the appropriate mathematical relations.

Another limitation which we consider inherent is complexity. It is our experience that it is possible to conceive of systems which are too complex to build. It can be argued that this is not the case, that given enough time, money, and people anything can be built. We do not accept this as a valid argument. It is even more the case that a system may be so complex that, while it can be built, it never works the way it was intended. There is always something wrong with it and its reliability is so poor that it is useless.

1.3.2. ECONOMIC LIMITATIONS

The other type of limitation is economic. This type of limitation is not inherent and can be overcome given enough money. It is, however, a genuine limitation since no project ever has an unlimited source of money. The optimal system design which can be achieved is limited, often rather severely, by a relatively fixed budget. Economic limitations on performance are often overlooked in formulating the design goals and unrealistic performance objectives are often attempted.

One obvious economic limitation is the cost of high performance hardware. The current state of the art in hardware technology is such that hardware can be built which has considerably higher performance than the hardware which is currently marketed. In addition, there is a wide range in performance among the currently available hardware and it is usually the case that the higher performance hardware is the more expensive hardware. Thus, up to a point, higher performance can be achieved by spending more money. This is not usually an acceptable method of achieving optimal performance due to the budget limitations of most projects. Hence, a limited budget imposes an upper bound on the performance of the system.

Another way that a limited budget can impose an upper bound on the performance of the system is to limit the search for more optimal algorithms. It is well known that additional work by a designer usually leads to improvements in the efficiency of an algorithm or even a completely new algorithm with much superior performance. This is especially true with a complex operating system. Thus, better performance can be obtained by having the designer spend more time on the design and implementation. How-

ever, the designer is paid and thus, the size of the project's budget
limits the total amount of time that the designer can devote to algorithm
improvement. Only rarely is the budget of sufficient size that all parts
of the system can receive equal attention. Usually only those parts which
are most critical in the system's performance can be considered for
improvement. For this reason it is vitally important that the system
designer understand the behavior of the system which he is designing so
that he can locate those parts which have the most critical affect on the
overall performance of the system. These parts of the system should be the
first to receive his attention in an attempt to discover more efficient
algorithms.

1.4 SUMMARY

In the preceding sections we gave an informal definition of performance
and briefly discussed the problem of measuring performance. We also pointed
out that there are limitations on the optimality of performance which we
can reasonably expect to achieve. Interest in performance analysis, while
increasing rapidly in the past few years, is not new since several papers
on the subject were published in the open literature more than ten years
ago. The number of published papers relevant to performance is large.
Crooke, Minker, and Yeh [1] list over 400 papers. In spite of this mass of
literature, satisfactory solutions do not exist for most of the problems
in performance analysis, especially performance prediction. There seems
to be no documented case where performance prediction was used effectively
and extensively in the design and implementation of a large, complex operating
system. The reasons for this are discussed in section 5.

The aspect of performance analysis which has received the most attention is the evaluation of the performance of existing systems. Lucas [2]
gives a good summary of the major techniques currently in use for performance analysis. Much work has been done on improving the performance of
existing systems. The improvement which is possible in most systems is
so substantial that several commercial organizations exist whose sole
business is performance evaluation and improvement [3].

2.   SYSTEM MODELING

We now focus our attention on the central problem of performance
analysis, system modeling. A model of a system expresses, in some form,
the relations which exist between the basic variables of that system. The
model of a system may be very simple or it may be quite complex, depending

on the complexity of the system and how the model will be used. If the
system is very simple the model may be so simple that it exists only in the
mind of the designer. However, most systems are of sufficient complexity
that any useful model will have to be expressed in some precise and formal
way. It is clear that a complete, detailed description of the system, such
as the actual code, is a model of the system. However, such a model is
generally not useful since it contains a large amount of unnecessary information and does not clearly exhibit the relations between the basic variables.
A model is an abstraction containing only the significant variables and
relations. Hence, it is usually much simpler than the system which it
models. How much simpler will depend heavily on the expected use of the
model and the precision desired in the results of its use.

Any form of performance analysis, even the measurement of performance,
is impossible without some kind of model. Conceptually a model is a function,
or set of functions, in which the system parameters used to characterize
the system's performance are expressed as a function of the system's basic
variables. When predicting performance, a sequence of jobs or requests is
expressed as a sequence of values for the basic variables. Using this
sequence of values and the model we obtain a sequence of values for the
performance parameters. This sequence of parameter values then describes
the performance of the system for the given sequence of jobs or requests.
If we wish to measure the performance of an existing system we need a
model to help us interpret the quantities which we can actually record.
The performance of a system is not a constant number, rather it is a function,
or several functions, whose values depend on the input. In order to characterize the performance of a given system we have to express these functions
and this expression is a model of the system. We can directly record the
values of only some of the system variables. The values of these variables
for different input sequences are then used to derive the values for the
coefficients of the functions in the model.

2.1. TYPES OF MODELS

There are many different kinds of models for systems, but basically
only two different types,analytical and logical. An analytical model is
a set of mathematical equations which express the relations which exist
between the basic system variables and the performance parameters. These
equations are then solved for the dependent variables, that is, for the
performance parameters. After solving these equations the system's performance is completely known since graphs of the performance parameters can
be plotted from the resulting mathematical expressions.

In general, an analytical model does not reflect the structure of the
system which it models, but only expresses the relations between its variables.
On the other hand a logical model mirrors closely the structure of the system
being modeled. A logical model usually cannot be solved in the sense that
an analytical model can be, that is, closed form expressions for the performance parameters are not derivable from the model. However, a logical model
often includes mathematical equations which express some of the relations
between variables.

In the following sections we will discuss analytical models and two
different kinds of logical models, directed graph models and simulation models.
In each case we will informally define the kind of model and give an example.
In sections 3 and 4 we will see how these particular example models can be
used for predicting performance. For that reason, the examples will not be
analyzed in this section. The purpose here is to show how they model a system.

2.1.1. ANALYTICAL MODELS

An analytical model is a set of mathematical equations which express
the relations which exist between the basic system variables and performance
parameters. As such, the number of different analytical models is large
and the kinds of mathematical equations appearing in these models covers
a wide range. However, practically all analytical models share one common
property, they are stochastic, that is, analytical models ordinarily contain stochastic variables. The exact sequence of values taken by a stochastic
variable is not known, however, its range of values and the probability with
which it will take these values is known or assumed to be known. Stochastic
variables are usually defined by functions which give the probability of the
variable taking the values in its range.

The stochatic nature of analytical models really reflects a basic
property of system performance. We seldom, if ever, know the exact sequence
of jobs or requests which will be presented to a system. Further, we do not
know the exact characteristics of the jobs or requests. Ordinarily the most
we know, or can estimate, is the probability distribution of such quantities as the job arrival time and its resource demands. Since this stochas-
ticness is basic to operating systems we should expect that it will also
show up in the logical models.

Much of the work on analytical models of systems has focused on the scheduling policy used in the system. Assuming that the performance of a system is
not noticeably affected by anything other than the scheduling policy, quite
simple analytical models can be constructed. The simplest such model is based

on a first-come-first-serve scheduling policy. We assume that our system consists of a single processor and a single queue for that processor, as in Figure 2.1. Time is divided into units called quanta, each of which is exactly

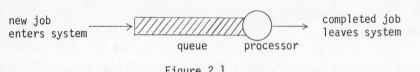

new job   completed job
enters system   leaves system
                            queue   processor

Figure 2.1
First-come-first-serve model

Q seconds long. At the end of each quantum a new job may enter the system,
if so it is put at the end of the queue. The processor is always allocated to
the job at the head of the queue. Once the processor has been allocated to a
job, that job executes until its execution is complete. The completed job
then leaves the system and the processor is allocated to the job now at the
head of the queue. If the queue is empty the processor remains idle until a
new job is placed on the queue. Thus, each job which enters the system is
queued until it gets its turn at the processor. Once a job gets the processor it executes to completion. This scheduling policy is frequently used in
the simpler, nonmultiprogramming, batch systems.

To construct an analytical model we have to specify the time when each
job enters the system and the job's execution time. The usual method of specifying this information is by probability distributions for both job arrival and execution times rather than giving actual sequences of job arrivals
and execution times. For example, we may assume that at the end of each quantum a new job arrives with probability λQ. This gives a job arrival distribution which is a special case of the discrete Bernoulli or binomial distribution. We might also assume that a job's execution time is an exact multiple of Q, nQ, and is chosen independently from a geometric distribution,

$$s_n = (1-\sigma)\sigma^{n-1} \quad , \quad n = 1,2,3,\dots \quad , \quad 0 \le \sigma < 1$$

where s_n is the probability that a job's execution time is exactly n
quanta, i.e., nQ seconds. In section 3.2 we will explore the performance

of the first-come-first-serve model with these probability distributions.

A slightly more complicated model is based on the round-robin scheduling policy sometimes used in time-sharing systems. In this model a new job entering the system is put at the end of the queue and the processor is always allocated to the job at the head of the queue. However, when the processor is allocated to a job, the job executes for exactly one quantum, Q seconds. At the end of the quantum if the job has completed its execution it leaves the system, otherwise it is returned to the end of the queue (see figure 2.2). The processor is then allocated to the job now at the head of the queue. Since a job's execution time is exactly nQ seconds, it will be put on the queue exactly n times before it has completed

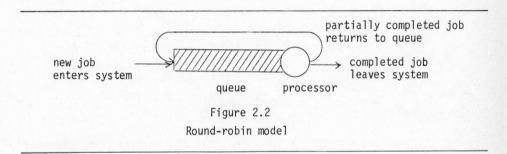

Figure 2.2
Round-robin model

its execution. The same distributions for arrival and execution times may be assumed for this model as were assumed for the first-come-first-serve-model.

Kleinrock [4] has studied models based on these as well as other scheduling policies, particularly policies involving priorities. Estrin and Kleinrock [5] have surveyed the results of analyzing a number of different models. Analytical models have been used to model many different aspects of a system's operation, such as; central processor scheduling, disk scheduling, memory partitioning, paging, and file organization. Since resource management usually requires the use of queues, many analytical models require the use of queueing theory in their analysis. Several interesting studies of analytical models appear in [6] and [7]. Good bibliographies appear in [8] and especially in [1].

2.1.2. DIRECTED GRAPH MODELS

One of the simplest models of a program is a directed graph, which is

basically a flowchart of the program in which some of the detail has been
suppressed and some additional information has been added. A directed graph
is a set of nodes and directed arcs. Each arc in the graph originates at a
node and terminates at a node, possibly the same node. More than one arc
may originate or terminate at a single node. For example, figure 2.3 shows
a directed graph consisting of five nodes (circles) and seven arcs (lines
with arrowheads).

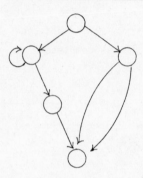

Figure 2.3
Directed graph

In modeling a program with a directed graph the arcs represent the
paths of possible control flow. Branch points are represented by nodes with
more than one arc originating at the node. Computation or other processing
may be associated with either the nodes or arcs depending on the particular
model. Additional information may be associated with the nodes and arcs,
for example, the probability that control exits from a branch point along a
given arc is often associated with that arc.
    As an example consider the following program fragment,

```
IF X<5 THEN W=X+2 ELSE W=6-X;
DO I=1 TO N;
    A(I)=B(I)*W;
END;
```

Figure 2.4 shows its flowchart. To construct its graph model let us make the following assumptions. N is always equal to 9. X is less than 5 half of the time. The instructions for addition, subtraction, comparison, load, store, and conditional transfer each take one time unit. Multiplication takes three time units. The index I is kept in a register and thus the subscripting does not take any additional time. Using these assumptions we can make the following assignment of execution times to the boxes in the flowchart,

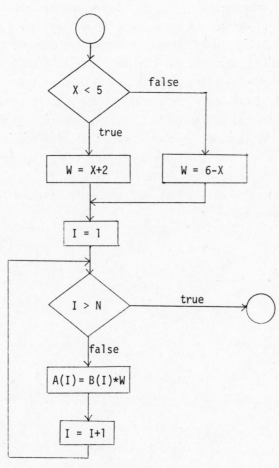

Figure 2.4
Flowchart of program fragment

flowchart box	execution time
X < 5	3
W = X+2	3
W = 6-X	3
I = 1	1
I > N	2
A(I) = B(I)*W	5
I = I+1	1

The box X < 5 takes three time units, one to load X into a register, one
to make the comparison with 5, and one to execute the conditional transfer.
The boxes W = X+2 and W = 6-X take three time units, one to load one
operand, one to do the addition or subtraction, and one to store the result.
The box I = 1 takes only one time unit since all that is necessary is to
load 1 into the register used for I. The comparison I > N only takes
two time units because I is already in a register. The box A(I) = B(I)*W
takes five time units, one to load B(I) (subscripting is free), three to
multiply by W, and one to store the result. The box I = I+1 takes only
one time unit for adding 1 since I is already in a register and the
result is to be left in the register.

Using these execution times we can construct the directed graph model
shown in figure 2.5.

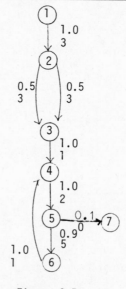

Figure 2.5

Directed graph model

In this model all execution time is associated with the arcs of the graph. The nodes are junction, branch, or separation points. Each arc has two numbers associated with it: the probability that control will exit from that arc's origin node along the arc, which is written with a decimal point, and the execution time for the branch, which is written without a decimal point. Notice that the execution time for a decision box in the flowchart has been associated with the arc which terminates on the corresponding node in the graph. Thus, the execution time for the flowchart box $X < 5$ is associated with arc (1,2) while the branching in this flowchart box is represented by node 2 which is the origin for the two arcs (2,3) which correspond to the two flowchart boxes $W = X+2$ and $W = 6-X$.

The model in the preceding paragraph is adequate for very simple programs, but needs to be extended in order to model some of the more common program constructions. The first situation in which the model is inadequate is when N is not constant. If the variation in N is small compared to its size, the model will probably be valid if the mean value of N is used to calculate the branch probabilities. However, if the variance of N from its mean value is high some modification of the model is required in order to obtain a valid model. One way of achieving this is to leave the variable N in the model, for example

where $\quad p = \dfrac{N}{N+1}$

A similar problem arises in connection with branch points in general. Another strategy for attacking the same problem is to associate a random variable with each arc and define its value as some particular probability distribution.

Another problem occurs when a computation box in the flowchart is a subroutine call. Usually a subroutine does not have a fixed execution time, rather, the time is a function of its input arguments. Again two strategies are suggested. The actual function which determines the execution time can be associated with the appropriate arc. Alternately, the execution time can be defined by a random variable. Beizer [9] proposes a model in which

the execution time is given by a mean value and its variance. In his model
a subroutine or function call would be modeled by an arc such as,

$$
\bigcirc \xrightarrow{\begin{array}{c} p \\ (\mu,\lambda) \end{array}} \bigcirc
$$

where μ is the mean execution time and λ is its variance.

Both of the extensions to the simple graph model which are suggested
in the preceding paragraphs make analysis of the model more difficult. However, these difficulties cannot be avoided if we wish our model to be valid
enough that analysis will provide reliable information about the performance
of the system. We will discuss these difficulties in a later section when
we consider how our model can be used for performance prediction.

A directed graph is conveniently represented by a Boolean matrix.
The properties of directed graphs and their manipulation in Boolean matrix
form have been studied [10]. Directed graph models of programs are useful
for many other purposes in addition to performance prediction. As a result,
many variations of the basic model exist. For example, Lowe [11] defines
a model which contains additional nodes, of a different type, corresponding
to disjoint data sets and additional arcs which represent data references.
Graph models of programs have long been used by compilers for optimization
of object code [12,13]. More recently graph models have been used for automatic program segmentation [11] and performance measurement [14]. A simple
graph model can easily be constructed directly from the source language program [14]. The construction of a complete, detailed model is straightforward
when it is part of a compiler for the source language [13].

2.1.3. SIMULATION MODELS

The most important kind of model is a simulation model. It is the most
general and flexible of all the different kinds of models. Practically any
kind of information can be included in such a model. Further, such a model
can be constructed at any level, that is, as much detail as desired can be
included in the model. Furthermore, concurrency [see Dennis C] is easily
modeled with simulation models, whereas it is difficult or impossible using
analytical models and many graph models, although some graph models are specially designed for modeling concurrency [15].

There are large number of different kinds of simulation models, just
as there are a large number of different simulators. Since a simulator is

required to interpret a simulation model, the form of model to be used is
determined by the simulator. For example, one simulator uses a model which
is similar to the directed graph model used as an example in the preceding
section [16]. There are a number of simulators which require the model to
be described in a special model description language. Some of these simulators are described in later sections where simulation and simulation models
are discussed in considerable detail.

Logical models in general reflect fairly directly the structure of the
system. There are several different ways to express this structure. The
directed graph model which was discussed earlier expresses structure by
directly representing the branch points in the program. Another way of
representing the structure is by modeling the flow of the entities with
which the system deals, such as, jobs and input-output requests. In a model
of this type the structure of the system is less explicit than it was in the
directed graph model. This entity flow type of model is most frequently used
in simulation. In the remainder of this section we will describe a model of
this type for a rather simple system. The model and its use for performance
prediction will be discussed in detail in section 4 which deals with simulation.

The system which we will model is a non-interactive, multiprogramming
system and is due to MacDougall [17]. The hardware in the system consists
of a central processor, central memory, and a movable head disk. For this
example we will not consider the effects of any peripheral devices such as
the card reader. Jobs are entered into the system whenever they are submitted
to the computation center. As soon as sufficient central memory space is
available the job is loaded for execution (we ignore the loading time in
this example). All of the loaded jobs compete with each other for use of
the central processor. Whenever a job makes a disk input or output request
it gives up the central processor. When a job finishes execution it gives
up the central memory space which it has been allocated. Since there may
be more than one job in the system at a time, it is possible that a job
requests the use of a resource which is not currently available. Thus, a
queue must be maintained for each resource. The resources the system has are
central memory space, the central processor, and the disk. Whenever a job
makes a request for one of these resources and the resource is already in
use or, for central memory, there is not enough resource remaining to satisfy
the request, the job is put on the appropriate queue. A job may be on only
one queue at a time and does not execute when it is on a queue.

Briefly, the system functions as follows. When a job first enters the system a request is made for central memory space into which to load the job. If sufficient central memory space is not available the job is put on the central memory queue. Otherwise the job is loaded and a request for the central processor is made. If the central processor is not free the job is put on the central processor queue. Otherwise, the job begins execution.

Whenever a job in execution makes a disk request several things happen. If the disk is free the requested disk input or output is started. Otherwise, the job is put on the disk queue. In either case the requesting job gives up the central processor. If the central processor queue is not empty the central processor is allocated to the job at the head of the queue. This job then resumes (or begins) execution. If the central processor queue is empty, the central processor is left idle until a request is made for its use.

When a disk input or output request has been completed the job which made the request is ready to resume execution. A request is made for the central processor. If this request can be satisfied, the job resumes execution. Otherwise, it is put on the central processor queue. If, upon completion of a disk input or output request, the disk queue is not empty the input or output requested by the job at the head of the queue is started. When a job completes execution, the processor is allocated to the job at the head of the processor queue if the queue is not empty. The central memory space allocated to the terminating job is given up. If the central memory queue is not empty then central memory space is allocated to the job at the head of the queue if there is now sufficient space to satisfy its request.

Our model for this system consists of a characterization of the flow of a job through the system. The job is the single entity which appears in the model. The flow of a job through the system is expressed by the flow diagram in figure 2.6. Each job which enters the system follows a path through this diagram until its execution is completed, at which time it leaves the system. Although the diagram is not exactly a flowchart of the system it is very close to it. Thus, the model closely reflects the structure of the system.

To use the model we must specify the relevant properties of the jobs which enter the system. We do this by specifying distribution functions just as we did for our example analytical models. There are five relevant job characteristics: job interarrival time, central memory requirement, central processor time requirement, I-O interrequest time, and I-O record length. The job interarrival time is the interval between arrival of successive jobs.

415

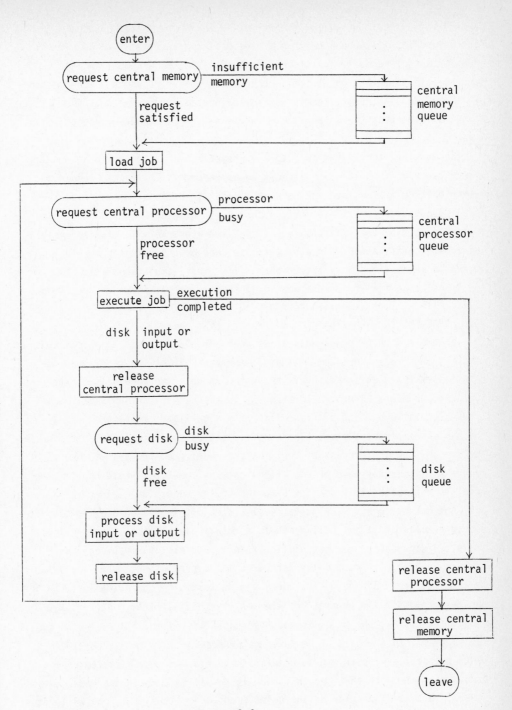

Figure 2.6
Job flow in the system

The I-O interrequest time is a distribution which specifies the length of time a job executes, whenever it gets the processor, until it makes a disk input or output request. The central processor time requirement and the I-O interrequest distribution determine the number of I-O requests which the job will make. The I-O record length is a distribution which specifies the amount of time that the disk will be busy servicing an input or output request.

The model of the system is completely specified by the flow diagram. In order to use it in simulation it must be expressed in the manner required by the particular simulator being used. The distributions for the five relevant job characteristics specify a particular class of input jobs. These must also be expressed as required by the simulator. We will examine one of the model specification languages which is used by a particular simulation system in section 4. In that section we will study simulation in more detail, including the use of the preceding example for performance prediction.

2.2. PROBLEMS IN MODELING

A number of problems always arise whenever one attempts to model a system. The most significant problem is that of the validity of the model. A model of a system is an abstraction of the system in which many details of the system's structure have been omitted or, in the case of an analytical model, a set of equations which express all of the significant relations between the variables of the system. The model is basically a simplified version of the system. In the process of deriving the model from the system some significant relations may have been omitted from the model. If this happens the model is not valid, that is, the behavior of the model for a given input will not match the behavior of the real system within reasonable limits. It should be clear that an invalid model is relatively useless. The problem of validity is probably the most difficult and certainly the most serious problem in modeling, especially for performance prediction. When measuring performance the validity of the model can be tested by comparing the behavior of the model with the behavior of the real system. If they disagree beyond acceptable limits, the model is modified until its behavior agrees with the real system. In the case of performance prediction this is not possible. Since the designer is trying to predict the performance of a system design before he implements that design, there is no way to compare the model's behavior with the behavior of the unimplemented "real" system. We will return to the problem of validity in section 5.

One way of solving the problem of validity is to include more detail in
the model. However, this leads to another problem, the inclusion of a large
number of irrelevant variables and relations. This problem is not as serious
as an invalid model, nonetheless, it may have serious consequences. A model
which includes many irrelevant variables and relations often becomes unmanage-
able. Analysis of such a model becomes difficult and simulation is time
consuming and inefficient. It is difficult for the designer to understand
the behavior of the system because the significant relations get lost among
the irrelevant ones. It is possible to have more than one model for the same
system, each different model being used for a different purpose. The level
of detail in these models would be different. The ideal model is one which
has just enough detail for its purpose, and no irrelevant variables and
relationships. The level of detail may also vary from part to part in the
same model. For example, the model used to get a rough indication of the
gross behavior of the system may be quite simple and include only a few
variables and relations. On the other hand a model used to analyze the performance of a particular disk unit for a particular file storage allocation
algorithm would have to be fairly detailed. Such a model would probably
contain a moderate number of variables and relations in order to reflect
such things as, the sequence of positions of the disk's read-write head,
the sizes of the files on the disk, and the distribution of the records on
the disk.

There are several problems which are unique, or especially severe, with
analytical models. The most obvious problem is that the equations which
express the relations between the system variables may be extremely difficult or impossible to solve, that is, the analyst is unable to derive any
closed form expressions for the performance parameters. In this case the
advantage of the analytical model over logical models is lost. Also, for
a complex system, the relations between the system variables may not even
be expressible as mathematical equations. Another difficulty with analytical
models is that usually the level of detail in the model cannot be changed
without constructing an entirely new model. This is generally not true for
logical models. Since a logical model is a fairly direct reflection of the
system's structure it is usually possible to change the level of detail of
the model or any part of it by techniques analogous to the system design
techniques which are based on hierarchical structure and levels of abstract
machines [see Dennis A, Goos A, Waite, and Poole A]. Logical models also
have the advantage that it is relatively straightforward to build a model of

a system by combining models of its subsystems or component parts. This process of combination is usually difficult or impossible with analytical models. In fact, it seems to be practically impossible to model a complex system in any reasonable detail with an analytical model.

Analytical models are most useful in modeling some part of the system. The information obtained from the study of such a model can then be used in a logical model of the whole system. It is usually possible to capture a great deal more detail with a logical model than with an analytical model. This is especially useful in the earlier stages of performance prediction when it is still unknown what variables and relations in the system are really significant. There is no sharp dividing line between analytical and logical models. For example, an analytical model can be used for simulation rather than deriving a closed form solution. Likewise some logical models yield a closed form solution, at least for certain aspects of performance. In an analogous fashion, no single modeling technique is always the most useful. Although simulation modeling is the most versatile, the other kinds of modeling are usually always useful in a complete analysis of a system's performance, giving information which is difficult or impossible to obtain from simulation.

3. USE OF MODELS IN PERFORMANCE PREDICTION

In this section and the next we will explore the use of models in performance prediction using the three models described in the preceding section as examples. Each different type of model will require a different technique for its use and will yield different kinds of information. As we have previously mentioned each different technique has its place in a complete analysis of performance. Before considering the different techniques and examples, we should be aware of some problems which we will encounter when using any kind of model to predict performance.

3.1. PROBLEMS IN USING MODELS

The major problems in using models to predict performance are validity of the model, characterization of job or request properties, and interpretation of the results. The problem of the validity of a model was discussed in section 2.2. The reader should not underestimate the significance and difficulty of this problem. The significance of the problem lies in the fact that predictions based on an invalid model are virtually useless and do not give the designer any reliable information on the performance of the

system he has designed. Constructing a valid model is difficult, especially
for a large, complex operating system. In order to make the model tractable,
considerable abstraction will have to take place during construction of the
model. Since the designer does not usually have a very good understanding
of the behavior of a new, complex system in terms of its variables and the
relations between them, it is easy for significant relations to get omitted
from the model. Since the proposed system design has not yet been implemented the model cannot be validated by comparison with actual operation
of the system.

Characterization of the properties of the jobs or requests which will
be submitted to the system is also a significant and difficult problem.
As we have noted earlier, the performance of any system is a function of
certain properties of the input to the system, namely their resource demands.
When using a model to predict performance, the model is applied to the sequence of resource demands which represent the system's input. The result is
a measure of the predicted performance of the system for the given input.
Assuming that the model is valid, the result of applying it to input other
than that which will be given to the system in actual use may be interesting but is not apt to be relevant to the desired performance of the system.
What the designer wants to know is how the proposed system will perform for
the kind of input it will receive when it is actually used. The system's behavior with other input may be interesting, since it might give the designer
some insight into the sensitivity of the system to unexpected input, however,
it is not the primary reason for performance prediction.

It may be quite difficult to find a valid and usable characterization
of the system's input. The significant properties of the input are usually
the sequence of jobs (or requests) in the input and the sequence of resource
demands made by each of these jobs. In the first place, the designer may
have only a vague knowledge of the types of jobs which will be submitted to
the system. He may know what kinds of applications the system will be used
for, e.g., payroll or heat transfer computations. However, this knowledge
needs to be translated into typical sequences of resource demands before it
can be used with the model to predict performance. In fact, the input must
be modeled, that is, the significant resource demands must be abstracted
from the anticipated real jobs. In this modeling of the input we have to cope
with most of the problems which have been discussed in connection with modeling of the system. In fact, for some simulators, models of the jobs input
to the system are expressed in exactly the same way as the model of the
system itself [16,18].

In any system where the user is able to write his own programs the problem of modeling the input is especially severe, principally because the system designer does not know what programs the user will write. Even knowledge of the class of problems the user will be solving is often of little help since there are many different ways of writing a program to solve a particular problem. Even if the designer knows exactly all of the programs which will be input to the system, the number of different programs is so large that it is usually impossible to explore the system's behavior for all possible combinations of programs in the input. For this reason the input is usually characterized as a small number of different mixes of several typical jobs. A typical job is a sequence of resource demands which is similar to the resource demand sequences of some class of real jobs.

A typical job is an abstraction from a class of real jobs. It can sometimes be deduced from the sequence of computation and data manipulation required to carry out the function which the job performs. For example, a master file update job will have to sequence through the records in two files, the master file and the file containing the update information. The computation performed between input or output operations is minimal. However, most jobs are not so simple and may be impossible to analyze. The usual attack in this case is to record the operational characteristics of a large set of jobs from a given class when they are executing in some other system. From this data it is usually possible to derive a valid model (typical job) of this job class.

Just as models of systems range from simple to complex, so do models of job classes. The simplest model of a job class consists of a set of distributions, one pair for each resource. One distribution in the pair gives the pattern (frequency) of requests for the resource while the other distribution in the pair gives the amount of resource demanded by each request. In addition, it is assumed that these distributions are all independent. More complex models of job classes may allow some resource demands to be expressed as functions of prior demands for the same or other resources, for example, the amount of memory requested and the frequency of requests for memory may be a function of the amount of memory already requested. Even though time can be considered as a resource, the dependence of resource requests on time is so important that we will consider it as a separate aspect. Most distributions are a function of time. However, there is another way in which the resource demand sequence may depend on time. The distribution which models the frequency of requests for a resource or the magnitude of request for that resource may be different from time to time. For example, a particular typical job may be modeled by a sequence of frequent requests for a short amount of execution followed by a sequence of less frequent requests for a longer amount of execution. A single distribution (at least one of the common, simple distributions) may not validly model the total sequence of requests for execution, whereas, two different distributions might be quite adequate as a model.

The third major problem in using a model for performance prediction has to do with interpretation of the results. If the results of performance prediction indicate that the performance is not acceptable, the designer must modify his design until the design exhibits acceptable performance. Even if the prediction results show acceptable performance, the designer may still need to modify the design in order to improve its performance since he may be trying to achieve an optimal design. In order to improve his design the designer needs to know what part of his design to modify to achieve performance improvement. This requires some interpretation of the result of applying the model of the system to a typical job mix. It is not sufficient to simply observe the values of the performance since this information only tells the designer how good or bad the performance is compared to the minimum acceptable performance. The inner workings of the model as it reacts to the input has to be observed. It is only by examining the values of the system variables which are internal to the model and considering the relations which exist between these variables that the designer can locate the bottle-necks in his design and thus learn where the design can be improved. For example, observing the average length of the resource queues and the average time spent by a job in these queues will reveal any mismanagement of resources.

It was mentioned earlier that the use of different kinds of models may require different techniques depending on the particular model. There are basically two classes of techniques for the use of models, closed form solution and experimental. Closed form solution is most commonly used for analytical models. The set of equations which constitute an analytical model are solved for the performance parameters. This solution, which is itself a set of equations, can then be plotted or further analyzed. Since the equations which constitute a solution are almost always functions of several variables, the graph of these equations is a family, or families, of curves. These curves usually display quite vividly the complete behavior of the system.

Since by definition a logical model does not yield a closed form solution, some other technique is required, even though parts of the model may be solved for closed form expressions. The basic way of using such a model is to conduct a set of experiments, that is, the model is applied to a set of differing inputs. Each application of the model constitutes an experiment. The results of each experiment are recorded and the set of results from all of the experiments is later analyzed. Usually this analysis includes plotting the values of some or all of the observed variables (the performance parameters and system variables), just as the results of experiments in the physical sciences are plotted to depict the relations between variables. If enough experiments are conducted, the designer may be able to discover simple mathematical equations which are good approximations to the true relations between the system variables and performance parameters.

Simulation always involves conducting a set of experiments. Thus, it is the most versatile of all the types of models and is useful at any level of detail and complexity. Actually, almost any model, including analytical models, can be used for simulation. However, while some logical models can be analyzed to some degree, most logical models are suitable only for use in some form of simulation, that is, to use them for performance prediction a set of experiments must be conducted. The use of simulation models will be discussed and illustrated in section 4. In the remainder of section 3 we will discuss the use of an analytical model and a logical model upon which some analysis can be performed.

3.2. PREDICTION USING AN ANALYTICAL MODEL

As an example of prediction using an analytical model we will explore the analytical models described in section 2.1.1. Recall that the first-come-first-serve model is a simple, single queue model without feedback, where the queue discipline used is first-come-first-serve, while the round-robin model is the same except for the addition of feedback and limitation of execution time for a job on the processor to a single quantum. Strictly speaking, the distributions which characterize the job arrival and execution times are not part of the model, but part of the input description. However, most studies of analytical models seem to include these distributions as part of the model. In our example we assume that jobs arrive according to a (discrete) Bernoulli distribution with probability λQ, where Q is the length of a quantum (in seconds). We also assume that a job's execution time is chosen independently from a geometric distribution,

$$s_n = (1-\sigma)\sigma^{n-1} , \quad n = 1,2,3,\dots , \quad 0 \le \sigma < 1 ,$$

where s_n is the probability that a job's execution time is exactly n quanta (nQ seconds).

Kleinrock [4] derives the following results for these two models. In both models the expected number of jobs in the system at any given time is,

$$E = \frac{\rho\sigma}{1-\rho} \text{ , where } \rho = \frac{\lambda Q}{1-\sigma} \quad .$$

Since λ is the average number of jobs arriving per second, $1/(1-\sigma)$ is the average number of quanta of execution required per job, and Q is the number of seconds in a quantum, then ρ is just the average number of seconds of execution time demanded per second by all of the jobs in the system. Clearly $\rho < 1$, otherwise the system overloads and never gets caught up. In fact, $E \rightarrow \infty$ as $\rho \rightarrow 1$.

For the first-come-first-serve (F) model the response time is given by,

$$R_F(n) = \frac{QE}{1-\sigma} + nQ \quad . \tag{3.1}$$

$R_F(n)$ is the total time that a job, which requires n quanta of time for execution, spends in the system. Its execution time is nQ seconds and it spends $QE/(1-\sigma)$ seconds in the queue. For the round-robin (R) model the response time is given by,

$$R_R(n) = \frac{nQ}{1-\rho} - \frac{\lambda Q^2}{1-\rho}[1 + \frac{(1-\sigma(\sigma+\lambda Q))(1-(\sigma+\lambda Q)^{n-1})}{(1-\sigma)^2(1-\rho)}] \quad .$$

Kleinrock has found that a good approximation to $R_R(n)$ is,

$$R_R(n) \cong nQE + nQ \quad . \tag{3.2}$$

Thus, in the round-robin model a job which requires n quanta of execution spends nQE seconds in the queue.

Let us look more closely at the response time. Notice first that both $R_F(n)$ and $R_R(n)$ are linear in n, since all of Q, σ, and λ are constant. Rewriting equations 3.1 and 3.2, we have,

$$\frac{1}{Q}R_F(n) = n + \frac{E}{1-\sigma}$$

$$\frac{1}{Q}R_R(n) = (E+1)n$$

We drop the constant factor $1/Q$ which occurs in both relations and plot the response time for the two models as a function of n in figure 3.1. In the graph the crossover point, n_a, for the two functions is obtained by equating them and solving for n,

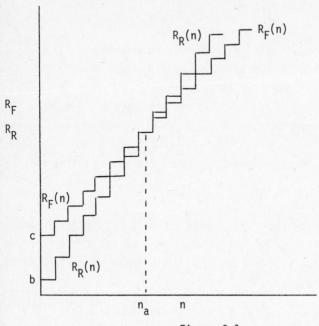

Figure 3.1

Response time as a function of execution time

$$n_a + \frac{E}{1-\sigma} = (E+1)n_a$$
$$n_a = \frac{1}{1-\sigma}$$

The crossover point is the place where the first-come-first-serve scheduling policy begins to give a shorter response time than the round-robin. In other words, if the execution time of a job is less than n_a quanta then its response time is shorter if a round-robin scheduling policy is used. Another way of looking at this is to say that a round-robin scheduler gives better service to short jobs, which is desirable in most time-sharing systems. Consider the case where $\sigma = 0.1$, then $s_1 = (1-\sigma) = 0.9$, that is, the probability that the execution time of a job is one quantum long is 0.9.

The crossover point is, n_a = 1.1. Thus, those jobs whose execution time is one quantum (about 90% of the jobs) get better service when a round-robin scheduling policy is used.

We can also examine the behavior of these two models as the system approaches overload conditions, i.e., as $\rho \to 1$. We will look at the amount of time a job spends in the queue, which is its delay time. The delay time is the response time minus the execution time. In [4] Kleinrock plots,

$$kD_F(n) = k(R_F(n) - nQ)$$
$$kD_R(n) = k(R_R(n) - nQ) \quad,$$

where $k = (1-\sigma)/(\sigma Q)$, rather than the true delay time. He also uses the true formula for $R_R(n)$ rather than the approximation since the approximation is quite bad as $\sigma \to 0$. Under the normalization factor k, $kD_F(n)$ is a function only of ρ. However, $kD_R(n)$ remains a function of n and σ as well as ρ. In figure 3.2 $kD_R(n)$ is plotted for two values of σ. In each case we get a family of curves, one for each value of n, and several members of the family are shown. The curve for $kD_F(n)$, which is the same for all values of n and σ, is plotted in each of the two graphs with small circles. There are three significant aspects of the system's performance which can be seen from the graphs. The service deteriorates as the system approaches overload conditions. That is, the more efficiently the processor is used, the longer the delay time. It is also clear that the rate at which service deteriorates gets larger as the system approaches overload. Finally, if a round-robin scheduling policy is used, the service deteriorates at a faster rate for jobs with longer execution times. This deterioration is particularly severe for small values of σ, i.e., when the input to the system contains a large percentage of short jobs.

The preceding analysis has derived practically all there is to know about the two models. We have seen how the response time varies with the execution time of the job. The actual response time depends on the values of λ, σ, and Q, however, for given values of these parameters it varies linearly with respect to job execution time. We also saw how the service deteriorates as the system approaches overload conditions. Both of the models studied are extremely simple, yet they include several variables and the mathematics required to solve them is not trivial. When predicting the performance of a system of any complexity use of either of these models will not give a complte and accurate picture of the system's performance. This is not to say that these models are useless. If the system follows a first-come-first-serve or round-robin scheduling policy, then using the appropriate one of these two models will give some broad indication of the system's performance, an upper bound to the best possible performance.

These models are inadequate for precise performance prediction because they are too simple. Many significant system variables and relations have been omitted from these models. For example, any system, except the most trivial, will have more than the single queue which is included in the above

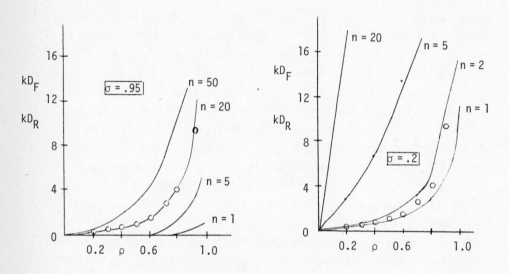

Figure 3.2

Delay time as a function of system load

models. We cannot expect that any model which omits all of these other queues will yield completely valid, detailed performance information. The movement of a job in and out of at least some of these queues (e.g., queues for input or output requests) will certainly have a noticeable effect on the job's response time. Multiple queue models have been formulated, but they are extremely difficult to solve.

3.3. PREDICTION USING A DIRECTED GRAPH MODEL

In this section we will analyze the directed graph model described in section 2.1.2 (figure 2.5). Our strategy will be to successively apply elementary transformations to the graph in order to reduce it as much as possible. Each elementary transformation will reduce the complexity and/or the size of the graph. The reduced graph which results will be equivalent to the original graph. Since we are interested only in performance, this equivalence will be equivalence of execution, but not usually equivalence of structure.

Beizer [9] defines three elementary transformations: series, parallel, and loop. The series transformation is applicable to a pair of arcs in series, i.e., the terminal node of one arc is the origin node of the other arc. The pair of arcs and the node between them can be replaced by a single arc provided no other arcs terminate or originate at the interior node. Figure 3.3 illustrates this replacement. Recall that the two numbers attached

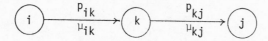

can be replaced by

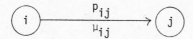

Figure 3.3

Simple series transformation

to an arc (i,k) are the probability, p_{ik}, that control leaves the origin node, i, along the arc and the execution time, μ_{ik}, associated with that arc. In the series reduction illustrated above, arcs (i,k) and (k,j) and

node k are replaced by a new arc (i,j). The probability and execution
time for this new arc are,

$$p_{ij} = p_{ik}p_{kj}$$
$$\mu_{ij} = \mu_{ik} + \mu_{kj} \quad .$$

This transformation can be generalized to apply to any node which is not
interior to a loop of length one, i.e., there is no arc for which that node
is both its origin and terminal node. The general transformation is illustrated in figure 3.4. Each different combination of two arcs in series is
replaced by a new arc and the interior node is eliminated. The probability
and execution time for each of the new branches are computed in the way as
for the simple series transformation, that is,

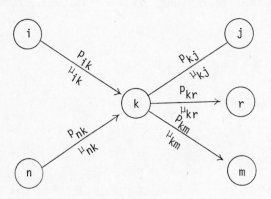

can be replaced by

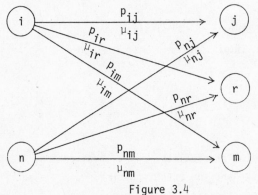

Figure 3.4
General series transformation

$$P_{nr} = P_{nk}P_{kr}$$
$$\mu_{nr} = \mu_{nk} + \mu_{kr} \quad .$$

and similarly for each of the other new arcs.

The parallel transformation is applicable to a pair of arcs in parallel, that is a pair of arcs both of which have the same origin node and the same terminal node. Figure 3.5 illustrates this transformation. The pair of

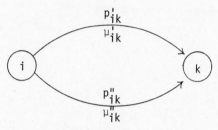

can be replaced by

Figure 3.5

Parallel transformation

parallel arcs is replaced by a single new arc. The probability and execution time for this new arc are,

$$p_{ik} = p'_{ik} + p''_{ik}$$
$$\mu_{ik} = \frac{p'_{ik}\mu'_{ik} + p''_{ik}\mu''_{ik}}{p'_{ik} + p''_{ik}}$$

If there are more than two parallel arcs between two nodes they can be reduced to a single arc by applying the parallel transformation repeatedly to one pair of arcs at a time.

The loop transformation removes an arc which is a loop of length one, that is, an arc which has the same node for both its origin and terminal nodes. This transformation is illustrated in figure 3.6. The arc which is a loop is eliminated and a new probability and execution time are assigned to each of the remaining arcs. These new values are,

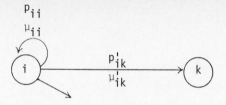

can be replaced by

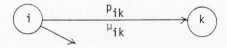

Figure 3.6

Loop transformation

$$p_{ik} = \frac{p'_{ik}}{1 - p_{ii}}$$
$$\mu_{ik} = \mu'_{ik} + \frac{p_{ii}\mu_{ii}}{1 - p_{ii}}$$

which must be calculated for each remaining arc which has node i as its
origin node.

If a directed graph has a single entrance node and a single exit node,
repeated applications of these elementary transformations will reduce the
graph to a single arc and two nodes. To illustrate this procedure we will
use the graph model from section 2.1.2, which is shown again in figure 3.7 (a).
Figure 3. shows the reduction of this graph model by repeated application
of the elementary transformations. The parallel transformation applied
to the two arcs (2,3) transforms the graph from (a) to (b). Two applications of the series transformation, first to the arcs (1,2) and (2,3)
with interior node 2 and then to arcs (1,3) and (3,4) with interior
node 3, transform the graph from (b) to (c). Another series transformation,
on arcs (5,6) and (6,4) with interior node 6, transforms the graph from
(c) to (d). The transformation from (d) to (e) is accomplished by a general
series transformation. In this case node 5 is the interior node and there
are three arcs involved, (4,5), (5,7), and (5,4). The result of eliminating node 5 is two new arcs, (4,7) and (4,4) which is a loop. Application of the loop transformation eliminates this loop and transforms the

431

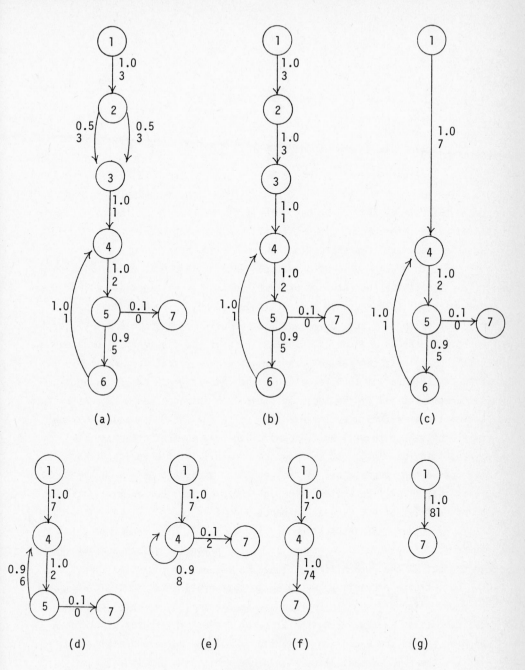

Figure 3.7

Reduction of graph model by elementary transformations

graph from (e) to (f). Referring to figure 3.6 we see that,

$$p_{ii} = p_{44} = 0.9 \qquad p'_{ik} = p'_{47} = 0.1$$
$$\mu_{ii} = \mu_{44} = 8 \qquad \mu'_{ik} = \mu'_{47} = 2$$

then,

$$p_{47} = p_{ik} = \frac{p'_{ik}}{1 - p_{ii}} = \frac{0.1}{1 - 0.9} = 1$$

$$\mu_{47} = \mu_{ik} = \mu'_{ik} + \frac{p_{ii}\mu_{ii}}{1 - p_{ii}} = 2 + \frac{0.9(8)}{1 - 0.9} = 2 + \frac{7.2}{0.1} = 74 \qquad .$$

Finally, application of a series transformation to arcs (1,4) and (4,7) with interior node 4 reduces the graph to (g) which is a single arc and two nodes, the entrance and exit nodes. The final reduced graph indicates that the execution time of the program is 81 time units.

The elementary transformations which we have been using are also applicable to graph models with multiple entrance and exit nodes. The only restriction is that no entrance or exit node may be eliminated. A graph model with multiple entrance and exit nodes cannot be reduced to a single arc. For example, figure 3.8 shows the reduction of a graph model with two entrance nodes and two exit nodes. Each of the transformations used in this example is the series transformation except that from (d) to (e) which is the parallel transformation. The reduced graph has three arcs which represent all of the possible paths from entrance nodes to exit nodes. Each of the arcs indicates the execution time for that path and the probability that the path will be followed given that control enters at the corresponding entrance. If we know the probability of entering at each entrance we can tabulate all of the paths and assign to each path the probability that it will be followed through the program. For example, assume the probability of entering at entrance node 1 is $e_1 = 0.9$ and the probability of entering at entrance node 2 is $e_2 = 0.1$. The three paths in figure 3.8 are tabulated in figure 3.9. The probability for each path is the product of the probability assigned to the arc representing the path and the entrance probability assigned to that arc's origin node, that is, the probability of the path represented by arc (i,j) is $p_{ij}e_i$. We can also compute an average execution time for the entire program by taking a weighted sum of the execution times for all of the paths where the weights used are the path probabilities. In our example this sum is,

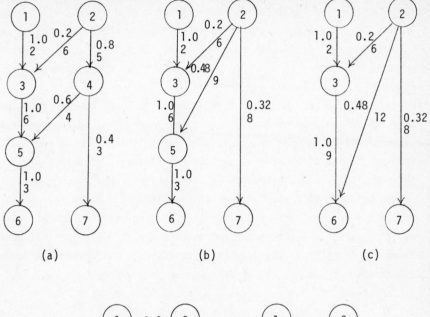

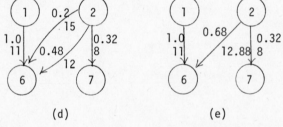

Figure 3.8

Reduction of a multiple entrance and exit graph model

path	probability of path	execution time of path
1,6	0.9	11
2,6	0.068	12.88
2,7	0.032	8

Figure 3.9

Paths in the multiple entrance and exit example

$$0.9(11) + 0.068(12.88) + 0.032(8) = 11.04$$

These figures are principally useful for getting a general idea of the magnitude of the average execution times for the paths and the program as a whole. When control enters the program it actually follows some particular path. The actual execution times for the paths in our example range from 8 to 15.

We mentioned in section 2.1.2 that in order to model some of the common program constructions, we needed to extend the graph model to include arcs whose execution time was not constant. Following Beizer [9], we propose representing the execution time by two numbers, the mean execution time and its variance (μ, λ). This extension is useful even in the simpler case illustrated by our last example. Even if the variance is zero for all of the arcs in the original graph, the result of a parallel transformation will not have zero variance if the execution times of the two arcs are not equal. The elementary transformations are easily extended to include the variance. The new variance for the series transformation is given by,

$$\lambda_{ij} = \lambda_{ik} + \lambda_{kj} \quad ,$$

for the parallel transformation by,

$$\lambda_{ik} = \frac{p'_{ik}\lambda'_{ik} + p''_{ik}\lambda''_{ik}}{p'_{ik} + p''_{ik}} + \frac{\mu'^2_{ik}p'_{ik} + \mu''^2_{ik}p''_{ik}}{p'_{ik} + p''_{ik}} - \mu^2_{ik}$$

and for the loop transformation by,

$$\lambda_{ik} = \lambda'_{ik} + \frac{\lambda_{ii}p_{ii}}{1 - p_{ii}} + \frac{\mu^2_{ii}p_{ii}}{(1-p_{ii})^2} \quad .$$

By associating a variance with each arc, the reduced graph will indicate the variation in execution time for the various paths as well as their mean execution time. This helps give a more accurate picture of the program's behavior.

If we include the variance in our last example, the variances are all zero up until application of the parallel transformation to the partially reduced graph in figure 3.8(d). The variance for the new arc (2,6) is,

$$\lambda_{26} = \frac{p'_{26}\lambda'_{26} + p''_{26}\lambda''_{26}}{p'_{26} + p''_{26}} + \frac{\mu'^2_{26}p'_{26} + \mu''^2_{26}p''_{26}}{p'_{26} + p''_{26}} - \mu^2_{26}$$

$$= \frac{0.2(0) + 0.48(0)}{0.2 + 0.48} + \frac{15^2(0.2) + 12^2(0.48)}{0.2 + 0.48} - 12.88^2$$

$$= 1.93$$

We can also apply the variance computations to the program paths and reduce the graph to a single arc if we assume a dummy entrance node which is the origin node of some new arcs, one to each entrance node in the original graph, and a dummy exit node which is the terminal node of some new arcs, one from each exit node in the original graph. Figure 3.10(a) shows the final graph of figure 3.8(e) modified in this way. In this graph the execution times are written as a pair of numbers (μ, λ). Two series transformations are applied to (a) and one to (b) to get (c). Then the parallel transformation is applied to obtain (d). Notice that the variance actually decreases. This is because the arc which had the higher variance also had a very low probability and the means for the two branches are quite close together. One more series transformation followed by a parallel transformation reduce the graph to a single arc which has a mean execution time of 11.04 with a variance of 0.39.

The modified graph model which we have just been discussing, which includes variances, is still not adequate for modeling some aspects of program behavior, especially loops and branches which depend on the arguments of the program. If this dependency can be expressed as a simple relation we may be able to find a mean value and variance for the execution time corresponding to the data dependent portion of the program. However, we may not be able to do this because the execution time does not follow a normal distribution closely enough for the mean and variance to be a valid representation. Also we may not be able to derive a numerical probability for all of the arcs. There are two basic directions in which to attack this problem. We can try to extend the basic model to allow more variety in the method of expressing the probability and execution time attached to an arc, either by allowing other distributions or symbolic expressions. In either case the analysis becomes more difficult and we soon experience great difficulty in analyzing the model, just as we did with the analytical model. The other direction is to go to some form of simulation. In this case, we can extend the model to include other

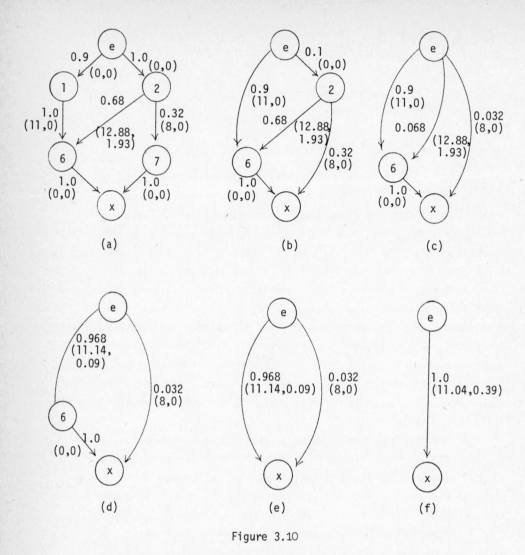

Figure 3.10

Reduction of multiple entrance and exit model with variances

distributions and symbolic expressions for expressing the branching probabilities and execution times. One extension of this model [16] is used
with a combination of techniques. After doing as much analysis as possible,
the partially reduced model is used for simulation. This extended model
and the techniques used on it are described in more detail in section 5.

4.   SIMULATION

Gordon [19] defines system simulation "as the technique of solving problems by following the changes over time of a dynamic model of a system." Basically, in simulation one does not attempt to solve the model analytically. Further, no specific attempt is made to isolate the relations between any particular variables, one just observes the way the variables of the model change with time. Relationships must be derived from these observations. Therefore, simulation is basically an experimental technique. In this section we will consider the methods and problems of simulation and explore the model described in section 2.1.3.

4.1. MAJOR METHODS

There are two major types of simulation: continuous and discrete. The model of a continuous system, where our interest is in smooth changes in time, is usually a set of differential equations. Continuous simulation is based on such a model. Analog computers are best suited for this type of simulation and are used extensively for this purpose. Digital computers can be used also, provided a small enough time interval is used to integrate the equations. If we are not interested in smooth time changes but in certain events, our model is essentially a set of logical conditions which are necessary for the event to occur. In this case simulation follows the changes in the system which result from a succession of events. This is discrete simulation. Computer operating systems are basically discrete systems so our discussion will be limited to discrete simulation.

To further clarify the definition of discrete simulation refer back to the simulation model described in section 2.1.3. There we described a model which represented the system by describing the flow of a job through the system. With respect to time only certain events were interesting, for example, putting a job on one of the queues, allocating the processor to a job, the entry of a job into the system, and so forth. What happens between these events (e.g., several seconds of uninterrupted execution) is uninteresting and, aside from the length of the time interval between two successive events, has no relevance to the performance of the system. Thus, our interest is focused on a succession of points in time which are separated by finite time intervals (which we allow to be of length zero).

There are three major computer based methods used for simulation: an analogue computer, a simulation system, and a do-it-yourself specific program. As we mentioned earlier the principal use of analogue computers is for continuous simulation. It is a relatively useless method for the simulation of computer operating systems, or any other discrete systems for that matter. Hence, this method will not be discussed further. A simulation system usually consists of a special modeling language, a translator or interpreter for that language, and a collection of support routines. The user describes his model in the modeling language. This description is then either interpreted directly to perform the simulation or translated into a program which performs the simulation when it is executed. In either case, the user is provided with a convenient way of specifying and changing the parameters in his model so that he can make a number of different simulation "experiments." The simulation system also provides him with data collection, analysis, and display facilities so that he can easily observe the changes in the variables of his model and derive the relations between them. Using the do-it-yourself specific program method the user writes a program to specifically simulate exactly his model. As a result he may have to program most of the functions supplied by a simulation system. However, if his model is quite simple, the resulting program may perform the simulation much faster than a simulation sytem would.

The technique for discrete simulation is essentially the same whichever of the latter two methods are used. A model of a system is concerned with one or more different classes of entities. In our example, job is one class of entity Each class of entity has a number of attributes associated with it which represent various properties of entities in the class. For example, the attributes of a job are its execution time, its central memory requirement, and its I-O requests. An individual entity from a certain class has a set of values associated with it, one value for each attribute associated with the class. The model consists of the definition of the classes of entities and their attributes, a set of activities, and a set of events. An activity is a process which acts on one or more entities and changes the state of the system. For example, an activity may be an input or output operation or execution of a program by the central processor.

The state of the system is a record of all the individual entities, with the values of their attributes, which currently exist in the system and the activities currently in progress along with an indication of which entities they are processing.

An event is a point in time at which a change in the system state occurs. An event has no duration. When an event occurs some activity takes place. Activities also cause events to occur. It is the execution of activities which actually cause the changes in the system state. Since simulation consists of following the changes in a model of a system, it is basically a program which follows a sequence of events. Except for the magnitude of its duration, the time between events is not significant and is ignored. While following a sequence of events the simulator keeps the system state updated.

Fundamental to simulation is the concept of time. The simulator must be aware of the passage of simulation time, which is the basis for time relationships in the model. Simulation time usually has no connection with the real time which it takes the simulator program to run.

The usual method of recording the passage of simulation time is to maintain a simulation clock. The simulation clock can be updated by small, uniform intervals of time. This method is normally used for continuous simulation. On the other hand the method normally used in discrete simulation is to advance the simulation clock to the time at which the next event is due to occur. Thus, the clock is updated by varying length time intervals whose length corresponds to the simulation time between consecutive events. In a sense, the simulator is unaware of the time between events. Indeed it need not be aware of this time since nothing happens between events.

One of the major functions of an activity is to determine that some event will occur in the future and compute the time at which it will occur. A major function of the simulator is to accept this information and record an identification of the event and the time at which it will occur. This action is called scheduling an event. The most common way of recording the information about a future event is in an event list which is ordered by time of occurrence of the event. The first event to occur in the future is the first event on the list. The second event to occur in the future is second on the list and so forth.

4.2. SPECIFICATION OF JOB PROPERTIES

Many of the interesting properties (attributes) of a job are stochastic variables. The most common way of specifying the values of such a variable, x, is by a probability distribution. There are two types of distributions, discrete and continuous. A discrete distribution is a finite set of values $x_1, x_2, \ldots, x_n$ each with an associated probability, $p_1, p_2, \ldots, p_n$, where p_i is the probability that the value of the stochastic variable x will be equal to x_i. The condition,

$$\sum_{i=1}^{n} p_i = 1$$

is imposed on the probabilities, that is, the stochastic variable must have a value equal to one of the x_i. For a continuous distribution, the value of the variable x is defined using a probability density function $f(x) \geq 0$. The probability that the value of x falls in the range x_1 to x_2, where $x_1 \leq x_2$, is given by the integral

$$\int_{x_1}^{x_2} f(x)dx \quad .$$

We can see from this that the probability of x having one specific value is zero. We also require,

$$\int_{-\infty}^{\infty} f(x)dx = 1 \quad .$$

A related function, the cumulative distribution function,

$$F(x) = \int_{-\infty}^{x} f(x)dx$$

is more often used in simulation. $F(x)$ is monotonic increasing and its value is positive ranging from 0 to 1. The value of $F(x_0)$ is the probability that the value of x is less than or equal to x_0. We can also derive a cumulative distribution function for a discrete distribution. We order the values x_i and change their subscripts (and also the corresponding subscripts on the p_i) so that, $x_1 < x_2 < \cdots < x_n$. Then,

$$F(x_k) = \sum_{i=1}^{k} p_i$$

is the probability that the value of x is less than or equal to x_k.

Actually what we really need is the inverse of the cumulative distribution function. When simulating our system we need to generate a set of values for the attributes of each new job which enters the system. For

each stochastic variable x in the attributes we need to generate a sequence
of random numbers which are drawn from the distribution corresponding to x.
If this distribution is not uniform (all values equally likely) it may be
difficult to generate the sequence directly. However, it is relatively easy
to generate sequences of uniformly distributed random numbers and most system
libraries have at least one subroutine which does this. It is fairly easy
to convert a sequence of random numbers which are uniformly distributed
over the range from 0 to 1 to a sequence of random numbers which satisfy
some other distribution by using the inverse of the cumulative distribution
function for that distribution. Recalling that $0 \leq F(x) \leq 1$, generate a
random number, y_r, uniformly distributed over $0 \leq y_r \leq 1$. Then let
$y_r = F(x_r)$ and solve for x_r, i.e., $x_r = F^{-1}(y_r)$ as shown in figure 4.1.

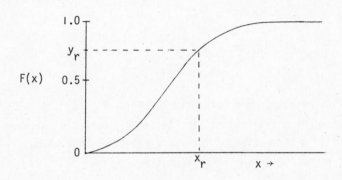

Figure 4.1

Graph of a cumulative distribution function

Of course this procedure requires that one be able to evaluate F^{-1}. This
procedure also works for discrete distributions, but in this case it is
basically a table look up. Again we generate a random number y_r which
is uniformly distributed, but we must restrict the range so that $0 < y_r \leq 1$.
Then we have to find a value k such that, $F(x_{k-1}) < y_r \leq F(x_k)$, with
the convention that $F(x_0) = 0$. The desired random number is then x_k.
The sequence of x's generated by either of these procedures is random and
has the desired (non-uniform distribution).

Another important characteristic of the jobs which are input to the
system is their arrival pattern, which describes the statistical properties
of the job arrivals at the system. The usual way of describing an arrival
pattern is in terms of the inter-arrival time, which is the interval between

successive arrivals. If the arrival pattern has no variability, the inter-arrival time is a constant. If the arrivals vary stochastically, the inter-arrival time will be defined by a probability distribution. It is common practice to define the arrival distribution $A_o(t)$ as the probability that an inter-arrival time is greater than t. Since the cumulative distribution function $F(t)$ is the probability that an inter-arrival time is less than t, we have, $A_o(t) = 1 - F(t)$.

A common arrival pattern is one in which the arrivals are completely random. This means a job can arrive at any time, subject only to the restriction that the mean arrival rate λ be some given value. With this arrival pattern the distribution of inter-arrival times is exponential. The probability density function of the inter-arrival time is,

$$f(x) = \lambda e^{-\lambda t} , \quad t \geq 0$$

and the arrival distribution is,

$$A_o(t) = e^{-\lambda t} .$$

The number λ is the mean number of arrivals per time unit. The actual number of arrivals in an interval of time t is a stochastic variable. With an exponential distribution of inter-arrival times, the probability of n arrivals occurring in an interval of time t is,

$$P(n) = \frac{(\lambda t)^n e^{-\lambda t}}{n!} \quad (n = 0,1,2,\ldots) .$$

This distribution is discrete and is called the Poisson distribution. For this reason a random arrival pattern is usually called a Poisson arrival pattern. The cumulative distribution function of the exponential distribution function is,

$$F(x) = 1 - A_o(t) = 1 - e^{-\lambda t}$$

and its inverse is,

$$\lambda t = -\log_e(1 - F(x)) .$$

The Poisson arrival pattern is one of the most commonly occurring arrival patterns.

We use the coefficient of variation σ/T_a (where σ is the standard deviation and T_a is the mean value) to measure the degree to which data is dispersed about the mean. Since the standard deviation for an exponential distribution of mean value T_a ($T_a = 1/\lambda$) is also T_a, the coefficient of variation is 1. If the coefficient of variation for the job mixes which will actually be submitted to the system is significantly less than or greater than 1, then an Erlang or hyper-exponential distribution [19], respectively, should be used.

While it may be possible to create a sequence of job arrivals before a simulation run is started, the usual procedure is to delay creation of the jobs until they are needed. The arrival of a job is an event. When the simulation clock reaches the time for this event to occur a new job (entity) is created. Using the inverse of the cumulative distribution for the inter-arrival times and a newly generated random number, the inter-arrival time for the next job to arrive is computed. The arrival of the next job is then scheduled to occur at a time equal to the current clock time plus the inter-arrival time for the next job. In addition to scheduling the arrival of the next job, the values of the attributes of the newly created job are computed and set. Thus, the job arrival event creates a new entity, sets the values of its attributes, and schedules a future event.

4.3. DATA COLLECTION

The particular data collected and the analysis performed on this data depend upon the model and the purpose of the simulation. However, there are some data which are so common that most simulations will collect this data. The same is true of certain basic analysis. A count of the number of times some event occurred, such as a request for disk I-O, or the number of entities in a particular class which were created, such as the number of jobs which enter the system, is one of the most common datum which is collected. Summary statistics, such as extreme values, mean values, and standard deviations are also usually computed. Suppose we are interested in central memory usage. The maximum and minimum amount of central memory occupied is easily obtained by comparing each new value for memory use, x_i, against the current values of the maximum and minimum. To obtain the mean M and standard deviation S the simulator must accumulate both the sum of the different memory use values and the sum of the squares of these values, since M and S are defined by,

$$M = \frac{1}{n} \sum_{i=1}^{n} x_i$$

$$S^2 = \frac{1}{n} \sum_{i=1}^{n} x_i^2 - M^2 \quad .$$

The sums are accumulated during the simulation run and the remainder of the computation is done at the end of the simulation. Another common datum collected is the fraction of time that some entity such as the central processor is in use.

Since queues usually play an important part in any system, data on the queue activity is usually collected. Some of the more important data are the variation in queue length, which may be expressed by the mean, standard deviation, maximum, and minimum, and similar statistics for the waiting time, which is the time a job spends in the queue. Often the time between certain events or the time it takes an entity to move from one part of the system to another is useful. Sometimes an event trace is desired. This is a record of every event and the state of the system after the occurrence of the event. Since this is usually a very large amount of data, a complete event trace is normally not desired, except in case of trouble in the simulator. However, a partial event trace may be quite useful. In a partial event trace only part of the system state is included in the output, or only selected events are traced.

Most simulation systems provide facilities for collecting all of the data mentioned above. In addition, they contain the most common analysis routines. Since the user may often wish to analyze the data in other ways, some systems allow the user to write analysis programs which can be incorporated into the simulation. Display of the simulation results is, in some ways, as important as the simulation itself. Thus, most simulation systems have facilities for printing the results in reasonably readable tables. A few systems have facilities for plotting graphs from the simulation results. A graph is often the ideal way of displaying simulation results, since the user is looking for relations which exist between the variables of the system.

4.4. SIMULATION LANGUAGES

In speaking of simulation languages we mean a language for describing a model and the other information necessary to simulate the system which is represented by the model. As such we would expect any simulation language to include features especially for describing entity classes and their attributes, activities, and events. This rules out languages like FORTRAN and PL/I which we do not consider to be simulation languages. We also expect a simulation language to include queues (or something equivalent), facilities for specifying a number of different probability distributions, and facilities for data collection and analysis.

There are two classes of simulation languages, general purpose and special purpose. A general purpose simulation language is designed to be used to simulate a wide range of dynamic systems, such as, computer systems, telephone systems, economic systems, factory assembly lines, supermarkets, and ocean ports. For this reason the underlying simulator for a general purpose language can have no built-in knowledge about the system being simulated. On the other hand, a special purpose simulation language is designed to simulate a specific kind of system, such as a computer operating system. Thus, its underlying simulator can have built-in knowledge about the kind of system which will be simulated, such as, knowledge of the operational characteristics of sequential and random access devices (e.g., tape and disk).

Four of the most popular general purpose simulation languages are GPSS, SIMSCRIPT, SIMULA, and CSL. Each of these languages presents a different view of system dynamics. Kiviat [20] has written a detailed analysis of simulation languages and compares the characteristics of these four languages. In addition, he gives examples of the use of each language. We will not attempt to duplicate that analysis here. What we will do is to briefly sketch the highlights of GPSS and SIMSCRIPT to give the reader a feeling for the character of general purpose simulation languages.

GPSS is a block diagram language. The model of the system to be simulated is described as a block diagram. Blocks represent activities and the lines joining the blocks indicate the sequence in which the activities can be executed. Moving through the system to be simulated are entities, such as jobs. In GPSS these entities are called transactions. An event is defined as the movement of a transaction from one block to another. Input to the GPSS simulator is a description of each of the blocks in the model plus some control cards which may define functions (probability distributions, etc.) and tables as well as control the execution of the simulator. In the model transactions are created by GENERATE blocks. Part of the

description of this block is the definition of the inter-arrival time of
the transactions generated by the block. The inter-arrival time can be
specified as a constant, a normal distribution, or some user defined function.

Normally it does not take any (simulation) time to pass through a
block, except for the ADVANCE block. This block is a delay and its description specifies the duration of the delay. When a transaction enters an
ADVANCE block an event, which is the movement of the transaction to the
next block, is scheduled to occur at a time in the future equal to the
current time plus the delay specified by the ADVANCE block. The simulation
consists of moving a transaction through one block after another until
it reaches a TERMINATE block, which removes the transaction from the simulation, or until it is delayed by an ADVANCE block or encounters a block
which cannot be entered at the current time. The simulator then considers
the next scheduled event, moving the associated transaction through as many
blocks as possible.

There are some blocks which cannot always be immediately entered, such
as the SEIZE and ENTER blocks. These blocks are used to control the use of
permanent entities which GPSS calls facilities and storages. A facility
is an entity that can be allocated to only one transaction at a time, such
as the central processor. A storage is a partitionable entity, such as
central memory. Portions of a storage may be allocated to several different
transactions simultaneously, a different portion to each transaction. The
portions need not be the same size. The SEIZE block applies to facilities
and the ENTER block applies to storages. The RELEASE block releases a
facility which has been allocated by a SEIZE block and a LEAVE block gives
up some or all of the storage allocated by the ENTER block. A transaction
is prevented from entering a SEIZE block if the requested facility is in
use. Similarly a transaction is prevented from entering an ENTER block if
the amount of storage available is less than the amount requested.

When a transaction is prevented from entering a block it is automatically queued, however, the simulator keeps no statistics on the activity
in these queues. If the user wishes to collect such statistics he must
explicitly queue and dequeue the transactions. This is done by the QUEUE
and DEPART blocks. The QUEUE block identifies a queue and increments the
length of that queue. The DEPART block identifies a queue whose length is
decremented. These blocks do not affect queue activity, they simply allow
statistics gathering. GPSS also has some blocks which allow the user to

specify other than the standard queue discipline. Two other blocks, MARK
and TABULATE, allow the user to record the time it takes for a transaction
to move between two points in the model. The MARK block indicates the
initial point. The TABULATE block records the amount of (simulation) time
which has passed since the MARK block. This time is recorded in a table
specified by the TABULATE block.

GPSS also contains blocks for branching, assigning values to variables,
and maintaining lists. However, since our purpose is only to give the
flavor of GPSS, not completely describe the language, we will not discuss
any of these additional features. Figure 4.2 shows a sample GPSS block
diagram. In this example the name of the block is written to th
left of the block.

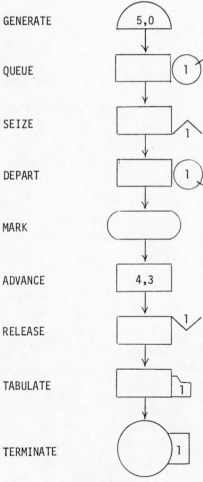

Figure 4.2
Example GPSS block diagram

The GENERATE block generates transactions at the rate of one every 5 time units. The 0 indicates that there is no variation in the inter-arrival time. The sequence for a transaction is to seize facility number 1, process for a period of time, release the facility, and leave the system. The ADVANCE block specifies that the processing time has a mean value of 4 and varies uniformly from 4 - 3 to 4 + 3. In order to gather statistics on the activity in the queue for the facility we have bracketed the SEIZE block with a QUEUE and a DEPART block. The inclusion of the MARK and TABULATE blocks causes the actual processing time for each transaction to be recorded in table number 1.

When using an actual GPSS simulator each block will have to be described on cards for input to the simulator. For example the first three blocks would be written,

```
GENERATE   5,0
QUEUE      1
SEIZE      1
```

In addition, table number 1 must be defined and various other control information specified. The length of a simulation run is defined by specifying the number of transactions to be processed. The TERMINATE block counts by 1 until its count reaches the number of transactions specified, at which time the simulation run ends.

SIMSCRIPT is a language which is similar in appearance to FORTRAN. It deals with entities and their attributes. Activities are described by event routines which are closed subroutines. When an event occurs its corresponding event routine is executed. All events must be explicitly scheduled by executing the appropriate statements in some event routine. For this reason SIMSCRIPT is classed as an event based language. There is no automatic queuing in SIMSCRIPT. Queues are managed by the event routines using data structures of entities called sets.

SIMSCRIPT has statements for creating and destroying entities. One special class of entity is the event notice. This entity is used for scheduling events. Whenever an event is to be scheduled an event notice is created. Then the CAUSE command is executed to schedule the corresponding event for some specified time. There are statements for maintaining sets, assignment of values to variables, branching, and collecting statistics. In addition there are minimal facilities for generating random values from various distributions.

It is a characteristic of SIMSCRIPT that the user has to program more of the action in the simulation than he does if he uses GPSS. This is the price that is paid for the advantage that SIMSCRIPT is a more flexible language than GPSS. If we translate our previous GPSS example into SIMSCRIPT we will need to write four event routines: one to get started, one to generate the entities (corresponding to the generate block), one to start processing (corresponding to the QUEUE, SEIZE, DEPART, and ADVANCE blocks), and one to finish processing (corresponding to the RELEASE and TERMINATE blocks). We will omit the MARK and TABULATE from our translation.

To get the simulation started we need the following special event routine,

```
EXOG EVENT START
    CREATE ARRV
    CAUSE ARRV AT TIME
    STORE O IN BUSY
    RETURN
    END
```

This event routine creates an event notice for the event ARRV and schedules it to occur at TIME. TIME is a system variable whose value is the current time. BUSY is a global variable indicating the central processor is free if its value is 0. The event routine ARRV generates an entity corresponding to a job which arrives at the system.

```
ENDOG EVENT ARRV
    DESTROY ARRV
    CREATE JOB
    CREATE PROS
    STORE JOB IN J(PROS)
    CAUSE PROS AT TIME
    CREATE ARRV
    CAUSE ARRV AT TIME+5
    RETURN
    END
```

This event routine creates a job, creates an event notice for the event PROS, and schedules it to occur immediately. The event routine PROS will begin processing of the job. The STORE statement stores the identification of the job to be processed in the event notice. The event routine ARRV must

also destroy the event notice which activated it and create a new event
notice for itself and schedule this event to occur at 5 time units in the
future.

The event routine PROS controls allocation of the central processor
and maintains a queue of jobs waiting for the processor.

```
ENDOG EVENT PROS
        STORE J(PROS) IN JID
        DESTROY PROS
        IF PQ IS EMPTY, GO TO 3
        FILE JID IN PQ
        RETURN
3       IF BUSY EQ 0, GO TO 2
        FILE JID IN PQ
        RETURN
2       STORE 1 IN BUSY
        CREATE TERM
        STORE JID IN J(TERM)
        CAUSE TERM AT TIME+RANDI(1,7)
        RETURN
        END
```

The identification of the job must be extracted from the event notice which
activated this event routine before it is destroyed. PQ is a set which is
the queue for the processor. If it is not empty the new job is added to
the queue by the FILE statement and this event routine is then finished.
If the queue is empty a test is made to see if the processor is busy. If
it is the job is put on the queue. If the processor is not busy it is
allocated to the job. In this case an event notice for termination of the
job's execution is created. This event, TERM, is then scheduled for the
time at which the job will complete execution. The execution time of the
job is a random number uniformly distributed in the range 1 to 7, as computed by the function call RANDI(1,7).

The termination event routine is activated when a job completes execution and releases the central processor.

```
ENDOG EVENT TERM
      DESTROY J(TERM)
      DESTROY TERM
      IF PQ IS EMPTY GO TO 2
      REMOVE FIRST JID FROM PQ
      CREATE TERM
      STORE JID IN J(TERM)
      CAUSE TERM AT TIME+RANDI(1,7)
      RETURN
   2  STORE 0 IN BUSY
      RETURN
      END
```

Both the terminating job and the event notice which activated this event routine are destroyed. If the queue is not empty, the first job on the queue is removed from the queue and the processor allocated to it.

In a complete SIMSCRIPT program the various variables, entities, and sets would be defined by declarations. Additional statements would be included for collecting data and generating reports. Cards to control the simulation run would also be needed. Some versions of SIMSCRIPT permit the inclusion of subroutines written in FORTRAN which may be called from the event routines. This feature makes it possible for the user to do things during simulation which would otherwise be difficult or impossible.

There are two special purpose languages which we will discuss briefly: CSS [18] and DES [16]. These are both languages which have been designed for use in simulating computer operating systems. However, their orientation is different. CSS is oriented toward the simulation of existing systems, while DES is oriented toward systems which have not yet been implemented. DES was actually designed to be used for implementing operating systems as well as simulating them. The other major difference between the two languages is that CSS is like assembly language while DES is like PL/I.

The simulators for both of these languages have built-in knowledge of computer hardware systems and the language contains statements and declarations which relate to hardware facilities. The user specifies a particular hardware configuration by declaring the values of various hardware parameters, such as, central memory size and cycle time, data transfer rates for I-O devices, latency for rotational devices, select time for tape drives, head movement time for disk drives, and the number of devices and processors.

They have statements for sepcifying processing time which are similar to the ADVANCE block of GPSS. There are also statements for synchronizing asynchronous operations which are necessary to model I-0 channel operation, interrupts,and concurrent processing (multi-tasking).A minimal computational ability is available in CSS, but DES, which is actually an extension of PL/I, has the full capability of PL/I for computation and decision making.

The following example taken from [18] illustrates the CSS language.

```
APPL PROCESS 3000        similar to ADVANCE
     WRITE   (file A)    initiate I-0
     READ    (file B)
     PROCESS 5000        overlapped with I-0
     WAIT    SCHEDL      wait for I-0 completion
     PROCESS 7500
     WRITE   (file C)
     WAIT    SCHEDL
     BRANCH  SCHEDL      end of program, go to scheduler
```

In addition to these statements there would be declarations defining the hardware configuration and other required information. The DES language will be discussed in section 5 so we will not include an example here.

4.5. AN EXAMPLE SIMULATION MODEL

In this section we will model the small system defined in section 2.1.3 using GPSS and discuss its use in predicting the performance of the modeled system. The reader should refer to the diagram in figure 2.6 which shows the flow of jobs through the system. We must translate this diagram into the GPSS language. This is a fairly straightforward task since a job will be a GPSS transaction and a GPSS program describes the flow of transactions through the modeled system.

The body of the GPSS program for our example is,

```
GENERATE    1,FN1,,,,2      job enters system
ASSIGN      1,1,FN2         set memory length
ASSIGN      2,1,FN3         set I-0 record count
QUEUE       1               memory queue
ENTER       1,P1            allocate memory
DEPART      1
```

453

```
     EXEC QUEUE        2                 processor queue
          SEIZE        1                 allocate processor
          DEPART       2
          ADVANCE      1,FN4             execute
          RELEASE      1                 release processor
          TEST G       P2,0,DONE         job completed?
          QUEUE        3                 disk queue
          SEIZE        2                 allocate disk
          DEPART       3
          ADVANCE      1,FN5             read or write disk
          RELEASE      2                 release disk
          ASSIGN       2-,1              decrement I-O record count
          TRANSFER     ,EXEC
     DONE LEAVE        1,P1              release memory
          TERMINATE                      job exits from system
```

A number of new GPSS features have been introduced into this example and
need a few words of explanation. When we initially defined our model we
gave a job five attributes: inter-arrival time, central memory requirement,
I-O inter-request time, execution time, and I-O record length. It turns out
to be easier to work with the number of I-O requests instead of execution
time, letting the execution time be the sum of the I-O inter-request times.
The transaction which represents jobs needs only two attributes since the
job inter-arrival time is specified in the GENERATE block while the I-O
inter-request time and I-O record length are specified in ADVANCE blocks.
In addition to specifying the inter-arrival time the GENERATE block specifies
the number of attributes for the generated transaction. The attributes are
referenced by number. The two ASSIGN blocks following the GENERATE set the
values of the job's two attributes. References to the current transaction's
attributes in blocks other than ASSIGN use the notation Pi for the ith
attribute, as in the ENTER block which allocates an amount of storage equal
to the value of the first attribute.

Queues, facilities, and storages are all referenced by number. Our
model has three queues: a central memory queue (1), central processor
queue (2), and a disk queue (3); two facilities: central processor (1)
and disk (2); and one storage: central memory (1). After completing a disk
input or output, the I-O record count, the second attribute of the job, is
decremented by 1 and the job is routed to the processor queue. The TEST block

determines if the job has completed by testing the I-0 record count to see
if it is greater than zero, if not the job is routed to location DONE which
releases memory and terminates the job.

The job inter-arrival time, memory length, I-0 record count, I-0 inter-
request time, and I-0 record length are each defined by a different function,
F1,...,F5. These functions must be defined by function definition cards.
Functions in GPSS are defined in tabular form and are considered as inverses
of cumulative probability distributions. Each time a function is referenced,
a uniformly distributed random number is generated and used as an argument.
When a function value is needed in a block it is referenced by k,Fn and
the value actually used is the product of k and the function value. Hence,
1,F1 is simply the value of function number 1.

In using this model it is very easy to vary the input job characteristics
by simply changing the definitions of the functions. Thus, we can make a
number of simulation runs (experiments) and see how the system performs for
different typical jobs. We can also easily see how different hardware configurations effect performance. Each GPSS storage must be defined by a definition card which specifies its capacity. Thus, we can easily change the
central memory size. We can also observe the effect of multiprocessing by
changing the central processor from a facility to a storage whose capacity
is the number of processors. The corresponding SEIZE and RELEASE blocks
would also have to be changed to ENTER and LEAVE blocks.

The GPSS program can also be modified so that the simulations can be
done with mixes of different job types. Jobs are given an additional attribute which is their job type. Then when other attributes are generated or
the job passes through ADVANCE blocks this new attribute is used to select
the appropriate function, for example,

ADVANCE   1, FN*3

computes the delay time by using the function specified by the third attribute. We have been assuming that the various job attributes, such as I-0
inter-request time, are defined by the same distribution throughout the
entire time the job is in the system. If this is not true our GPSS program
gets more complicated. The attributes of a job must be expanded to include
the specification of each of the different distribution functions involved,
the sequence in which they are used, and the time interval or other conditions
which cause the shift from one distribution to the next. As the job progresses

through the system its progress will have to be monitored to detect when to change distributions. This modification to our GPSS program is quite complicated.

The observant reader will have noticed that our simple model does not take into account any system overhead. This of course must also be included before our simulation results can possibly be a valid prediction of the system's performance. In some ways this is very easy, in other ways it is very difficult. The overhead resulting from the loader can easily be modeled by including an ADVANCE block at the point where memory is allocated. The loading time will be a function of the program size. Therefore, the memory length for the job should be specified as two numbers, program length and total length. If we wish to record statistics on loader overhead the new ADVANCE block will be bracketed by MARK and TABULATE blocks. This simple modification assumes that the loader overhead is some simple, known function of program size. This is usually not the case. The function may not be simple and it is usually not known for an unimplemented system. For this reason the loader itself may need to be modeled and included in the simulation. This model will have to model the library search which loaders usually perform. This involves disk input, assumptions about the organization of the system library, and so forth. In addition, additional job attributes will be required to specify the job's use of library procedures. As all of this is incorporated into the model of the system it rapidly grows quite complicated.

It should be clear that simulation is an extremely flexible and powerful tool. However, simulation models for a complex system are likely to be complex themselves. Thus, they are difficult to construct. However, none of the other prediction techniques seem to be capable of providing the kind of detailed performance information which the designer needs. Clearly, since simulation seems to be necessary to do the job, better techniques for building simulation models are required. The special purpose simulation languages discussed earlier are attempts to provide the required improvements in model building.

5. INTEGRATED PERFORMANCE PREDICTION, DESIGN, AND IMPLEMENTATION

It is not unusual for a complex system to be designed and implemented only to find that it's performance does not even meet the minimum acceptable performance. This is largely due to the lack of any attempt by the designers and implementers to evaluate (predict) the performance of the proposed design. The solution to this problem seems to be to make performance evaluation an integral and continuing part of both the design and implementation of the system.

5.1. THE PROBLEMS WITH NON-INTEGRATED PREDICTION

There are many problems involved in evaluating the performance of a system design. However, the two critical problems seem to be the validity of the evaluation and the provision of timely performance information. We have seen that all performance evaluation requires a model. This model must faithfully represent the system actually being implemented. If it does not, the evaluation is apt to be misleading. In fact, if the designer modifies his design in response to these results it may well lead to performance degradation rather than improvement. Even if the evaluation is valid, it is of little use if it is not available until after the system has been implemented. In fact, the sooner the evaluation is available the more likely it is that costly redesign and reimplementation will be avoided.

A number of factors contribute to the lack of timeliness. Except for simulation, current evaluation techniques make little or no use of a computer. Most analysis is done by hand. Thus, any deep analysis takes a long time and the results are too late. Since evaluation is not automatic, it almost always has only second priority and is continually postponed because of the pressure resulting from over optimistic schedules and deadlines. No easily accessible, central repository exists which contains all of the knowledge about the proposed system, both the software components and the hardware. Obtaining the information needed for evaluation may be difficult, or even impossible, resulting in a considerable delay in producing the desired results. Even though simulation usually uses the computer, a model of the proposed system has to be coded and debugged in some language which is different from that being used to specify the design and implementation. The process of interpreting the written documentation, designing the model, coding it, and debugging it is a major project of long duration. By the time this project has been completed the proposed system design will either have changed significantly or already have been implemented.

Validity is an even more serious problem. Since use of existing evaluation techniques requires considerable time and effort it is usually not practical for the designer to do the evaluation. Thus, the design

specifications must be interpreted by someone other than the designer. Any
interpretation by someone other than the designer is open to question, principally because of a lack of precision and uniformity in the specification.
Another factor which makes the validity of an evaluation questionable,
especially simulation, is that in abstracting to a model it is very difficult, and frequently even impossible, to identify the significant variables.
If any of these are omitted from the model the results will be invalid.
Since all existing evaluation techniques require a model which is separate
from both the design specification and the implementation, changes in either
may not get reflected in the model. Minor software or hardware changes may
have an effect which, when propagated throughout the system design, significantly affect performance. It is difficult to prevent the model being used
in evaluation from drifting away from the system actually being implemented
when this model's description is separate from the implementation description.

5.2. SINGLE LANGUAGE APPROACH

A system which integrates design specification, implementation, and
evaluation has been proposed [16] and a pilot version has been implemented
[21]. This system is called DES (Design and Evaluation System). The two
most significant features of DES are a single high level language, which
is used for both design specification and implementation, and a single data
base containing all known information about the proposed system, both software and hardware. In a sense DES is a combined management information
system, simulator, and compiler. The DES language is an extension of PL/I,
the extensions making it into a special purpose simulation language.

The key idea in DES is to use a single language to describe the proposed
system at all stages of its design and implementation. This evolving source
language description of the proposed system is used as direct input to the
analysis and simulation routines. The initial sketch of the proposed system's
structure and data bases, which is the gross design specification, evolves
into a final, detailed implementation specification which can be compiled
into executable object code. As soon as any part of the object system is
specified some evaluation information is available. As the design becomes
more detailed this information becomes more precise. Thus, a fairly detailed
and precise picture of the proposed system's performance is developed before
it is completely implemented.

The central data base for the proposed system contains a description of both the hardware and the software. The hardware description includes the memory size, instruction and cycle times, standard configurations, and device descriptions. A device description specifies the properties of the device which influence its behavior, such as, seek time, latency, transfer time, and number of access paths. The software description includes both procedure and data components. A procedure component description identifies its entry points and a description of the corresponding arguments (data type, structure, etc.), names of external data components and procedures which it references, its resource requirements, and so forth. A data component description includes information on its structure, the data type of its elements, the way or ways it will be accessed, its average and maximum size, and so forth.

As soon as any part of the proposed system design is known it is expressed in the DES language and entered into the central data base. Initially this information may be no more than component names and types (procedure, data, or hardware). As the design progresses the designer gradually fills in additional information until the central data base contains a complete description of all components in the proposed system. The evaluation routines in DES give performance information consistent with the degree of detail and completeness of the component specifications. Whenever a change is made in the specification of a component, DES automatically propagates this information throughout all components which are affected by the change and the persons responsible for these components are notified that there has been a change.

The DES language is an extension of the implementation language, in this case PL/I, with additional statements which allow the designer to express the design at whatever level of detail he desires. This allows the total system design to be captured in a processable format beginning with the initial design phase. The intent of these extensions is to make it possible for the designer to sketch his inital design in the extensions with little or no use of the standard PL/I statements or declarations. As the design progresses the designer fills in missing parameters in the statements of the extended language, inserts additional PL/I statements, and completes the data descriptions in the object system data base. Each iteration of a component's design is automatically combined with all others to ensure that the total system is consistent at all times. Variations in the level of detail between components and within a single component can be noted for project control, but do not prevent evaluation of parts or the whole at any time.

Three types of language elements are defined. The first is a data structure description which allows declaration of generalized data structures such as queues and tables. For example, the statement,

$dcls 1 d_free(queue,fifo);

declares a local data structure, d_free, which is a queue with fifo access characteristics. The description of the data items within an individual queue entry can be added when its detailed description is known. The statement,

$dclg fr_list(table,key);

directs DES to include in the source text a data declaration which is stored in the central data base. It further indicates that the declaration is that of a table to be accessed by a key.

The second type of language element is used to specify conceptual operations, such as create, find and insert, on the generalized data structures. The statement,

$find fr_list;

indicates a search of the structure fr_list to locate an element. The statement,

$insert d_free;

specifies the insertion of an element into the structure d_free. The third type of language element is used to indicate the use of system resources such as input or output devices, memory, and central processor utilization. The statement,

$read(disk);

indicates a read operation on a disk device. The statement,

$process(1000);

indicates the use of the central processor for 1000 time units.

The following example shows how these language elements can be used to describe a basic system function:

```
get_element:  proc;
              $dcls 1 d_free (queue,fifo);
              $dclg fr_list (table,key);
              $find d_free;
              $process (100);
              $insert fr_list;
              end;
```

In this example an element on the queue d_free is located, an estimated amount of processing is performed, and an element is stored in the table fr_list.

5.3. INTERACTION WITH THE DESIGNER-IMPLEMENTER

There are three major phases in the evaluation analysis performed by DES. The first phase analyzes each procedure component individually. Certain static information is output from this phase, such as, the estimated size of the procedure, a list of external references, and a list of interface violations. However, the principal output is a directed graph model of the procedure. This model is similar to the one described in section 2.1.2. This model has been reduced as much as possible using the techniques discussed in section 3.3. In constructing this model execution times and other timing information are calculated from the hardware description which is contained in the central data base. These computations take into account the structure of data which is accessed as well as the operations performed on the data.

The second and third phases of evaluation demand interaction with the designer (who should also be the implementer). The second phase consists of exercising a component model interactively with the designer to ascertain which of the variables remaining in the model are significant. This exercising may require some simulation of the component. In the course of this analysis the designer supplies additional information, such as, the distribution of the values of the variables in the model and the probabilities of various branches. The result of this analysis is a more simplified model.

The third phase of the evaluation is simulation of the entire system. The model of the system is the collection of component models produced by the first two phases of the evaluation. DES provides an easy way of specifying input job mixes for the simulation runs. Each typical job is programmed in the DES language using actual calls to the proposed system. These

461

programs are then subjected to the same analysis that is applied to the system components. The result is a set of models, one for each typical job. These models can be combined with the models of the system components for simulation runs. This results in a very flexible way of simulating the system's performance for differing job mixes.

5.4. AIDS TO PROJECT MANAGEMENT

Although not directly part of performance prediction the DES approach provides a number of useful aids to project management. The existence of the central data base and the ability to express the early design in machine processable form certainly aids documentation. By controlling access to the central data base, unauthorized changes in the global data bases or interfaces of the proposed system can be prevented. Since the DES analysis routines and the compiler, which will ultimately produce object code for the implemented system, both refer to the central data base for component descriptions, constraints on the use of certain language features, hardware devices, and software components can be continuously enforced.

Utilizing the information in the central data base, periodic reports on the status of the project can be produced. Information in such a report includes,
-- a list of all procedures called and global data referenced by each procedure in the system
-- estimates of the memory and other resource requirements
-- indicators of progress, such as, the frequency of component updates, the date of the last update, and the ratio of execution time specified by process statements to execution time resulting from other statements
-- a list of all recent changes to interfaces and the components affected
-- a list of all inconsistencies and other constraint violations
By itself, this information is inconclusive as to the state of system development. However, when the project manager combines this information with his own knowledge of the development effort within his department it can give him a much more accurate and complete picture of his project than has usually been the case in the past.

462

6. REFERENCES

1. Crooke, S.; Minker, J.; Yeh, J.: Key Word in Context Index and Bibliography on Computer Systems Evaluation Techniques. Technical Report TR-146, Computer Science Center, University of Maryland, College Park, Maryland (January 1971).

2. Lucas, H.C. Jr.: Performance Evalution and Monitoring. Computing Surveys 3, 79-91 (September 1971).

3. Hart, L.E.: The User's Guide to Evaluation Products. Datamation, 32-35 (December 15, 1970).

4. Kleinrock, L.: Time-Shared Systems: A Theoretical Treatment. J. ACM 14, 242-261 (April 1967).

5. Estrin, G.; Kleinrock, L.: Measures, Models and Measurements for Time-Shared Computer Utilities. Proc. ACM National Meeting 1967, 85-96.

6. Proceedings of the Third Symposium on Operating System Principles (held at Stanford University). ACM, New York (October 1971).

7. Proceedings of the SIGOPS Workshop on System Performance Evaluation (held at Harvard University). ACM, New York (April 1971).

8. McKinney, J.M.: A Survey of Analytical Time-Sharing Models. Computing Surveys 2, 105-116 (June 1969).

9. Beizer, B.: Analytical Techniques for the Statistical Evaluation of Program Running Time. Proc. FJCC 1970, 519-524.

10. Ramamoorthy, C.V.: Analysis of Graphs by Connectivity Considerations. J. ACM 13, 211-222 (April 1966).

11. Lowe, T.C.: Analysis of Boolean Program Models for Time-Shared, Paged Environments. C. ACM 12, 199-205 (April 1969).

12. Allen, F.E.: Control Flow Analysis. Proc. SIGPLAN Symp. Compiler Optimization (held at the University of Illinois). ACM, New York, 1-19 (July 1970).

13. Allen, F.E.: Program Optimization. Annual Review in Automatic Programming, Vol. 5, Pergamon, New York, 239-307 (1969).

14. Russel, E.C.; Estrin, G.: Measurement Based Automatic Analysis of FORTRAN Programs. Proc. SJCC 1969, 723-732.

15. Patil, S.S.: Coordination of Asynchronous Events. Project MAC Technical Report TR-72, MIT, Cambridge, Massachusetts (June 1970).

16. Graham, R.M.; Clancy, G.J. Jr.; Devaney, D.B.: A Software Design and Evaluation System. Proc. SIGOPS Workshop on System Performance Evaluation (held at Harvard University). ACM, New York, 200-213 (April 1971).

17. MacDougall, M.H.: Computer System Simulation: An Introduction. Computing Surveys 2, 191-209 (September 1970).

18. Seaman, P.H.; Soucy, R.C.: Simulating Operating Systems. _IBM Systems Journal_ 8, 264-279.

19. Gordon, G.: _System Simulation_. Prentice-Hall (1969).

20. Kivat, P.J.: Simulation Languages. Appendix C of; Naylor, T.H.: Computer Simulation Experiments with Models of Economic Systems. John Wiley (1971).

21. Carlson, B.: Forthcoming MS Thesis, Department of Electrical Engineering, MIT.

P E R F O R M A N C E   M E A S U R E M E N T

C.C.Gotlieb
Department of Computer Science,
University of Toronto, Canada

1. INTRODUCTION

Performance measurements are needed when:

(1) installing a new computing system

(2) changing the configuration or "tuning" it to improve throughput

(3) comparing systems to determine technological improvements, econo-
    mies of scale and cost/benefit ratios

The available techniques are to:

(1) establish a figure of merit based on component ratings

(2) run a set of "kernel", "benchwork" or synthetic problems

(3) make observations and measurements by using
    (i) hardware instrumentation
    (ii) software monitors

(4) model the system either
    (i) analytically, or
    (ii) by simulation.

Modeling and simulation are often the only tools available during the
design and planning stages. They are also useful in identifying the important parameters (see Graham). The first three techniques are more
often used in evaluating existing systems and alternative configurations.
We concentrate on these.

2. FIGURES OF MERIT

The cost *should* be an overall measure of performance. In computing, the economic principle known as "economy of scale", (which states that large production units and processes are more efficient than small ones) finds its expression as *Grosch's Law*. According to this:

$C = K \sqrt{E}$ where C is the cost

                     E is the effectiveness measured in

                        speed, throughput etc.

                 K is a constant

If we assume that $S \propto C$ and $CPU \propto C$ where S = storage capability and CPU = central processor speed, and further that $E \propto S.CPU$, Grosch's Law follows. Simple as it is, it seems to be an observablyconfirmed relation (Solomon 1966). Generally we want some measure of effectiveness that it is related to ability to process jobs, and in any case, when alternative systems are being considered it is usual to compare systems of equal cost in order to eliminate this factor.

One approach is to define *machine features*, by associating a number of attributes with each feature, and attaching a weight to each attribute. The figure of merit is calculated as a weighted sum of the features. The example in Table 1 is given by Sharpe (Sec. 9.4).

      Table 1 Features for Evaluating a Computer System

Feature	No. of attributes	Weight of attributes
Hardware	38	0.27
Supervisor	18	0.27
Data management	8	.08
Language processors	31	.16
Programming support	4	.02
Conversion difficulty	8	.12
Vendor reliability support	16	.08
		1.00

The objection to this is that the choice of weights (usually arrived at by a group of experts) is inevitably arbitrary and the method therefore has limited credibility. A somewhat more objective approach is to weight the various types of machine instructions and compute an overall weighted instruction time. The weights are determined by analyzing typical problems, and to allow for the difference between scientific and data processing applications different sets of factors are produced for each. Table 2 shows examples of sets of weights. (See also Solomon 1966).

Drummond (1966) suggests the *maximum storage bus rate (MSBR)* as a merit figure.

MSBR = data length x degree of interleave/storage cycle time.

Table 2   Instructional Weights

Instruction Type	Scientific Mix[*]	Commercial Weight[**]
Fixed add (subtract) and compare		.25
Floating add	.095	0
Multiply	.056	.01
Divide	.020	0
Load/store	.285	
Indexing	.225	
Conditional branch	.132	
Miscellaneous	.187	.74
	1.000	1.00

[*] Arbuckle 1966
[**] K.E.Knight A Study of Technological Innovation
         PH.D. Thesis, Carnegie Inst.of Technology 1963

Merit figures determined by calculating weighted means of the instruction times are too simple, for they do not take into account such important factors as word length, I/O rates, channel speeds, overlapping, buffer stores etc. It is possible to devise much more complicated figures of merit in which these factors are included and Knight and others have done this (see Knight 1968 and Sharpe Ch. 9, Section D). For example Knight defines:

Computing power = memory factor x operations per second

$$\text{Memory factor} = \frac{[(L-7)N \ (WF)]^P}{K} \quad \text{where}$$

K = a constant

L = word length (in bits), N = no. of words in high speed memory

WF = 1 for a fixed word length memory, 2 for a variable length memory

P = 0.5 for scientific computation, 0.333 for commercial computation

$$\text{Operations per second} = \frac{10^{12}}{t_c + t_{I/0}}$$

where t_c = time in μs for one million operations

$t_{I/O}$ = non overlapped time (in μs) for one million I/O operations.

(determined from channel width, transfer rate, start, stop or rewind times etc.)

It is clear that even these more complex ratings do not include factors which are important in time-shared, multiprogrammed or highly parallel systems, and for this reason such formula are not applicable now. They have been used however to study the effects of technological innovations both for computing systems as a whole, and for subsystem components, over time (See Knight 1968, Sharpe Ch. 9, Harman 1971 and Solomon 1966).

Table 3   Observations on Kernel Problems

	Job#	Step#	Core(KB)	370 ERT *	360 CPU **	360 ERT	360 CPU	I/O cost
1	1	1	100	212	40	278	100	0
2	1	2	96	36	5	42	10	350
3	2	1	130	34	30	115	113	134
4	3	1	200	21	2	17	4	0
5	3	2	96	24	3	27	6	0
6	3	3	200	76	21	69	50	109
7	4	1	100	6	4	18	16	0
8	4	2	96	12	2	14	3	0
9	4	3	76	59	58	294	293	120
10	5	1	140	21	18	69	66	195

 * ERT is the Expected Run Time, computed by adding a fixed time for
** each I/O interrupt issued during the job step.

   in units of .01 minutes

From C.A. Ford, A report on CUC/UTCC Pricing Data University of Toronto Computer Centre, January 1972.

3.   KERNELS, BENCHMARKS AND SYNTHETIC PROGRAMS

A *kernel* is a representative program which has been partially or comple-tely coded and timed. (Arbuckle 1966, Calengaert 1967, Lucas 1971). The programs may be short or extensive and the timing is often based on manu-facturer-provided data or machine characteristics.

A widely quoted set of kernels is described by Auerbach in the EDP Reports (See System Performance Charts, and also Hillegass, 1966). The problems used are:

      Updating sequential files
      Updating files stored on a random access disk storage
      Sorting
      Matrix inversion
      Polynomial evaluation

To achieve useful comparisons the parameters of the problem are carefully specified (size and number of records, activity factor, etc.) and the machines are standardized (core size, number of channels, type divisors, etc.). On the other hand file arrangements and detailed coding methods are left flexible so that advantage can be taken of the special characteristics of each machine. The results are displayed in a series of charts, e.g. "Time to Process a Master File of 10,000 Records" vs Activity Factor" and vs "Average System Rental/Month".

It is necessary to accept the result of comparisons based on kernel calculations (or runs) with caution.

- there is no agreement about the relative importance of kernels -
  i.e. how frequently they arise or what weights should be attached to
  them

- The results are dependent on the quality of the programming as well
  as on the system

- important factors such as I/O considerations, overlapping operations
  and software overhead are usually omitted since these are difficult
  to predict and require actual operation within a larger context.

In spite of these reservations, kernels can be very useful, especialy when comparing configurations which are not too different. Table 3 shows excerpts from a comparison of an IBM 360/65 with a 370/165, based on 36 distinct computer jobs (54 job steps) run with the same operating system on the two machines. The study from which these results are taken was made to determine the ratio of the computer speeds and to compare the cost of running a job on the 165 with that of running it on the 65, using an agreed-upon pricing formula in each case. For the jobs run, the ratio 360 CPU time/370 CPU time was 3.67 and the 360 cost/370 cost was 980.65/639.20 or 1.5 as compared with the 1.4 which was intended.

A *benchmark* is an existing program that is coded in a specific language and executed on the machine being evaluated (Lucas 1971). With a benchmark the complete software system is used, and it is possible to evaluate factors other than job time, e.g. compile and execute speeds, turnaround, diagnostics etc. This method of evaluation is widely used in competitive situations, e.g. where government regulations require open bidding and objective performance tests. It is also used by manufacturers in introducing new computers so that their customers can compare the new configurations with the old. For example, on the bases of benchmark runs, IBM quote a speed advantage of 2-5 for the 370/165 as compared with the 360/65.

There are still two serious reservations about the use of benchmarks in evaluating systems. It is very difficult to assess the relative importance of different problems, unless one can be sure that the computer will be mainly dedicated to one application. Even more important however, the performance of a particular program or a particular system may be limited because of some bottleneck which is not obvious (lack of core storage, contention for a channel or disk etc.). Thus speed may be improved dramatically by some relatively minor hardware or software change in the system, and the conditions under which benchmarks are run do not allow one to know whether this is possible. While the benchmark comparisons provide information about the systems actually run, they do not necessarily reflect how the systems would compare in a well run environment where at least the obvious bottlenecks have been eliminated.

Synthetic programs are used to validate the operation of a system by exercising as many component functions as possible, or by subjecting it to extremum conditions. Such programs have long been used by hardware engineers during design and maintenance, and they are now commonly used to test software as well. OS/360 for example includes a set of jobs which may be run after local system generation, and most commercial software packages include similar tests.

Synthetic programs can be used to test any phase of system operation (see Lucas, Table II). They are in fact very much like kernel and benchmark programs, and also like software monitors. Their greatest value is in conjunction with monitors. Their disadvantage is that they have to be specially written for the system on hand, often in assembly language.

All of the methods described here, along with modelling, come into use in computer selection. In a survey of 69 installations reported by Schneidewind (1967), the relative use of evaluation methods in computer selection was given as follows:

1. Use of benchmark problems   61 %

2. Published hardware and software reports 64 %

3. Use of kernel problems   52 %

4. Computer simulation   16 %

5. Mathematical modelling   7 %

Kernels, benchmarks and synthetic programs are not in themselves capable of quantitatively analysing systems or adequate for determining how effectiveness can be increased. For this it is necessary to take a more analytical, engineering approach and go to detailed measurement and observation on individual system components.

4.   DATA COLLECTION AND ANALYSIS

There is no difficulty in listing quantities which might be monitored in a computing system. Statistics can be gathered at three levels:

the user job level - here we can measure the programs called in, estimated job times, elapsed times for job steps, compilation, execution etc., the run-time options selected, core used, cards read and punched, lines printed, turn-around time, priorities selected, cost, diagnostics called in

the system level - here we measure resource allocation, channel and I/O activity, job and system queue lengths and service times, various overlapped activities

the installation level - here we measure job traffic and flows, service utilisation, resource allocation, operator actions and interventions, user enquiries, requests and complaints, cost and income statistics. Many of these quantities are observed directly; others are calculated or derived quantities. They are suggested from analytical and simulation models of the system, from observation of input stations, disk-arm movements and console lights, and from **reflection on what parameters** are likely to be important. The difficulty comes in choosing from this large list of possibilities, in deciding which tools to use, how frequently to collect data (continually, at intervals, upon request, under extreme conditions) how to display and store the data, and most of all, in knowing what kind of analysis to do.

The two general classes of monitors, hardware and software each have
their own advantages. Hardware monitors are easy to attach, but they
do require the services of a maintenance engineer and are more limited
in the ways they can be used. They impose no system overhead and can
therefore be used continuously or selectively as desired. Software monitors are more versatile and can be used to observe system functions (such
as queue lengths and program usage) which are not at all accessible to
hardware monitors. They interfere to some extent, at least, with the
operation, and may require that tape units or other resources be allocated to them. The observations can be displayed more imaginatively and
dependent and related quantities can be calculated simultaneously. The
essential components of a monitor are common to both types. These include:

Probes - devices or program-interrupts which are inserted at points where
data is to be gathered

an *analyzer* - a device or program which receives data from a set of
probes, applying selection integration or conversion as needed

the *control* - the system which directs and synchronizes the activities
of the other components, either through programmed procedures, or directions applied by the operator or automatically by the system on the occurrence of certain events

an *output unit* - this displays and records the output directly in the
case of the hardware monitor; for software monitors the output may take
the form of a program which processes the contents of a *data buffer* in
which the data is retained until it is ready for output.

5. *HARDWARE MONITORS*

The earliest devices were outgrowths of the equipment used by engineers
in the design and development of computing systems - oscilliscopes, meters and counters. At the extreme ends of simplicity and complexity are
the program-accessible hardware clock and a full scale computer. The
standard 60 cps clock available in all systems is not adequate for monitoring because its resolution is not high enough. A clock which counts
in tens-of-microseconds, or even smaller units of time is needed.

5.1. ONE COMPUTER MONITORING ANOTHER

There are many examples of one computer being used to monitor another.
Table IV lists some cases reported in the literature.

Table IV - One Computer Monitoring Another

Primary Machine	Monitoring Machine	Environment	Reference
IBM 7090	IBM 7044		Conte 1964
UNIVAC 1108	UNIVAC 1108		MacGowan 1970
CDC 6600	Peripheral processor	Lawrence Radiation Lab.	Stevens 1968
Variable	SNUPER	UCLA	Estrin et al. 1967
GE 648	PDP.8	MULTICS	Saltzer and Gintell 1970

Clearly this technique permits the full power of the monitoring computer to be used for collecting, recording, reducing and analysing of the
data. Although a special interface must be designed (e.g. a channel-to-
channel connection) such dual systems allow the primary machine to be
operated with minimal interference. If the monitor computer is fast
enough most of the data can be evaluated as soon as it is collected. If
it is not it is necessary to halt the monitored system until the processing
catches up, (at some cost in elapsed testing time) or else to provide
buffers and intermediate storage. With a computer as monitor, data
gathered from the test system can be fed back to the primary computer,
providing two-way operations. The disadvantage of having a computer as
monitor is, of course, the extra cost, which is prohibitive except under
research, as opposed to operational conditions.

5.2. MONITOR LOGIC

The basic monitor device is an *event counter*. This is essentially an
"and" gate which allows a clock pulse through to a counter when a register which is being monitored records the event sought (Fig.1). The
high impedance probe buffers (isolates) the monitor circuit from the
system being monitored. With a more elaborate control unit it is possibl

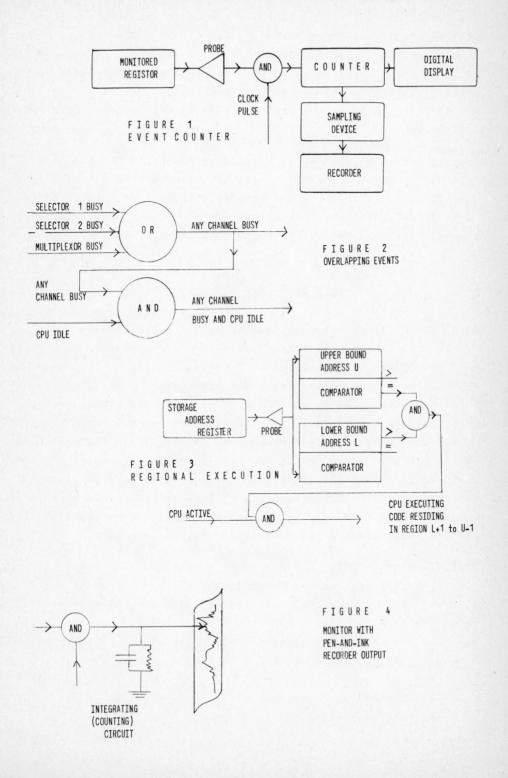

F I G U R E   1
E V E N T   C O U N T E R

F I G U R E   2
OVERLAPPING EVENTS

F I G U R E   3
R E G I O N A L   E X E C U T I O N

F I G U R E   4

MONITOR WITH
PEN-AND-INK
RECORDER OUTPUT

to recognize when certain instructions are encountered, record overlapping events, etc. (Fig.2). By attaching a decoder network to the
storage protect bits it is possible to recognize when instructions in
certain regions of the store are being executed. In particular it is
possible to record when the computer is executing from the part of store
reserved for the operating system and thus measure system overhead.
Alternatively, if the monitor unit has comparators, it is possible to
measure the time spent by the CPU in executing instructors out of any
part of store. (Fig.3).

As shown in Fig.1 the counter is sampled periodically and the results
recorded for subsequent analysis. Instead the counter can be replaced
by an integrating circuit and the results displayed on a meter or recorded on a pen-and-ink strip recorder. The output from several points
can be presented simultaneously on the same chart.

5.3.   EXAMPLES OF CURRENTLY AVAILABLE HARDWARE MONITORS

Initially the monitors were constructed by the manufacturers who used
them in special configurations or loaned them to customers where there
was some problem requiring analysis. Examples are the Basic Counter
Unit (BCU), the Machine Usage Recorder (Apple 1965) and the monitor
described by Bonner (1969), all IBM produced. The usefulness of these
was such that monitoring devices or various complexities have been built
into computers, particularly time-sharing systems where the configuration
was not completely determined in the initial design. Examples of such
monitors are TS/SPAR - (Schulman 1967), the Multics instrumentation
(Saltzer and Gintell, 1970). Recently self-contained hardware monitors
have been marketed commercially. To indicate the current availability,
four present-day hardware monitors are described briefly.

(1) The System Utilization Monitor (SUM) - Manufactured by Computer Syne-
tics Inc. This company was the first to market hardware monitors. Model
SM-416 provides 16 six-decimal independent counters. The counting rate
can be varied from 1 KHZ to 1 MHZ. Any one of them can be displayed,
and they are all recorded on magnetic tape. The whole system (except for
probes and input cables) is mounted in a single chassis.

(2) Boole and Babbage Hardware Monitor Units - These are separately
packaged devices, consisting of:

Event Monitor - six counters - 10^4 t 10^6 counts/sec - removable logic
plugboard
Measurement Probe
Measurement Printer - records data digitally from four event monitors
Magnetic Tape Unit - for storing
Trend Recorder - plots output
Data Summary Program - A program for analyzing data or magnetic tape

(3) System Activity Meter. This is a standard component of the IBM 370/
165 (IBM 370/65 Functional Characteristics p 24).
A switch allows any one of seven functions to be selected:

(1) I/O - I/O overlap (e.g. between channels) (2) I/O

(3) I/O and Compute (4) Off (5) Compute in Supervisor (6) Compute Total

(7) Compute Problem (PSW bit 15 equals 1)

A counter or strip recorder can be attached.

(4) University of Toronto Hardware Monitor (HARDMON II) (Milandre 1971)
This is a subsequent development to a unit built at the University of
Waterloo. It has 108 probes (20 are required for each address). An address
- compare circuit, a signal comparator, a logical plugboard, a 6-channel
recorder, a general purpose counter, etc. An important feature is that
the cost of the probe is small enough (less than $ 5 each) that it is
practical to leave them permanently attached to the computer, and use
the monitor without interrupting normal operations. Fig. 5 shows a
typical output of the strip recorder.

5.4.   ANALYSIS OF OUTPUT OF HARDWARE MONITORS

We conclude the discussion of hardware monitors with some illustrations
of how the results were useful in improving system performance.

(a) Analysis of a telecommunication system (Bonner 1969). The CPU time
spent in the portion of core storing the message processing system was
compared with the time used elsewhere. By plotting this against the number of inquiries it was found possible to reduce the polling rate without degrading performance.

(b) Distribution of access to direct-storage (Bonner 1969). A study of
access to the modules in a 5-module disk storage device revealed that
one module had excessive requests and seek time. Transfering a catalogue
to another module improved performance.

476

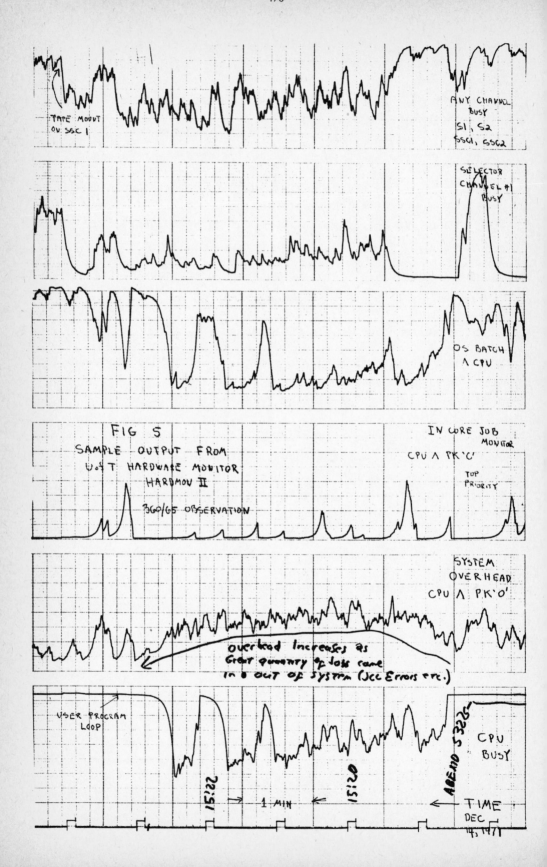

FIG 5
SAMPLE OUTPUT FROM
U of T HARDWARE MONITOR
HARDMON II

360/65 OBSERVATION

(c) Balancing Channel Loading (Kohn 1971).
Bottlenecks due to excessive activity on one channel are common. The
continuous surveillance permitted by a hardware monitor makes it easy
to avoid this. This is probably the most frequent use of the hardware
monitor on the 370/165.

(d) Direct-Storage Contention (U. of T. Computer Centre - T. Sellgren,
oral communication).
Two direct storage devices were configured so that A had a dual path
to the CPU, through its own channel and also through the channel of B.
The activity on A pre-empted B's channel. The hardware monitor provided
the clue which enabled the key routine to be transferred from a disk
to a drum with a much faster channel capacity.

(e) Analysis of operator actions (U. of T. Computer Centre - T. Sellgren,
oral communication)
Examination of the traces revealed poor operating practices in mounting
tapes, failing to recognize program loops and assigning disk packs. The
monitor enabled better procedures to be specified.

Two features of (metered) hardware monitor are valuable:

(1) The *simultaneous* recording of several event streams make it possible to recognize concurrent actions which cause trouble.

(2) the *continuous* (as opposed to the sampled) output allows events
which happen in a short time (seconds) to be recognized. Important observations can be lost because of averaging.

There is a need to develop techniques which will allow the monitored
output to be used continously by operators, and to develop standard
analysis procedures to the traces.

6. SOFTWARE MONITORS

Hardware monitors point to places in the system where the flow of work
is constrained because of bottlenecks, device contention, inadequate
operation attention, etc. To pinpoint the trouble spots, and eliminate
the difficulty it is often necessary to obtain much more detail, e.g.
the exact location of heavily used program modules or the waiting time
in queues. Some of this information can only be obtained with a software monitor. The general approach is essentially that of a diagnostic
routine - at appropriate points in the program (corresponding to the
point where a hardware probe is inserted) there is a transfer of control to a routine which collects data and stores it for later analysis.
The sampling rate and amount of data collected must be low enough so
that the overhead due to the monitor is acceptable. We can distinguish
three types of monitors:

(a) System accounting programs which gather data as part of the normal
    job-accounting for users and management.

(b) Standard packages which are run periodically or to obtain informa-
    tion arising out of some special problem.

(c) Programs written in conjunction with system design and development.

6.1. MONITORING FROM JOB-ACCOUNTING DATA

The normal job-accounting information which is given to users and which
is collected for billing purpose is an extremely rich source of data.
This is particularly true if billing is based on resource usage (CPU
time, core-residence time, connect-time, etc.). The information is useful in setting up price structures, in scheduling, in predicting turnaround, and in advising users how to reduce the costs of their work. We
give some examples.

(1) Cumulative distributions of:
    - job execution times   These are useful in setting times
    - job-step times   for priority limits and classes
    - core usage   in multiprogrammed job streams and
                               for selecting benchmark problems

(2) distribution of
- turnaround time   These will require time-stamps on
- time users take to   the job card - they are useful in
  call for their work   setting prices for priority work and
                           in user-relations

(3) machine loading statistics
- daily, weekly and   Necessary for scheduling, configura-
  monthly averages and   tion planning, budgeting, determin-
  peaks   ing the dependence of turn-around
- connect-time in time-   on load etc.
  sharing etc.

(4) I/O statistics
- cards read and punched   Useful in designing benchmark
- lines printed   problems, budgeting for supplies etc.

(5) Analysis of
- program advice sought   These help to bring to light de-
- diagnostic messages   ficiences in distributed material,
- user refund requests   operating procedures and user under-
                           standing

There should be standard programs to prepare most of this information, and also regular procedures for displaying it to users - either as charts or in newsletter distribution. It helps them in preparing the job submissions and helps maintain good relations with the computing centre.

There are several commercially available program packages for obtaining this information. Biggs-Matthews have a set of tabulation programs, and in Canada, Systems Dimensions Limited (SDL) market ACCOUNTPAK (both for IBM systems).

ACCOUNTPAK takes a very detailed profile of the user job because the pricing scheme used by SDL is based on charges for every identifiable component of the system - CPU time, core and disk residence, channel usage, I/O volumes etc. There are about thirty program "hooks" at appropriate points in the program software. In addition to the quantities listed above, records are produced for:

. channel usage - time allocated, block and byte traffic
. program module usage
. tape and disk mounting activity

The data are displayed in tabular form and as histograms. In detail the data recorded approaches that available in the special-purpose software monitors described next, but the program efficiency and system overhead ($\approx 3\%$) is such that it is practical to use the program as regular practice.

6.2. *PACKAGED SOFTWARE MONITORS*

Most of the quantities observable by means of hardware monitors can also be observed with software monitors, but at greater cost in time. To illustrate the possibilities two 'packaged' monitors will be described.

(1) Boole and Babbage Systems Measurement Software (SMS).
This is the first company to market software monitors. There are several distinct programs, available for IBM Ard Spectra computers.

. Problem Program Efficiency (PPE). This program, operating in the same partition as the problem program, samples every 1/60 sec. to record the percentuage of time the CPU spends executing instructions out of specified core regions. It also records when a supervisor call (SVC) has been issued within the sample bounds, and data on I/O waits.

. Configuration Utilization Efficiency (CUE)., collects data on hardware usage (channels, CPU etc.) disk head movement, supervisor calls etc. Both programs contain an *extractor* which collects the data and an *analyser* which analyzes it. The results are displayed in tables, and histograms.

. Data Set Optimizer (DSO) records disk head movements and suggests reorganization of the data sets to reduce average head movement time. Tables V(a), (b) and (c) show representative outputs for each of the three programs.

(2) SUPERMON - An MVT Software Monitor, operating as a system task under OS/360 MVT, written at SLAC, Stanford University (SUPERMON, 1970). In addition to the types of measurements already mentioned it is possible to observe various aspects of core storage use, including the "high water mark" (the maximum used), the amount available for additional programs, and the fragmentation of unused storage.

Table VI shows a sample output from SUPERMON, the Direct Access Device

Utilization report, and the summary report issued at the end of a run.

Monitors such as SUPERMON have been developed for many computers and at many installations (See Stevens 1968 for the CDC 6600, Kohn 1971, and Katonak 1971 for other OS/360 monitors and MacGowan for UNIVAC). One valuable way they can be used in multiprogrammed systems is to help operators load the processor efficiently. In most installations there are ten or so programs which typically account for 50 to 80 % of the computer use. These programs deserve careful study. Their resource utilization should be observed and all combinations of one or two of them which can just be fitted into the processor should be determined. It is almost certain that one or more of the frequently occurring jobs is always waiting for service. As a general multiprogramming strategy, exactly one of the combinations should be in the machine at all times. (Cantrell and Ellison).

Software monitors are not yet used regularly at most installations to tune the system by relocating important modules, balancing channel use or deriving frequently used load combinations. Although much remains to be done in the way of systematizing the analysis of monitor outputs, and we are a long way from being able to have the results of measurements automatically set operational parameters, there is already enough experience that software (and hardware) monitors should be considered standard tools in software engineering. Further, instruction on their use should become a regular part of the computer curriculum.

6.3. SPECIAL MONITOR AND TRACE PROGRAMS

We consider finally, special analysis and trace programs, written in conjunction with research investigations and system design studies. Of course most of the monitors just described were first used as system analyses tools before they were incorporated into job-accounting programs or standard operating procedures. The greatest efforts have gone into programs for gathering statistics and carrying out analysis on time-sharing virtual memory systems, in view of the difficulties experienced with memory and device management in these systems. As illustrated in Table VII each major time sharing system has its monitor.

Table V   Sample Outputs from Boole and Babbage Software Monitors

(a) Problem Program Efficiency Report

```
DISTRIBUTION OF DSOW WAIT

    DATA SET
      NAME                              PERCENT OF ACTIVITY

      JOBLIB                                    0.0
      SYSOUT                                    0.0
      SYSIN                                     0.0
      UNBLKED                                  22.73
      BLKED                                     2.37
                                               ------
      TOTAL                                    25.10

                                 * * * * *

MODULE MAP

    MODULE     FIRST BYTE   LAST BYTE   PERCENT OF   MODULES WITH   MODULES FOR WHICH
     NAME       ADDRESS      ADDRESS     RUN TIME      OVERLAYS     REPORTS ARE PROVIDED

    COBLTEST    001820       002B38       61.55                            X
    IGG019CC    02BDA8       02BE68        2.83
    IGG019AQ    02BC10       02BC88       34.84
    IGG019AA    02BB90       02BBF8        0.78
    IGG019CF    02BA48       02BB48        0.00

                                 * * * * *
```

(b) Configuration Utilization Efficiency Report

EQUIPMENT SAMPLED	AMOUNT OF TIME	PERCENTAGE OF TOTAL TIME
CHANNEL 1 AND CHANNEL 2 BUSY	181.44 SEC	2.52
CHANNEL 1 AND CHANNEL 3 BUSY	75.60 SEC	1.05
.	.	.
CHANNEL 0 BUSY	79.20 SEC	1.1
MULTIPLEXOR CHANNEL IN USE	5909.76 SEC	82.08
CHANNEL 1 BUSY	2298.24 SEC	31.92
CHANNEL 2 BUSY	802.08 SEC	11.14
CONTROL UNIT 03 BUSY	0.0	0.0
CONTROL UNIT 13 BUSY	1285.20	17.85
NO DEVICE BUSY	1231.92	17.11

DEVICE TYPE	DEVICE ADDRESS	AMOUNT OF TIME BUSY	PERCENTAGE OF TOTAL TIME BUSY	RATIO OF TASKS WAITING TO TOTAL SAMPLE INTERRUPTS	RATIO OF TASKS WAITING TO TOTAL SAMPLE INTERRUPTS WHEN DEVICE NOT BUSY
					(WHEN CPU IN WAIT STATE)
2540	00C	3751.20 SEC	52.10	0.620	0.100
2540	00D	6.48 SEC	0.09	0.011	0.004
1403	00E	3243.60 SEC	45.05	0.112	0.070
2311	130	21.60 SEC	0.03	0.0	0.0
2311	131	3610.08 SEC	50.14	0.284	0.020
2311	132	1190.88 SEC	16.54	0.079	0.001
.	.	.	.	.	.
2314	282	4710.24 SEC	65.42	0.670	0.010
2314	283	2534.96 SEC	35.18	0.382	0.005
2314	284	0.0	0.0	0.0	0.0
2314	285	404.69 SEC	5.62	0.004	0.001

(c) Data Set Optimizer Report

```
DATA SET HEAD MOVEMENT ON VOLUME BOOL70
```

DATA SET PAIRS	NUMBER OF TRAVERSALS BETWEEN DATA SETS	HEAD MOVEMENT TIME	PERCENTAGE OF HEAD MOVEMENT TIME	AVERAGE HEAD MOVEMENT TIME
PBFILE (01) - PBFILE (02)	108127	8758287 MS	49.00	81.01 MS
PPFILE (01) - PPFILE (02)	86920	5997480 MS	34.50	69.00 MS
PBFILE (01) - PBFILE (01)	19529	637817 MS	8.18	32.66 MS
.	.	.	.	.
.	.	.	.	.
	------	----------	-----	--------
	238680	17378290 MS	100.00	72.81 MS

Table VI   Sample Output from SUPERMON

MVT OS/360 Monitor

(a)   Direct Access Device Utilization

Address	Serial No.	Use Count	Allocated	Not Ready	Cu Busy	Seek	Data Trans
ICO	TICDO1	1 - 1	100.00%	.00%	.00%	.00%	11.97%
140	TIC950	10 - 24	100.00%	.00%	4.23%	40.85%	25.35%
241	TIC108	0 - 0	.00%	.00%	.00%	.00%	.00%
242	TIC035	0 - 0	.00%	.00%	.00%	.00%	.00%
143	TMD001	2 - 2	100.00%	.00%	13.38%	4.23%	30.99%
144	TIC019	12 - 12	100.00%	.00%	1.41%	.00%	.00%
145	TIC103	0 - 0	.00%	.00%	.00%	.00%	.00%
146	SPOOL1	1 - 1	100.00%	.00%	1.41%	9.86%	4.23%
247	TIC070	4 - 4	100.00%	.00%	4.93%	28.87%	13.38%
230	TIC954	1 - 1	100.00%	.00%	.00%	.00%	.00%
231	TIC106	0 - 1	61.27%	.00%	1.41%	.70%	2.11%
232	TIC008	0 - 0	.00%	.00%	.00%	.00%	.00%
233	TIC069	1 - 1	100.00%	.00%	.00%	.00%	.00%
234	TIC022	13 - 16	100.00%	.00%	.00%	1.41%	8.45%
235	TIC014	1 - 2	100.00%	.00%	.00%	.00%	.00%
236	SPOOL2	1 - 1	100.00%	.00%	.00%	2.82%	5.63%
237	TIC071	2 - 3	100.00%	.00%	.00%	4.93%	11.97%

Table VI   Sample Output from SUPERMON (con't)

MVT OS/360 Monitor

(b) Machine Activity at a Glance - Monitoring Completed

DATE: 72.007
ENDED: 13.33.26
TIME MONITORED: 2.00 MINUTES

PARAMETERS

CYCLE RANGE

CORE	4
MODULES	3
QUEUES	2
I/O DEVICES	4
CHANNELS	1

CYCLE TIME   0.20 SECONDS

CYCLES COMPLETED   569 OUT OF   600

ACTIVITY

ANY SELECTOR CHANNEL BUSY	84.18%	
I/O ACTIVITY INDEX	79,016	
I/O INTERRUPTS	13,779	6,890 PER MINUTE
DEVICES USED	37	
RQE USE SINCE LAST IPL	61	
TOTAL SUPERVISOR CALLS	38,750	19,375 PER MINUTE
EXCP	12,453	6,227 PER MINUTE
OPEN	14	7 PER MINUTE

POSSIBLE BOTTLENECKS

ENQ WAITS	100.00%
070K REGION AVAILABLE	100.00%
AVERAGE CORE WASTED	117K
TAPE CU WAITING	59.15%
DISK CU WAITING	26.76%
TAPE NOT READY	.00 MINUTES
DISK NOT READY	.00 MINUTES

Table VII   Software Monitors for Time-Sharing Systems

System	Monitor	Reference
CTSS		Scherr, 1967
MTS		Pinkerton, 1969
TSS/360	SIPE	Deniston, 1969
		Schulman, 1967
360/67 CP-67	DUSETIMR	Bard, 1971
MULTICS	(a set of programs)	Saltzer, 1970
GE Dartmouth System		
GECOS	MAPPER	Cantrell and Ellison 1968
SDC Time-sharing		
system		Totscheck

The basic components of the monitors record the resource utilization, display memory maps, determine the time spent in program segments, and do all the other things we have already mentioned. A program of the type used for diagnostic tracing is essential.

Paging quantities of interest include:

. instructions issued by users and by the system to virtual memory
  I/O devices.

. counts on pages read in and swapped out

. records on pages that belong to users in active queues and that are
  overwritten by incoming pages.

- average running time between page faults, and average duration of the
  time a page is idle until its space is revised.

. performance of associative memory hardware.

The result obtained from monitors are, on the whole, specific to the system being investigated, but it is possible to make some general observations.

. The most useful part of a monitor is some version of the standard
  diagnostic trace program which indicates how the CPU time is spent
  while executing a defined program segment. Once the heavily used
  programs are identified this in itself almost invariably produces
  significant improvements, both for user and system programs (Cantrell
  and Ellison).

. Monitors can be designed so that they impose a 1 to 5 % overhead due
  to their presence (Trace Monitors, running interpretively will be more
  expensive). This is small enough to allow them to be used over very
  long periods.

. In attempting to evaluate the worth of a hardware or software change,
  it is necessary to observe the system under heavy load conditions
  (Bard). This means that in a time-sharing system, for example, the
  frequency of sampling should be increased when many users are on.
  Alternatively, it may be useful to create a synthetic job which simulates the presence of user terminals (Saltzer and Gintell). To do this
  it will be necessary to have a profile of the load, and this can be
  found from monitor statistics.

. A way to use monitors which has already proved useful, and promises
  to become even more so, is in connection with simulation to produce
  what has been called *Trace Driven Modelling* (Sherman, Basket & Brown
  1971, and Katonak 1971). A very detailed profile of a job stream,
  down to almost a microscopic level is observed. In this, statistical
  distributers are fitted to the all job features considered important -
  e.g. I/O request, CPU service time for each job segment, etc. The
  type of distribution (Gaussion, Poisson, Uniform) as well as the averages and variances are filled to each feature as as to correspond to
  the observations. Then a model is constructed with different strategies and the performance (as measured by throughput or CPU utilisation)
  is simulated for each strategy. The strategy might be a scheduling
  algorithm in time-sharing (round-robin, FIFO, shortest requested time
  first etc.), placement of modules on drums vs disks etc. The observed
  performance of the system on the job stream is used to "calibrate"
  the model. In essence the technique is a combination of using monitor
  results, a set of kernel jobs, and simulation.

6.4. ESTIMATING MONITOR STATISTICS FROM THE OBSERVATIONS

The statistical techniques which are used to estimate system parameters
from the monitor observations are usually very simple, but some consideration of them is in order (Denning and Eisenstein 1971). In general a
quantity such as a queue length, or a channel delay is represented by a
set of possible wave forms $(x_1(t),...x_s(t)...)$ called an ensemble or
random process. Often what is wanted is an *ensemble measurement* , taken
at fixed t for various s, but what is observed is a *temporal measurement*,
taken at various times. If the system is *ergodic* temporal averages are

equal to ensemble averages. In effect this means that there must be no periodicities in the system's behaviour.

The simplest statistic (representative) of (x), given $(x_1...x_k)$ is the average

$$\hat{x}_k = \frac{1}{k} \sum_{i=1}^{k} x_i$$

It is unbiased, i.e. has expected value equal to $\bar{x}$, the true mean.

An unbiased estimate for the variance is $\hat{\sigma}_k^2 = \frac{1}{k-1} \sum_{i=1}^{k} (x_i^2 - \hat{x}_k^2)$

x_k is calculated iteratively by

$$\hat{x}_0 = 0 \qquad\qquad \hat{x}_k = \hat{x}_{k-1} + \frac{1}{k}(x_k - \hat{x}_{k-1})$$

It is always better to use a *stochastic approximation*. given by

$$\hat{x}_0 = 0 \qquad a_1 = 1$$

$$\hat{x}_k = \hat{x}_{k-1} + a_k (x_k - \hat{x}_{k-1})$$

The simplest is the *exponential estimator* where $a_k = \alpha$, $0 \leq \alpha \leq 1$

Another useful estimator is given by $\hat{S}_0(T) = 0$

$$\hat{S}_k(T) = \hat{S}_{k-1}(T) + \frac{1}{T} (x_k - x_{k-T})$$

where T determines the size of a "window" through which the measurements are observed.

Stochastic estimators have the advantage that the effect of initial errors eventually fades away, they require less storage than is needed for recording the complete sequence and calculating the estimate later, and they provide a current, timely estimate which is available for immediate uses, e.g. in carrying out some resource allocation.

In conclusion we may note a strong interest in all methods of performance evaluation, including especially the use of hardware and software monitors. This is evidenced by the appearance of a large number of papers on the subject in the last three years, and by special con-

ferences devoted to the subject (see ACM Workshop on System Performance
Evaluation, April 1971, and Computer Monitoring Workshop schedule for
April 1972 at Brigham Young University). There is general agreement that
there are still some important open questions, especially on methods of
analysis.

7. REFERENCES

ACCOUNTPAK A Proprietary Software Package of Systems Dimensions Ltd.,
            Ottawa, Canada

Apple, C.T. The Program Monitor - A Device for Program Performance
            Measurement Proc. ACM 20th National Conference Aug.1965,
            pp 66 - 75

Arbuckle, R.A. Computer Analysis and Thruput Evaluation Computers and
            Automation, Vol. 15, No.1, January 1966, pp 12-15

Bard, Y.   Performance criteria and measurement for a time-sharing
            system.IBM Systems J. Vol. 10 No. 3, 1971, pp 193-231

Basson, Alan; Brundage, Robert Performance Measurements on a Virtual
            Memory Computer System in a Batch-Processing Environment -
            Workshop, April 1971

Bemer, R.; Ward, A.L.; Ellison Software Instrumentation Systems for
            Optimum Performance Pwc. IFIP Congress 68, North Holland,
            pp 520-524

Boehm, B.W. Computer Systems Analysis Methodology - Studies in Measur-
            ing, Evaluating and Simulating Computer Systems,R-520 NASA,
            Rand Corp., Santa Monica, Sept. 1970

Bonner, A.J. Using System Monitor Output to Improve Performance,
            IBM Syst.Journal Vol 8 (1969) No. 4, pp 290-298

Bordsen, Donald T. UNIVAC 1108 Hardware Instrumentation System -
            Workshop April 1971

BUC Component Description and User's Guide. Form no. 7X22-6953 IBM Corp.

Calengaert, P. System Performance Evaluation: Survey and Appraisal Comm. ACM Vol, 10, No. 1, January 1967, pp 12-18

Campbell, D.J.; Heffrer, W.J. Measurement and Analysis of Large Operating Systems
During Development AFIPS Proc.33, (FJCC 1968,Vol 2),pp 903-914

Cantrell, H.N.; Ellison, A.L. Multiprogramming System Performance and Anylysis, AFIPS Proc.32 (SJCC, 1968), pp 213-21

Choosing a Computer 1971-72, Data Systems, Dec. 1971

Crooke, S.; Minker J. Key Word in Context: Index and Bibliography, Computer System Evaluation Techniques, Technical Report 69-100, Dec.1969, University of Maryland, Computer Science Dept.

Deniston, W.R. "SIPE: A TSS/360 Software Measurement Technique" Proc. ACM 24th National Conf. 1969, pp 229-245

Denning, Peter J.; Eisenstein, Bruce A. Statistical Methods in Performance Evaluation - Workshop, April 1971, pp 284-307

Esthin, G.; Hopkins,D.; Coggar, B.; Crocker, S.D. Snuper Computer: A Computer in Instrumentation Automation, AFIPS Proc. 30 (SJCC, 1967), pp 645-656

Freibergs, I.F. The Dynamic Behaviour of Programs. AFIPS Proc. 33, (FJCC 1968, Vol.2,) pp 1163-1167

Gotlieb, C.C. and Mac Ewen G.H. System Evaluation Tools in *Software Engineering*. NATO Scientific Affairs Division, 1969, pp 93-98

Hart, L.E. User's Guide to Evaluation Products.Datamation 16 (Dec.1970) 17, p 32

Harman, A.J. The International Computer Industry. Harvard University Press, 1971

Hillegass, J.R. Standardized Benchmark Problem Measure Computer Performance Computers and Automation Vol.15, no. 1, Jan.1966, pp 16-21

IBM System/370 Model 165 Functional Characteristic, GA22-6935-0
            May 1971, p 24

Joslen, E.O. and Aiken, J.J. The Validity of Basing Computer Selections
            on Benchmark Results. Computers and Automation Vol.15,
            No.6 , June 1966, pp 22-23

Katonak, P.R. Use of Performance Analysis Statistics in Computer
            System Simulation - Fifth Conference on Applications of
            Simulations. Association for Computing Machinery,
            December 1971, pp 317-325

Kohn, Carl E. Techniques and Results of Systems Monitoring. University
            of Waterloo, 1971, Computer Centre

Knight, K.   Evaluating Computer Performance 1962-1967. Datamation,
            January 1968, pp 31-35

Lucas, H.C.   Performance Evaluation and Monitoring Computing Surveys,
            Vol.3, No3, Sept.1971, pp 79-91

MacGowan, J.M. UNIVAC 1108. Instrumentation in *Software Engineering
            Techniques*. NATO Scientific Affairs Div. 1970, pp 106-
            110

Metzger, J.   Monitoring Computing Systems. M.Sc.Thesis. Dept. of
            Computer Science. University of Toronto, December 1970

Milandre, G.   Hardware II - University of Toronto, Hardware Monitor
            Project. Internal Report V, November 1971. University of
            Toronto Computer Centre

Minker, S.; Crook and J.Yeh Analysis of Data Processing Systems. Techni-
            cal Report 69-99. University of Maryland, Computer Science
            Centre, Dec. 1969

Pinkerton, T. Performance Monitoring in a Time-Sharing System.
            CACM 12, Nov. 1969, Vol.12, No.11, pp 608-610

Saltzer, J.H.; Gintell, J.W. The Instrumentation of Multics. CACM 13,
            No.8, Aug.1970, pp 495-500

Scherr, A.L.   An Analysis of Time-Shared Computer Systems. M.I.T.Press,
            Cambridge, 1967

Schneidewind, N.F.   The Practice of Computer Selection. Datamation,
          February 1967, pp 22-25

Schulman, F.D. Hardware Measurement Device for IBM System 1360 Time
          Sharing Evaluation. Proc. ACM 224. National Conf. 1967,
          pp 103-109

Share-Session Report on "Hardware vs Software". Share XXXIV Proc.Vol.1
          (1970) pp 380-405

Sharpe, W.F.   The Economics of Computers. Columbia University Press 1969
          Ch.9. The Cost and Effectiveness of Computer Systems

Sherman, S.; Browne, J.C.   Forest Baskett III. Trace Driven Modeling
          and Analysis of CPU Scheduling in a Multi-Programming
          System - Workshop, April 1971, pp 173-199

Solomon, M.B. Jrs.   Economies of Scale and the IBM System/360 Comm.
          ACM Vol.9, No 6, June 1966, pp 435-440

Stanley, W.I.; Hertel, H.F.   Statistics Gathering and Simulation for
          the Appollo Real Time Operating System. IBM Syst.J.
          Vol.7 (1968), No 2, pp 85-102

Stevens, D.G.   System Evaluation on the Control Data 6600. Proc.IFIP
          Cong. 68, Aug.1968, pp 542-547

SUPERMON   Systems Technical Memo No. 30, January 1970. COSMIC, Barrow
          Hall, University of Georgia, Athens, Georgia

System Performance Comparison Charts - in Standard EDP Reports, Auer-
          bach Corp. sec. 11 00.101-115

System Utilization Monitor: User's Manual. Form no.A/B-416. Computer
          Synetics Inc., Sept.1969

Warner, C.D.   Monitoring: A Key to Cost Efficiency. Datamation
          Jan.1971, pp 40-49

Workshop on System Performance Evaluation, Harvard University, Cambrid-
          ge, Mass., ACM, April 5-7, 1971

Wulf, W.   Performance Monitors for Multiprogramming Systems.
          Proc.2nd ACM Symp. on Op.Syst.Principles.Princeton,N.J.
          (Oct.1969), pp 175-181

CHAPTER 4.E.

P R I C I N G   M E C H A N I S M S

C.C.Gotlieb
Department of Computer Science
University of Toronto, Canada

Pricing serves an important role in allocating service resources and
rationalizing planning. In the long run its alternatives turn out to
be not as satisfactory. Price levels are determined by costs, but also
by policy considerations. Different methods of setting levels are examined, along with some of the resulting implications and requirements.

1.   THE RATIONALE OF PRICING

In a market situation prices are a device for recovering costs and
making a profit. But even in the situation where a centralised computer
facility provides services to internal departments, as prevails in a
university, a government computing bureau or a large company, there are
equally strong reasons for adopting a policy where prices are charged
for the services. Prices (with budget allocation) are a means of allot-
ing scarce resources and obtaining an efficient use of resources over
time. They do this because they help control demand, smooth loads (when
used appropriately), rationalize planning and acquisition of new facilities, and provide a basis of comparison with other service centers.

There are other methods of recovering costs - e.g. levying an average
cost, applying overhead charges, or instituting priority services, but
in the long run these do not work as well as pricing (Kanter and Moore,
1968). Average costs preclude the ability to provide service at marginal costs (sometimes desirable), encourage use during peak periods, and
do not protect against over investment since a return is guaranteed.
Overhead simply fail to provide the proper incentives either to the
user or the administration for sensible use of the facilities. Priorities are in essence a surrogate for prices without the advantage of
competitive testing, and are unlikely to cost less to administer.

2.   DETERMINING FACTORS

The factors which determine price levels are:
. Costs - these should be realistic. They are discussed in more detail
   in the next section.

. Policy decisions - the first decision is to apply prices and transfer
   payments between divisions.

Other important questions are:
- is each identifiable service to be priced in relation to cost or are
   certain services (and users) to be subsidized?

- will prices be set by overall average costs or will certain users be
   permitted to pay marginal costs?

- what will be the "convertability" of the funds which users are given?
   Will they be good only for alternative in-house computer services?
   for computer services elsewhere? for other types of products (Smidt,
   1969)

- the level of use which is considered necessary **or desirable. High uti**-
   lization implies greatest efficiency in one sense, but less flexibility and room for growth in another.

. Complexity of equipment and services - the complexity increases
   significantly as we go from a single processor to time-sharing and
   multiprocessor facilities, and as the variety of services is increased (tape and disk storage, special outputs, plots, keypunching
   etc.)

3.   COSTS

In addition to their use in pricing, costs are important for cost effectiveness determination. We need a method of going from expenses and
distributing these to the different users, but this is difficult in a
general purpose multiprogramming situation, and the policy decisions
mentioned above are needed. The problem is a particular case of the general problem of cost accounting in any production processes.

The *cost components* are not difficult to identify.
These are:

Salaries   - management, operational, applications, development, fringe benefits (pension, insurance, health plan contributions etc.)

Equipment   - purchase or rental payments, maintenance, communication costs, office equipment

Supplies   - cards, paper, tapes, documentation

Software   - purchased, leased, developed in-house

Site   - space, preparation costs, utilities

Overhead   - use of purchasing and maintenance services, library

Miscellaneous - travel, advertising, user manuals, etc.

A major decision is that concerning the method of amortizing the purchase costs of the equipment. In business it is usual to show depreciation allowances for equipment but this does not seem to have been common in computer financing and costing - perhaps because the major asset is so often acquired with the aid of grants or special financing, and it is difficult to determine what value should be imputed to it. There are arguments for always including an amortization cost (Report of Task Force on Computer Charging). Among other things this places the decision on purchase vs renting vs third-party leasing of equipment on a more rational basis. To analyze the purchase cost we must know the *useful life* of the equipment. A lower bound can be estimated from R/C the ratio of the monthly rental cost to the purchase cost as determined by the manufacturer. If L is the useful life in months, r the annual rate of return on capital, and M the maintenance part of the rental cost; approximately

$$R - M = \frac{C}{L} - \frac{r}{12} \cdot \frac{C}{2}$$

For example if $\frac{C}{R}$ = 48, M = $\frac{R}{4}$ and r = 10% then L $\approx$ 66 months.

In commercial service bureaus the computer is usually amortized in a time which is very short compared to that usually found in other equipment investment e.g. 3 or 4 years compared with the 10-20 years common elsewhere. Ten years is clearly long for the life of a computer in view of the rapidity of technological change, but 3 years makes the cost of services very high.

4. THE FACTORY MODEL

The recent trend, both in commercial and University installations is to view the computer facility as a "factory" which delivers a number of products, i.e. various types of services, and determine cost and prices for these (Nelsen 1968, U. of T. Computing Centre Reports 1971). A number of distinct services are identified, and cost accounting techniques are used to assign cost components to each of these services. For example at the U. of T. in 1971 the following services and cost components were defined.

SERVICE	COST $
Time sharing service (CPS, APL, ATS)	258,723
Batch service (OSon 360/65)	1.309,610
High-speed batch service	299,120
7094-service	300,000
Remote Job Entry Service	239,176
Miscellaneous services (Plotters, unit record)	136,071
	2.542,700

There is inevitably some arbitrariness in identifying a service. Thus programming advising, which might have been called a service, was redistributed into the others. These costs were determined by a careful analyses of the annual budget. In some cases, e.g. salaries and supplies, it is easy to allocate the budget line items to the services. The most difficult to assign are the capital (amortization) costs, and this was arrived at by measurements on the core and c.p.u. usage for the three types of usage identified on the 360/65, namely OS batch, high speed batch (HSJS) and time-sharing.

It was a policy decision that users of the remote job service would pay no more for their computing than time local users, and therefore the costs for this service were redistributed into OS, to be added to the input/output charges.

5. PRICING A SERVICE

Having determined the total price for each of the services there is still a great deal of choice in arriving at a *unit price.* Different strategies are appropriate for the different services. We have:

- Single Price Scheme: This is the average cost mentioned earlier. It was adopted for HSJS. For such jobs there are strict upper bounds on core usage, c.p.u. time, cards read and lines printed. Much of the cost is in I/O and it is more efficient *not* to record c.p.u. time. The load runs about 5000 jobs/day, leading to a cost of $\approx$ 20¢/job.

- Prime Shift Definition: A prime shift is defined and prices are set below this for less desirable times - e.g. at nights or on week-ends. This was common when users were allocated the whole computer (See Table 1 from Sharpe), but it is less useful in multiprogrammed systems.

- Multiple Input Queue: Queues with different priorities are set up, and prices are charged according to the priority, e.g. Rush (at double rate)

Table 1 - Typical Shift Rates

Shift	Period	Price as a percentage of prime-shift price	Approximate percentage of time sold at this price
Prime	Working days 8:00a.m.-6:00p.m.	100	42
Second	Mon.-Fri. 6:00p.m.-midnight	85-90	28
Third	After midnight	60-90	25
Weekend	Sat. and Sunday	negotiable	5

From Sharpe - Economics of Computers p.504

ASAP (As Soon as Possible-at the standard rate)
IOI (If Otherwise Idle-at 60% standard)
It would be preferable to charge according to turnaround time, but this cannot be guaranteed.

- Resource Usage: This is the mechanism now used widely for time-sharing and multiprogramming installations. The resources for which charges are made include: CPU time, memory usage, terminal connect time, cards read or punched, lines printed, number of tapes or disks mounted etc.

- Market Scheme: Users bid for a "share" of the computer. There are many possible variations; for example the share may be alloted daily, and a share not used lapses. Priority may be given to those who have used least of their share to date. A variant of this scheme is used by the University of Waterloo in allocating service on the IBM 360/65.

Special problems arise in multiprogrammed systems. If prices are charged according to resources committed, in general the cost will depend on the program mix and users will find different prices for the same job run at different times. Also, the CPU time chargeable directly to users adds up to considerably less than 100 % of CPU time because it is difficult to keep the CPU fully occupied. A scheme developed by Douglas Aircraft was to calculate for each job an *expected run time* (ERT) which is found by adding a constant time (about 25ms.) for each I/O interrupt issued by the user program, and adding this to the measured CPU usage.

The result is that relatively complicated methods of computing job charges in a multiprogrammed system are often used. The Appendix gives the formula for computing run charges presently in effect at the University of Toronto (along with the rate structure for other services). A similar system is used in other universities and commercial installations.

6. SOFTWARE REQUIREMENTS

It is apparent that a pricing mechanism requires considerable backup in the form of software. Among the programs needed are:

a) A job authorization routine - this maintains credit balances and checks every job for sufficient funds before it is run. Preferably applied on-line.

b) Job accounting routine - this computes job charges, posts them to the accounts and displays them on the user output

c) Billing routine - prepares statements and summary statistics about earnings

d) Job analysis routine - this collects statistics about the number of jobs in each service so as to allow the effects of changing the pricing mechanism to be predicted.

These programs each have components. It is doubtful if a set of comprehensive job accounting programs can be written in less than ten men-
years. Commercial versions are available (SDL ACCOUNT PAK). The job
statistics collected are very detailed and useful for performance
measurement and system evaluation.

7. EXAMPLES FOR PRICING MECHANISMS

7.1. RATE SCHEDULE FOR THE UNIVERSITY OF TORONTO, 1 JAN 1972

A. SYSTEM/370 SERVICE – The General Purpose Job Stream

    JOB CHARGE = SF(($CPU*CPUTIME)+(SCORE*COREUSAGE)+UR+PDC)

    where:SF   = Service Factor of 2.00 for RUSH
                                               1.00 for ASAP
                                               0.60 for IOI
        $CPU   = $ 8.50 per CPU minute
        CPUTIME   = measured CPU time in minutes
        ¢CORE   = ¢ 1.05 per hundred kilobyte minutes of
                              core usage
        COREUSAGE   = (RA/100)*(1+RA/500)*ERT
        RA   = Region Allocated (KB)
        ERT   = Equivalent Run Time (in minutes)
                            = CPUTIME + I/O WAITTIME
        I/O WAITTIME   = (.0245 sec. per I/O event)/ 60 min
        UR   = Unit Record Service Charge
                            = ¢ 0.80 per thousand cards read,
                              plus
                              ¢ 0.80 per thousand lines printed,
                              plus
                              ¢ 2.00 per thousand cards punched

        PDC   = Peripheral Device Charge
                            = ¢ 4.00 per job requiring disk, tape, or
                              special printer set-up

B. *7094 II/1401 SERVICE*

Computation (7094)   = ⌀ 96.00 per system hour

Unit Record Service (1401)   = ⌀ 0.80 per thousand cards read,
plus
⌀ 0.80 per thousand lines printed,
plus
⌀ 2.00 per thousand cards punched

C. *INTERACTIVE TERMINAL SYSTEMS SERVICE*

1. Conversational Programming System (CPS)

⌀ 2.00 per CPU minute, plus
⌀ 1.20 per core page per hour, plus
⌀ 3.00 per connect hour

2. Administrative Terminal System (ATS)

⌀ 3.60 per connect hour

3. APL Service

⌀ 3.00 per CPU minute, plus
⌀ 3.00 per connect hour

4. IBM 2741 Typewriter Terminal Rental

⌀ 95.00 per month for a leased line, or
⌀ 105.00 per month for a dial-up line

(This rental is not payable in allocated or subsidy funds; it is
a real dollar charge).

5. Disk Storage Space

⌀ 0.30 per track per month for ATS permanent storage records, APL
workspaces, and CPS load/save and file space

D. *MISCELLANEOUS*

1. SYSTEM/360 On-line Disk Storage

⌀ 0.30 per track per month

NOTE: 7294 bytes   = one track
          20 tracks   = one cylinder
          200 cylinders   = one 2316 disk

(The minimum is one month and the charge is payable in advance).

PRICING MECHANISMS

7.2. *DISK PACK RENTAL (OFF-LINE)*

$ 25.00 per month
(The minimum is one whole disk pack for one month and the charge
is payable in advance).

7.3. *DISK PACK STORAGE*

$ 25.00 initial charge, plus
$ 10.00 annual renewal

7.4. *DISK TO TAPE BACKUP*

$ 20.00 per cycle

7.5. *TAPE RENTAL*

$ 1.00 per tape per month
(The minimum is one month and the charge is payable in advance).

7.6. *TAPE STORAGE*

$ 5.00 initial charge, plus
$ 1.00 per tape per month

7.7. *TAPE CLEANING AND TESTING*

cleaning = $ 1.50 per tape (double pass)
testing = $ 2.00 per tape

7.8. *NEGOTIATED CONTRACT SERVICES*

Job turnaround handling = $ 10.00 per man hour
Programming Assistance = $ 12.00 per man hour

Analytical Assistance   = $ 15.00 per man hour

(These services are not payable in allocated or subsidy funds; they are real dollar charges).

7.9. *CALCOMP PLOTTING*

$ 20.00 per plotter-hour

7.10. *CARD PROCESSING*

Reproduction	= $ 2.00 per thousand cards
Interpretation	= $ 2.50 per thousand cards
Reproduction and Interpretation	= $ 3.50 per thousand cards
Labels	= $ 5.00 per thousand cards
Listing	= $ 1.00 per thousand cards
Keypunching	= $ 5.00 per hour
Keypunch Verifying	= $ 5.00 per hour

8. REFERENCES

ACCOUNTPAK   A Proprietary Software Package of Systems Dimensions Limi-
            ted, Ottawa, Canada.

Diamond, D.S. and Selwyn, L.   Considerations for Computer Utility pricing
            policies. Proc.ACM Nat.Conference Brodon System Press 1968,
            pp. 189-200.

Gill, S. and Samet P.A.   Charging for computer time in universities.
            Computer Bulletin, 13, No.1 (Jan.1969) pp. 14-16.

Hootman, J.T. The pricing dilemma. Datamation in 15, 8 (Aug.1969) pp. 61
            66.

Leppik, J.J. "Proposal of Terms of Reference of the Institute of Compu-
            ter Science". University of Toronto, November 1969.

Marchand, M. Priority pricing with application to timeshared computers.
            FJCC 1968, AFIPS, Part I, pp. 511-519.

Nielson, N.R.   Flexible pricing: An approach to the allocation of com-
            puter resources. FJCC 1968, AFIPS Part I, pp. 521-531.

Report of the Task Force on Computer Charging. Computer Coordination
            Group, Ontario Council of Universities, June 1, 1970.

Sharpe, W.F. The Economics of Computers, Columbia University Press,
            1969 Ch.9 and 11.

Singer, N.M.; Kanter, H. and Moore, A.   Prices and the allocation of
            computer time. FJCC 1968, AFIPS, Part I, pp. 493-398.

Smidt, S.   The use of hard and soft money budgets and prices to limit
            demand for centralized computer facility. FJCC 1968, AFIPS,
            Part I, pp. 499-509.

University of Toronto Computing Centre - Internal Reports Pricing Sub-
            Committee - June 1970
            A Paper on Pricing - C.A. Ford, May 1971
            A Cost Accounting Model - C.A. Ford, February 1971

CHAPTER 4.F

EVALUATION IN THE COMPUTING
CENTER ENVIRONMENT

H. J. Helms
Technical University of Denmark
Northern Europe University Computing Center

1. INTRODUCTION

In the following we will consider some of the aspects of the utilization made from software. We are moving from the problems concerning
the design and construction of programs and systems of programs into
the environment of the users. We are no longer dealing with software
engineering in itself, but rather with the applications of the products of the software engineers.

We shall move around in the computing center environments, and while
we shall try to describe them it must be admitted, it is by now
difficult to give a precise definition. In former times this was
rather easy. The computing center simply was the physical location of
a computer, and the environment the staff servicing the computer, as
well as the users most of whom were programmers themselves and, on
many occasions, also operators.

The situation is no longer that simple. With the proliferation of terminals attached to distant computers and even development of computer
networks,it is more difficult sharply to provide a definition of a
computing center environment. We may still find it around the physical
location of a computer, but it may as well be found around the physical location of a terminal connected to a remote computer. There are
indeed examples of important computing environments using terminals
and never giving considerable thought to the fact that the computer
itself is located far away.

For the purpose of our discussion let us define the computing center
environment as the community of people using the services of a given
computing system.

A user is a member of this community and we may mention as examples
An airline ticket agent using a seat reservation system.
A typist using a text editing system.
A bank teller using an on-line accounting system.
A manager using a management information system.
A consulting engineer using standard engineering programs from a terminal in his office.
A chemist developing programs to solve his own research problems.
A student solving exercises for his informatics course.
A programmer developing programs for a customer.

While the above mentioned examples of user categories by far are exhaustive, it does lead to a recognition of various classes of users. Roughly we may describe them as non-specialists in computer usage and specialists in computer usage. We may also describe the users as falling into the categories non-programmers and programmers, but here reservation on the skills and abilities may be made for the persons falling in the category programmers.

The users we shall consider in the following, mainly fall in the latter of the two categories. We find them in computing center environments in amongst others computer firms, computing centers serving administration, business, hospitals, industry, libraries, research institutions and universities.

The largest variety of these categories of users are found in university computing center environments also often characterized by a large variety of applications, a large variety of problems to be solved, a vide scope of need for computing facilities as well as a broad spectrum of varying degrees of experience and skills in computer usage.

With the above broad definition of a user it is of course rather difficult to provide statistics of the number of users.

There does exist many statistics countrywide and worldwide of the number of computers, and as an example in the Federal Republic of Germany the company Diebold, Deutschland has published that in early 1971 there were the following approximate number of computers

60 large computers
8.300 medium sized computers
13.500 small computers

of a total value of 11.6×10^9 DM.

A large computer is defined as a machine whose purchase value exceed
8 mill. DM.

It depends of course entirely from the application, how many users a
given machine or a given computing center have. At least on an European scale a computing center in a large research institute may have
some 1000 users and a large university computing center will have
2000 or more.

At NEUCC, Technical University of Denmark, where we provide a university computing service on a regional basis i.e. also to universities
and research institutes outside our own university, we have around
1000 valid account numbers and a user population of 2000-3000.

The computer system, actually an IBM 360/75 is largely terminal-
oriented and besides a high-speed terminal there are at present 14
medium-speed terminals attached to the mainmachine, as well as the
users have around 80 typewriter terminals, which connect with us on
a dial-up basis.

During a typical month we find that some 40-45.000 jobs are passed
on the machine. 20.000 of these are typical student jobs. Around half
of the jobs come from the terminals some of which are located far
away, up to 200 km.

North American university computing centers may serve a community of
30.-40.000 students and a faculty of some 3.000 members. Quite typical
are some 20% of the students in professional or graduate schools.

Our computing center environments are thus operating on a very large
scale and draw their users from large populations.

2. *THE USER AND HIS NEEDS*

It is often claimed that the user has great difficulties in specifying
his needs and do not know, what he really wants in order to solve his
problems. This is perhaps not surprising, but it is most dangerous
for the user as well as for us, if we do not try to perform a further
analysis both of the user and his problems and thereby try to provide

a specification in greater details of his needs and requirements. It is
surprising to find how seldom this is done in an intelligent and workable fashion, and how often decisions in reality are made in a nearly
random way or as a result of a coincidence of circumstances.

There is often a large amount of goodwill involved in reaching the
right decisions also letting the users exercise influence through an
appropriate committee structure. Without underestimating the value of
this, it must be admitted, that the reasons for their existence sometimes are psychological. Anybody who live in the environment will by
the way know only too well that a complicated structure for mutual information, decision making on several levels etc, in a computing center
environment as in many other organizatorial environments by far is the
only line of communications. Perhaps just as important also when it
comes to influence on decisions are the many informal contacts.They
may be sound, stimulating and inspiring, but by their very nature may
lead to decisions based on coincidences. A strong element of influence
directly or indirectly is also exercised by software firms and computer
firms.

The start of any systematic measurement technique must be a very good
set of accounting routines. They should provide records of the facilities used such as total time, CPU time, core store used, use of input/
output facilities. It is surprising that routines of this type to do
accounting are relatively rare when the computer system is delivered
from the manufacturer. The machine may even lack an internal clock.
It is for this reason there is a large number of papers in the literature describing what was done at a particular installation to provide a reasonable accounting scheme for their utilization.

Accounting routines are used for keeping record of the utilization of
the computer, charging the users and provide a basis for prognosis on
further computer use and thereby aid the budgeting plans and establish
the procurement policies.

The data collected may also be used to the establishment of a user
profile, and here we find surprising similarities between university
computing centers.

From the individual figures in the accounting schemes we can get the distribution of jobs by time and by number in particular time intervals. The general shape of such distributions are very alike.

P.A. Samet [1] , University College, London, Computer Centre, which is equipped with an IBM 360/65, reports that about 90% of the jobs run for less than 5 minutes, but took only 50% of the time. Almost 50% of the jobs run for less than one minute. What is a job? In this distribution batches of small jobs run under the WATFOR compiler are counted as one job, and each of these batches usually contain between 5 and 10 jobs. Each such batch typically takes 1 minute.

P.A. Samet [1] also reports that the London University CDC 6600 machine from its first months of operation in handling more than 33.000 jobs, it was found that 83% took less than 30 seconds and 88% took less than 1 minute.

These figures relate to the same university. In 1968 at NEUCC we reported [2] from our IBM 7094 operations that 92% of the jobs run for less than 6 minutes. They took 45% of the machine time. The similarity is striking.

At present on the IBM 360/75 at NEUCC we find (not taking WATFIV and Algol W jobs into account) that 63 % of the jobs take less than 1 min CPU time and use 12% of the total CPU time.

It is distributions like these which explains the interest of university computing centers in fast compilers like WATFOR and justify their concern for small overheads.

The distributions of the number of jobs and the time used of course reflects the use of the computer facilities both for research and educational purposes. At NEUCC we found in 1968 from the IBM 7094 operations that the distribution of the machinetime was

Education	19%
Research	80%
Other use	1%.

At present on the 360/75 installation it is

	Account units	Normal jobs
Education	14%	31%
Research	85%	66%
Other use	1%	3%

Many accounting routines also allow us to obtain information about
the utilization of the software modules available. It is based on these
we at NEUCC estimate 50% of the machinetime is used on Fortran jobs,
20% on Algol jobs and 30% on other languages.

It is, however, necessary to provide even more detailed studies of
the user profiles and the usage characteristics.

We may estimate that their will be no major changes in the type of
computing done in many environments over the next few years. The
number of users may, however, increase and it is thus important to
know the major characteristics of the increasing population in order
to anticipate the bottle-necks and to plan for the necessary expansion.

This is true for the computing center but is also true for the users.
An instructor must be able to estimate the cost of his programming
class. A leader of a research project should also be provided with
applicable averages to estimate correctly his needs for computer resources in the development of production programs. His programmers
go through cycles of planning, debugging, program modifications and
reprogramming. It is important to know what this costs.

Earl Hunt et al. [3] has reported on an analysis of computer use in
the university computing center at Washington University, Seattle
equipped with a CDC 6400 machine.

A more detailed study of programming practices has been conducted by
D. Knuth [4] as an empirical study of Fortran programs written and run
by users at Stanford University, Computation Center and at the computer center of Lockheed Missiles and Space Corporation in Sunnyvale,
California.

A static statistics provide a picture of how frequent certain constructions are used in practice.

The conclusion is that compilers spend most of their time doing surprising simple things. Anybody who has tried to consult with users
at a university computing center can subscribe to this conclusion.

More detailed studies were performed by dynamic statistics. In the
method of frequency counts or program profiles, counters are inserted
at appropriate places in the program in order to determine the number
of times each statement is actually performed.

The frequency counts are highly revealing and indeed tell the programmers that much that they ought to be provided as a standard tool.
This could also [4] be used to govern selective tracing and to locate
untested portions of a program i.e. it is a useful tool for debugging
purposes.

The collection of debugging counts is called the profile of the
program [4] . The programs often have a profile with a few sharp peaks.

It was also found that less than 4% of a program generally accounts
for more than half of its running time. There are few such studies,
but if this is common it means that programmers can make substantial
improvements to their own programs by being careful only at a few
places. Moreover optimizing compilers can be made to run faster as
they do not need to study the whole program with the same degree of
concentration.

More detailed studies of programs written by a population of programmers provide even more information on the use of compilers and hence are
useful both for the programmer and the compiler builder.

The frequency counts give an important dimension to programs and show
programmers how to make their routines more useful and efficient with
relatively little effort. A study [5] has shown that this method may
lead to an eleven-fold increase in a particular compiler's speed.

It might be a challenge to develop interactive systems which immediately tell the programmer the most costly parts of his programs. This should strongly motivate him to make the necessary changes.

The studies described are only too rare and it may be expected that many will be encouraged to continue and to report their results.

This should provide a solid base for feed-back to the software engineers about the users behaviour both on a global basis when we study the operatings of a computing center and on a more local basis when we study the behaviour of the programmers.

These methods can lead to a better economy in computer usage and undoubtedly make the users more motivated to proper economy than the various administrative schemes derived in the computing center environments.

Only to a limited extent do they tell us about new facilities needed and they only provide a limited basis for a marked analysis.

3. SOFTWARE AND THE COMPUTING CENTER

We may find computing centers with expensive facilities who are unable clearly and sharply to define their objectives and purposes. In particular this is too often the case with university computing centers.

One of the reasons is that some university computing centers not yet clearly have recognized where they want to place themselves on the scale ranging from research laboratories to purely service facilities. Many make gradual moves back and forth while others have gone through major organizatorial changes. In many cases the objectives of such redefinitions have been to distinguish clearly the service functions from the academic functions. Several cases could be discussed including an assessment of the advantages and disadvantages of the various schemes.

It is also important to recognize the distinction between a commercial service bureau and a university computing center.

The organizatorial structure of the two types of centers may be rather identical, but while a commercial service bureau often provide a specialized service - a time-sharing service as a typical example - the university computing center mostly have the task to make a multitude of services and facilities available. Moreover, most service bureaux only try to provide services which are found to be economical profitable over longer or shorter periods of time. The university computing centers are often required to provide services independent of their profitability. Indeed many such centers by their very nature are forced to provide non-profitable services. In this respect they may be compared with other public services like postal services or transportation services.

Another important difference is that most commercial computing services are operated in a highly competitive market, while a majority of the university computing centers enjoys a monopoly or an almost monopoly. This increases the responsibility and in itself it contains a danger of unsatisfaction amongst the users.

All these aspects also influence the software situation in university computing center environments. The multitude of services and facilities available is of course only possible with a similar large amount of software available including a vast number of application programs.

The cost components of the computing center are described by Gotlieb [6] . It is of particular interest that at most university computing centers the software budget as it is shown directly on the accounts still is rather marginal. This will of course change as the policy of computer companies of separate pricing for hardware and software is developing. At NEUCC we currently spend as little as 2% of the total cost of operating the center on directly renting or purchasing software, and within a few years we estimate this figure to grow to more than 5%.

However, if we look into our staff expenses we may estimate that 60% of these are for staff members involved in developing, evaluating and maintaining software.

The major sources for software from outside the computer center environment are

        manufacturers
        software houses
        program libraries
        private communications.

The manufacturer normally also deliver the basic software like operating systems, compilers, assemblers, translators, etc. and, moreover,
utilities and a variety of applications software. The availability of
software is often both an important argument in the offer for sale of
a computer, and one of the elements in the choice made by the customer. It is, however, also found that computing centers only use a
limited amount of the software offered and indeed even develop their
own operating systems. For more specialized purposes we find important software developments performed in a collaboration between
the manufacturer and the customer. The policy of separate pricing
on software is still new for many manufacturers, but one of its
effects may be a shift from the manufacturer to other sources for
software.

The software houses are characterized by providing either software
for a customer on a special contract or developing software packages
for sale or for lease. Software may also be developed for a manufacturer to enhance the software selection available to his particular
machines.

The whole range of applications software and basis software is available on the market, but most of the offers are for systems or rather
big programs of more general usability such as Fortran compilers,
linear programming systems, flowchart programs etc. Of particular
interest are programs for accounting of the usage of a computer system,
system measurement software and simulation programs used in determining the optimal configuration for well-defined applications.

The services of many software houses often go beyond making the products available to the clients and are often combined with consulting
services.

Close to the software house concept is the university computing center
or computer science department which develop software for research

purposes or own purposes and subsequently make the products available
to other interested installations.

Large exchanges of software has been made in that way and mostly on
an informal basis at no cost or a nominal cost covering merely the
expenses of replication, materials and shipping.

Beside ensuring the distribution of such university developed software through a program library there is at present a trend that the
distribution, maintenance and other services are ensured by a software
house.

There are also several examples that university groups themselves
form and organize software houses which are university-based. The
idea is that a gap exists between research innovations in universities
and research institutes and the state of the software arts in industry.
These companies are often centered around a particular large piece of
software like an operating system or a compiler.

A more conventional way of stimulating the contact between industry
and the research environments at universities is by individual con-
tracts and large amounts of software are developed in this way.

Program libraries are a well-known and much used source for software,
but the concept is broad and many of the libraries suffer under
serious deficiencies.

The manufacturers often keep libraries where routines, programs and
larger packages are available for the customers. The items of the
library is mostly classified according to the degree of service which
the company guarantees for the programs. A low class of service is
attached to the programs furnished by the customers to the library
and in many cases are the contents of this section of the library
of varying quality or of virtually no value at all.

There are many of these general purpose libraries and they are normally best when they are organized as systems for handling abstracts
of computer programs or other information pertinent to information
on software items rather than distributing the programs themselves.

Special purpose libraries concentrating on programs for use in a specific scientific discipline or a particular line of applications are normally at a limited size. It is for this reason they often are able to offer a rather homogeneous quality and thus provide a highly useful service. In particular are such libraries often a fine adjunct to the special libraries kept in the university computing centers.

Close to the library concept are the publications of algorithms in journals. They should be compared to normal publications and are often subject to the same degree of referee examination which largely guarantee their quality.

In [7] M. D. McIlroy suggest a factory for mass produced software components. Here he clains that the CACM algorithms, in a limited field, perhaps come closer to being a generally available product than do commercial products. However, such collections of algorithms also suffer certain deficiencies. They are an ingathering of personal contributions and are often quite varying in style. Moreover, they fit into no plan, for the editor can only publish what the authors volunteer. It is further criticised that algorithm sections of journals of learned societies can not deal in large number of variants of the same algorithm. Variability which makes the algorithms more useful for a large number of users can only be provided by expensive run time parameters.

The review indicates that there are many types of formal sources of software. In the university computing center environment we find that besides these sources both the center and its users to a large extent also draw on more informal sources and many pieces of software are obtained through private communications.

For the computing center it is important to keep an exact record of the software independent of its origin. This is done through the software inventory which ought not only to list the software but also contain a summary of the documentation available, status of maintenance, implementation characteristics and degree of responsibility taken for the particular piece of software.

Many computing centers have found it feasible to combine the software inventory with the function of exercising central control over quality of all software available in the center and provided to the users. This function provide the needle-eye between software under development or consideration and software for operational purposes and offered by the computing center to the users on a regular basis.

With software stemming from many sources it is quite difficult to maintain an adequate standard of documentation. It is, however, a necessity that there for every piece of software in the inventory is documentation satisfying a set of requirements [8],[9].

There are four different categories of persons who need information about a piece of software.

-Users of the software. Based on the documentation they need to assess the suitability of the software for their problems and they need also to see how the software may be used.

-Programmers. Based on the documentation they perform eventual corrections and further developments of the software.

-Systems staff at the computing center. Based on the documentation they perform the implementation on a particular computer.

-Operations staff at the computing center. Based on the documentation they assure the runs of the software on the computer.

Besides this documentation the computing center also need a centralized service called the software advisor. This should not be confused with the ordinary programming consulting service whose tasks mainly are to help users in debugging programs under development.

The software advisor will

-assist users in defining their problems

-advise an available software either within the environment or obtainable from elsewhere

-provide guidance on eventual new development of software necessary for solving the problem

-accumulate experiences.

The services of the software advisor are supported by suitable know-how on the software available in the software inventory.

In all considerations costs should play a proper role. Here we may distinguish between the open costs and the hidden costs.

Open costs for software in the computing center are for

-developing software

-purchasing or renting software

-installing software

-documentation.

Those cost items will normally be recognized for each individual piece of software.

The more hidden costs are for

-storing software

-replicating software

-servicing software

-maintaining know-how.

In particular the latter item is very important and the ambitious computing center with a long inventory may find itself in a situation where it has far too many items in its inventory in comparison with its staff resources for servicing the software and to provide know-how and assistance on the software.

There are also the cost of using the software available. Are the software pieces reasonable efficient and are users aware of the operational costs? It is also the duty of the software advisor to provide guidance to the users about these matters.

The awareness of costs may provide a better basis for a decision to use the available standard program, to adapt an available standard program or to develop a new program to solve the specified problem.

An encouragement for the recommended solution may be provided through the pricing scheme of the computing center for its software services.

4. INSTALLATION AND MAINTENANCE OF A PIECE OF SOFTWARE

In the following we shall follow a piece of software from the need
has been established through the installation phase and into the
phase where it is made available for the users on a regular service
basis.

The piece of software under consideration may form part of the basic
software like an operating system or a compiler or it may form part
of the applications software like a package for linear programming or
statistics.

From whom does the initial motivation occur to increase the inventory
of software at the computing center? This is perhaps not possible to
answer in general, but we may list
     -users
     -software advisor
     -systems programmers.

They are all concerned with problems to be solved and may recognize
that existing facilities including existing software do not satisfy
a new problem range.

At this stage the new piece of software should be documented in the
form of a proposal. This should explain why the new software is
desirable, provide proper specifications and also outline the likely
costs concerned with the software including the hidden costs.

Each appropriate section of the computing center must review the proposal and comment it based on its area of responsibility.

At this stage the proposal may give occasion for feed-back to the
software producer. It may be found that changes should be made or
indeed that another version of the software is likely to provide
better service than the originally proposed.

At the phase of decision there should be a document describing in
some details the product's operations and also its performance. Those
are the specifications. Its level of detail should be deep in order
it really provide a clear set of expectations to the software.

It is assumed that the software producer provide a proper testing of
his product before he pass it on to his clients and that he satisfies
himself it is fit for release. This testing may be done entirely without collaboration with the client or it may be combined with a field
test. The latter procedure is to be encouraged, but only if it is
clearly underlined that the responsibility still is fully with the producer.

Once the product is provided to the client he often accept it on its
face value or at most run a demonstration to prove that the main
features are working as expected. At a later stage he may discover
the inconveniences, the errors, the omissions and in general that his
expectations have not been fulfilled.

The consequences of this are only too well-known and lead to wasted
time and efforts as well as they create a lack of confidence in any
changes or improvements to existing software.

To prevent this the computing center must provide its own acceptance
test to be applied rigorously on any piece of software before it is
put into operations and in turn made available to the computing center
environment.

The aim is to ensure that we get the software we expected which means
that it fulfil the specifications drawn up at the stage of deciding
the acquisitions.

Hopefully this acceptance test will also provide an incentive for the
producer to improve his own testing procedures and quality control
before he releases software.

The test procedure should include

(i)   Documentation
(ii) Availability
(iii) Verification af facilities
(iv) Performance assessment.

For each of the items there must be stated criteria of acceptance and
only when these are fulfilled the software is approved.

The procedure is not trivial and it may request considerable efforts.
In [10] Llewelyn and Wickens describe an acceptance scheme for software and find the cost for a typical currently available operating
system to be 75 man-months, together with the use of 47 machine-hours.
They find the total cost of the exercise to be approximately £ 25.000
spread over a period of a year.

The National Computing Centre, Manchester has suggested a procedure
for a formal verification and certification of a program with the
following stages.

1.   The identification of the type and purpose of a program, the
     configuration on which it is known to run, mode of use and
     language.

2.   The identification of the level of documentation, technical
     support and level of use.

3.   The carrying out of tests, either by an independent authority of
     jointly with a user group to check that the program operates in
     accordance with the instructions given in the user manual and
     that the program actually does what the manual claims it will do.

A verification service of this kind is certainly a great improvement,
but it would never completely make the acceptance test by the computing
center superfluous.

Once the software is tested and accepted it will be installed on the
machine during which process there will also be made a decision of the
installation dependent parameters. For those it may be important to
have a prior estimate of the likely usage of the software as well as
the setting of the parameters may influence on the performance during
the operations.

The software available for the users in the computing center environment should be properly introduced to ensure on the one hand that they
take advantage of the new facility and on the other hand to ascertain
that its usage is limited to those purposes for which it was intended.

This is the task of the software advisor who will provide mechanisms
for the initiation and the formation of the users on the new piece of
software. This may take place in the form of courses and seminars and

may also involve development of new documentation to supplement the users manual.

Furthermore, methods are provided for ensuring the distribution of the software. It may be placed permanently on a primary or secondary storage on the machine with direct access for the users or it may be placed remotely on cards, tapes or discs. In the latter case there should be good facilities to secure replication and rapid distribution.

During the life-cycle of the software it is under constant evaluation with respect to

-performance
-quality
-usability.

These experiences should be collected in a continuous way with an easy procedure for deciding on

-error correction
-changes of implementation parameters
-changes of facilities.

The procedure should also include a procedure to determine when a piece of software is to be removed from the inventory of the computing center.

Clearly the procedure includes a mechanism for feed-back to the original software producer either to encourage him to perform changes in his product or to provide inspiration for new products.

5. CONCLUSION

There has in recent years been much concern over software, its bad quality, delays in delivery, cost which exceed the estimates etc.

We may not be able to improve the situation in a drastic way on a short term basis, although the seeking for basic principles in the concept of software engineering does give occasion to more optimism.

The users of software, however, must be aware that they also have a large responsibility for the improvement, and if a larger awareness of this aspect has been obtained through the present paper one of the goals has been obtained.

6.*REFERENCES*

[1]   P.A. Samet: Measuring the efficiency of software,
                                Proceedings SEAS XIV, Grenoble,
                                France 1969.

[2]   H. J. Helms et al.:   Experiences from operating NEUCC
                                (in Danish), Forskning, december 1968.

[3]   E. Hunt, G. Diehr,   Who are the users? -An analysis of
       D. Garnatz: computer use in a university computer
                                center, AFIPS Conference Proceedings
                                Vol. 38, 1971. Spring Joint Computer
                                Conference, 1971.

[4]   D. Knuth: An empirical study of FORTRAN programs,
                                Software Vol.1, No 2, 1971.

[5]   S.C. Darden and   Streamline your software development,
       S. B. Heller: Computer Decisions No.2, 1970.

[6]   C. C. Gotlieb: Pricing mechanisms, Advanced Course on
                                Software Engineering, 1972.

[7]   M.D. McIlroy: Mass produced software components, in
                                P. Naur and B. Randell (eds.): Software
                                Engineering, Report on a conference,
                                October 1968.

[8]   H. J. Helms (ed.)   Guidance in Construction of Datamatic
                                Systems (in Danish), Studentlitteratur,
                                Lund, 1972

[9]   G. Goos: Documentation, Advanced Course on Soft-
                                ware Engineering, 1972.

[10]   A. I. Llewelyn and   The testing of computer software, in
       R. F. Wickens: P. Naur and B. Randell (eds.): Soft-
                                ware Engineering, Report on a conferen-
                                ce, October 1968.

Appendix

S O F T W A R E   E N G I N E E R I N G *

Friedrich L. Bauer

Technical University, Munich
Germany

"Our problems arise from
demands, appetites and our
exuberant optimism. They are
magnified by the unevenly
trained personnel with which
we work".

Alan Perlis

This lecture was presented by F. L. Bauer on August 28, 1971
during the IFIP-Congress 1971 at Ljubljana, Yugoslavia, and
was published in 1972 by the North-Holland Publishing Company,
Amsterdam-London, in the "Proceedings of the IFIP Congress 71"
edited by C. V. Freiman (pp. 530-538).

Software Engineering seems to be well understood today, if not the subject, at least the term. As a working definition: software engineering is that part of computer science, which is too difficult for the computer scientist.

1. WHAT IS IT?

1.1. The common complaint

When the word software enginnering was introduced a few years ago, it was done in a provocative way. The use of the word was intended to signal a certain deficiency in the computer world, and "software engineering" by analogy pointed out a certain remedy.

What have been the complaints? Typically, they were

- Existing software is produced by amateurs (regardless, whether it is done at universities, software houses or manufacturers)

- Existing software development is done by tinkering (at the universities) or by the human wave ('million monkey') approach at the manufacturer's

- Existing software is unreliable and needs permanent 'maintenance', the word maintenance being misused to denote fallacies which are expected from the very beginning by the producer

- Existing software is messy, lacks transparency, prevents improvement or building on (or at least requires too high a price to be paid for this).

Last, but not least, the common complaint is

- Existing software comes too late and at higher costs
  than expected, and does not fulfill the promises made
  for it.

Certainly, more points could be added to this list.

1.2. The aim

Clearly, nobody likes software having the characteristics
mentioned above. But a negative definition of software
engineering would not be the right answer. Positively,
the aim may be stated:

To obtain economically software that is reliable and
works efficiently on real machines.

Software engineering would then mean the establishment and
use of sound engineering principles in order to reach that
aim. Before considering the question what these principles
are or might be we have to look at the existing situation
again and to ask ourselves: What differences between the
computer field and other fields of science and technolgy
exist which give rise to the difficulties outlined above.

1.3. The paradox of non-hardware engineering

An answer lies in the paradox that is inherent in the
combination of the word engineering and software.
Engineers usually deal with material subjects, with hardware
in the widest sense, from chariots to steam engines and
airplanes, from jungle footbridges to the Verrazano Narrows
Bridge, or, to use the word «ingenieur» in the meaning of the
17th century French builders of fortresses, from ramparts to
Maginot lines. One may object to this that electricity is
not a material, and indeed, electrical engineers see to be
somewhat more abstract, somewhat more noble than others, but
in common with other engineers they deal with physical objects.
And here, the difference comes up: software is not a
physical object, it is non-material.

It needs physical objects as carriers only, and it is altogether unspecific about the carrier.

Since the material is cheap - paper as a carrier is sufficient - - and the tools are at hand - usually one's own head - to produce some software is a common puberty rite for beginners in the computer field.

As CHEATHAM says in his lecture at this Congress, things can be sensed in normal engineering, thus they can be judged easily whether they are reasonable. The abstract nature of software disallows this.

Indeed, software is an abstract web, comparable to mathematical tissue, but it is a process and in so far very different from most of usual mathematics, too.

The difficulties with software can already be observed in the problem it poses with respect to the German patent law. Is software patentable? According to the German patent law, software consists only of 'instructions to the human mind' and is therefore not patentable, despite the fact that it usually needs 'ingenuity' and that its protection may be important to the national economy.

So something is different about software, something, which has the effect of prohibiting software engineering from being simply a copy of other engineering fields. My impression is that this difference has not been given proper recognition and attention in the past, and that many of the complaints are based on after-effects of this neglect. Of course, the mere fact that in the early days progress was strongly associated with the hardware engineer explains this somewhat, and the idea of software as an industrial product, to be purchased at regular prices in an open market, is even now not fully accepted. Something that is given away free might very well not attain more value than a gold plated car medal one obtains with gasoline. More-over, a hasty buildup in the computer industry has not provided the best climate for satisfactory development of good software. ED DAVID ([G], p. 73) said: "In computing, the research, development, and production phases are often telescoped into one process. In the competitive rush to make available the

latest techniques, such as on ·line consoles served by
time-shared computers, we strive to take great forward leaps
across gulfs of unknown width and depth. In the cold light
of day, we know that a step-by-step approach separating
research and development from production is less risky
and more likely to be successful. Experience indeed indicates
that for software tasks similar to previous ones, estimates
are accurate to within 10-30 % in many cases. This situation
is familiar in all fields lacking a firm theoretical base.

Thus, there are good reasons why software tasks that
include novel concepts involve not only uncalculated but
also uncalculable risks".

But the situation is improving and has even improved
already to some extent. The economical importance of software
is now fully recognized. Estimates that the software used
with large machines often costs just as much as pure hardware
costs are now viewed by manufacturers. This has had, of
course, the effect that in the software field an extra
inflationary tendency was introduced; but even if no
world-wide recession cools the overheated market,
the recession in the USA - insofar as it applies to
computers - will already act as a regulator.

1.4. The role of education

But it seems that the core of the difficulties lies
deeper, and the situation outlined above has only brought
it to the open - fortunately, I may say. My observation
is that the problem that is meant by the provocative use
of the phrase 'software engineering', is in fact an
educational one. Surprisingly enough, there seems to be
agreement about this point from two extreme sides of the
software gang: from the 'theorists' as they are sometimes
called, and from the 'practicioners'.

Perhaps it is less surprising that the practicioners
are uneasy. Computer Science, as exercised in the United
States, is not only sometimes somewhat highbrow, it also
has a tendency to neglect the practicioner's immediate
needs. Rightfully so, if one thinks that the only
orientation academic education has is towards a Ph. D.,
but this ideal picture does not hold. Attempts in Europe,
to define «informatique» in France, "Informatik" in
Germany in a way so as to strengthen the practical side
of programming have still a way to go in order to prove
their effectiveness. What the practicioners want, is
the introduction of sound engineering techniques in Computer
Science teaching. Said D'AGAPEYEFF ([G], p. 24):

"We need a more substantial basis to be taught and
monitored in practice on the structure of programs and
the flow of their execution, on the shaping of modules
and an environment of their testing, and on the simulation
of run-time conditions".

In any case, the 'theorists' are even more upset
(DIJKSTRA: "the massive dissemination of error-loaded
software is frightening" ([G], p. 16) and they propose
real changes in programming habits. LUCAS, from the
Vienna IBM Lab, reporting about a mechanical correctness
proof, which by failing indicated an error, said ([R], p. 21):

"The error was not found by the compiler writers. I am
quite convinced that making this proof was cheaper than
the discussion I have heard among highly-paid people on
whether or not this allocation mechanism would cover the
general case".

And DIJKSTRA says "Testing shows the presence, not the
absence of bugs" ([R], p. 21). How the concept of
structured programming which he advocates combines with

engineering needs, will be seen later. In its tendency
to go from the general to the particular, to detail the description
of a system step-by-step, it coincides with modern top-
down teaching. In particular it helps the student to develop
a sense for the conscious discipline that is needed in
programming, and early in the education it supports the
production of clean, gimmick-free, defensive programming.
In the course of such an education, it may be hoped that
a code of good practice for professional programmers
will develop.

2. SOFTWARE DESIGN AND PRODUCTION IS AN INDUSTRIAL ENGINEERING FIELD

> 'On the Division of Mental Labour'
>   Charles Babbage, Chapter heading in his book
>   'On the Economy of Machinery and Manufacturers'.

2.1. Large projects

For the time being, we have to work under the existing
conditions, and the work has to be done with programmers
who are not likely to be re-educated. It is therefore all
the more important to use organisational and managerial
tools that are appropriate to the task, in particular to
large projects - i.e. projects which essentially cannot
be carried through by one man within the specified time.
It also goes without saying that a code of good practice,
as stipulated above, will be of utmost importance if the
work has to be divided by groups. Communication within
the group is the main problem; and whether the resulting
work increases with the square root, or with the dual
logarithm of the number of co-workers, or even decreases
after some critical size, depends on the degree of
commonality.

2.2. Division into manageable parts

If software is to be designed and produced in an
industrial process, the problem of division of labour
is the main obstacle. Frequently, there are no natural
boundaries to suggest a division into manageable parts.
More important, in contrast to a normal industrial
process which gains its efficiency from the economization
of frequent repetition, the situation in software is
different from day to day, from case to case. Moreover,
as software is usually highly interwoven, breaking it
into manageable parts frequently leads to a host of
interface specifications. The solution can therefore
not be sought in a mosaic-like sub-division (fig. 1).

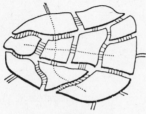

Fig. 1.

Instead, a hierarchical structure is needed, in the
simplest case a tree-structure (fig. 2) where no (or only
few) connections exist between pieces at the same depth.
The gain is to be found in stepwise detailization, which
establishes the vertical interfaces in a natural way and
keeps them to a minimum. The main difficulty rests,
however, in finding the appropriate layers.

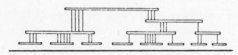

Fig. 2.

As an example of such a structure, I would like to take the organization of the project BS Munich, an operating system for a Telefunken 2-processor configuration, being built by a working group at the Technical University, Munich (fig. 3). The example for the hierarchical structure supporting one arbitrary user process has been taken from routine material and has not been made up for our purpose; in particular it would be difficult to answer the anticipated question 'what do the lines mean?' - nevertheless, it illustrates the point.

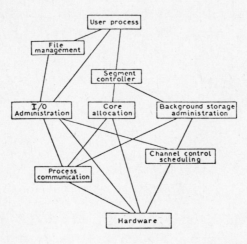

Fig. 3.

2.3. Division into distinct stages of development

Also in contrast to the usual situation in engineering, the division into distinct stages of development is a problem. The need for thorough feedback from construction to design, from use to construction is usually given as a reason. But this is not new at all, it is in fact characteristic in industrial manufacturing. It may, however, be that there more feedback is needed from production because of the poor status of the design, and more from maintenance because of poor construction. Again, the haste in the build up might be held responsible, including the fact that in the computer field PETER's principle is not valid.

Nobody seems to reach the level of incompetence, because
probably erverybody is incompetent (D'AGAPEYEFF: "those
who are incompetent find each other's company congenial").
Therefore, nobody will ever do something again as soon
as he somehow understands it.

The hope, that time will cure these ills, is insufficient.
The inner complexity of large software projects needs a
careful treatment of organizational hazards. Fortunately,
the computer itself can help.

2.4. Computerized surveillance

The whole design, production and maintenance process
has to be subjected to computerized surveillance. The
points to be looked at are in particular:

- Automatic updating and quality control of documentation
- Selective dissemination of information to all project
  staff
- Surveillance of deadline plans
- Collection of data for simulation studies
- Collection of data for quality control
- Automatic production of manuals and maintenance material.

It is clear that a house well equipped with programs and
an underlying philosophy for doing these things, can be
regarded as a modern software plant. The tools are to a
large extent at hand, although they are sometimes used to
"nibble at the periphery", as someone from a leading
manufacturer has stated. Many excellent remarks about
the theme will be found in the Reports on the Software
Engineering Conferences in Garmisch (October 1968, [G])
and Rome (October 1969, [R]).

More modest, but probably earlier successful efforts are those
described by LANDY and NEEDHAM [15].

2.5. Management

Needless to say that successful operation in an
industrial engineering field requires the full repertoire
of management artifices that is at hand. Yet, many
project managers in software design and production have
never heard of such things and even if they are aware of
this deficiency, they have neither time nor opportunity
to acquire the necessary knowledge. As soon as the
software market enters into a competitive situation, this
will change. Education should be particularly concerned
about providing the elementary knowledge and the willing-
ness to apply it. About management problems, the
Garmisch [G] and Rome [R] reports contain many interesting
details - it would go too far to mention here all the
names.

3. THE ROLE OF STRUCTURED PROGRAMMING

3.1. A hierarchy of conceptual layers

The essential point, however, is to organize the software
project in conceptual layers. This technique is known under
different names. It is essentially what DIJKSTRA (1969)
does in his "Notes on Structured Programming" ([3], see
also [R], pp. 84-88).

Stepwise abstraction is advocated; the writing of a
program should start with the most abstract form. Doing
the labour mentally, one does not have to introduce formalized language at different levels. But doing so, one
arrives at the use of a sequence of languages, from the
highest being the user's language, problem-oriented in
the main, to the lowest, usually the machine language.
In this form, the technique has been used somewhat widely
since first described (to my knowledge) in the 1958
UNCOL Report [11], where three levels of languages were
advocated, the one intermediate level being the 'Universal

Computer Oriented Language' ([11], Appendix A). The
essence of such a hierarchical structuring, however,
was given in 1968 by ZURCHER and RANDELL [14]. They
speak, like DIJKSTRA, of design "from the outside
inwards", using different "levels of abstraction" and
achieving "successively greater detail".

The technique is also advocated by J. I. SCHWARTZ in
a most interesting contribution at the Rome Conference
[10].

The direction is here 'top-down', and interestingly
it is the same as in modern top-down teaching of programming.
There is, however, also the choice of adopting a bottom-up
approach to the design, illustrated by POOLE and WAITE [7],
who start from machine level, which is defined by a real
machine, then introduce a sequence of <u>abstract machines</u>,
each one being defined in terms of one or some of its
predecessors. For the final structure neither the
direction matters nor is there any fundamental difference
between abstract machines and intermediate languages.

In the simplest case, we will have a linear ordering
(fig. 4) of levels or layers. More generally, the ordering
will be a partial ordering only. The levels as such
disappear, we may speak of layers only and incomparable
layers may exist (fig. 5).

Fig. 4.

Fig. 5.

Since one man and/or one machine is not necessarily
implied by the picture, we have the most general
situation of fig. 6. Such a structural scheme means
that everything in the meaning of a certain layer is based
directly on the layers immediately below.

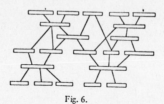

Fig. 6.

3.2. Communication between layers

At any interface between layers, we may consider whatever
means of intercommunications we find as a language, by
which the concepts of the higher layer are expressed in
terms of concepts of the lower layer.

There is no logical reason, however, why the same language should
not be used at different interfaces. In fact, the UNCOL
idea meant that UNCOL would be used in <u>every</u> communication.
We know today, that under most practical circumstances more
than one intermediate language is worthwhile. However, extensible languages (CHEATHAM) allow to develop within <u>one</u>
language different styles, appropriate for the respective
layer.

The use of the same language at two levels also allows one
to make use of recursive descriptions. In these descriptions,
we find - seemingly in contradiction to the partial ordering - closed loops of descriptional reference. Fig. 7 (A)
shows such a situation - the arrow between $\mathcal{A}$ and $\mathcal{B}$
meaning: "In the description of the concepts of $\mathcal{A}$, use
of the concepts of $\mathcal{B}$ is made". Nevertheless, we should

hope that the <u>recursive</u> description does not lead to a circle definition, that is, that we have a partially ordered conceptional structure like the one in fig. 7 (B).

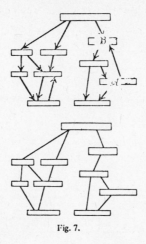

Fig. 7.

Concepts and their descriptions are different things. This is important in the following respect: The language used at a higher conceptional interface does not have to be a 'higher level' language. Neither the degree of redundance to be used nor the syntactical complexity, are necessarily correlated with the conceptual layers. But usually the more detailed, lower layer will use a less compact notation. It is also not necessary that the languages be formalized - in particular those used at higher layers will frequently not be completely formalized. Thus, we are not so much concerned with the language as such to be used, as with the style of use. Religious aspects in the use of some current programming languages are irrelevant.

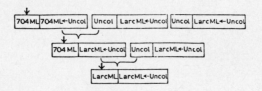

Fig. 8.

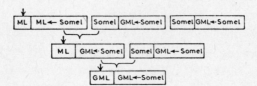

Fig. 9.

An important matter, however, is the kind of communication between layers. In simple cases, it can be strictly
operative or strictly descriptive ("communication of
control" and "communication of information" in the sense
of ZURCHER and RANDELL). It usually is a mixture, and
sometimes does not show the pragmatic distinction between
control and information at all. It may, in special cases,
require a finite number of parameters of predetermined
importance, quite similar to subroutine parameter sequences.
Then one speaks of 'parameterized generality'.

3.3. Software engineering aspects

Apart from the obvious conceptual discipline and economization structured programming brings forth, it has
special technical merits. A system of layered structure
easily lends itself, as is well known, to bootstrapping
techniques.

This has been demonstrated already in the UNCOL report
[11]*. For the simple portability problem - the transition
from 704 ML to LARCML, having a description of a translator
from UNCOL to LARCML, written in UNCOL, and using a 704 -
in a first run a description of this translator, written in
704 ML, is obtained by using the existing UNCOL to 704 ML
translator, and in a second run with the help of this translator, the wanted UNCOL to LARCML translator, written in LARCML,
is obtained (fig. 8).

Moreover, if a translator description of SOMEL into ML,
written in SOMEL, concentrates all efforts on making the
translator very efficient both in the compiling process and
the run-time characteristics of the code produced, then
bootstrapping with a crude translator of SOMEL into ML, written in
ML, obtains in one run (which may take long time) a translator of SOMEL into a good ML, written in ML, which may

---

*- the UNCOL project, although being 'spectacularly
unsuccessful' and 'an exercise in group wishful thinking',
as two leading scientists have stated , was nevertheless
the first software engineering attempt.

now be applied again to the original description, resulting
in an efficient translator from SOMEL into good ML
irrespective of the crudeness of the bootstrap translator. 'Good' ML, obviously a subset of ML, is abbreviated
GML in fig. 9, which shows that this frequently used bootstrapping process is technically identical with the one
of fig. 8. Thus, using layered description, simulation
can be greatly simplified, as ZURCHER and RANDELL [14]
have pointed out in particular. They stress the evolutionary
aspect of the software design labour. To begin with,
inefficient realizations of lower layers may be used -
highly interpretative schemes for example - which may be
easily built, checked and changed. These will be replaced
towards the end from above to below by final, efficient
schemes. During the design labour, or in construction,
intermediate layers can be expressed fully by lower ones.
This is the situation resembling the use of open subroutines, and will to some extent have advantages. Very
often, however, it is worthwhile to keep the layered
structure. DIJKSTRA has shown this in his design and
construction (1967) of the T. H. E. multiprogramming system [2].
This offers great flexibility for later changes. More
details, in particular about the formation of the
layers by introduction of abstract machines, are given
in a working paper in [G], pp. 181-185.

One more remark may be in order: Structured programming
may even go down to include the microprogramming level.

3.4. Flexibility: portability and adaptability

The flexibility structured programming offers with respect to
the changes that occur during the work are particularly
evident in the two ends that have been at so far regarded

as fixed: the <u>machine end</u> and the <u>user's end</u>. The
latter means that a changing situation with the user
enforces changes, adaptations to new foreseen or unforeseen
situations. The situation has been called <u>adaptability</u>
[RP]. The former means changing machine characteristics,
foreseen or, as usually the case with a new machine,
unforeseen ones. This situation has been called <u>portability</u>
[RP]. The case of foreseen changes offers in fact nothing
new, since then the problem can be considered as being
taken care of from the beginning. (The word <u>availability</u>
that has been used sometimes in this connection is misleading.)

Portable software and adaptable software mean, however,
that something has to be changed, depending on the unforeseen change. The hope is to keep this to a minimum, and
as in the previous case, to achieve this by suitable structure
so that perhaps only the immediate neighbouring units will
have to be changed, or at least very few of them. In
general, the effect of changes should rather be damped
at more remote layers.

3.5. Some existing examples

There exist a number of examples for software which is
sufficiently portable or adaptable so that its portability
ratio or adaptibility ratio, resp., is less than 5 %, the
ratio in question being the effort necessary to make
changes, in relation to the total effort. An early example
is the ALCOR ILLINOIS compiler for ALGOL 60, which was
built for an IBM 7090 and was transferred by DAVID GRIES
to an IBM 7044 in two weeks [5]. Its portability was
achieved mainly through parameterization.[*] More recently,
MARTIN RICHARDS with his BCPL compiler has given several

---

[*] The problem was thoroughly discussed by S. Warshall at
the Rome Conference [16].

examples of successful portability, to a KDF 9 ([R], p. 29) and recently to a Telefunken TR 440. Very impressing are the experiments POOLE and WAITE made, using a 'mobile programming system' with the macro processor STAGE 2 as tool ([7],[12],[13]). STAGE 2 itself is highly portable and has been implemented on 20 different computers, requiring about one man-week of effort to obtain a running version in each case [8]. They have ported, among others, several compilers to a number of machines of quite different characteristics. D. T. ROSS with his system AED [9] claims portability, through a complex bootstrapping approach, too ([R], p. 29), and favours macro-expansion ([G], p. 150). There are many more interesting approaches scattered in the literature.

On the side of adaptability, examples have been given, too. Parametrizing 'generic software' has been used, e.g., for varying precision of calculation and arguments range in numerical approximation. Mc ILROY proposed to use 'software components' which allows software to be built mosaic-like from a multitude of mutually harmonized small pieces, to be ordered from a catalogue [6]. Such an ambitious goal is not likely to be attacked successfully in near future, but theoretically it falls fully within the 'structured programming' idea.

Keeping in mind that our definition of user and machine is relative, we obtain a number of further examples through macro generators which allow the specification of new macros, and more generally through extensible languages. In these examples, although the extra work is practically negligible, the possible changes are, however, also narrowly restricted.

3.6. The trade-offs

Known successes in making software portable and/or
adaptable have often accepted considerable inefficiency
as the price to be paid for this. This has been the
practical result, but it is not a logical necessity. Even
with this present situation, the advantages of portable
and adaptable software have overcome the accompanying
inefficiencies in many cases. The values implied by this
trade-off point to the urgent need for further research.

In this connection, it is important to develop system
evaluation tools. A detailed survey has been given by
GOTLIEB and MAC EWEN [4], and most recently some very
interesting results came from ASLANIAN and BENNET [1].

4. CONCLUDING REMARKS

Software engineering has probably a long way to go
before it can repay the costs that have to go into it.
The discussion of structured programming as a software
engineering approach has left a number of questions
open: how to find the right layers, for example. All
experts agree that this is the most important thing, and
it seems to require so much intuition that it cannot
be taught simply. But although no one would suggest
that software engineering now can be left to a robot:
it is important that - to use a phrase of LEIBNIZ -
"excellent men should not loose hours like slaves in
the labour which could be safely relegated to any one else
if machines were used".

Progress in software engineering can be expected only
if the available techniques are more widely used and
applied to a variety of situations. Comparison can then

show the advantages and disadvantages. Such a comparison
between commercial manufacturers is hardly imaginable,
and therefore a cooperative effort of governments has been
proposed. The result of an international, non-commercial
activity in the development of software engineering techniques
could at the same time be some help for the user who finds
it more and more difficult to obtain the software he needs
in view of the growing complexity of the computer system.
Such an enterprise should, however, be in contact with
manufacturers and software houses in order to avoid a
drift into the purely academic direction, and should in
particular publish its final products for free use. In view
of the long time the preparations took so far, however, it
is doubtful whether such a thing would come at all in time.

In the four years since autumn 1967, when the phrase
'software engineering' was introduced to a wider public,
many people - scientists, educators, managers, businessmen -
became aware of the problem. Software houses commence to
reorient themselves, tutorial meetings are held, like one
by Infotech in London this year, and the scientific affairs
divisions of governmental agencies support further development; for example an International Advanced Seminar on
Software Engineering, under EEC auspices financed by the German
Federal Ministry for Education and Science, is under preparation
and will be held in Munich in February/March next year,
hopefully providing the computing community with well-
organized teaching material in some form. Last not least,
the fact that IFIP has taken up this subject in its congress
program is a most encouraging sign.

Some of the effects software engineering may have may
not be liked universally. From a list DIJKSTRA compiled,
I take: It may be necessary to change our tools - which
is expensive, to change our hardware - which is upsetting
balance, to change the organizational set-ups in which our
work has to be done - which is alarming for some supervisors.
It may mean that we have to change our thinking habits -
which a majority of the computer community may dislike.

Unemployment of unskilled programmers may very well be
a result of software engineering. The gold-rush will
not last forever. The computer, one of the greatest
inventions of engineers, has to go the complete way of
engineering to its end.

ACKNOWLEDGEMENTS

I have heard many views and learnt about the details
at the Working Conferences sponsored by the NATO Science
Committee, held in 1968 at Garmisch and in 1969 at Rome.
For a systematic approach, I owe thanks for fruitful
discussions to Dr. E. DAVID, formerly at Bell Teleph.
Lab., and Dr. W. MORTON, Culham Laboratory, UKAEA, and
to many of my academic colleagues. My particular thanks
go to Prof. C. C. GOTLIEB for editorial help.

REFERENCES

[G]   (Garmisch Report) P. NAUR and B. RANDELL (ed.)
       Software Engineering. Report on a Conference,
       Garmisch, October 1968.

[R]   (Rome Report) J. N. BUXTON and B. RANDELL (ed.)
       Software Engineering Techniques. Report on a
       Conference, October 1969.

[RP]   Recommendation of the Planning Board for an Inter-
       national Computer Science Institution. Working
       Document, Rome Conference on Software Engineering
       Techniques, October 1969.

[1]   R. ASLANIAN and M. BENNET. Computer Oriented Operating
       System Design Using Evolutive Modelling and Evaluation.
       CII Working Document (May 1971) submitted to the Palo
       Alto October 1971 Symposium on Operating Systems
       Principles.

544

[2]   E. W. DIJKSTRA: The Structure of the T. H. E. Multi-
Programming System. ACM Symposium on Operating
Systems Principles, 1967. See: Comm. ACM 11 (1968),
341-346.

[3]   E. W. DIJKSTRA: Notes on Structured Programming.
Report Nr. 241, Technische Hogeschool Eindhoven
(1969).

[4]   C. C. GOTLIEB and G. H. Mac EWEN: System Evaluation
Tools. In: [R], pp. 93-99.

[5]   D. GRIES, M. PAUL and H. R. WIEHLE: Some Techniques
Used in the ALCOR ILLINOIS 7090, Comm. ACM 8 (1965),
496-500.

[6]   M. D. Mc ILROY: Mass-Produced Software Components.
In: [G], 138-155.

[7]   P. C. POOLE and W. M. WAITE: Machine Independent
Software. Proc. ACM Second Symposium on Operating
Systems Principles, Princeton, N. Y., October 1969.

[8]   P. C. POOLE and W. M. WAITE: The Design of Portable
Abstract Machines. Culham Lab. Report CLM-P 258
(1971).

[9]   D. T. ROSS: News About AED. Periodical Publication
by Softtech, Waltham, Massachusetts.

[10]   J. I. SCHWARTZ: Analysing Large-Scale System Development. In: [R], 122-137.

[11]   J. STRONG, J. WEGSTEIN, A. TRITTER, J. OLSZTYN, O. MOCK,
T. STEEL: The Problem of Programming Communication
with Changing Machines. Comm. ACM 1, No. 8, 12-18,
No. 9, 9-15 (1958).

[12]   W. M. WAITE: Building a Mobile Programming System
        Comp. J. 13, 28 (1970).

[13]   W. M. WAITE: The Mobile Programming System:
        STAGE 2 Comm. ACM 13, 415 (1970)

[14]   F. W. ZURCHER and B. RANDELL: Iterative Multi-
        Level Modelling. (Submitted Paper) IFIP Congress
        1968.

[15]   B. LANDY and R. M. NEEDHAM: Software Engineering
        Techniques used in the Development of the Cambridge
        Multi-Access System, Software Practice and Experience 1,
        167-173 (1971).

[16]   S. WARSHALL: Software portability and representational
        form. Paper, submitted to the Rome Conference.

Lecture Notes in Economics and Mathematical Systems

Vol. 69: S. Ashour, Sequencing Theory. V, 133 pages. 4°. 1972. DM 16,–

Vol. 70: J. P. Brown, The Economic Effects of Floods. Investigations of a Stochastic Model of Rational Investment Behavior in the Face of Floods. V, 87 pages. 4°. 1972. DM 16,–

Vol. 71: R. Henn und O. Opitz, Konsum- und Produktionstheorie II. V, 134 Seiten. 4°. 1972. DM 16,–

Vol. 72: T. P. Bagchi and J. G. C. Templeton, Numerical Methods in Markov Chains and Bulk Queues. XI, 89 pages. 4°. 1972. DM 16,–

Vol. 73: H. Kiendl, Suboptimale Regler mit abschnittweise linearer Struktur. VI, 146 Seiten. 4°. 1972. DM 16,–

Vol. 74: F. Pokropp, Aggregation von Produktionsfunktionen. VI, 107 Seiten. 4°. 1972. DM 16,–

Vol. 75: GI-Gesellschaft für Informatik e. V. Bericht Nr. 3. 1. Fachtagung über Programmiersprachen · München, 9–11. März 1971. Herausgegeben im Auftrag der Gesellschaft für Informatik von H. Langmaack und M. Paul. VII, 280 Seiten. 4°. 1972. DM 24,–

Vol. 76: G. Fandel, Optimale Entscheidung bei mehrfacher Zielsetzung. 121 Seiten. 4°. 1972. DM 16,–

Vol. 77: A. Auslender, Problemes de Minimax via l'Analyse Convexe et les Inégalités Variationnelles: Théorie et Algorithmes. VII, 132 pages. 4°. 1972. DM 16,–

Vol. 78 : GI-Gesellschaft für Informatik e.V. 2. Jahrestagung, Karlsruhe, 2.–4. Oktober 1972. Herausgegeben im Auftrag der Gesellschaft für Informatik von P. Deussen. XI, 576 Seiten. 4°. 1973. DM 36,–

Vol. 79 : A. Berman, Cones, Matrices and Mathematical Programming. V, 96 pages. 4°. 1973. DM 16,–

Vol. 80: International Seminar on Trends in Mathematical Modelling, Venice, 13–18 December 1971. Edited by N. Hawkes. VI, 288 pages. 4°. 1973. DM 24,–

Vol. 81: Advanced Course on Software Engineering. Edited by F. L. Bauer. XII, 545 pages. 4°. 1973. DM 32,–